CAMBRIDGE STUDIES IN AMERICAN LITERATURE AND CULTURE

Henry James and the "Woman Business"

Henry James and the "Woman Business"

ALFRED HABEGGER
University of Kansas

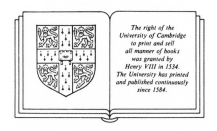

The right of the
University of Cambridge
to print and sell
all manner of books
was granted by
Henry VIII in 1534.
The University has printed
and published continuously
since 1584.

CAMBRIDGE UNIVERSITY PRESS

Cambridge

New York   Port Chester   Melbourne   Sydney

Published by the Press Syndicate of the University of Cambridge
The Pitt Building, Trumpington Street, Cambridge CB2 IRP
40 West 20th Street, New York, NY 10011, USA
10 Stamford Road, Oakleigh, Melbourn 3166, Australia

© Cambridge University Press 1989

First published 1989

Printed in the United States of America

Library of Congress Cataloging-in-Publication Data
Habegger, Alfred.
Henry James and the "woman business" / Alfred Habegger.
p.   cm. – (Cambridge studies in American literature and
culture)
Bibliography: p.
Includes index.
ISBN 0-521-36635-6
1. James, Henry, 1843–1916 – Political and social views.   2. James,
Henry, 1843–1916 – Characters – Women.   3. Feminism and literature.
4. Sex role in literature.   5. Women in literature.   I. Title.
II. Series.
PS127.F44H33   1989
813'.4 – dc19   88–38545
CIP

British Library Cataloguing in Publication Data
Habegger, Alfred
Henry James and the "woman business". –
(Cambridge studies in American literature
and culture).
1. Fiction in English. American writers.
James, Henry, 1843–1916. Characters: women
– Critical studies
I. Title
813'.4

ISBN 0-521-36635-6 hard covers

Contents

Acknowledgments

Writing this book would have been inconceivable if I had not been granted access to several collections of unpublished letters and other manuscripts. Permission to quote from these materials has been kindly granted by the following individuals and associations:

Caroline H. Dall Papers and Annie Adams Fields Papers – Massachusetts Historical Society

de Kay and Gilder family papers, including Mary Temple's letters to Helena de Kay – Gilder Palmer

Ralph Waldo Emerson's letters – by permission of the Ralph Waldo Emerson Memorial Association and the Houghton Library, Harvard

Mary Hallock Foote Papers – Evelyn Foote Gardiner and Stanford University Libraries (Special Collections)

Robertson James Papers – Henry James Vaux

Katharine Prince Papers – Colby College Library (Special Collections)

All other James family papers – by permission of Alexander R. James and the Houghton Library, Harvard

Letters of Robert and Mary Temple, Frances Macdaniel, and Elizabeth Stoddard – by permission of the Houghton Library, Harvard

I am also obliged to the many librarians who have opened their collections and facilities to me or taken the time to answer my questions. My thanks to the helpful staffs at Houghton Library, Widener Library, Harvard Law School Library Treasure Room, Boston Public Library, Massachusetts Historical Society, Swedenborg School of Religion Library, Butler Library at Columbia University, Suzzallo Library at the University of Washington, Stanford University Libraries (Special Collections), University of Virginia Library (Manuscripts Department), Minnesota Historical Society, Museum and Library of Maryland History, Enoch Pratt Free Library, Library of Congress, British Museum Library, Archives Nationales in Paris, New York Public Library, and Watson Library at the

University of Kansas (where I want to single out Evelyn Gelhaus, Rob Melton, the Reference Department in general, and Interlibrary Loan).

To recall the many intellectual debts I have incurred to fellow scholars and others during the writing of this book is to relive much of the past six years. For help in locating privately held papers, I am grateful to Evelyn Foote Gardiner, Paul R. Baker, Ormonde de Kay, and W. deKay Palmer. Gilder Palmer graciously allowed me a free hand with family papers, and Jane Maher turned me loose in her research files and passed on some good stories. Addy Tintner, Taylor Stoehr, and Jonathan Beecher sent prompt and productive answers to my inquiries. My spring 1988 Henry James seminar made a significant difference in the final version of this book, thanks in part to the stimulating contributions of Brad Born, David Davis, Jennifer Dean, Gardner Mein, Jan Martin Moreno, Dan Murtaugh, and Steven Trout. This is also the place to memorialize some challenging conversations and exchanges with Carol Holly, Ian F. A. Bell, Dan Fogel (whose backing has been deeply appreciated), and Bill Veeder (who showed me the holes in a chapter I thought I had completed). June Howard, William T. Stafford, George Monteiro, Tom O'Donnell, Warren Rosenberg, Linda Smith Rhoads, Lou Budd, Addy Tintner, and Ian F. A. Bell all provided me with opportunities to get preliminary versions of my work out in public. Ian Bell and Charles Swann gave me some excellent practical advice. Thanks to Leon Edel for encouragement and a keen critique of some of my ideas; to Tony Tanner for saving me from some flat-footed stumbles; and to Nina Baym, Susan Gilbert, Joel Porte, Wendy Martin, Michael Johnson, and Lou Budd for aid, comfort, and correction over the years the book has consumed. Special thanks to my copy editor, Mary Byers.

Finally, because the writing of a book consumes more than time, I express gratitude to the National Endowment for the Humanities for a timely Senior Research Fellowship; to the Hall Center for the Humanities for travel grants, a semester's research leave, and more; and to the University of Kansas for a sabbatical, two GRF grants, and supplementary aid (from the College of Liberal Arts and Sciences).

Abbreviations

Chapter 1

Introduction

════════════

Gerty MacDowell in "Nausicaa"

Although this book is not about James Joyce, the best avenue of approach to my subject is by way of the chapter in *Ulysses* known as "Nausicaa," where a timid, deformed, and depressed girl named Gerty MacDowell sees Leopold Bloom on the beach and has an intense fantasy about him. Gerty imagines that the handsome middle-aged stranger remembers "an old flame he was in mourning for from the days beyond recall" (299), and she dreams that the two of them might each make up the other's loss: He would "love her, his ownest girlie, for herself alone" (294). The only two books Joyce mentions as being read with enjoyment by Gerty are *The Lamplighter* and *Mabel Vaughan*, both produced in the 1850s by the popular American novelist Maria Cummins. Evidently Cummins's euphemistic fictions channel Gerty's blocked carnality. The girl leans back and lets the unknown man look up her dress, while Bloom, also a fantasizing animal, seizes the opportunity to masturbate. After his orgasm, as Gerty limps away, he experiences the coarse epiphany – "O!" (301) – that explains her pathetic sexual compliance. She is lame.

"Nausicaa" enjoys a remarkable air of authority. Marilyn French may have spoken for most of Joyce's readers, male and female, when she concluded that "there is no question of Joyce's accuracy: the world of Gerty MacDowell is as true and recognizable as that of Barney Kiernan's pub" (157). Another Joycean, Suzette Henke, who has read *The Lamplighter* and observed the close links between its heroine (also named Gertrude) and Gerty MacDowell, has demonstrated the canniness of Joyce's appropriation of Cummins's novel. Not only do both Gertrudes feel "emotionally orphaned and socially ostracized," but when Joyce's character imagines that Bloom is mooning over an old flame, she is attributing to him a "history similar to the plight of Philip Amory in Cummins's *The Lamplighter.*" Amory, a mysterious and melancholy older man, proves in the end to be the heroine's long-lost father. It was partly *her* he was in mourning for – and *his* first and last names denote two kinds of

1

love. As Henke points out, Joyce's Gerty "dreams that eventually, like Gerty Flint, she will be saved from her present fate by . . . a father-lover" (133, 139, 134). Thus, what is plot in Cummins's mid-Victorian novel turns out to be weak euphemistic fantasy in *Ulysses*. This relationship increases one's awe of Joyce, for not only has he dissected a young woman's fiction-prompted fantasy life, showing how her imagination integrates novels with her bleak physical and social existence and thus insulates her from life, but he has also cast a backward light on popular and sentimental women's novels, which now seem to be built on the same sickly evasions. "Nausicaa" appears to enclose women's fictions and fantasy lives in an unchallengeably authoritative manner.

But Joyce's authority must be challenged, for two reasons: The weakness he attributed to Gerty was in part his own, and not that of the female culture she represents; and *The Lamplighter,* the book that to some extent formed Gerty, is in crucial ways a stronger work than "Nausicaa" lets us assume.

Richard Ellmann, and Fritz Senn after him, have shown how in writing "Nausicaa," Joyce made use of his own amorous pursuit of Marthe Fleischmann in Zurich. Joyce had sent this woman a postcard in which he called her Nausicaa and signed himself Odysseus. His sentimental plea – "*j'ai vécu et péché et créé*" – reappears in Gerty's fantasy "that Bloom 'had erred and sinned and wandered' " (Ellmann 462–65). Emphasizing the strain of "romantic *kitsch*" in Joyce, Senn argues that his own "sentimentality and doubtful taste and the languishing are projected on to the girl." Senn also conjectures that "an element of spite . . . may have been at play too in the malicious reversal of roles" (287–90, 310), and this strikes me as a very good guess.

The favorable, two-column review of *The Lamplighter* that ran in the *New York Tribune* (in 1854 the James family newspaper) shows the sort of respect the novel commanded. Neither Cummins nor her heroine resorted to smarmy archaisms or glib commercial phrases or gave a second thought to cosmetics like "eyebrowleine which gave that haunting expression to the eyes" (286). The author's prose had many of the qualities that add up to dullness, being correct, bland, always well balanced, and often vague and unspecific, especially in the later novel, *Mabel Vaughan*. The fact that Cummins had a story brought out by the *Atlantic* and had one of her novels reviewed there shows that her taste was better than Gerty's, and less interesting. It is incorrect to say that "Joyce parodies Cummins's saccharine style" (Henke 134), since Cummins did not have a saccharine style. It might be argued that saccharinity is what you get when you translate Cummins's sentiments into style, but even this possibility seems doubtful in view of Joyce's remarkable transformation of the character of *The Lamplighter*'s heroine – his suppression of her leading trait.

Who would ever guess, reading about Gerty MacDowell, that her eponym in Cummins had a tough and fiery power of resistance? Gertrude's flinty character (Flint is her provisional last name until she learns who her father is) comes out in high relief in those scenes where she resists the will of bossy men. One of these, Mr. Graham, is an old and well-to-do gentleman who regards himself as Gertrude's protector. Used to getting his way, Mr. Graham pressures her to accompany him and his daughter on a vacation, chiefly because he depends on Gertrude's expert care. But instead of admitting his dependency, he only says, "You are under my care, child, and I have a right to say what you shall do" (177). Gertrude knows he does not have the right, not being her legal guardian. When she refuses to go along, he childishly loses his temper, venting his pompous resentment in a speech he pretends to direct to his daughter, but which is actually aimed at the nearby Gertrude: "Here I plan my business, and make all my arrangements, on purpose to be able to give up this winter to travelling . . . and, just as everything is settled, and we are almost on the point of starting, Gertrude announces that she has concluded not to go. Now, I should like to know her reasons" (178). Like A. A. Milne's Eeyore, this man's dignity is such that he cannot speak directly to the inferior who has offended him. When Mr. Graham resorts to threat – "I utterly withdraw my protection and assistance from you. You must take care of yourself, or trust to strangers" – Gertrude merely replies, "I intend to earn a maintenance for myself" (185–86). She derives the strength to defy him in this way from her conviction that she has an ethical obligation elsewhere (caring for a destitute family in Boston) and from the fiery spirit she has sought to govern from childhood on.

Mr. Graham is not the only man whose smug sense of authority arouses Gertrude's sense of independence. When Mr. Bruce proposes marriage and Gertrude turns him down, he gives her a complacent scolding: "Such a chance does n't occur every day, especially to poor schoolmistresses; and if you are so foolish as to overlook it, I'll venture to say you'll never have another" (294). Gertrude forces herself to return a civil answer to this insulting speech, and in the end Mr. Bruce's air of authority dissolves into petulance. Like Mr. Graham, he delivers an angry exit speech and then slams the door on his way out. The episode has a didactic function, of course, for it demonstrates the proper way to heap coals of fire on your enemy's head. The moral lesson of the two Cummins novels read by Gerty MacDowell is that you have to redirect your natural selfishness; anger and rebellion must be turned into caring for others.[1] It does not matter that Joyce did not take this lesson at face value, but I am struck that his own transcription of Gertrude would entirely eliminate her anger, her dignity, her self-reliant spirit, her ability to support herself, and her skill as a domestic manager. Nobody reading "Nausicaa" could possibly suppose that the Joyce character closest to Gertrude is not Gerty at all but the able, energetic tomboy, Cissy Caffrey, who, like Cummins's heroine, skillfully governs the turbulence of men and boys.

"Nausicaa" has a duplicity, therefore, that is undetectable unless one gives The Lamplighter a fair reading. On the one hand, Joyce's account of Gerty MacDowell's inner life represents a wonderful appropriation and interpretation of some key aspects of Cummins's novel – the heroine's orphan status, the missing girlhood sweetheart. But Joyce also distorts the novel, appropriating it in such a way that his most scrupulous reader would necessarily gain a mistaken sense of the book Gerty has taken to heart. Joyce regales us with his impersonation of a certain kind of feminine weakness and duplicity; his authority overwhelms. Yet to the degree that Joyce exaggerates Gerty's weakness and prevents us from guessing at the strong spirit of Cummins's heroine, his authority exhibits the secrecy and evasiveness of authoritarian regimes. We have to read The Lamplighter, in other words, in order to prevent Ulysses from misleading us, and that is because of the faint parallel between Cummins's Mr. Graham and James Joyce himself. Each of these men is a strong masculine authority on women, and each, finding himself challenged by Cummins's sturdy orphan, seeks simultaneously to face down and to evade the challenge.

Henry James and Women

Joyce's handling of Cummins's Gerty is a paradigm of the complicated topic I explore in this book, namely, Henry James's appropriation, masterly and distorting, of American women's fiction. Just as "Nausicaa" necessarily misinforms us unless we read the literature it resists, so James cannot be fully and rightly understood unless we confront the enormous culture of nineteenth-century literary women against which he often wrote. Also, The Lamplighter was an important book for him, too, as a boy, and in his adult novels – Watch and Ward, The Portrait of a Lady, What Maisie Knew – he returned again and again to the basic fantasy material that caught Joyce's attention, the orphaned girl and the father-lover.

James's own narratives have all along professed great authority on the subject of women. Many of his readers have been impressed by his astute representation of women's characters and lives. As early as 1867, when James had done only a handful of stories and reviews, Gail Hamilton wrote that "his women, if they are wicked or foolish, have their own way of being so. They are not the old block women handed down by tradition" (Dodge 1: 588–89). Clover Adams, reading "Daisy Miller" with more sympathy than many offended compatriots, "stoutly defended Henry James and Daisy Miller to stout Mrs. Smith of Chicago . . . and protested that the latter [Daisy] was charming and that the author adored her" (Kaledin 78). Constance Fenimore Woolson, in despair at the spectacle of James's mastery, once asked him, "How did you ever dare write a portrait of a lady? Fancy any woman's attempting a portrait of a gentleman!" (HJ, *Letters* 3: 535). In our own time some strong feminists have praised even *The Bostonians* for its insights into women's lives, Nina Auerbach, for instance, extracting from this challenging novel a view of female community similar to that of *Little Women* (120–21).

I think all these views are incomplete and erroneous in that they seriously underestimate James's condescending view of women. Even Judith Fetterley tries to obscure his condescension in her imposing discussion of *The Bostonians*. She has no trouble seeing that Basil Ransom "wins because he knows he will and he knows he will because that is the way things are and the way things are is right," and that this "massive egotism" of his has a systematically incapacitating effect on the female characters. Olive's morbidity is not pathological but the result of her helpless knowledge that she is bound to lose; Verena's attractive talent as a speaker is the effect of her availability "for the projective fantasies of those who observe her." Yet Fetterley's essay is compromised by a need to rehabilitate James for feminism. She admits in passing that the novel exhibits a "contempt" for movements, and she also allows that "no one would want to make a claim for James as an ardent or perhaps any other kind of feminist,"[2] yet in the end she sees "a revolutionary message latent" in *The Bostonians:* In Olive's character and "in the fate of Olive and Verena" James grasped "the central tenets of radical feminism: women will never be free to realize and become themselves until they are free of their need for men, until they know that their basic bonds are with each other, and until they learn to make a primary commitment to each other" (126–27, 142, 117, 116, 152–53).

But could *Henry James* have produced a novel with this unspoken message? Fetterley is too partial, in every sense. She does not consider some of the opposing evidence, such as Olive's covert manipulation of Verena, and she is too disposed to forget that "contempt" she alludes to so briefly. Conspicuously absent from her essay is any consideration of the historical situation of *The Bostonians,* in particular its reception by contemporary women readers. The most detailed private response I know of, in Mary Hallock Foote's 10 January 1886 letter to Helena de Kay Gilder, shows what a cultivated reader opposed to women's rights made of the novel:

And isn't the *Bostonians* like a story *sent* just at this time on a mission?

Basil's declaration of his own beliefs – about saving his own sex – about the cant and sentimentality and emasculation of the age – I think one of the finest things we have had from anyone [?] for years.

It is a most important story and it troubles one to think that so many people *will* not read it. I feel like saying, well you must for the good of your soul. Howells' Indian Summer is an enforcement of the need of Basil Ransom's crusade. I mean that Howells has presented just the sort of man; (just as he is, loveable, charming, good, but not a *man*); that shows what we have come to. And *dont we know* what women are when they become lovers of each other – There is no *slavery* like it! (Foote Papers, Stanford University)

Although Foote wrote this before the final installment came out in February 1886, I would guess that her reading was not greatly altered by the last wrenching scene at the Music Hall. I also think she correctly divined some of James's authorial intentions. Her correspondent and close friend, Helena Gilder, knew James socially and was married to the editor of the magazine that serialized *The Bostonians*.

James may have known that good fiction does not force the author's opinions on the reader, but he could not keep his ideas, prejudices, and conflicts out of his writing. He was not only a man, of his time, with a collection of opinions about the differences between men and women and a strong point of view on the women's rights movement, but his own masculinity was problematic in the extreme. There is another way to read *The Bostonians* besides the "phallic" way and Fetterley's resisting way, and that is to assume that the novel is gravely disunified, incoherent, or fractured, split by the same system of injustice and inhumanity that Fetterley has seen so clearly within it. Such a hypothesis – that the novel is itself divided between its allegiances to its male oppressor and its female victims – would explain why both radical feminists like Fetterley and sexual conservatives like Foote and Philip Rahv and Lionel Trilling have been attracted to *The Bostonians*. This hypothesis would also accord with the facts – some known, some not – about James's life, views, and times.

The basic fact is that up until his late middle age Henry James was for the most part contemptuous of women's suffrage and women's entry into the professions. An early letter of his makes a passing pejorative reference to "free thinking young ladies" (*Letters* 1: 44). A later letter, dating from the period when James was at work on *The Bostonians*, hints at his opposition to universal suffrage: "I don't think all the world has a right to it [marriage] any more than I think all the world has a right to vote" (*Letters* 3: 54). In the late 1870s, shortly before writing *The Portrait of a Lady*, James read a conservative essay, "The Future of English Women," which warned that female emancipation would entail certain fatal consequences: Children would fail to learn a "sense of difference" between the sexes, womanly tenderness would disappear, and so would love. The essayist saw sexual difference as inborn: "That men possess the productiveness which is called genius, and women do not, is the one immutable distinction that is bound up with the intellectual idea of sex." Once emancipated, women "will not be improved women; they will only be inferior men" (Orr 1027–28). Soon after reading these contentions, James wrote a letter to one of his closest friends in which he praised the essayist, Mrs. Sutherland Orr, as "a very nice woman who writes in the '19th Century' against the 'emancipation' of woman (sensible creature)" (HJ to Grace Norton, 8 June 1879, MH-H).

When *The Bostonians* was published, the reviewer for the *Woman's Journal*, Lucia True Ames, saw with clarity the novel's inaccurate and hostile representation of the women's suffrage movement. In our own time Patricia Stubbs discerns in James an "antifeminism so subtle and fused so completely with the form and texture . . . that it can be overlooked altogether. . . . Ultimately his artistic control is so complete that the reader is tricked into accepting the unacceptable" (155–56). But Ames and Stubbs remain minority voices. Very few of those who have thought about James's female characters have questioned his authority in writing about women or have looked with any energy for the political commitments and historical determinants that underlie his treatment of women's lives.[3] One explanation for this blindness or disinterest is that the texts of this writer have been divorced from his privately expressed opinions. There is a consensus that in reading James the fiction *should* be read without reference to external print or circumstances. In addition, James's fervent defense of the private life against intrusions from the public has gone unquestioned – has not been permitted to reflect on his own narratives. So successful has he been at persuading readers that the political must not infect the personal that his own politics become invisible. James was haughty, circumspect, devious, and inconsistent in expressing his views on the "Woman business" (HJ to HJSr, 14 January 1870, MH-H). It is not that his mind was too fine to be violated by an idea, as T. S. Eliot wrote, but that his mind already had been violated and he was extremely anxious about this.

Given James's inconsistencies, there is some excuse for ignoring his antifeminism. In 1868 he ridiculed a sensational attack on modern women by writing: "It seems to us supremely absurd to stand up in the high places and endeavor, with a long lash and a good deal of bad language, to drive women back into the ancient fold."⁴ Yet only the previous year he had wound up a review by asserting: "Here, alas! is the objection to these high-toned, free-thinking heroines, in whose favor . . . we just now entered our voice. At the crucial moment they are certain to do something utterly pedantic and unnatural and insupportable." James's various comments about George Eliot, for instance, cover the spectrum of possible views. An 1866 article says that Maggie Tulliver in *The Mill on the Floss* is "worth a hundred of her positive brother, and yet on the very threshold of life she is compelled to accept him as her master. He falls naturally into the man's privilege of always being in the right" (*Literary Criticism* 1: 24, 598–99, 929). Yet when James talked about George Eliot's own mind, he sounded suspiciously like Maggie's older brother. He wrote Grace Norton that "a marvellous *mind* throbs in every page of *Middlemarch*. It raises the standard of what is to be expected of women – (by your leave!) We know all about the female heart; but apparently there is a female brain, too" (*Letters* 1: 351). To his brother William he admitted that "your remarks on *D.D.* [*Daniel Deronda*] were most sagacious. The book is a great *exposé* of the female mind" (12 January 1877, MH-H).⁵ The same kind of ambivalence runs through James's characterizations of his most important heroines. *The Portrait of a Lady* may appear to have a rounded perfection, but there are good reasons, external and internal, for regarding even this novel as the product of a divided mind. James loves Isabel, loves her when she struggles to do the right thing under oppressive circumstance, loves her all the more because she is hamstrung by that fatal female mind.

Another thing that should put us on our guard with James is that, more than most writers, he tended to live and make fiction behind a mask. In spite of the Herculean labors of Leon Edel, our image of James remains in many respects precisely the image he designed for us. He was very careful to doctor certain facts about his life and to conceal others. He sifted and destroyed documents, just as his aunt Catharine Walsh burned many of his father's letters after his death in 1882. Many surviving family letters allude by date to others that are no longer extant; some of this missing correspondence undoubtedly requested the recipient to burn the letter after reading it. Henry Sr.'s 18 March 1873 letter advises Henry Jr. to "destroy this."⁶ Furthermore, many of these missing letters date from certain critical periods in the lives of one or more of the Jameses. There are thus many ambiguities about Henry James that we cannot sort out, and there are probably many important facts we do not even suspect.

When James wrote his memoirs in 1912–13, he conveyed the impression that his family had lived abroad without interruption from 1855 to 1860, thus suppressing a fifteen-month residence in Newport in 1858–59. He justified this distortion to his nephew Henry III and his old friend

Thomas Sergeant Perry by claiming that he wanted to make his father appear less vacillating and the narrative read more smoothly (Edel, *Untried Years* 137–39; Harlow 344). What he did not reveal was that his deception already had a long history. Back in 1882 W. D. Howells had told the same story in his sketch of James's life and works: "In his twelfth year [actually his thirteenth] his family went abroad, and after some stay in England made a long sojourn in France and Switzerland. They returned to America in 1860, placing themselves at Newport" ("Henry James, Jr." 25). It was undoubtedly James himself who fed this misinformation to Howells and thus made his youthful years appear more stable and regular.

This book probes the prehistory and deep structure of some of James's narratives about women from his early and middle periods – particularly *Watch and Ward*, *The Portrait of a Lady*, and *The Bostonians*. Although these narratives offer themselves as high-gloss artifacts, there is a great deal to learn if we strip away the varnish and look for evidence of the long and circumstantial process of growth that created them.

The prime circumstance to keep in mind is that James reached maturity and found his calling at a time when the air was thick with theory and controversy about women. "Woman's mind, body, social and political condition are now the subject of constant debate," wrote E. L. Godkin in the *Nation* in 1867, going on to express his scorn for women's "literary 'culture,' if we may apply that term to the wild race after popular novelists, popular divines, popular essayists, and popular periodicals which unhappy women are now forced to keep up in order to be able to make a decent figure in polite society" ("Other Side" 316–17). One of these periodicals was the *Galaxy*, which ran an article by Eugene Benson the following year, 1868, attacking Godkin's view: "It is no longer possible to patronize women as writers without taking rank in the mental classification which comprises prigs, pedants, and pretenders" (788). A few years earlier the *Atlantic* had run Thomas Wentworth Higginson's essay, "Ought Women to Learn the Alphabet?" which ridiculed the attempt to exclude women from literature and which, according to the author, enjoyed "a wider circulation" (*Cheerful Yesterdays* 184) than any other essay written by him. The telling fact is that James, like his father and older brother, strongly inclined to Godkin's side of the debate – did so in the last years of the 1860s, when the *Nation*'s original liberalism on women's issues was rapidly eroding. James himself joined the assault on women's literary culture in those years. His reviews of American women writers had a tone ranging from condescension to outrage, and his references to literary men who spoke up for women's rights, Benson and Higginson in particular, show a conspicuous distancing effect.[7] In 1868 James even raised a storm against a novel he admitted he had not read, Anna Dickinson's *What Answer?*, an earnest but inartistic novel assailing white American prejudice against blacks (*Literary Criticism* 1: 224; see note 27 in Chapter 8).

Henry Jr. took his cue in the women's rights ferment from his father, who attempted to set everyone straight in countless lectures, essays, letters to editors, and other public and private utterances. Henry James, Sr., was a kind of Victorian sage on the vexed questions of womanhood and marriage, and was recognized as such during his life. Since his death one prevailing image of him has been that of the benign eccentric, liberal and egalitarian, a friend of the women's movement. Jean Strouse's biography of Alice James makes it abundantly clear, however, that there is something wrong with this view. The father's teachings on women and marriage were full of contradictions and strange dark corners and hints of weakness, sickness, and self-loathing. And there was more: In back of the essentially reactionary philosophy of marriage that he worked out, there lay a lifelong struggle with radical nineteenth-century feminism and free love. The full story, told for the first time in Chapter 2 of this book, sheds a startling light on the younger Henry James's novels about women, particularly *The Bostonians,* that "very *American* tale" about "the situation of women, the decline of the sentiment of sex" (*Complete Notebooks* 20).

It appears that at some point in the radical 1840s, Henry James, Sr., began to dream of perfecting the sexual relationship in a utopian society. He translated and wrote a laudatory preface for a Fourierist pamphlet called *Les Amours au phalanstère*. His version, titled *Love in the Phalanstery* and generally faithful to the original, argued that in the future monogamy would be replaced by a variety of types of marriage. Some people, for instance, would have multiple sexual partners. The pamphlet was of course attacked, and Henry Sr., whose name was not on the title page, acknowledged and defended it and himself in a long series of letters in the *Harbinger*. He backed away from the pamphlet only to the extent that he refused to determine "whether the marriage of any two parties will allow or exclude love relations on the part of either towards others" ("Love and Marriage" 203).

For the rest of his life, Henry Sr. would find himself tarred from time to time as an advocate of free love. In 1874, during the Beecher–Tilton divorce trial, he was drawn into an embarrassing controversy in the pages of the most scandalous periodical of the day, *Woodhull & Claflin's Weekly*. Yet all along, as if to defend himself against the contamination of the disreputable free lovers, Henry Sr. preached a strange, and strangely familiar, scenario that explains how man succeeds in transcending his brutish egotism *within* marriage, and thus enters the spiritual life. In this scenario, marriage seems to be essentially a lifelong spiritual discipline for man, who first desires one particular woman, then grows dissatisfied with her, and finally learns from her how to transcend his selfish carnality. It is woman who makes this process of male redemption work – woman as nonintellectual, affectionate, and self-sacrificing angel. Once, when Henry Sr. spoke on the subject of marriage before the Radical Club in Boston, the recording secretary who summed up his talk found it "as remarkable for the orthodoxy of its spirit as for the heterodoxy of its form" (M. Sargent 208), and this formula aptly categorizes the intellectual style of this extremely deceptive thinker.

Interestingly, the senior James's most appreciative follower and interpreter in England was none other than Mrs. Sutherland Orr, the essayist who predicted in "The Future of English Women" that female emancipation would be the death of idealistic love. In 1880 Mrs. Orr wrote a detailed and sympathetic review of one of Henry Sr.'s books, and thereafter they seem to have corresponded, with Henry Jr. as prompter and intermediary. And after the father died, she was one of the small number of people – and the only known woman – to whom the novelist gave a copy of the memorial volume, *The Literary Remains of the Late Henry James*.[8]

Henry Sr.'s views on women formed a large part of Henry Jr.'s intellectual birthright. And at the precise moment that the young writer was discovering his craft in his late twenties, the father was arguing more forcefully than ever that the sexes were more or less different species, with opposite natures and social roles. In letters home the good son heartily agreed with the father's conservative insistence "upon the distinction of sexes" (*Letters* 1: 188). In 1883, when Henry Jr. mapped out his big novel about the "decline of the sentiment of sex" in the United States – a book that would have a tremendous influence on the New York Intellectuals following its republication in 1945 – one of his primary motives was to vindicate his father's antireformist views on women. This study will dispel some of the staggering misconceptions about the senior James and disclose his actual social and political commitments and their by no means salutary influence on his anxiously loyal son and on *The Bostonians*.

But the son's loyalty was not unmixed. Only in the context of his muffled struggle with his father's dogmas can one seize the real importance of Minnie Temple for the novelist. Leon Edel's biography emphasizes Minnie's charm and intrepidity and suggests that these qualities led Henry James to memorialize her in the characters of Isabel Archer and Milly Theale. But there is another reason why Minnie interested and inspired James: Both tacitly and openly she challenged his father's opinions. Not only was she a sterling example of the earnest, restless young woman, a much publicized type in the late 1860s that the Jameses and many other Brahmins tended to frown on, but she denounced the philosopher's ideas to his face. She disliked the way he habitually attacked human egotism and self-well, and she once "manifested plainly unto him" that she considered his ideas "not only highly unpractical, but ignoble & shirking" and "wanting in earnestness & strength" (fair copy, MT to John Chipman Gray, 25 January 1870, MH-H). There is evidence that Henry Sr. and his wife, Mary, and also William and Alice James, all felt some dislike for this bad girl. But Henry Jr. was so captivated by this image of a challenging doomed girl that he made Minnie the basis of Isabel Archer in *The Portrait of a Lady*. The fact that the father died soon after this novel appeared left the son alone with a tremendous guilt. The effort to atone for this betrayal of his father engendered a great deal of the confusion in James's next novel, *The Bostonians*.

Henry James, Sr., and Minnie Temple are the major supporting figures in my consideration of James, but the biggest item of all will be American women's fiction of the 1850s and 60s, especially the novels James is known to have read and reviewed between 1864 and 1867. Just as he was immersed at an early age in narratives by and about women, often against his will, so, when he began writing for the public in the mid-sixties, almost all the American novels he reviewed were feminine.

Again and again the literary female captured James's attention, only to be haughtily dismissed. His first "instructors kept being instructresses," and he remembered their gender as a "humiliation," "a grave reflection both on our attainments and our spirit" (*Small Boy* 16). A youthful letter that plays with the fancy he has died and gone to literary heaven makes a point of saying that "there are no women" there (Harlow 272). His manner of expressing first memories of magazine authors establishes a curious distinction between the sexes: "There were authors not less, some of them vague and female and in this case, as a rule, glossily ringletted and monumentally breastpinned, but mostly frequent and familiar, after the manner of George Curtis and Parke Godwin and George Ripley and Charles Dana" (*Small Boy* 59). Although the women in this passage are anonymous bespangled performers and only the men have the dignity of names, the men would seem to be nothing *but* names. The "glossily ringletted" authors evidently made the greater impression – though only as a condemned group. Decades later, when James wrote *The Portrait of a Lady*, the curls rematerialized. As the Countess Gemini attempts to make sense of modern Henrietta Stackpole, she contrasts the journalist with the "literary ladies" of a former generation, chief among whom was the countess's own mother wearing her "multitude of glossy ringlets" (*Portrait* [1881] 394).

In *A Small Boy and Others* the first " 'grown-up' novel" James remembered reading was *The Lamplighter*, Gerty MacDowell's favorite. If this happened about the time of publication, James would have been ten or eleven years old. Almost sixty years later, dictating his memoirs, he recalled his "absorbed perusal" of Cummins's best-seller, and also his "secret reserves." He had his doubts whether the book was "really and truly grown-up," and he also felt (like Joyce) that there was "no rage" in it – or so at least the aging twentieth-century memoirist claimed he once felt, no doubt forgetting the episode in which Gerty hurls a rock through the window of a woman who once tormented her. His *real* first grown-up novel, he afterward decided, must have been *The Initials* by Jemima Montgomery. In a later chapter he concluded that *Uncle Tom's Cabin* would have been his "first experiment in grown-up fiction" (*Small Boy* 77–78, 159). All three books, one notes, were written by women.[9] One notes as well that the American heroines of James's "Poor Richard" and *The Europeans* bear the same name as Cummins's heroine, Gertrude.

James's account of *The Lamplighter* illustrates two stable aspects of his response to women's novels – fascination with the narrative, dismissal of the childishness. In 1865 James defended the length of his review of Carlyle's translation of *Wilhelm Meister* by recalling his unusually long reviews of women's novels: "When we entertain a giant, it is a pity to cramp him: and I too have been so hospitable to little men, or rather – little women!" (*Letters* 1: 58). In 1902, James was still using the diminutive: "The *little* American tale-tellers (I mean the two or three women) become impossible to me the moment they lengthen. Mary Wilkins I have found no better than any other Mary, in the fat volume; and dear Sarah Jewett sent me not long since a Revolutionary Romance, with officers over their wine . . . , that was a thing to make the angels weep" (*Letters* 4: 222–23). Jewett's *Tory Lover,* a historical romance, was ill-conceived, and Wilkins's short stories are agreed to be superior to her novel-length narratives. But James overlooked Jewett's *Country of the Pointed Firs* because of his prejudice against all the Marys who had done fat popular novels, including perhaps a residual animus against the original Maria Cummins herself.

The reviews James wrote during the five years before his first independent trip to Europe in 1869 – a period when he was trying to become an American writer and did not dream of a conquest of London – suggest an almost unimaginable sense of the literary landscape, one which our own boundaries and classifications cannot easily accommodate. The following excerpt from an 1865 review makes a strained connection between French realism and Anglo-American religious fiction by women:

It is just now very much the fashion to discuss the so-called principle of realism, and we all know that there exists in France a school of art in which it is associated with great brilliancy and great immorality. The disciples of this school pursue, with an assiduity worthy of a better cause, the research of local colors, with which they have produced a number of curious effects. We believe, however, that the greatest successes in this line are reserved for that branch of the school which contains the most female writers; for if women are unable to draw, they notoriously can at all events paint, and this is what realism requires. For an exhibition of the true realistic *chique* we would accordingly refer that body of artists who are represented in France by MM. Flaubert and Gérôme[10] to that class of works which in our own literature are represented by the "Daisy Chain" and "The Wide, Wide World." (*Literary Criticism* 1: 827)

The Daisy Chain was by the English writer Charlotte Yonge, best known for her popular 1853 novel, *The Heir of Redclyffe,* and *The Wide, Wide World* was the extremely influential 1851 novel by the American Susan Warner. James was saying that the final consequences of advanced French realism are to be seen in the stupid domestic narratives of best-selling Anglo-American women writers. As it happens, women's fiction did have a great deal to do with realism, yet there is something willful in James's icy declaration that Susan Warner has already arrived at the point Flaubert is aiming at. James not only began writing as an antirealist, but his early antirealism was bound up with a contemptuous view of women's domestic fiction: To be down-to-earth was to be far too undignified and female. Writing to William in 1869 from Switzerland: "I have unwound this string of homely details in the belief that it may amuse mother & Alice & gratify their feminine love of the minute & the petty" (12 July 1869, MH-H). Reviewing Stowe's *We and Our Neighbors* in 1875: "The reader remains in an atmosphere of dense backstairs detail which makes him feel as if he were reading an interminable file of tradesmen's bills" (*Literary Criticism* 1: 619).

The point from which James's writing took its departure has not yet been brought into clear focus. In the first volume of the biography, Leon Edel considered James's early reviews of Harriet Prescott's *Azarian* and Louisa May Alcott's *Moods,* and summed things up in this way: "In a society addicted to happy-ending tales, he was a confirmed realist" (*Untried Years* 213). The truth is exactly the opposite. From 1860 to 1867 American women were writing their darkest books of the century, and in almost every case James thought they were far too grim and pessimistic. Sarah B. Daugherty's survey of James's reviews and critical essays corrects the preconceptions in Edel's summation. Noting the young writer's aversion to Trollope and Flaubert, in fact to any intense representation of material and social determinants, Daugherty points out that James was "one of a number of reviewers [in the 1860s] whose idealism prevented their wholehearted acceptance of the commonplace" (20). What I would add is that James's animosity to the commonplace received an immense stimulus from his father's anticarnal doctrines and from his own appalled reading of the most recent phase of women's novels.

But it is necessary to take a longer, closer look at the many women's narratives that helped compose the literary cosmos James grew up in. This book is a study not simply of one particular male writer but of the interaction between him and a whole insurgent culture of female writers, who, from his point of view, often looked like usurpers wrongly established from the first. What I have to tell is to some extent the story of the collision and interaction of two different ways of dreaming the world, male and female. The opposing daydreams mesh, and do not mesh; but they meet in James's powerful imagination.

Today there are many Jamesians and others who continue to speak of a "master" whose artistry and cultural insight – and understanding of women – remain beyond question. There are also opposing readers who, in restoring to visibility some women writers, tend to put *them* beyond question, seeing them as an entirely separate tradition or instructing critics not to ask whether they are any good, or as good as James and the other men. I want to chronicle the long war that was fought in James's narrative imagination, and between him and the women, in order to break up the stalemate that has hardened over time into our own canonical or countercanonical pieties.

Fifties Best-sellers and Sixties Agonists

The Wide, Wide World, the American novel young James lined up with *Madame Bovary* in order to shoot the latter down, was one of the epoch-making feminine narratives of the 1850s, the only decade in American literature when women wrote practically all the best-sellers. Like *The Lamplighter, The Wide, Wide World* had an incalculable influence on readers all over the world and down through later decades, shaking millions of people in ways they could not forget. We get a vivid sense of the power of Susan Warner's novel from the episode in *Little Women* where Jo March carries the book up into her tree house on the first day of summer vacation and spends the day there reading and crying (123). *The Wide, Wide World* was a favorite with Vincent van Gogh also, who regarded "the first chapters" as "very fine, and so true and simple" (1: 80). Van Gogh gave the book to friends, and when he taught school in England in 1876 he assigned it to his pupils.

According to *Golden Multitudes,* Frank Luther Mott's survey of best-sellers in the United States, there were thirteen American novels published in the 1850s that were so popular they sold more than 225,000 copies in the succeeding one hundred years (307–8). If we exclude from consideration those works whose appeal had to do with religion and political reform (*Uncle Tom's Cabin, Ten Nights in a Bar-Room, The Prince of the House of David*), and those that attracted later generations of readers by virtue of becoming classics (*The Scarlet Letter, The House of the Seven Gables,* and *Moby-Dick*), we are left with seven novels written by women:[11]

The Wide, Wide World by Susan Warner
The Curse of Clifton and *The Hidden Hand* by Emma Southworth
The Lamplighter by Maria Cummins
Tempest and Sunshine and *'Lena Rivers* by Mary Jane Holmes
Beulah by Augusta J. Evans

These seven narratives tell us a great deal about the story preferences of a dominant segment of the American reading public. Ordinarily, if we are looking for information about real people in works of fiction, the most we can assume is that we learn certain secrets about the authors, or the authors' enemies. But the best-sellers of the 1850s, selected as a result of a national unplanned survey, have the information value of systematically gathered statistics. They open a special window into their readers' collective mind.

Up until the early 1970s, the few critics who paid attention to *The Lamplighter* or *The Wide, Wide World* consigned them to the deadliest literary category of all time, sickly fluff. (It is sickly fluff that fills Gerty MacDowell's mind.) Today, thanks to the work of Ann Douglas, Nancy F. Cott, Nina Baym, Mary Kelley, Judith Fetterley, and many others, mainstream women's fiction from the middle of the nineteenth century has emerged from the fog. The key discovery, presented by Baym in 1978, is that almost all the novels written by American women from 1820 to 1870 tell "a single tale." The heroine of "woman's fiction" is a young girl or woman who first assumes that she will be well taken care of in life but then finds herself basically alone, far more insecure and vulnerable than she had dreamed. She may be compelled to accept the protection of more powerful people, who variously alarm, insult, deceive, and torment her, but she keeps a self-reliant spirit and gradually acquires the skills, resources, and connections that enable her to survive on her own. She also shows a strong sense of duty and an unrelenting control of her desires. She generously assists those whose hardships are greater than her own, slowly acquires a circle of her own, and eventually wins "her own way in the world" (Baym 11).

It was one of Baym's chief points that this story formula embodied a reasonable strategy for overcoming the unfair social disabilities women had to face, and for this reason the novels were, if not revolutionary, definitely progressive. They accompanied a growing impulse to condemn feminine dependency, an impulse articulated by Elizabeth Stoddard in 1856: "I maintain that most women live with the view of being provided for in some way; they unhesitatingly adopt the idea of their female helplessness" (Matlack, "*Alta*" 296). The story formula also had a vital literary potential, stimulating writers to regard familiar social institutions from the point of view of the dispossessed, bringing in a great deal of gritty, mundane, domestic detail, and thus opening an approach to realism that would in time lead to *Sister Carrie*.[12] Along with the nascent realism went a hardy strain of heroism. But while this sometimes produced some very moving episodes, it more often gave rise to heroines who became monsters of exemplary and long-suffering righteousness.

The seven best-selling novels of the 1850s that were written by women told another story, however, which Baym did not discuss. This was the story of the heroine's temporarily ill-starred love, and it almost always culminated in a prospect of happy married life. Love was a standard feature of woman's fiction, along with Baym's successful struggle over privation and dependency. Together, these two stories defined the genre. The obvious problem is that the stories were not compatible. In Baym's summary, the heroine learns to be shrewd, determined, and self-directing, to manage her affairs, make alliances, assume adult responsibilities. Yet in every best-seller except *The Hidden Hand*, the male lead looks suspiciously like a savior at the end. The opening chapters of each book question male power and unearned female privilege, but in the end, after the heroine has fought the good fight, it appears that her reward is to be protected by a good strong man. To a modern reader, this conclusion looks like a sellout, as if the heroine's hard-won independence has been all along a temporary expedient. There was a signal contradiction in woman's fiction, and this contradiction was particularly glaring in the seven novels readers took most to heart.

There is a curious feature of the love story in these books that has escaped notice. In every single novel, even though the heroine learns how to take care of herself in a very rough and unjust world, the love she comes to feel for the boy or man who will in the end become her husband *first arises before she attains adulthood and independence.* The man she marries (or is destined to marry, in *The Wide, Wide World*) may or may not have passed puberty at the time she first becomes fixated on him, but one fact is invariable in the chronology of all seven books: She herself, at the time, is never quite grown up.

In three of the novels the person the heroine romantically binds herself to before becoming independent is a kind of older brother. In *The Hidden Hand* Capitola regards herself as promised to Herbert Greyson after residing with his family. In *'Lena Rivers* the heroine finds out that her fiancé is her stepbrother and then goes ahead and marries him. And in *The Lamp-*

lighter there are actually two pairs of quasi brother-sister lovers, and in the end both couples are united in marriage. One of the happy brides in this novel explains her life's romance by drawing a startling equation between sibling friendship and matrimony: "She and Philip," Emily says, "had loved each other in their childhood; before that childhood was fully past, they had parted; and as children they met again" (492). What marriage does, here, is to renew a lost childhood paradisiacal union, and this view finds apparent confirmation in the fact that the leading nuptial couple, in two of these three novels, originally lived in the same household on the footing of sister and brother. In Harriet Beecher Stowe's 1862 novel, *The Pearl of Orr's Island*, Moses and Mara are brought up in the same home. She sees him as "all the brother I ever had" (269), and he thinks of her as his little sister. In this narrative, however, as in *Wuthering Heights*, paradise is not of this world.

The same pattern may be observed in three of the other best-sellers, with this crucial difference: It is not the "brother" the heroine grows up to marry but the "father." In *The Wide, Wide World, The Curse of Clifton*, and *Beulah*, the orphan-heroine falls in love with her husband-to-be at a time when he is already a grown man and she is still a little girl; and not only that, but man and girl reside for a time in the same household, where he is clearly the person in authority and she is a dependent and insignificant-feeling child. The fact that the little girl marries this man even after winning her way in the world casts grave doubt on the nature of her hard-won independence. It should be observed that none of these men exhibit anything like Rochester's intermittent helplessness.

The best-seller that displays the gravity of this contradiction most blatantly is *Beulah*, the 1859 novel by Augusta J. Evans, who wrote her first novel in her teens and gave it to her father as a Christmas gift (Fidler 39–41).

The heroine, an orphan, begins by enduring the most terrible hardships and humiliations. Also, she feels she is not attractive and is especially sensitive about the mark that signifies her great intelligence – her large, overhanging forehead. She has the highest ideals and a dogged self-reliance, and she insists on supporting herself as a domestic servant rather than accept handouts. But when Beulah becomes too ill to survive on her own and is in danger of dying, she is rescued by a rich doctor named Guy Hartwell.

It was partly because of the similarity between Hartwell and Rochester that Evans was sometimes honored as "the Charlotte Brontë of America" (Davidson 622). Guy Hartwell is "proud, gifted and miserable," with "a chaotic, passionate and moody nature" (*Beulah* 61, 79). He insists on adopting Beulah even though she dislikes being dependent on him, and he tries to direct her upbringing. Once, when he seeks to introduce her into polite society, she resists:

"I cannot! I cannot!" cried Beulah, firmly, though tears gushed over her cheeks.
"Cannot? cannot?" repeated the doctor, pressing heavily upon her shoulders.
"Will not, then!" said she, proudly. (176)

Beulah is sixteen, Hartwell thirty-six (136, 137). She again asserts her will when she chooses to attend public school rather than accept tuition money from her guardian for a private institution. Graduating, she delivers the valedictory address on the topic "Female Heroism." Afterward, although Hartwell disapproves, she insists on supporting herself by teaching school, a decision she defends by declaring: "What was my will given to me for, if to remain passive and suffer others to minister to its needs? Don't talk to me about woman's clinging, dependent nature" (141). Force of will was a leading theme in all Evans's fiction. In her later and phenomenally popular *St. Elmo,* the heroine, Edna Earl, actually overcomes an incurable heart condition by imitating Ligeia's refusal to die. As Edna puts it, "You know Glanville said, and Poe quoted, 'Man doth not yield himself to the angels, nor unto death utterly, save only through the weakness of his feeble will.' Mine is strong, invincible" (*St. Elmo* 439).

Through most of *Beulah,* the emphasis is on the heroine's determination to think for herself. She reads widely in contemporary philosophy and soon finds she has lost her Protestant faith (for many, *Beulah* was the novel that dared to confront doubt). She defends her freethinking by employing the imagery of Ephesians 6 in a way that might have displeased patriarchal St. Paul: "I tell you there is nothing a woman cannot do, provided she puts on the armor of duty, and unsheathes the sword of a strong, unbending will" (233). Of course Hartwell, himself a skeptic, still condemns Beulah's double quest for self-support and philosophic truth. As she finishes an article "designed to prove that woman's happiness was not necessarily dependent on marriage," he declares his love and presses "a long kiss on her lips" (404).

A terrible sense of isolation overcomes Beulah. "She loved him above all others; loved him as a child adores its father; but how could she, who had so reverenced him, consent to become his wife?" (416). She says no, but when he leaves in disappointment for a five- or six-year trek through the deserts of Asia, she feels guilty and uncertain and begins to fall apart. Another man gives her Sir William Hamilton's "Philosophy of the Conditioned," and suddenly Beulah realizes that it is a great sin to try to make up her own mind about the world she has been born into. She despairs, goes down on her knees, praying "My God, save me! Give me light; of myself I can know nothing!" (452); and of course she is "saved."

When Hartwell returns from exile, Beulah lovingly embraces him but he stands unforgiving, leaning against the door jamb with his arms folded. Then without warning he clasps "her to his heart with a force that almost suffocated her" (500). With an authoritarianism quite different from that of Rochester, he says:

> "Beulah Benton, do you belong to the tyrant Ambition, or do you belong to that tyrant, Guy Hartwell? Quick, child, decide."
> "I have decided," she said. Her cheeks burned; her lashes drooped.
> "Well!"
> "Well, if I am to have a tyrant, I believe I prefer belonging to you?" (500)

One of the saddest details in this scene is that the punctuation mark at the end of the sentence announcing Beulah's shamed capitulation is not a period but a question mark. So complete is her philosophic and erotic submission that the act itself is left to her master to define, determine, and enforce. She speaks like a scared child trying to guess the correct answer to the question of her fate. And yet the author insists that it will now be Beulah's lifework to convert her husband to Christianity.

Beulah exhibits in an extreme and unstable form the contradiction at the heart of popular fiction during Henry James's formative years. In some ways this contradiction applies to all humans, male or female, caught between a desire to do what they want and a need to be cared for by others. But the contradiction had a special pertinence for women of the 1850s. Some may argue that the best-sellers set forth a childish concept of female sexuality in equating girlish affection or worship with adult attachment. Others might counter, more sympathetically, that "to be married figuratively to one's sibling was to be safe from outside forces" (Ziff 170), especially in a culture that insisted home was women's sphere. Either way, the fictive heroines who displayed an exceptional resourcefulness and power of endurance only to go happily – or un-happily – passive in the end would seem to be, finally, rather conserva-tive. They vented the reader's dissatisfaction yet shored up a beleaguered commitment to ideality, nurturance, marriage, and the home. The 1848 Seneca Falls women's rights convention represented what was then a militant minority. Mainstream women, judging from the best-sellers, shared the minority impulse to break their bonds – but felt an even stronger impulse to reaffirm them. Readers were profoundly satisfied by the story of a heroine who began as a free and spunky orphan and ended as a victorious wife lapped in coziness.[13]

The inherently unstable formula for women's fiction began to break up at the end of the 1850s. *The Hidden Hand,* an engaging novel by Emma Southworth serialized in 1859, stretched the formula to the limit by turning the defenseless orphan-heroine into a cross-dressing tomboy who passes for a boy in a tough section of New York City. After a policeman discovers this unusual heroine's gender and arrests her, she is remanded to the protection of an old-school Virginia aristocrat. The idea of the novel is to display the insouciant success with which she defies him and all the other older, richer, stronger men who seek to control or entrap her. In the end she marries, but with no sentimental feelings at all. It is understood that she, not her husband, will wear the pants. *The Hidden Hand* was the one best-seller of the 1850s whose heroine never sold out, and thus it necessarily subverted the romantic dependency that was essential to the denouement of earlier books. Southworth's novel broke the mold, yet it appears to have been one of the five or ten best-loved American books of the century.[14]

But *The Hidden Hand* was basically a romp. The book was fun and good, but what about novelists who chose not to forswear the realistic potential in the orphan's story, a potential many novels by women had partly realized since *The Wide, Wide World* appeared in 1851? What story would a woman tell who tried to resolve the contradiction between dependency and independence within the context of recognizable social fact?

Russel B. Nye has pointed out that a new theme emerged in women's fiction after 1860, the "loveless marriage" (9), meaning one in which the wife does not – cannot – love her husband. One of the first writers to tackle this tricky new theme was Louisa May Alcott. During a five-year period beginning in 1860, she wrote and rewrote what would prove to be one of her few grown-up novels, *Moods,* which tells how Sylvia marries Geoffrey when she really loves Adam. By coincidence, shortly before *Moods* was eventually published in 1865 by A. K. Loring, another Boston publisher, Ticknor and Fields, brought out a novel with the identical story, *Emily Chester,* written by a Baltimore woman named Anne Moncure Crane; Emily's story is that she marries Max but feels a supersensuous magnetic pull toward Frederick. The resemblance between *Moods* and *Emily Chester* was noticed by contemporary readers, among them young Henry James, Gail Hamilton, and Alcott herself, who was displeased.[15] A reviewer wrote, "Just as there is a lull of that excitement which the publication of 'Emily Chester' produced, there comes . . . a work upon the same theme, called 'Moods' " (advertisement in the *New York Evening Post* [7 January 1865]: 2). Eighteen years later Mark Twain came upon a note in the *Boston Post* about the close parallel between *Moods* and *Emily Chester,* and he innocently added the account to his article, "Mental Telegraphy" (98). He evidently believed that the two young writers had flashed messages to each other, between Concord and Baltimore.

But there is no need to invoke magic. The coincidence had another cause. In the early 1860s the time had come for the novel about a heroine trapped in a loveless marriage. The unhappy wife had been everywhere in fiction of the fifties, but not one of the best-sellers had permitted the *heroine* to marry badly. The fact that she began to do so around 1860 shows that novelists were trying to work out the contradiction at the core of feminine narrative. Why should the heroine alone escape female misery? The emergence in the 1860s of the novel about the loveless marriage means that something inevitable had begun to happen: Women's fiction was beginning to grow up. The doughty orphan-heroine was fading, and so was her happy concluding union with a fatherly lover. In other words, at the very time when Henry James was trying to break into the world of letters, a younger generation of women writers was taking a more unflinching look at women's lives than ever before.

Suddenly there was a sizeable group of narratives with a very grim tone, intimating that death or misery is the only possible issue and implying that there are thousands of cases like the one we are reading. Rebecca Harding Davis's first novel, *Margret Howth* (1862), was about the suffering of a single woman who tries to still her starved heart through philanthropic devotion. Originally *Margret Howth* had an unhappy ending, but the revision that was pressed on Davis by her editor at the *Atlantic* allowed the heroine to marry the man she loves (Austin 46). Davis did not confine herself to treating the ordeal of womanhood; later in the sixties she wrote two novels about racial and economic oppression, *Waiting for the Verdict* and *Dallas Galbraith*. Two other writers, however, Adeline Whitney and Elizabeth Stoddard, continued to focus on women's themes and to do so more uncompromisingly than had earlier writers. Whitney's 1865 novel, *The Gayworthys,* narrating several female lives simultaneously, told about bad matches that should not have been made and good marriages that are either delayed (for seventeen years) or altogether frustrated. Stoddard, a daring and original New England pagan, was the grimmest and most unflinching novelist of this group, and easily the best. Her first novel, *The Morgesons* (1862), had a fearlessly sensual heroine named Cassandra, and the rendition of her maturation was taut and bitter. Nathaniel Hawthorne was so impressed by the book he wrote Stoddard a congratulatory note. But young Henry James hated *The Morgesons,* and in 1865, when he read Stoddard's second novel, *Two Men,* which refurbished the story of the orphan-heroine who marries her guardian, the notice he dashed off for the *North American Review* was so vituperative it did not see print for a century (Kraft). In Stoddard's third novel, *Temple House* (1867), a hearty egalitarian character observes a marriage ceremony and, when the priest says, "Whom God hath joined, let man not put asunder," laughs to himself and thinks, "curious stuff, that, for a couple of children" (58).

These five writers – Louisa May Alcott, Anne Moncure Crane, Rebecca Harding Davis, Adeline Whitney, and Elizabeth Stoddard – form a clearly defined group. They all began writing fiction in the late 1850s or early 1860s, picking up the traditional women's story that formed the basis of earlier novels but exploiting it in order to make a much less inhibited analysis of what it meant to be a woman, and what the prospects were. Their work was circulated by the best magazines and publishing houses and generated a lot of talk. The writers themselves all peaked in the sixties, and then either died or stopped producing fiction or turned to children's literature or churned out works so mediocre and preachy they may safely be ignored; and before long their serious sixties novels had been forgotten. Because these associated women novelists are central to my study, I have found it convenient to give them a common name: the Civil War women agonists.[16] I regret that the limits of this book forbid any consideration of the poet with such close affinities to the agonists, Emily Dickinson, who shared some of their stylistic experiments and their treatment of unsatisfiable desire and the fatherly lover. The agonists constitute Dickinson's lost cohort.

One reason I give extended attention to the agonists is that they were the heirs of traditional women's novels of the 1850s; another is that they helped bring Henry James, Jr., into being. He read *all* of them, and during his first years as a magazine contributor he reviewed all their more important novels. It is the Civil War women agonists who link James to women's fiction. His reviews were long, detailed, and very strongly felt, full of disapproval veering to outrage yet punctuated with an occasional confession that his own imagination had received a jolt. That is to say, James was the vital witness, at the formative stage of his career, of the tortured climax of nineteenth-century women's fiction in the United States.

But of course James was hardly a disinterested witness. Not only was he a struggling young writer, but in the 1860s, more than in any later period of his life, he saw himself as American, like the agonists. The readers he felt he had to reach were American readers, and the competitors he had to reach across were American writers, mainly all the modern little women, who commanded too much uncritical public attention. Later on, James would seek to conceal these American roots, and Leon Edel would inadvertently propagate the image of a European James, one who acquired next to nothing from the American literary culture of his formative years.[17]

Another reason James could not be disinterested as he read the agonists was that he had conspicuously failed to get himself initiated in male American society (as I have argued elsewhere), and he was very sensitive about this (Habegger, *Gender*). He had a remarkable rapport with his unstable sister Alice (Strouse 48–49, 139), and he would later develop close friendships with Minnie Temple and Grace Norton and, as Edel has shown, a number of older ladies, chief among them Fanny Kemble, the actress who had run away from her Southern slaveholding planter-husband. Still, he shared many of the prevailing views of what it meant to be a man or woman and what kind of behavior and aspirations were appropriate for women. Most important of all, he was the extremely good and loyal son of a philosopher whose theory of woman's redemptive role entirely excluded the possibility that she herself might be dissatisfied. And according to one hostile witness, Lilla Cabot Perry, James's mother, Mary, "was the very incarnation of *banality*" (Strouse 44).

Thus, in the middle 1860s, when the brilliant son of a philosopher of marriage and his possibly banal wife undertook to review a group of novels in which the agonists, the daughters of woman's fiction, were conducting a tortured inquiry into the contradictions of marriage and femininity, something very interesting had to happen. Again and again the son's reviews defended the father's anticarnal views of women, and attacked the claims of "temperament" and personal "affinities" and "magnetic" attraction – all contemporary code words for sex and free love. The new generation of women's novels carried a strong whiff of physicality and social disorder. They threatened to release once again that obscene beast that had shattered the elder Henry in 1844, and the younger Henry did what he could to keep the beast, now strangely female, under wraps. And yet at the same time, particularly in his review of Anne Moncure Crane's second novel, *Opportunity* (1867), young James found himself unexpectedly responsive to the portrait of an ardent and independent girl struggling against an intangible bondage. According to Daugherty's survey of James's early reviews, "When he discovered a spirited heroine in the author's works, his attitude changed from condescension to respect" (22). This was especially the case if the heroine was oppressed: "Lady Glencora, young and fascinating, torn from the man of her heart and married to a stranger, and pursued after marriage by her old lover, . . . touches at a hundred points almost upon the tragical" (*Literary Criticism* 1: 1320). The youthful male writer's imagination was the field of battle on which the huge collision between female insurgency and male resistance took place.

As this young man read all the new novels about unhappily married wives, he was forced against his will to recognize one of his major subjects, to recoil from a treatment of it that appalled him, and to begin imagining his way toward *The Portrait of a Lady*. His early fiction, like his reviews and his after-dinner lecture to Louisa May Alcott, *answered* the women, showing them how they should have told their story. His first novel, *Watch and Ward,* took one of the women's favorite stories – the orphan heroine who grows up to marry her guardian – but tried to get it right by transforming the guardian from a tyrant into a tolerant encourager and by making the girl grow up to be a proper lady. Indeed, in this novel James lifted a scene from one of the agonists' novels (the same scene his review had singled out) and laundered it of its flaw (the same flaw the review had ridiculed).[18] James's early reviews establish an unbroken line between the agonists' novels and his own corrective narratives. Once he started retelling the ladies' fictions, however, their original logic began to assert itself and work against his own gentlemanly impulses.

One of the most important and fascinating continuities in the bestsellers of the 1850s, the agonists' novels of the 1860s, and certain of James's own narratives is the frequent pairing of an independent and original girl-heroine with a much older lover. Often the lover is already a father, like Gilbert Osmond. Often he is the heroine's own guardian, as in *Beulah,* Alcott's "A Marble Woman; or, The Mysterious Model" (1865), Stoddard's *Two Men* (1865), and James's *Watch and Ward* and *What Maisie Knew.* The older lover is not only much more experienced (like Basil Ransom, who has a variety actress for a mistress), but he may have been the lover of the heroine's mother – Sir Claude, in *What Maisie Knew,* Vanderbank in *The Awkward Age.* Whenever James reviewed a novel in the 1860s that contained this romantic pair, he took notice of them and recorded his distaste. He called them "the precocious little girl" and the "middle-aged lover" (*Literary Criticism* 1: 189–90), and he claimed, I suspect accurately, to have encountered them in a hundred narratives. He put them into his own narratives, but with a crucial difference: After *Watch and Ward* he would always regard their relationship with a critical disbelief that is absent from most women's novels. For what the fatherly lover does in James is to threaten the precocious girl's freedom.

James's best work thus turns out to be saturated with American literature and life in ways he may not have been fully conscious of. In the bestselling women's novels, in the agonists' work, in Alice James's madness, and in James's own narratives we can discern a common passion or yearning, and that yearning is incestuous. To the extent that James's fiction was rooted in American society, it was rooted in incest – in incestuous acts, perhaps, but even more in incestuous daydreams.[19] The acts cannot be documented, but because of the best-sellers we know the daydreams existed and were widespread and greatly enjoyed. In novel after novel the heroine ends up marrying her guardian, stepfather, or preceptor after undergoing a terrible ordeal. In novel after novel, we build up to a warm reciprocal love between an orphan girl and the man who provides her with shelter *before* she reaches physical maturity. One of James's basic obsessions in his fiction was to control, to master, this disturbing family romance – a romance that, within his own family, his sister Alice may have struggled against, without success. Many critics have pointed out that *The Portrait of a Lady,* the first novel in which James made his play for fame and greatness and centrality, is about the heroine's own imagination. Another way to say this, in historical terms, is that *The Portrait* is about the collective imagination that wrote and read all those novels – that loved to relive the precocious girl's love for a middle-aged man who (in words James wrote in an 1865 review) "spends his time in breaking the hearts and the wills of demure little school-girls, who answer him with 'Yes, sir,' and 'No, sir' " (*Literary Criticism* 1: 190). Much of James's distinction – and Joyce's in "Nausicaa" – came from a deep engagement with a mass feminine daydream, one whose symbolic incest was an unavoidable consequence of patriarchal family life.

Yet James – again like Joyce in "Nausicaa" – also betrayed woman's fiction. This body of narrative represented a struggle against patriarchy from within. If the heroine submits, she also defies. If her imagination has been to some extent subverted by her life of bondage, so that she dreams of surrendering, she also dreams of independence and fights hard for it. Where woman's fiction was contradictory, James's fiction resolves – but in the wrong way. Why does Verena Tarrant allow Basil Ransom to wrest her away from the speech she has her heart set on delivering? Why does Caspar Goodwood's forceful kiss finally show Isabel that she must return to a tyrannical husband and a failed marriage? Once, after two of Minnie Temple's sisters married men over twenty years their senior, Minnie wrote James a proud letter saying *she* would never follow suit. When one reflects that James made the character based on Minnie do precisely what the real girl said she would not, having Isabel marry a middle-aged man who is so expert in breaking the heart and will of his demure little school-girl daughter, one is face to face with the elusive male authoritarianism of James's narratives. To make Isabel marry Osmond, and then go back to him once she knows better, was to be unfair and illiberal to the memory of a free spirit. It was to insist that even the American girl, the freest woman of all, finds freedom too much of a burden, and it was to forget that any heroine worth making an ado about can be defeated only against her will. With few exceptions James's heroines would either connive at their own defeat, or their creator would weaken their powers of resistance at the critical moment. Why is Daisy Miller the one who dies of malaria, even though Giovanelli and Winterbourne are also exposed? Behind James's narratives there is found the ancient theory that women are weaker than men. Daisy, Isabel, and Verena, like Joyce's Gerty, have been lamed in secret by their author.

Chapter 2

The Lessons of the Father

Henry James, Sr., on Sexual Difference

When Henry James, Jr., wrote his memoirs in his late sixties, he was surprised at the number of times he could recall accompanying his father away from home – he alone without any of the other four children (*Small Boy* 68). The aging son interpreted this public father-and-son companionship as an odd reflection of mid-nineteenth-century American manners, but I should like to propose an alternative interpretation: The father wanted his second son, his namesake, to inherit his own sense of social life. Henry Sr. would show the public world to Henry Jr., and explain it to him.

The impression the younger Henry gives of his father in the two volumes of memoirs, *A Small Boy and Others* and *Notes of a Son and Brother*, does not wholly agree with what one can learn about this father from other sources, especially his own writing. The son drew a portrait of a man devoted to a doomed, yet heroic, intellectual labor. The senior James never succeeded in getting anyone to believe in him, or really listen to him, but he never lost heart. He was a droll Olympian, completely without pomp or public honors, a magnificent man and father. He would not force his cherished ideas on his children, and yet these ideas saturated the home and rendered it all the more sacred. Convert the literal into the symbolic and spiritual, Henry Jr. remembered being taught. Scorn moralistic thought. Don't be selfish. Be social (*Notes of a Son* ch. 6).

Although Henry Jr. admitted he had really learned next to nothing of his father's vast and original system, he was proud that he had "never . . . been so *bête* . . . as to conceive he might be 'wrong,' wrong as a thinker-out, in his own way, of the great mysteries" (*Notes of a Son* 228). Henry's first friend, Thomas Sergeant Perry, remembered how loyal the son had been in his teens: "Harry had heard his father describe the great reformer's [Fourier's] proposal to establish universal happiness, and like a good son he tried to carry the good news further" (*Letters,* ed. Lubbock 1: 7). Another anecdote told by F. O. Matthiessen indicates that James never lost this half-blind loyalty: "When Bernard Shaw indulged his love of trying to shock by declaring to Henry Junior that the most interesting member of his family was neither himself nor his brother but their father, he found that no praise could have been more welcome" (7).

The question of the senior James's influence on his second son and his fiction has exercised more than one scholar and biographer,[1] but the subject remains vexed and obscure. There is a rich and tantalizing mystery here, involving two powerful minds bonded by filiality. Why did the son want the father to gain recognition, to be vindicated, when the son himself did not understand him? If the father's ideas saturated the home, why *didn't* the son understand? And just how benevolent *was* the father if the one sure thing his son learned was that the paternal thinker could not be understood or doubted or in any way separated from his investiture of clouds?

Unlike Henry Jr., William wanted to see through the clouds, and he systematically read the elder Henry's books, reporting to Henry Jr. that their father's "ignorance of the way of thinking of other men, and his cool neglect of their difficulties is fabulous in a writer on such subjects" (2 October 1869, MH-H). While William dared to read the father in the light of what other men thought, Henry simultaneously protected him from public exposure yet nursed a secret hope that his thought would be admired by all.

Most of those who have written about Henry James, Sr., in the twentieth century have seen him as an admirably nonconforming, adventurous, and above all liberal and tolerant thinker, but recent biographies of his other children – William, Wilkie, Bob, and Alice – have shown how misleading this image is. Jean Strouse shows that Henry Sr. had a confusing and stifling effect on his only daughter, and Howard M. Feinstein argues that he visited on his eldest son the same forceful pressure he had been subjected to by his own father. Bob, Jane Maher reveals, was unrelentingly advised to do his "duty." There is no doubt the senior James sought to indoctrinate his children: Among his manuscripts is a "Dialogue between a Parent and Child" in which a father explains the meaning of spirit. It is also clear that a great deal of coercion was brought to bear on Henry Jr. A scrupulous reading of his memoirs spots many hints of the father's (and mother's) manipulativeness. In Geneva, for instance, the parents persuaded their second son to give up what he most cared for and attend a technical school. "I puzzle it out to-day that my parents had simply said to themselves, in serious concern, that I read too many novels, or at least read them too attentively – *that* was the vice; as also that they had by the contagion of their good faith got me in a manner to agree with them" (*Notes of a Son* 4). It would appear that young Henry Jr. was not only subjected to a rigorous and unnecessary discipline but was also made to believe – "in a manner" – that this discipline was good. When such a son grows up and writes his memoirs of childhood, how reliable will they be, even if he does puzzle things out today that he had not quite understood earlier? Do we take him at his word when he assures us that it was the *contagion* of the parents' *good faith* that led him to endorse their discipline?[2]

The task this chapter assumes is to try to discern the conscious and unconscious intellectual inheritance that passed from Henry Sr. to Henry Jr. To do so, we must leave the confines of the son's texts and explore the father's own writings, trying to understand them both in themselves and in the context of the ways of thinking of other men – and women. The usual approach to the thought of the senior Henry James has been to regard it as a strenuously original reconstruction of the Calvinism he thought he left behind in his youth. But this is not the only approach. As it happens, the one department of the father's thought that the son paid close attention to was the doctrine on "woman" and marriage. In 1870 – the same year Henry Jr. wrote in three different letters that he strongly agreed with his father's views on the difference between the sexes – E. L. Godkin pointed out in the *Nation* that Henry Sr. had "made the philosophy of marriage, one might almost say, a special study" ("Society and Marriage" 332).[3] For over three decades Henry Sr. poured out an astonishing number of essays, reviews, lectures, and letters to editors explaining his philosophy of marriage, and at his death he left a large number of manuscripts on the subject.[4] These unexplored materials shed a startling light on who the Jameses were and what they were saying in their writings and why those writings seem to keep so much behind a veil. The father's doctrines shaped the son's response to the women's novels he read in the 1860s and helped shape the son's own narratives about women.

Free Love

Over fifty years ago Austin Warren (107) turned up something in the James family record to which no biographer, historian, or critic has paid much attention. In 1848, the year of revolution, Henry James, Sr., translated and wrote a laudatory preface for a Fourierist tract, *Les Amours au phalanstère* by Victor Hennequin. *Love in the Phalanstery,* as James called his translation, was sponsored by the American Union of Associationists. Like some of the other works advertised on its back cover, it explained how life would be organized in the perfect and harmonious social unit – the phalanx – of the future.

It was well known that Charles Fourier had certain heterodox French notions about the relations between the sexes. Five years earlier, Bronson

Alcott had talked to Emerson about "marriage & the fury that would assail him who should lay his hand on that institution, for reform: and spoke of the secret doctrines of Fourier" (*Emerson in His Journals* 318). In 1846–47 Henry J. Raymond had been so successful in attacking Fourier's views on marriage in the pages of the *New York Courier* that his opponent, Horace Greeley, editor of the *New York Tribune*, effectively backed away. The *New York Observer* had run a series of articles on Fourier and marriage that was so aggressive it elicited a statement from the master's disciples disowning his teaching on this subject (Muncy 70–71).⁵ If there was one thing that most American Associationists were agreed on in 1848, it was that the less said about Fourier and marriage, the better. Not so Henry James, Sr. Of the eleven passages he marked in Parke Godwin's *Popular View of the Doctrines of Charles Fourier*, three were in the short and cautious chapter on marital arrangements (84–90, HJSr's unbound copy at the Swedenborg School of Religion). Unlike Godwin's diplomatic presentation, the pamphlet James put before American readers offered an uncompromising statement of Fourier's "passional series," and the preface James added called attention "to the truths involved in these views."

Fourier had taught that monogamy was only one of several legitimate kinds of marriage. People were animated by a variety of passions, and the ideal society would evolve a variety of institutions to satisfy them. Women who wished to remain single would be able to support themselves; those women or men who preferred to marry and be faithful to their spouse could so do; provision would be made for those who wanted a series of sexual partners, or who needed more than one spouse at the same time. Fourier had evolved a series of technical terms – the *damoisellat*, the *faquirate*, the *pivotate* – for these varying categories, and Hennequin's tract pedantically set them forth, as did James's translation.

The translator's stated motive was "to give the public some true information concerning Fourier, in place of the scurrilous falsities with which our unprincipled newspaper censors have regaled it." James apparently believed that if Fourier's critics could read his own doctrine on marriage, their mouths would be stopped. No "well-meaning man" could read Hennequin's tract "without cordially assenting to its *conclusions*." James took the offensive (he would *always* take the offensive) and attacked "our present erotic institutions and manners." Marriage failed because it gave each spouse "an absolute *property* in the affections" of the other. This material relationship, James argued, "directly instigates deception, adultery, domestic tyranny, and dissension throughout the land." It is not Fourier, then, but the present system of marriage and its defenders that promote "a promiscuous intercourse of the sexes." Fourier himself was innocent: All he did was to sound "the death-knell of our profuse prostitution and licentiousness."

James was thirty-seven years old at the time he wrote these words. He had been married eight years, he had fathered five children, and he had had one nervous collapse. His preface bristles with rage and grandiose condemnations, and inevitably raises a number of questions. Did James seriously expect to convince Fourier's American critics that *they* were the supporters of licentiousness? How far was he prepared to accompany Fourier in his passional series? The translator proclaimed his lofty and pious "hope for the eventual extinction of the present adulterous and promiscuous commerce of the sexes" – and yet Hennequin's own pamphlet seemed to endorse almost every type of sexual impulse (except the "*vice de Sodome*" and that "*de Sapho*" [*Amours* 50]). And there was a strange wild card in James's method of arguing, as everything seemed to metamorphose into its opposite. He defined promiscuity, for instance, not as multiple sexual relations outside marriage but as that "intercourse which takes place between man and woman, unsanctioned by any ties of the heart, or by the reciprocal personal preference of the parties." This idiosyncratic "spiritualized" definition suggests that promiscuity may be found chiefly within marriage, and this was evidently James's point. "But where this mutual preference does not exist, where the husband does not inspire the highest affection of the wife, nor the wife that of the husband, then their intercourse is truly promiscuous, being the intercourse of consenting bodies merely, and dissentient souls. However much the law may declare these bodies united, their own souls pronounce the union adulterous." Interesting. But suppose an *unmarried* couple happened to feel the highest affection for each other: Would their union be promiscuous? James's answer is startling: "Where this mutual preference for each other exists between the parties, there Love exists, and in a true social order *every expression* of it would be divinely beautiful and sacred" (italics mine). Evidently Henry James, Sr., had a dream of what used to be called free love.

On publication *Love in the Phalanstery* brought forth a laconic prediction from the *New York Tribune*'s book reviewer: "We . . . presume the anti-Fourierites can find something in it which they might quote to great advantage" ("New Publications"). This was correct, and James was soon involved in bitter and strenuous controversy. The *New York Observer*, an influential Presbyterian weekly representing the denomination that William James of Albany had supported and Henry Sr. had renounced, devoted two columns to an attack on the pamphlet, which proved that "*Fourierism*, is only another name for *promiscuity*" ("Love in"). *Love in the Phalanstery* showed once and for all how sinister the American Associationists were in their aims. Other papers chimed in. Alfred E. Ford, formerly an Episcopalian clergyman and now sympathetic to utopian socialism, wrote to the *Harbinger*, the official organ of the American

Fourierists, and reminded them that they would be well advised to abjure the master's views on marriage ("Letter").[6]

James rose to the occasion. Answering the *Observer*, he identified himself as Hennequin's translator and sought to clear the American Union of Associationists of all discredit. Instead of supporting Hennequin's "truths" as he had in his preface, he now claimed that he was neither "prepared to endorse Fourier's details of the organization of the love relations" nor "disposed to gainsay them"; he only wanted to get people to think. He doubted, however, that "the unchangeable will of God" forbids "all erotic intimacies" ("Observer and Hennequin" 197) between unmarried men and women. James defended himself even more vigorously in his replies to Ford, sometimes retreating into obscurity or arcane definitions and at other times giving vent to extremely defiant and unusual opinions. The reason men are licentious and lustful, he argued, is that love is not free: "If you bind a man in whom the passion of Love is highly organized, to the intercourse of one woman, whether he feel any love to her or not, you not only provoke his unmerited disgust towards her unoffending sweetness, but you are sure to inflame his passionate longings towards every other woman from whom you have excluded him" ("Concluding Remarks" 61). Fortunately, a new order was at hand: "I presume a day will come when the sexual relations will be regulated in every case by the private will of the parties; when the reciprocal affection of a man and a woman will furnish the sole and sufficient sanction of their material converse" ("Remarks" 37). When that "divine time" arrives, the law will no longer require couples to adhere to "any past act or promise." Instead, the law "will declare the entire freedom of every man and woman to follow the bent of their private affections, will justify every alliance sanctioned by these affections. . . . Thus, if a man's or woman's affections bind them to an exclusive alliance all their days, the law will approve. If, on the contrary, they lead the subject to a varied alliance, the law will equally approve" ("Remarks" 37). James went so far as to allow that "technical fornication" may under certain circumstances be considered "spiritual marriage" ("Concluding Remarks" 60).

If one compares James's opinions on the marriage controversy to those expressed by other contributors in the *Harbinger*, it becomes clear that in 1848 James belonged to the radical wing of utopian socialism. Most of the other contributions either defended monogamy or hinted that this was a topic the Associationists had better steer clear of.[7] But James did not take the hint. He believed, like Swedenborg, that a revolution had taken place in the spiritual world. The foul present order was being transformed into a perfect future; legal institutions were about to be spiritualized; the letter of the law was even now passing away. There was a new and much less restrictive sexual order in the making, and James meant to proclaim it. He contributed $78.86 to the *Harbinger* (6 [26 February 1848]: 134), and his alarming pronouncements on passion and law, appearing in nearly every issue, clearly dominated the magazine during its last months of existence. When publication ceased, following two of James's longest and most contentious articles, a fellow radical at the Oneida Community wondered whether James's "subjects and ideas" had "proved to be too heavy 'freight' for the Harbinger" ("Movements and Changes"). It appears that the most important socialist journal in antebellum America was finally done in by James's imprudence and belligerence.

Of course there were many other Americans besides James in the 1840s who dreamed of a new social harmony that would unchain human sexuality. There were the Mormons with their still-secret polygyny, and there was the amazing John Humphrey Noyes and his Perfectionist community at Oneida, New York, where each member of one sex was married to all the members of the opposite sex, and nearly everyone practiced a carefully supervised promiscuity. Years later Henry James, Jr., would dismiss the moral and social life at Oneida as "simply hideous" (*Literary Criticism* 1: 567) and his novel *The Bostonians* would make a veiled allusion to the colony, renaming it Cayuga and hinting that Selah Tarrant had been "associated" (*Bostonians* 73) there with Mrs. Ada T. P. Foat. But thirty-five years earlier the novelist's father had himself preached "association,"proclaiming in his lectures, articles, and a book that "nature and society should have no power to identify me with a particular potato-patch, and a particular family of mankind all my days" (quoted in review of *Moralism and Christianity* 89). So fascinated was he by the Oneida experiment that he more than once visited its Brooklyn branch, probably in 1849 or 1850. A few years later, recollecting his encounter there with the "leading men," he described them as "*ultra* – that is to say, consistent – Calvinists" whose fanaticism had led them beyond "common sense," and he claimed to have lectured them on their "disorderly lives" ("N.Y. Observer and Mr. James"). An Oneidan who was present, however, remembered the debates rather differently. According to this spokesman, who was probably Noyes himself, James criticized the community for "our narrow-minded views of the value of the Bible" and "the foolishness of our slow way of propagating our sentiments." So far from restraining Noyes, James had urged him to do what he himself would soon attempt – "to operate on the public mind through such established journals as the *Tribune*" ([Noyes?] "Mr. Andrews").

There is no doubt James felt a strong solidarity with the "honest, upright souls" of the men at Oneida. "They were fathers and husbands and brothers like myself, disfigured to be sure by a morbid religious conscience, but no less capable of suffering on that account whatever I suffered" ("N.Y. Observer and Mr. James"). This wistful and obscure statement (what *was* this masculine suffering James had in mind?) informs us of an extremely important affinity: James and Noyes, both born in 1811, were part of the same generation, and the two men developed in different ways their generation's dream of a revolutionary sexual utopia. A writer for the *New York Observer* saw in the Oneida Perfectionists "the same tendency which is so strikingly manifested by Mr. James . . . namely, to clothe an essentially sensuous dogma in a spiritual dress" ("Marriage and Reformers" 366).[8]

This can be a costly dream. In 1852 a wild book was published, *Love vs. Marriage,* that pressed James's antinomian impulses far beyond anything he had imagined. It was written by Marx Edgeworth Lazarus, who a few years earlier had contributed several articles and translations to the *Harbinger.* The Jameses once had Lazarus to dinner to discuss the prospects of Associationism (HJSr to James T. Fisher, 7 June 1849, Fisher Papers, MHS). Since that time Lazarus had been doing some heavy traveling. His new message was summed up by the New Testament verses he ingeniously conjoined in his epigraph:

> For in heaven they neither marry nor are given in marriage, but are as the angels of God.
> Thy kingdom come, thy will be done, on earth as it is done [*sic*] in heaven.

The book developed James's own view that love and marriage were not compatible in the present civilization. Giving an exposition of the same passional series that *Love in the Phalanstery* had presented, Lazarus pushed on to argue that humans were promiscuous by nature: Love "requires for its vigor and permanence in action, the charm of variety, the alternation of its objects. . . . Hence, monotony, monogamy, or exclusive constancy, are for love a true suicide" (251). What Lazarus did was to reduce James's ideals to practice, offering "Practical Suggestions to Lovers" (ch. 4) and a great deal of physiological information on the formation of semen, the ovulation cycle, the steps to avoid pregnancy, and so forth. James may have been troubled to discover that *Love in the Phalanstery* and two other books of his were included in Lazarus's bibliography (326). Most alarming of all was the author's stated wish

> to clear away that confusion of opinions and of action which has hitherto compromised the efficiency of our propagandism and of our practical efforts; *to reveal men to themselves* and to each other. . . . I take pleasure in acknowledging the substantial integrity of the writings of *Henry James,* of John S. Dwight, of Albert Brisbane, and Dr. C. J. Hempel among our American friends, although considerations

entirely personal may prevent them from taking openly the same ground as myself. (250; italics mine)[9]

(A few months later an editor of the *New York Observer* wrote that an "elevated and decent style of argument" could not be expected from James because of his "present views and associations" ["Letter to Mr. James"].)

James retaliated with a long essay-review in the *New York Tribune*, "The Marriage Question," that worked out an obscure and allegorical view of marriage. Only in concluding did he turn briefly to *Love vs. Marriage*, dismissing it in a few contemptuous phrases – "a very needless affront to public decorum," "mere childishness, mere imbecility." This lofty air was quite disingenuous, as James, waked up from his revolutionary slumbers, was fighting for his name, and he was also resisting Lazarus's effort to reveal James to himself. His review was in effect a fervent defense of monogamy as a legally sanctioned institution. He still dreamed of "a perfect society," but now it must be one in which every man finds "an exhaustless ideal charm" in "the wife of his bosom" and in no other woman; it was time to cultivate one's private potato patch. James kept his old view that marriage is a disappointment for the husband because his wife can never "fulfil the promise which the unappropriated woman held out," but he now preached that this disappointment is precisely what man needs to raise himself from the physical to the spiritual. The history of each man and of civilization itself follows the same path: First man glimpses in the "downcast eyes" of the woman he has enslaved a radiant glory; he binds himself to her for life; and eventually the confinement of marriage proves to be a saving discipline for him through which he transcends himself.

In this redemptive fable, James apotheosized the very thing – monogamy – he had set out to reform. Still believing (like Lazarus) that marriage was the death of love, James now abandoned the pursuit of happiness and instead proclaimed that all men must follow a long and painful process of self-correction. James preached this gospel for the rest of his life; it formed the core of his doctrine. Because so many students of the Jameses have simply accepted the doctrine as a given in his thought, it is of the first importance to understand the pressures that led him to elaborate and espouse it – his own heartfelt tendency to free love, the fear of being claimed by Lazarus as a brother-in-arms, the final loyalty to "public decorum," and the deep self-betrayal. James's philosophy of marriage was created to defend James himself from an antimatrimonialism that was so seductive he could resist it in no other way.

It is also important to note the completely unconscious egotism of

James's little fable. Everything is calculated with certain male needs in mind, and women's own dissatisfactions or desires or liberties never once enter into the matter. Woman is man's angel, a totally different kind of being from himself. James announces from on high how man can escape his selfish nature, and the remedy he thunders out is sublimely selfish. A revision in one of his lecture manuscripts, which speaks of woman's influence on "our ultimate social evolution" and then replaces "our" with "man's," neatly sums up his blindness to the other sex ("Philosophy of Marriage," sheets 32–33). This is the man who would be regarded by some of his children – among them Henry Jr. – as a marvelously unselfish father and devoted husband.

Slave Love

Having spurned what he believed in 1848, James now had a new set of enemies to contend with, the free-love radicals. This hard-pressed faction needed all the help it could get, and the loss of James, with his wealth, prestige, energy, and wit, was a severe blow. Few Americans of the time grasped that the essential issue in free love was one of civil liberty rather than morality. Almost everyone, including James, associated the cause with fringe movements like homeopathy, vegetarianism, and spiritualism. They could not imagine that a time would come when most Americans would apparently take for granted that the state should not regulate the sexual lives of citizens. (It is ironic that even under rulers as hostile to civil liberties as Reagan and Bush and the Rehnquist Supreme Court, we can now say that the principle of free love has won – temporarily.)

Of all James's new enemies, the most adept and tenacious was Stephen Pearl Andrews, the philosopher of "individual sovereignty." Andrews was angered by James's "saucy and superficial" review of Lazarus, and two months later, when James publicly defended his old position in favor of more liberal divorce laws, Andrews struck back. He had been looking for a way to introduce the dubious topic of free love into a large-circulation paper. He sent a letter to the New York Tribune and James was soon enticed into a lively public debate. Andrews showed how James's own statements on divorce meant that marriage was at times oppressive and should be terminated. James defended divorce in a strange way: "If our conjugal . . . ties . . . can be safely discharged of the purely diabolic element of outward force, they must instantly become transfigured by their own inward, divine, and irresistible loveliness." Andrews, seeing just where James was vulnerable, approved of his preference for the "sexual union of loving souls" over "the sordid considerations of a marriage settlement." Insofar as James trusted to "the self-regulative powers of freedom, in the place of regulations imposed from without" (Andrews et al., *Love* 14, 41, 5, 98), he was pushing free love.

James was very neatly caught. What was particularly upsetting was that the editor of the *Tribune,* Horace Greeley, who opposed divorce and of course detested free love, pointed out to his readers that Andrews's libertinism was the logical consequence of James's own position. Worse, Greeley contended that "Mr. James's liberty of divorce, no matter what *his* intent may be, . . . would practically open to the licentious and fickle a prospect of ridding themselves of the obligations of marriage at pleasure." To discredit Andrews, Greeley cited a newspaper report: "Henry Schriver eloped from this city last week with the wife of a neighbor, leaving behind a wife and several children" (Andrews et al., *Love* 39, 53). If this was Andrews's tendency, then it was Henry James's as well.

The rich and respectable father once again saw himself classed with a shady crowd. The contradictions of his social thinking were out in the open. Losing his temper, he blustered at Andrews's "lurid and damnable falsehood" that his own opinions served in any way to sanction "license" (Andrews et al., *Love* 59).

Now James had to retreat even further, and some of the intellectual strategies by which he did so are nothing less than appalling, especially his redefinition of freedom. Mankind, he dogmatically announced, lives under a "threefold subjection, first to nature, then to society, and finally to God." Perfect freedom is to be found only in total submission to these three: "It constitutes the express and inscrutable perfection of the divine life that he who yields himself with least reserve to that most realizes life in himself" (Andrews et al., *Love* 59–60). In this sentence, James is still concerned with "perfection" (like Noyes) but he has lost sight of choice and social institutions. Although he began by defending desire or will against law or force, he now feels a pressing need to surrender to something inscrutable. He abandons a political argument questioning the right of society to constrain individual choice, and he abandons it in order to embrace a psycho-universal process in which choice has no part. In this way, a dreadful new equation moves to the center of James's social thought: Slavery is freedom. The unknown scandal of James's obscure metaphysics is that it was designed, under intense pressure, to limit civil freedom in the guise of enlarging it.[10]

Another strategy James followed involved women. He had already begun to think of "woman" as a different kind of being from man, a *deus ex machina* who redeemed him from his carnal selfishness, but in his 1853 essay, "Woman and the 'Woman's Movement,' " James pushed this argument to its political conclusion. He now ridiculed feminism, opposed the entry of women into the learned professions, and insisted with remarkable emphasis that women were intellectually inferior to men. At the heart of his essay was the banal idea that home is woman's sphere, an idea James developed to the point of claiming that woman was not an individual but "a form of personal affection." It is "only in ministering to man" that she "finds her life." The "woman's movement" (a phrase Henry Sr. would always put in quotes) did not in his opinion "presage any directly valuable results" (286, 287, 279).

"Woman and the 'Woman's Movement'" brought out some strong responses in the New York Tribune, where James's old socialist friend, George Ripley, was literary editor. Undoubtedly aware of the author's identity, Ripley praised him as "some golden mouthed Chrysostom of our own day" ("March Magazines") but remained noncommittal on the points at issue. Two others, however, Antoinette L. Brown and the unknown writer of a striking opinion piece called "Man and Woman," took the new Chrysostom severely to task. The latter writer pronounced James's essay "the most liberal and candid of any we have read on the conservative side" of the woman question but regretted that the author had not "seen fit to consider what is desirable and necessary for Woman, instead of looking at the subject as if the only point to be considered were how Woman shall render herself most bewitching and serviceable to Man." This skillful controversialist developed his/her argument by creating a dialogue between "Man," who utters James's words and sentiments, and "Woman," who voices some keen feminist rejoinders. Thus, to "Man's" claim that women are not suited to the learned professions, "Woman" asks, "Why enact laws at Albany and Washington to fortify Nature's resistless fiat?" To "Man's" praise of woman's "delicious weaknesses and softnesses . . . which constitute the arms of her omnipotence to the imagination of Man," "Woman" scornfully points out that those of her sex who are deficient in these attractions still need to earn a living. She accuses "Man" of an ulterior economic motive: It is to ensure an abundant supply of cheap labor that he excludes women from the best-paying work. At the end of the dialogue "Woman" brusquely rebuffs "Man's" – and James's – "greasy gallantry and sterile flattery." This was one of the few public attacks to which James did not issue a rebuttal.

Unlike James, Andrews did not lose sight of the problem of individual liberty in marriage. He argued that present statutes turned wives into "helpless dependents," who were "liable at any time to be thrown upon their own resources, with no resources to be thrown upon." This dependency fostered "mental imbecility and bodily disease" or else transformed wives into clever slaves who concealed their real aims and thoughts from their husbands, and often from themselves. As an institution, marriage was a "house of bondage" (Andrews et al., Love 18–19). The difference between the two thinkers is that while Andrews spoke for the rights of individuals trapped in an often oppressive institution, James spoke for the institution. One of the contradictions at the heart of his son's novel, *The Portrait of a Lady*, is that it represents marriage as a house of bondage yet never supports the obvious idea that Isabel would be wise to escape. It is because slavery is freedom that Isabel is refined by her oppressive life with Osmond.

Henry Sr.'s evolution reminds us of the familiar truths that millennialism and sexual antinomianism often go together, and that radical dreams are often succeeded by pompous sound and fury. We get a sharper sense of the meaning of his social thought, however, if we locate it in the context of the tensions and oppositions of his own time and place. It helps, for instance, to distinguish two opposed tendencies in the radical ferment of the 1840s and 1850s. The first shows up in the Mormons, who reserved the privilege of sexual variety for men only and placed women in an inferior social category, and the second shows up in those dreamers – Noyes, Lazarus, Andrews – whose millennialism was transformed into a secular vision of greater freedom for both sexes.[11] One type of millennialism reverted to an archaic, patriarchal order, and the other turned into a modern kind of civil libertarianism. The Mormons came to regard marriage as the central institution of their sect, while the free lovers often joined the feminists in arguing that for women marriage was a form of dependency. Although James had strong Eastern upper-class affiliations, he was surprisingly close to the Mormons.

Another way to plot James against the larger tensions of his day is to compare the disagreements between him and Andrews with the central contradiction in popular women's novels of the 1850s. The first chapters of *The Wide, Wide World* or *Beulah* are a vivid narratization of Andrews's position: The suddenly orphaned heroine figures women's political and economic dependency. But the segments of the novels telling how the heroine learns to devote herself to others, or how, like Beulah Benton, she capitulates to a man who controls her and whom she will somehow save, duplicate James's own later philosophy of marriage. The contradictions in James were to some extent homologous with the contradictions in his changing society and in that society's fiction. In spite of his monstrous show of originality, his key ideas were often familiar and banal.

Yet there remains an elusive personal aspect to James's social thought: The heart of his mystery is not to be plucked out. Late in life he wrote Henry Jr. that Mary "really did arouse my heart, early in our married life, from its selfish torpor." To his son Robertson the father confided that his wife had preserved him from "envy, hatred, contempt of others, ill-will, lasciviousness, memories, unchaste nay unclean desires."[12] These confessions, which would be perfectly in character for St. Elmo, seem less than candid in the light of Henry Sr.'s often repeated claim that marriage kills love rather than rouses it. The confessions are also incomplete: What *were* those "unchaste nay unclean desires" that Mary preserved him from? And how odd to find the neutral *memories* lurking in this catalog of sins. What did James want to forget? Back in 1848 he once issued a strident declaration that he was perfectly clean: "I am unconscious . . . of any desire after greater passional liberty. . . . I have never that I remember brought myself either by look or word or deed into illicit relation with any woman living or dead whether that relation be conceived as dating from my own existing conjugality, or that of the opposite party" ("Further Remarks" 53). But this seems like too much candor rather than too little: Surely the man protests too much. Why are there so many legalistic provisos – "that I remember," "living or dead"? Why does he insist he is "unconscious" of desire rather than say he does not desire? And does not the last long clause exclude from consideration any relationship *preceding* his "existing conjugality"?

The senior James may have had more of a past than we realize.[13] This much is obvious, however: To trace his social thought from 1848 to 1852 is to see in action a shocking self-disgust. The thing desired turns into the thing that must be repudiated, and desire itself is first holy, then filthy. In 1848, using the imagery of fountains for human sexuality, James wrote that in an ideal marriage the husband and wife "each drinks in a plenary refreshment from every inmost and covert fountain of the other's spirit" ("Concluding Remarks" 61). Four years later, however, wetness was wicked: James hoped that a perfect society would shame man "out of this odious *slang and slaver* of personal adulation now called love" ("Marriage Question"; italics mine). Slang suggests the demotic associations the patrician James generally avoided, and slaver is a frothy secretion that has connotations of animality, fierce appetite, disease, and insanity. Henry Jr.'s readers have often noted in his fiction an appalled sense of human carnality and a tendency to see love as a kind of vampirism. Were these also lessons of the father?

Sweet waters turn bitter, and freedom suddenly reeks of hell: Such was the pattern of James's famous breakdown in Windsor, England, in 1844. According to his account written decades later, he had been relaxing comfortably after a meal when he experienced a total and inexplicable panic. The only way he could account for it was on the supposition of "some damnèd shape squatting invisible to me within the precincts of the room, and raying out from his fetid personality influences fatal to life" (*Literary Remains* 59). James did not see this spirit-creature, but he was in no doubt about its gender and noxious attributes. It is hard to avoid the inference that the squatting personality was a projection of James himself. It was perhaps the way he secretly regarded himself as a carnal and self-engrossed man. So alienated was he from his feelings that he could sense them only in someone wholy *other*.[14] Yet he also was at times aware that his beast lurked within. Speaking of his "audacious faith in selfhood," James wrote: "When I sat down to dinner on that memorable chilly afternoon in Windsor, I held it [this faith] serene and unweakened by the faintest breath of doubt; before I rose from table, it had inwardly shrivelled to a cinder. One moment I devoutly thanked God for the inappreciable boon of selfhood; the next, that inappreciable boon seemed to me the one thing damnable on earth, seemed a literal nest of hell within my own entrails" (*Literary Remains* 71). The telling detail here is that James located his selfhood in his digestive organs, as if he saw himself as essentially a greedy beast. It was not simply his carnality, his physical appetites, that appalled him, however, but the combination of this carnality with a kind of wild ego – one whose restless pursuit of satisfaction and vindication necessarily kept it blind as to what it really was. James's philosophy of marriage was the structure that allowed a phantom called spirit to usurp the place of this greedy, wild, and unacceptable self.

Thus, the senior James devoted himself to a lifelong project of self-evisceration. He developed a blatantly defenseless yet overpowering personality, which confused his children about the limits of his authority, and he tinkered all his life with a universal scenario explaining that men must be forced to yield up their fetid personalities and pass from egotism to society. His effort to destroy his own "selfhood" left him averse to any and all individual quests for greater personal freedom, autonomy, or self-expression. He came to believe, as W. D. Howells put it in a review, "that whatever conception of human freedom involves the notion of a completed and independent existence [of the creature] is false" ("Reviews" 762). This belief was fatal to any concept of individual political liberty. Yet, as is customary with authoritarian regimes, James's social thought pursued its goals behind a veil of secrecy, obscurity, and disingenuousness. It was a complex fate having such a man for a father.

Stopping Their Mouths

As Henry Jr. passed through his unhappy youth and early adulthood and entered his vocation of writing, his father gained recognition as a leading seer on the modern questions of "woman" and marriage. In his extensive correspondence with his disciples, he handed down the truth with perfect self-assurance, explaining to one female inquirer, for instance, that for a woman "to yield herself up to mere passion, is to renounce her nature. . . . She degrades herself out of womanhood therefore whenever she disobeys affection, and seeks her own satisfaction primarily" (HJSr to Julia A. Kellogg, 2 June [1866?], MH-H). When a New York congressman shot and killed his wife's lover in 1859, Henry Sr. contributed three long letters to the *New York Tribune* – "The Lesson of the Sickles Tragedy" and two pieces titled "Marriage – Divorce."[15] An almost identical crime ten years later inspired his *Atlantic* essay, "The Logic of Marriage and Murder." He read versions of his lectures, "Marriage" and "Woman," to numerous audiences, and he incorporated his ideas on these topics in his books. The list of his essays and letters to editors dealing with his views on sexual difference is surprisingly long, and some of these productions made a great impression. At his death in 1882 an obituary writer still remembered that "a discussion of his with Horace Greeley in the columns of the *Tribune*, about 1858, on the marriage question, apropos of the Sickles case, was a rich entertainment for those who could enjoy masterly declamation, even if they by no means shared his somewhat mystical views of the relation of husband and wife" ("Henry James").

But the more Henry Sr. wrote and lectured, the more confused his listeners became. Although he again and again excoriated free love as nothing but "free hell," some of his listeners heard a very different message in his words. A British journalist named William Hepworth Dixon identified James in *Spiritual Wives* as a free lover (2: 242–43). Dixon was careless and sensational, yet William Henry Channing also believed that James tended to apotheosize "instinct" (170). Godkin of the *Nation* darkly suspected that his views had a tendency to do away with marriage ("Society and Marriage"). Noyes himself, the founder of Oneida, felt in 1870 that James had "continued faithful to both Swedenborg and Fourier, to the present time" (*History of American Socialisms* 546).

James had a particularly confusing effect on some of the women who regarded him as sympathetic. On 25 April 1866, Caroline Dall, a Boston feminist then separated from her husband, paid James a visit and talked about an accusation of some kind that had been made against her by Elizabeth Peabody. According to her journal, James did a strange and unexpected thing as she was saying good-bye. Apparently divining her wish for "a fuller richer life," the seated man

> drew my head down with a gaze – as compulsory as a blow – and kissed me on the mouth.
> I received this kiss – prolonged, steadfast – and compelling – as I might have received an electric shock – making all the time keen intellectual inquisition into its purpose. A divine Pity seemed to stream from his eyes – but I felt as if the kiss sealed a compact.
> "People shall not talk about you in this style – I will not let them" – he said as I rose & said coolly "thank you" – and then I laughed – as if any handful of dust could check the current of this world's petty hate! (Dall Papers, MHS)

It is anyone's guess what Henry Sr. meant by this kiss, but one thing is clear: It confused Dall. It was like the philosopher's doctrine of marriage – intense, vehement, mystifying.

James had a bitter quarrel about the same time over his teachings on "woman" with Julia A. Kellogg, one of his most faithful disciples. After he mentioned his 1853 *Putnam's* article to her, "Woman and the 'Woman's Movement,' " she evidently challenged him with some of its less creditable passages. He claimed to "have no distinct memory of its scope & contents; and what you quote of it doesn't reassure me." But he couldn't understand why Kellogg took issue with him. He summed up his views on the suffrage question in this way: "My opinions as I expressed them to you the morning we talked remain unchanged. I told you then that I thought suffrage ought to be universalized & would be. But I told you at the same time that women wouldn't avail themselves of it when it was granted. I think so now still" (HJSr to Julia A. Kellogg, 7 January [no year], MH-H). This rigid certainty that women would not vote once they were able to do so shows that James had not changed his mind since writing the *Putnam's* essay. He was still absolutely sure that women took no real interest in their own freedom.

In 1868 the New England Women's Club approached James and requested him to read a lecture on "woman." He agreed on the condition that they "invite him afterward to deliver it in public" (M. Howe 80). It is not known how many women heard him read his talk on 7 December. A letter he wrote earlier that day to Emerson expressed the fear that the bad weather would keep everyone away and that the lecturer would be his own "sole auditor" (Perry 1: 98). Some clubwomen attended, however, and a lengthy summary published in the first issue of the *Woman's Advocate* tells us what they heard. Evidently James set forth the same basic scenario he first worked out in his 1852 review of *Love vs. Marriage*. He informed his listeners that man represents a "descending movement" and his "distinctive activity is physical and moral, being more particularly identified with the civic consciousness of the race. Woman's action is of a higher or more spiritual scope." The implication of the speech was that women reformers who sought to expand their civic role were overlooking their real calling. Although the speaker disdained to comment on the famous woman issue – "the petty altercation which was springing up between *men* and *women*" – he blithely predicted that "men would probably continue to claim the highest place in the synagogue" and "women would continue to accept the lowest seats." The reason for this inequality is that "what is high [woman spiritually considered] always gives precedence to what is low" (Field 31, 33).

What would a group of moderate feminists of the late 1860s think of this speech that simultaneously ennobled and abased them? At the end of the *Woman's Advocate* summary, there is a brief paragraph containing a sentence that seems to be at variance with the lecture's conservative flavor: "Mr. James would have every barrier destroyed to women's freest activity in any line they themselves pleased" (33). One modern historian has quoted this sentence out of all James's voluminous writings on women to indicate his sympathy with feminism (Leach 274).[16] My own guess is that the sentence represents the speaker's conciliatory response to an uneasy or even hostile question from the floor. None of the lecture manuscripts on "woman" in the James collections at the Houghton Library ends with a passage similar to this one. According to Annie Fields, the wife of the influential *Atlantic* editor, the Boston clubwomen "disliked" (M. Howe 80) the talk – and no wonder.

The club kept its bargain, however, and the following March Henry Sr. was given the opportunity to deliver the same lecture to the public. Only twenty people attended. One of them was Fields, who kept an extremely informative private record in spite of being attached to "Le Brun's motto for women . . . 'Inspirez et n'ecrivez pas' " (journal entry for 19 February 1866, Fields Papers, MHS):

> In the evening we went to Cambridge to hear Mr. James read his paper on "Woman." We took tea first with the family and afterward listened to the lecture. He took the highest, the most natural, and the most religious point of view from which I have heard the subject discussed. He dealt metaphysically with it, after his own fashion showing the subtle inherent counterparts of man to woman, showing to what extremes either would be led without the other. He spoke with unmingled disgust of the idea of woman . . . forsaking the sanctity and privacy of her home to battle and unsex herself in the hot and dusty arena of the world. (journal entry for 13 March 1869, Fields Papers, MHS)

It was because of that "unmingled disgust" that the feminist clubwomen had disliked Henry Sr.'s speech. Yet their response to him was so carefully edited that a casual reader of Fields's journal and the *Woman's Advocate* would probably not have realized that they were summarizing one and the same lecture.[17]

The clouds enveloping Henry James, Sr., will not easily dissolve, yet in this instance the more conservative listener undoubtedly caught the real tendency of his words. In a very illuminating passage, Fields wrote that James

> . . . helps to lay that dreadful phantom of yourself which appears now and then conjured up by the W. rights people, haranguing the

crowd and endeavoring to be something for which you were clearly never intended by heaven. I think I shall never forget a pretty little niece of Mrs. Dale Owen, who was with her at the first [Sorosis] Club meeting in New York. Her face was full of softness & Madonna-like beauty but she was learning to contract her brow over ideas and become "strong!" in her manner of expressing them – It was a kind of night-mare. (journal entry for 13 March 1869, Fields Papers, MHS)

The women's rights advocates gave Fields an uncanny sense of a phantom self – an ugly contorted face behind the pretty wallpaper. It was nightmarish to see this phantom emerge from the face of a young "Madonna-like beauty." (In fact, the pretty little niece was Mrs. Ella Dietz Clymer – a separated wife, experienced clubwoman, and actress in training.) There had to be a Henry James, Sr., to exorcise the phantom of liberty in women. He seemed to embody all that was liberal, energetic, exuberant, human, but his real job was to reanesthetize women, so that their brows could relax and they could give up the effort to be "strong!" He stopped their mouths by kissing them, and that is one reason why there has been so much confusion about the drift of his thought.

The most clear-sighted response to James's lecture came from the pen of Frances ("Fanny") Macdaniel, a former resident of Brook Farm whose egalitarianism had survived an extended residence in the Paris of Napoleon III. Expressing herself in sentences that read like translations from the French, Macdaniel recognized that James's purpose was to buttress an old-fashioned social and political ideal:

The first word of the season – here in Boston has been given by Mr. Henry James in his lecture on "Woman" – before the New England Woman's Club. The philosophy of Mr. James you are acquainted with – this lecture is full of it – its main point – is his declared antagonism to woman's entering upon a political & professional career in society in its present form. – sending her back with a compliment which might turn her head by its devotest adoration – to a deeper *home* sphere than any she has yet realized. But any light from him – how to gain this deeper freedom in her womanhood is not given. (letter to William Aspinwall Tappan, 23 January 1869, MH-H)

What would it be like to be the daughter of such a man? The only real mystery in connection with Alice James is not that she was psychotic but that we have had to wait for Jean Strouse's 1980 biography to begin to understand why. Strouse has shown in convincing detail how confused Alice was by the treatment she got from her father, who stimulated her to think for herself but also convinced her that as a female she had an inferior intellectual capacity and had better keep still. Strouse's case is strengthened by a letter from Gail Hamilton to Henry Sr., which confirms that he was opposed in principle to the education of women: "I agree with you in desiring to have women distinct and different from man, . . . but you, O faithless and perverse man, have not trust in nature. You seem to think that woman must be kept away from the tree of knowledge lest she should thereby become *manny*" (Dodge 1: 433; letter dated 12 August 1864). On this issue, Henry Sr. was in agreement with the most conservative opinion of his time. He was aligned with Dr. Edward H. Clarke, whose influential 1873 book, *Sex in Education; or, A Fair Chance for the Girls,* argued that the modern trend toward the education of young women deranged their reproductive system and ignored the natural distinctions between the sexes; feminists bitterly opposed this book (see Gay 213–15).

The four James boys all went away to school at one time or another, but in the winter of 1866–67 Alice went away to the home of the New York orthopedist, Dr. Charles Fayette Taylor, who was opposed to "so-called 'higher education' for women." Taylor's diagnosis of Alice's trouble may be surmised from the paper he presented several years later, when an association of dentists invited him to speak on "Necrosis," or decay. Taylor took this opportunity to unload his views on decay at all levels – in the city, the family, and the mind no less than in the teeth and bones. He was certain that the universal cause of all the malformation and deterioration he had observed was the excessive stimulation of the emotions, particularly in the childbearing and -rearing gender. He recounted the case history of a girl who showed signs of intermittent languor and irritability and gave "evidence of curvature of the spine." On investigation, the cause proved to be her occasional visits to a grandmother, "a very intellectual woman," whom the girl "looked forward" to seeing "with great anticipations." Once the visits were stopped, on the doctor's orders, the girl cheered up and her back became "perfectly straight" ("Emotional Prodigality" 361, 359, 366). The man to whom Henry Sr. sent his daughter to be straightened out was convinced that women would develop kinks and twists if their minds were stimulated.[18]

At home no less than at Dr. Taylor's, Alice was a classic victim of a systematically disabling regimen presented as the kindest possible treatment of her sex. She worked hard to believe that her father loved her dearly. Strouse thinks she felt a helpless but overwhelming rage against him but directed it against herself. She would feel a "violent inclination" for "knocking off the head of the benignant pater as he sat with his silver locks, writing at his table," yet conceived of the struggle to restrain her violent impulses as "a fight simply between my body and my will"

(Strouse 118). The phantom of liberty that the father had stilled with his magic words, written at a table, had to be kept down no matter what. And yet, if you were alert and questioning, you could not help undergoing sudden shifts in your vision, so that the placid Madonna face itself became the nightmare and, sensing what the truth was, you broke out screaming and thrashing because something so *opposite* could not possibly be endured. And suppose you were that daughter's novel-writing brother and enjoyed a remarkably close bond with her, as Strouse (139, 249–51) has demonstrated that Henry had with Alice. Maybe you would be especially good at showing how a sinister father – Dr. Sloper, Gilbert Osmond – exercises an eerie tyranny over a daughter.

Your Article on the Woman Business I Decidedly Like

Because of the paternal Jamesian resistance to self-awareness, and because of the connected impulses in Henry Jr. – the need to muffle, to ennoble, to protect family privacy – it is no easy task to know with certainty what the son learned from his father's lessons on marriage and womanhood. Our aim will now be to discern, from firm documentary evidence, exactly what Henry Jr. made of the father's confusing philosophy of marriage and exactly how these lessons began to shape the novelist's fictions.

In 1869 the Jameses were confronted with a clear challenge to their commitment to sexual difference – John Stuart Mill's brilliant and epochal plea for liberty, *The Subjection of Women*. William probably read the book while on summer vacation with his family in Pomfret, Connecticut; Henry Jr. read it by himself during his summer in Switzerland.[19] Apparently he left no record of his direct, personal opinion of the book, but once he learned how his family was dealing with it he began to speak up. William and Henry Sr. each reviewed Mill in conjunction with an antifeminist book by Horace Bushnell, *Women's Suffrage; The Reform against Nature*. The reviews appeared in New England's leading literary and intellectual magazines, the *North American Review* and the *Atlantic Monthly*. With these reviews, the Jameses deployed their peculiar family doctrines on women to stake out a position in a larger theater of thought and politics. As we shall see, Henry Jr. allowed the two older male Jameses to mediate and guide his own responses.

William worked long and hard on his review. On 6 September 1869, Mary wrote Henry Jr. that William was "writing a notice of Mill & Bushnell's books for the North American which interests but tries [or "tires"?] him I fear" (MH-H). When she wrote two weeks later, William had "just been writing" and the notice had now lengthened to an "article" (21 September [1869], MH-H). It was published in October. On the critical question of women's participation in civic processes, William

clearly felt much more sympathetic to Bushnell than to Mill. William
quoted Bushnell at length: "All government belongs to men. . . . Where
agreement is impossible, one of the two clearly must decide, and it must
be the man. The woman's law . . . requires it of her . . . to submit
herself to his fortunes. . . . If he has no sway-force in him . . . to hold
the reins, he is no longer what Nature means when she makes a man"
(WJ, Review 557). It was hard for any son of Henry James, Sr., to see
anything wrong with this. William's own comment was: "So far so
good. If Dr. Bushnell is contented to urge this as an ideal, a matter of
inexplicable sentiment, he remains in a strong position" (557). Unfortunately, instead of simply resting on his sexist feelings, Bushnell made the
mistake of producing two arguments that William found unconvincing –
the claim that because of women's "subject nature" they can achieve
"ascendancy" only through submission and suffering, and the claim that
women will be unsexed if they vote. William refuted both arguments,
labeling the former "the good old Catholic doctrine" (557), which had
been used over the ages to console "sick men" and "many a slave" (558).
In making this point, William was backing off from his father's extreme
emphasis on bondage and the superiority of abasement.

In confronting Mill, however, William proved himself a loyal son
after all.[20] The "inexplicable sentiment" of male dominance and female
dependency, which was Bushnell's strong suit, now came to William's
aid as he sought to answer Mill. William admitted that *The Subjection of
Women* built a rigorous case on the basis of the ideas of equality and
liberty, but he made no effort to meet Mill on his own ground. Instead,
William evaded the issue of justice by psychologizing it; the argument
from "justice" (558) gets metamorphosed into "Mill's fervid passion
for . . . 'justice' " (565). Consistently focusing on the "hot vehemence"
(560) that motivated Mill, and suggesting more than once that he had not
kept his feelings under control, William made it his chief point that *The
Subjection of Women* had a "sentimental kernel" (561) lurking in all its
apparently rational arguments. Mill's basic sentiment, William suggested, was a strange, idiosyncratic ideal of equal friendship, and an
accompanying aversion to what most men understood by love. William's
review sought to discredit this "sentimental ideal" (561) in a surprisingly
dogmatic fashion: He simply asserted that "the ideal of the representative
American [man] is opposed to this. . . . The wife his heart more or less
subtly craves is at bottom a dependent being" (562–63). The unmistakable implication of William's review is that Mill, for all his logic, is
wrong simply because he refuses to recognize the American man's need
for a dependent wife.

On 7 October Henry Jr. commanded his brother to "*cut out* & send me
your article in the N.A.R." (MH-H). The article reached him by the end

of the month, and Henry wrote back: "Your notice of Mill and Bushnell seemed to me (save the opening lines which savored faintly of Eugene Benson) very well and fluently written" (*Letters* 1: 161). This sentence seems mildly approving but essentially noncommittal on the important question as to what Henry Jr. thought about the content of his brother's review. The reference to Benson, however, yields significant clues, especially in view of the fact that William's opening paragraph anatomized Bushnell's exuberant and inelegant style. Only a few months earlier, Benson had an article in the *Atlantic*, "French and English Art-Writers," that strained to characterize various prose styles. But more was involved than style: Benson was a well-known magazine essayist who championed art against philistine morality and decorum, yet also pushed for social reform. Reviewing Gail Hamilton, he offered an unusually detailed critique of her style but also praised her "new gospel of married life" ("Woman" 121). He defended American women novelists, George Sand, Thoreau, and the value of the Brook Farm experiment, but he also spoke up for manners and repose and against familiarity (Benson to Church, 12 October 1866, William Conant Church Papers, NYPL). He wished that American men of letters could "nourish themselves on all the succulent and opulent things of life," and he admired "the force and felicity" of Henry Sr.'s language ("About the Literary Spirit" 489).[21] In some ways Benson looks like an alternative version of young Henry himself – more democratic, less proper and moral, less adroit. It is suggestive that Henry thought he heard the voice of "the irrepressible" (*Letters* 1: 372) Benson in William's heavy-handed opening paragraph and that he did not like it.

Henry Jr. did not commit himself openly until he read his father's own remarks on Bushnell and Mill in the *Atlantic Monthly* of January 1870. Henry Sr.'s "The Woman Thou Gavest with Me" sought to answer several recent contributions to the woman problem, among then Epes Sargent's very interesting book-length poem in blank verse, *The Woman Who Dared*. (Linda, the child of a loving but unmarried couple, supports herself as a painter and dares to propose to a man.) But Henry Sr.'s essay gave only the most cursory attention to what these books had to say. He chiefly tried to set everyone straight once again by repeating his old argument that "if woman is dependent upon him [man] for her outward subsistence and honor, he is dependent upon her influence for all those inward or spiritual qualities which lift him above the brute." Mill is wrong because he is blind to the inherent "rational or moral" difference between man and woman. Also (as William had said) Mill is too passionate, and because he ignores "the interests of order" in favor of individual liberty, he is not even a proper philosopher. As for free love, there shall be no more Lindas: Men and women "have no right" to live together "without the amplest previous social authorization." Everyone must remember that "the welfare of society is primary" and "the welfare of persons altogether secondary" (68, 69, 71). All in all, the essay virtually completes Henry Sr.'s progress from the rights of the individual to the rights, so to speak, of society. (A few months later he wrote that "the only way in which harmony can ever be promoted" between the individual and society is "the *forcible and permanent subjugation* of men's private to their public interests ["Logic" 748; italics mine]). His mystifying title, taken from the excuse Adam gives God for eating the forbidden fruit, omits the *to be* that the Authorized Version added to the Hebrew – "the woman thou gavest to be with me." What does James's title-phrase possibly mean by itself? To give a woman *to* a man would be correct English, but what does it mean to give a woman *with* a man? Like everything Henry Sr. wrote, the very title of this essay flashes yet conceals an inadmissible message – in this case, that it is right for one person to own another. That strange "with" is nugatory, and sometimes, as in his 5 May [1866] letter to Julia A. Kellogg, Henry Sr. dropped it: "the woman thou gavest me, said Adam" (MH-H).

Henry Jr. borrowed the January *Atlantic* from friends and read his father's essay. Now at last his opinion was strong and clear:

> I read at the same time . . . your article on the Woman business – so you see I have had quite a heavy blow of your genius. Your *Atlantic* article I decidedly like – I mean for matter. I am very glad to see some one not Dr. Bushnell & all that genus insist upon the distinction of sexes. As a mere piece of writing moreover I enjoyed it immensely. (14 January 1870, MH-H)

This passage is a key document in understanding what the Jameses were about. Bushnell was a Congregational theologian. It was to be expected that he and his "genus" would oppose female suffrage. Henry Jr. was enthusiastic about his father's article because it proved a nonsectarian thinker could *also* insist on the old idea that women were not as men and ought to occupy a separate sphere. When the loyal son singled out "the distinction of sexes" as the point at issue, he was endorsing the most reactionary element in his father's thought, an element that underlay the father's tormented scenario for the salvation of the male and that also ensured a continuing coolness toward women's rights.

Back in 1852 the senior James had cited the notion of sexual difference to distinguish between his opinions and those of Elizabeth Oakes Smith. In his view, this early feminist lecturer was "engaged in a very arduous crusade against the natural and obvious distinction of the sexes, the which distinction I meanwhile set great store by" ("N.Y. Observer and Mr. James"). By 1870 this distinction had become the basis of the Jameses' family life, their individual identities, their deep intellectual commitments, their writing. Men had the "sway-power," and women were affectionate, selfless, and yielding, and the "sentimental" consequence of this natural difference was a powerful feeling of attraction between the sexes. This feeling was by nature asymmetrical: the man's sentiment for the woman necessarily included his sense of her sweet dependency, and the woman's sentiment for the man was based on his superior force. Because of this reciprocal but asymmetrical bond, no true man could love a managing woman and any woman would pervert herself if she tried to emancipate herself or otherwise match man's force. Henry Jr.'s 14 January letter to his father is extremely important because it informs us that he *bought* "the distinction of sexes," and also because it clears up the enigmatic note he wrote himself in 1883 about his plans for *The Bostonians:* "I asked myself what was the most salient and peculiar point in our social life. The answer was: the situation of women, *the decline of the sentiment of sex,* the agitation on their behalf" (*Complete Notebooks* 20; italics mine). *The Bostonians* was conceived partly as a final demonstration of the decay of New England society now that radical democracy and the women's rights movement had rooted out the natural sentiments that accompanied sexual difference. *They should have listened to Henry James, Sr.*

The *Nation's* conservative backlash on women's issues in 1867–70 forms an important context for Henry Jr.'s endorsement of his father's views. Two articles from 1866 illustrate the magazine's original liberalism: "Female Suffrage" by Charles Eliot Norton stated that "the moral judgment of the more thoughtful portion of the community is already convinced that it is not only right but wise that woman should take her place as the political equal of man," and George Perkins Marsh spoke up for "The Education of Women." The next year E. L. Godkin felt, ominously, that "anything which promises to make the female mind a little more masculine in its way of working will be a positive gain for society" (" 'Female Influence' " 73). A few months later Octavius B. Frothingham attacked the more vigorous supporters of women's suffrage (principally Stanton) for harming the cause ("Women vs. Women"). Two years later the same writer assailed the "apostles of 'a-sexualism,' " announced that the sexes "neither think, feel, wish, purpose, will, nor act alike," and spoke of suffrage as an "experiment" that might well fail ("Is There Such a Thing As Sex?" 87, 88). Godkin was now wondering why women activists never mentioned "the passion of love" ("Neglected Side"). He gave high praise to Mill's *Subjection of Women* in 1869 but devoted the bulk of his review to objections: Mill was wrong to argue that the nature of the two sexes remains unknown, and he overlooked sexual drives, especially woman's "maternal function" ("Mr. Mill's Plea for Women" 73). In 1870 Godkin ran two series of articles opposing female suffrage (James Miller McKim's

"Vexed Question" and Lulu Gray Noble's "Notes on the Woman's Rights Agitation") and he himself wrote a bitter satire urging that babies be given the ballot ("Baby Suffrage").

Henry Jr. followed this development closely. In 1869 he wrote William, "You must have received my message about the *Nation:* I miss it sadly" (*Letters* 1: 113). In a postscript to his 27 February 1870 letter to Alice, he asked, "Who is the author of the *Notes* on the Woman's Rights Question in the Nation?" and on 8 March 1870 he repeated the question in a letter to William: "Whose are the three female papers on Woman? they are 'so very clever' " (MH-H). In writing this series on the Cleveland convention of the National Woman Suffrage Association, Lulu Gray Noble first assumed an air of neutrality but finally opposed female suffrage. James's ambiguous comment, mimicking a supposedly British formula of bland approval (see *Letters* 1: 209), should be compared to a series of articles in *Woman's Journal* in February harshly criticizing Noble's reporting.

Henry Jr.'s letter endorsing "The Woman Thou Gavest with Me" crossed a much cooler evaluation from William: "Father has been writing a couple of articles on 'woman' & marriage in the Atlantic. I can't think he shows himself to most advantage in this kind of speculation" (19 January 1870, MH-H). On 8 February, soon after reading Henry Jr.'s much more enthusiastic response, William wrote a second time to his brother, this time enclosing "an article of father's" (HJ to AJ, 27 February 1870, MH-H).[22] The article may have been "The Woman Thou Gavest with Me" or an early proof of "Is Marriage Holy?" which appeared in the March *Atlantic*. Henry Jr.'s next letter home, addressed to Alice, ignored William's cool assessment and instead requested Alice to "tell father I read his article with real pleasure. It's a good thing. All England just now is engrossed with the Mordaunt trial – a hideous tissue of [misery?]. It strengthens the ground under father's feet" (27 February 1870, MH-H). The Mordaunt trial, one of the more scandalous cases of the time, had terminated two days earlier. Sir Charles Mordaunt had petitioned for divorce on the ground of his wife's adultery, and the Prince of Wales himself, evidently suspected as one of her lovers, had given testimony (*Official Report* 76). For Henry Jr., the trial justified his father's idea that divorce should be readily available to those who were blind to the sacramental significance of marriage.[23]

A week later Henry Jr. endorsed his father's ideas a *third* time in a letter to William: "Among the things I have recently read is Father's *Marriage* paper in the *Atlantic* – with great enjoyment of its manner & approval of its matter" (8 March 1870, MH-H). It is striking how much the son wanted to let his family know that he accepted the father's philosophy of marriage.

Not every reader of Henry Sr.'s first *Atlantic* essay was quite so impressionable as Henry Jr. A regular feature in both the *Independent* and the *Nation* was a monthly review of current magazine articles and serials. The readers of the former journal were told that Henry Sr. "discourses of the sexes and the woman's movement in that peculiar style of metaphysics which characterizes all he writes" and that his essay "has little merit" ("Magazines of the Month" 6). The *Nation* had warm praise for most of the *Atlantic,* but the notice of the James essay unmistakably insinuated that the author was a crank:

"The Woman Thou gavest with me," by Mr. Henry James, will be to many persons agreeable reading. For one thing, it proves that both parties to the woman's rights dispute are all wrong, or nearly so. Mr. Epes Sargent, and Mr. Mill, and Dr. Bushnell, and Mr. Fulton, and Dr. Todd, and G. F. Train, and the women of the *Revolution* – none of them has the rights of the matter; and none of them will, nor any more will any of the rest of us, till he or she comes to look on man and woman as "two contrasted terms of a great creative allegory in which man stands for what we call the World, meaning thereby human nature in moral or voluntary revolt from God; and woman, for what we call the Church, meaning thereby human nature in spiritual or spontaneous accord with its divine source." ([Dennett?], "Magazines for January" 589)

Over and over the philosopher of marriage had tried to still the troubled waters with his magic allegories of man and woman, but now his persistent intervention in the women's movement was giving him the reputation of a public nuisance. This trouncing from the magisterial *Nation* was precisely what he had been asking for.[24]

On the other side of the Atlantic Ocean, Henry Jr. was signing his letters to his father "Your H." or "Your faithful son" (*Letters* 1: 193, 217). When he finally had a chance to read the *Nation*'s sarcastic comment, he was disturbed: "I have lately received three *Nations,* for wh. thanks. The notice of your *Marriage* paper seemed to me rather flippant. I heard some time since that the great Dennet had left the Nation & come to Cambridge; but I still detect his hand" (19 March 1870, MH-H).[25] The son resented the *Nation*'s lese majesty toward his father and hoped to pin the blame on a particular staff-writer. In this case, however, the writer, almost certainly John Richard Dennett, happened to be one of the sharpest minds of the time. If he is known today, it is for his eyewitness report after the Civil War, *The South As It Is,* but in 1870 he was famed for his incisive and slashing tone in the *Nation.* W. C. Brownell later wrote that "Dennett was from a literary point of view the most remarkable talent New York journalism has ever had" (42). Another reader recalled that

Dennett "had no mercy for ignorance or stupidity or affectation or quackery, and very little reverence for tradition" (Holt 46). The tradition-loving son of a father whose system was riddled with quackery could not help but be upset when that father was publicly ridiculed by a first-rate wit.

Henry Jr. wished to make his father's gods his own gods, yet he was often mortified by the public criticism directed at his father.[26] Once, when Charles Eliot Norton snubbed Henry Sr. by refusing to see him, Mary wrote Henry Jr., "I fancy he feels a very strong antagonism to Father's views" (8 December 1873, MH-H). When the third of Henry Sr.'s marriage papers came out in the *Atlantic* in June 1870, the *Nation* ran a long rebuttal. Henry Sr.'s two verbose letters of rejoinder turned out to be his final contributions to the magazine. Either they had had enough of him or he had had enough of them. The first of these letters had an outlandish phrase that was tagged and stored by the most famous Gilded Age wit of all. James had written: "We must either come to regard marriage as a finality – *i.e.*, as existing solely in its own right – or else expect *the hideous carnival of crime* in which, so far as the sexual relations are concerned, we are now festering, to prolong itself eternally" ("Mr. Henry James on Marriage" 367).[27] In responding, the editors could not resist quoting the ludicrous phrase I have italicized. Six years later the *Atlantic* brought out Mark Twain's piece, "The Facts Concerning the Recent Carnival of Crime in Connecticut." Wonderfully, the figure that represents the speaker's conscience, "a shriveled, shabby dwarf" about two feet tall and covered "with a fuzzy, greenish mold" (641, 642), recalls the evil being that had caused the senior James's collapse in 1844. We seem to be dealing with a regular outbreak of little green men.

A Hideous Invasion by the Press

The worst was yet to come. When the eminent Congregational minister, Henry Ward Beecher, was accused in print of seducing Mrs. Tilton, Henry Sr. was moved to write a foolishly indiscreet letter that eventually found its way into the pages of the infamous *Woodhull & Claflin's Weekly*. This episode, one of the memorable events in the James family annals, had a tremendous impact on Henry Jr. and his fiction.

It was *Woodhull & Claflin's* that published the famous accusation against Beecher, on 2 November 1872. At once Victoria Woodhull and others were arrested for sending obscene materials through the mail. All over the country newspaper editors condemned "the Woodhull" for scandalmongering – but they also informed their readers of the exciting news that Beecher had been charged with "gross sensualism." One such newspaper was the *Saint Paul Daily Press* in Minnesota. Its printer, Harvey Y. Russell,[28] wrote Henry James, Sr., to ask his opinion on Beecher and free love, and James, famous now for his philosophy of marriage, replied. His letter to Russell rehearsed his argument that marriage stimulates man's spiritual growth by confining his sexual desire to one woman only. Unfortunately, the letter contained a passage that could easily be construed as confessional:

> I marry my wife under the impression that she is literally perfect, and is going to exhaust my capacity of desire ever after. Ere long I discover my mistake. . . . My good habits, my good breeding, my hearty respect for my wife, . . . prevent my ever letting her suspect the conflict going on in my bosom; but there it is nevertheless, a ceaseless conflict between law and liberty, between conscience and inclination.

Others may get divorced, he proclaimed, "but as for me I will abide in my chains" ("Morality").

For a little over a year the letter collected dust. In early 1874, however, Beecher was once more in the news. He had been named correspondent in the Tilton divorce suit, and minutely detailed accounts of the affair were appearing in respectable newspapers, along with a remarkable amount of opinion and hearsay. The broad campaign for "no secrets" in sexual matters (Leach 38–63) had taken effect and the limits of obscenity had receded dramatically. On 19 February 1874, a long extract from Henry Sr.'s private letter was published in the *Saint Paul Daily Press*. Russell, a follower of free-love doctrine for twenty years, clipped the article and sent it along with his own commentary to *Woodhull & Claflin's*, which was edited by none other than Henry Sr.'s old enemy, Stephen Pearl Andrews, who had been lying in wait. Back in 1852, the *New York Tribune* had refused to print Andrews's rejoinder to James. Now Andrews had his revenge. On 18 April 1874, the whole world could read in the most outrageous paper of the day Henry James, Sr.'s, own confession that his wife had not afforded him full sexual satisfaction. Henry Sr.'s radical ghosts were out of the closet with a vengeance, and this time Henry Jr. was old enough to have to deal with them.

Up to now, in all his roaring contests over the years, Henry Sr. generally roared the loudest and the longest. He sent two lengthy rejoinders to *Woodhull & Claflin's* to defend the role of suffering in human life and to attack enjoyment, liberty, and free love. Andrews's replies were wise and penetrating. He wondered why James was so fond of the imagery of punishment – "stigmatize," "scourge," "bondage" ("Free Love" 4) – and rightly drew the connection between James's concept of marriage and the institution of slavery. James, refusing to understand that the issue of free love was political, had accused free lovers of seeking to turn men into monkeys: "I am not a chimpanzee, either in origin as Mr. Darwin would argue, nor in destiny as the free-lover would have it." Andrews, who seems to have understood why his old opponent was so obsessed with carnality and ape-men, now turned James's crude attribution of motive back on the accuser:

> It is surprising that Mr. James should not sufficiently well understand the working of spiritual laws, to know that in charging on others the predominance of low and animal desires and manifestations simply because they demand a free field to live their own true lives, that he convicts them of nothing, while he implicitly confesses that he is *such,* and that he would habitually so manifest himself, if outward constraint were not so laid upon him; in other words that he, individually, is still a chimpanzee. (HJSr et al., "Morality vs. Brute Instinct" 5, 6)

Andrews could not have been more right if he had been present in the dining room in Windsor on that chilly day in 1844, when the beast in Henry James jumped, or rather squatted. Andrews himself was "not conscious of sweating so hard, spiritually, over the effort to be good as Mr. James deems it requisite" ("Comments" 6), and he concluded the exchange by asking a good question: "Why insist that the love of freedom is synonymous with the proclivity to evil – unless it be to reveal a dark chamber of conscious diabolism in one's own soul?" ("Free Love" 5).[29]

This sensational public debate not only took place in a paper that was seen as a blackmailing scandal sheet by those who belonged to the Jameses' social and intellectual cohort (J. Howe 356), but it also let out a painful family secret: Henry Sr. was not the husband and father he seemed to be. The family was surely disgusted by Andrews's ripping away of the veil, and perhaps they were even more appalled by the low associations. In the past, no matter how thick and fast the brickbats flew, Henry Sr. never seemed to know when he was hit. Did he know now? Probably not, for after the Beecher-Tilton storm had blown over, he wrote an ill-considered letter to Emerson, seeking to muster a general condemnation of the times. The letter, evidently conceived as a public statement, was probably never released to a newspaper or magazine. Emerson saw to that, beginning his reply, "No, once & forever No" (3 November 1874, MH-H).

On one point Henry Sr.'s letter was inconsistent and helplessly insinuating. The writer proclaimed, choosing his words strangely, that he was "blessedly innocent myself of any opinion" as to Beecher's guilt. Yet Henry Sr.'s argument that civilization must forgive adulterers and other transgressors of the law clearly assumes that Beecher was guilty as charged. A contemporary letter to Robertson James exhibits the same

assumption of guilt: "Every man feels that he himself, given the tempta-
tions . . . to which Mr. Beecher has succumbed, would probably exhibit
the same infirmity" (modern typescript, [summer 1874?], Vaux). Both in
this passage and in the letter to Emerson, Henry Sr. stressed his identification with the accused: "He is a human being precisely like myself, neither
better nor worse, subject like myself to a remorseless outward law – the
law of the community in which we both dwell – and liable therefore to
be called upon to expiate any thoughtless moment, any moment of in-
sane and silly passion, by a life of infamy" (Draft, sheets 10 [5th] & 11). In
writing this, Henry Sr. not only took Beecher's culpability for granted,
but the intensely sympathetic identification went back twenty-two years
to something the uneasy philosopher of marriage once wrote about the
male leaders at the Oneida colony: "they were fathers and husbands and
brothers like myself" ("N.Y. Observer and Mr. James").

These documents disclose an almost uncontrollable urge to step onto
the scaffold with dishonored and fallen men. It is as if Beecher and Henry
Sr. both bore the same mark of the beast – one openly, the other secretly.
Both men had, in fact, been exhibited to the public in the same radical
weekly. The philosopher of marriage looks to be a real-life version of the
most famous secret sinner of all, the Reverend Arthur Dimmesdale.

We get a rough sense of what the whole storm meant to Henry Jr. by
recalling his many fictions – all dating after 1874 – about intrusive journalists and publishing scoundrels and honorable people trusted with sensitive personal documents that must be destroyed.[30] Indeed, one of the
reasons biographers have missed the scandal of Henry Sr.'s exhibition in
Woodhull & Claflin's is that the family documents pertaining to it *were*
destroyed. Few of the letters that crossed the Atlantic between Henry Jr.
and his family in the spring and summer of 1874 are extant. Of those that
survive, not one mentions the father's troubles. His only existing commu-
nication to his second son for the whole of 1874, dated 21 June, mentions
a letter sent "the other day" (MH-H). An acknowledgment in Henry Jr.'s
letter home of 6 July [31] suggests that this vanished letter may have been
written 11 June – three weeks after Henry Sr. had dispatched his last
rebuttal to *Woodhull & Claflin's*. What appears to be the sole surviving
record of the children's interest in Henry Sr.'s public embroilment is
found at the end of his 19 June [1874] letter to Bob: "I will send you the
magazines you require – though they are generally pretty trashy" (modern typescript, Vaux). William's two surviving letters to Henry Jr. from
the time touch only on the Beecher scandal. The first of these condemns
the "Puritanic pruriency" (25 June 1874, MH-H) of the press. The second
is "glad for human natures sake" that Beecher has been found innocent
but regrets this verdict on aesthetic grounds – "so colossally dramatic
wd. his figure of hypocrisy have been" (26 July 1874, MH-H).[32]

Henry Jr. returned to the United States in September of 1874. In the two years since his departure, the limits of public candor had undergone an enormous expansion, and Henry Sr. had recently participated in an embarrassing exchange in the least respectable national journal of the day. The son who had signed his name more than once to the father's conservative doctrines on woman and marriage was shocked by the whole *Woodhull & Claflin's* business. What Andrews had said was an outrage against decency. The lesson drawn by the faithful son, however, was not that the father was in some sense part chimpanzee but that the radical democratic press sought to invade the private life. Henry Jr.'s dislike of newspaper vulgarity hardened into a lasting hatred of investigative candor. In the future he would not only associate social reform with the violation of family life by the press, but would also exaggerate the power and reach of American radicalism. In this way the father's deep apostasy – his willed refusal to know himself and to let himself be known – was visited on his son. Something negative and powerful and antidemocratic moved from one generation to the next.

Late in 1874 Henry Jr. wrote a book review that gives us a vivid glimpse of his outrage and partisanship. The book was Charles Nordhoff's imposing survey of utopian groups, *The Communistic Societies of the United States*. In effect this book put before the young reviewer's eyes the practical results of the radical dreams his father had abjured. The important part of the review was the discussion of Nordhoff's chapter on Oneida. Here the reviewer not only showed how angry he was about the radicals' recent exposure of Henry Sr. but Henry Jr. also allowed his pen to slip in an amazing way. His lapse, never before noticed, is uncanny and extreme and tells us much more about the son's anxious sense of his father's dark side than the son would have wanted us to know.

The anger is unmistakable. Henry Jr. bridled at Nordhoff's impression that the people living at Oneida were commonplace. Only four sentences later, however, the reviewer abruptly reversed himself. Commenting on Nordhoff's report of a session in which a young man went through an ordeal of group criticism, Henry Jr. insisted with great vehemence that this account showed how commonplace and typical the Oneidans were. "The whole scene," he wrote, "is an attempt to organize and glorify the detestable tendency toward the complete effacement of privacy in life and thought everywhere so rampant with us nowadays" (*Literary Criticism* 1: 567). This idea – that a tiny and unique separatist group expresses the larger society's sense of privacy and communality – seems unlikely. Henry Jr. was angry at the public criticism of *his* father in *Woodhull & Claflin's*, and he was lashing out.

It was Nordhoff's account of group criticism that evidently caused Henry Jr.'s pen to slip. The story concerned a young man named Charles, who had allowed himself to get too attached to a temporary sexual partner, a woman who had become pregnant by him. It was forbidden to show special preference for any one spouse at Oneida, since Noyes believed that monogamy was the death of communalism, and thus Charles broke a signal law by falling in love. According to Nordhoff's book, the young father-to-be was taken to task by Noyes and other Oneidans during "Criticism" and was persuaded "to isolate himself entirely from the woman, and let another man take his place at her side" (293). It was this communal act that elicited Henry Jr.'s heated condemnation of the invasion of private life.

Now, if we attempt to read this story through Henry Jr.'s eyes, to see what he would have seen in it, we sense a disturbing resemblance between Charles and Henry Sr. as a young man. Although there is a crucial difference, Charles recapitulates Henry Sr.'s great life-crisis. Both loved a single woman. Both were pressured by invasive communists. Indeed, that publishing scoundrel at *Woodhull & Claflin's* who had only recently defamed the father belonged to the same gang that misled Charles and convinced the poor man that fidelity (his great though unconscious virtue) was a crime. But there was this difference: While Charles was tragically persuaded to give up the woman he loved, Henry Sr. had emerged in triumph long ago from the mire of free love and socialism, and he had done so precisely by fathering both a family and a philosophy of marriage. Charles's "error" – loving one woman faithfully – was the virtue that saved Henry Sr. Thus, Oneidan Charles presented a defamiliarized image of the reviewer's own father.

Is all this fanciful? Henry Jr.'s bizarre lapse persuades me it is not. Evidently forgetting Charles's name, Henry Jr. came up with what he thought was the correct one, and the name he selected was *Henry*.[33] The reviewer urged his readers to go directly to Nordhoff and read the story of "young man Henry" for themselves (*Literary Criticism* 1: 567). For Henry Jr. this story simultaneously enforced a cautionary social lesson about the complete effacement of privacy and expressed his feeling that his father was essentially a victim, like Charles, of radical American democracy.

Buried completely out of sight, in 1874, was the queer fact that the proclamations issued a quarter-century earlier by the James father sounded exactly like the views of Charles's oppressors. "The most perfect society will be perfect simply by virtue of its men acknowledging a higher inspiration than woman, and its women acknowledging a higher divinity than man; and this acknowledgement will absolve both parties alike from every motive to that personal abasement and debauchery, which constitutes the present impure life of love" (HJSr, "Marriage Question"). Pending explanations, Noyes could have endorsed this repudiation of private affection and attachment in the quest for sexual perfection. They even had a song at Oneida that expressed the idea:

> I love you, O my sister [or brother],
> But the love of God is better;
> Yes, the love of God is better –
> O the love of God is best.   (Nordhoff 300)

Two or three months after the Nordhoff review, Henry Jr. disclosed his anxiously protective filiality a second time in a review for the *Nation*. The book was *Ezra Stiles Gannett*, a biography of a Unitarian minister, and it touched the reviewer's own life at some key points: Its subject was a Boston religionist who lost the use of one leg and had a nervous collapse, and the story of his life was written by his son. Not surprisingly, Henry Jr.'s chief criticism was that the biography was so frank it violated its "filial standpoint" (*Literary Criticism* 1: 278). The minister had got about with the aid of two crutches and his son wrote that his "quick leaps between them, as he fled clicking along the sidewalks, used to make the boys turn and shout" (*Gannett* 207). This sort of candor had a long pedigree in New England, but Henry Jr. detected a modern type of immodesty. He felt that the unfilial biographer had turned his father's disability into "picturesque touches," and he pitied "the venerable subject in his extreme bereavement of privacy" (*Literary Criticism* 1: 278–79).

When Henry Jr. converted the events of 1874 into the notion that American democracy destroys privacy, he was defending the part of his father that he knew and trusted and had sworn allegiance to against a part he had heard disturbing rumors of and wanted, passionately, to bury. In committing himself to an image of his father as victim, however, the son committed himself as well to a hostile and uninformed image of American life. The sign of "democratization" became the aggressive "invasion" (*Complete Notebooks* 40) by newspaper editors and reporters. The fuller truths were unacceptable: His father, victim and victimizer both, had given himself up to a profoundly unstable and foolish radicalism; a hotheaded controversialist, he had actively collaborated with those editors who exploited him. All along, the person who wanted most of all to efface Henry Sr.'s privacy was Henry Sr. himself. Perhaps the reason he persistently courted exposure and humiliation was that he truly did believe, as he so often announced, that his selfhood was damnable. But the only way a faithful son could honor such a father was by externalizing the demons that scourged him.

On 8 April 1883, four months after the father's death, Henry Jr. undertook an ambitious novel about American life that sought to prove – and for many readers, apparently, *has* proved – that these demons were to be found in sleazy Gilded Age feminists and propagandists. Henry

Sr.'s death had been a painful and drawn-out affair. During his last weeks he "talked constantly about the spiritual life, objecting to food and railing against 'this disgusting world' " (Strouse 208). When he learned he was seriously ill, he stopped eating. It is uncertain whether he would have died if he had not refused nourishment. His death may have been an act of suicide by self-starvation – as if at last he had found the sure way to punish those damnable entrails where his selfhood had its seat. Perhaps his death was the ultimate step in the path he had been following for three decades, "culminating his life by this drama of complete detachment from it," as William wrote Henry Jr. (9 January 1883, MH-H). Of course, he also wished to rejoin his much-loved and recently deceased wife.

Henry Jr., returning to the James home in Boston three days after his father died and one day after his burial, was stirred to his depths. Alice's friend, Katherine Loring, had moved in and was "painfully prominent," and Alice's "imperativeness of speech and manner" was more insistent than ever. Henry Jr. was laid up with a five-day "rheumatic" headache, "the worst . . . he ever had" (AHJ to WJ, 21 and 22 December 1882, MH-H). The father's willingness to leave his children behind imposed a great burden of guilt upon them, and Henry Jr. had other reasons to feel guilty. The steps he took to change Henry Sr.'s will, so as to prevent Wilkie from being disinherited, caused William to accuse Henry Jr. of failing to honor their father's last desires. More important, Henry Jr. was no longer quite so sure about the value of his father's intellectual labors, and he knew now that marriage was not for him. Partly because of all these derelictions, the son felt compelled to uphold and defend his heroic father against the callous world, especially those radical publishing scoundrels who seemed to have hounded him for twenty years.[34] After copying his formal prospectus, the novelist added a private memorandum: "There must, indispensably, be a type of newspaper man – the man whose ideal is the energetic reporter. I should like to *bafouer* the vulgarity and hideousness of this – the impudent invasion of privacy – the extinction of all conception of privacy" (*Complete Notebooks* 19). How similar this passage is to the angry sentence Henry Jr. wrote about Oneida eight years earlier, soon after his father's trouble with *Woodhull & Claflin's*: "The whole scene . . . is an attempt to organize and glorify the detestable tendency toward the complete effacement of privacy in life and thought everywhere so rampant with us nowadays" (*Literary Criticism* 1: 567).

In addition to avenging the dead father, *The Bostonians* was intended to vindicate his ideas on woman. Henry Sr. had fought a long rearguard defense of separate spheres and sexual difference, and his son would now show that the New England radicals who had ignored him only caused greater vulgarity, disorder, and dissension. Annie Fields had seen that

Henry Sr.'s lecture "Woman" helped to "lay that dreadful phantom of yourself," the woman who speaks up in public. Henry Jr. now took as his central character (his first title was *Verena*) a young female orator whose public speaking represents not a surging self-expression but a lesson learned by rote that bears no relation to her true feminine nature. The son's story – Verena leaves her friend in the women's movement to marry the dominating Basil Ransom – was designed to bear out the truth of the father's (and Bushnell's) teaching that female emancipation was against human nature.

But the family ghosts would not lie still. They rose in their chains and wrecked Henry Jr.'s plans for his novel. His commitment to the paternal notion of sexual difference was so brittle, so personally unfelt, that his effort to concretize it in narrative led him to turn against it. Was there anybody *less* like Henry Sr.'s definition of man – brutal, woman-dominating, carnal – than Henry Jr., or who was in *less* need of gentling by the other sex? As Henry, now no longer Jr., wrote *The Bostonians*, Basil inevitably became more and more of a repressive force. His success in winning Verena away from Olive backfired. Intended to show that feminism was weak and constricting because it went against nature, Basil's victory was so brutal that it only served, ironically, to vindicate feminism. Yet the fact that Verena's femininity can be freed only if she is forcibly carried off and confined shows that the novel articulates the bitter contradiction – slavery is freedom – at the heart of the thinking of Henry Sr. And in Olive Chancellor, the character whose rich complications overwhelm the other figures, all the buried James demons came out at once. What else but a witch would a family produce that sought so systematically to reduce woman to a "form of personal affection"? Because the father's philosophy was a weapon turned on himself – and on the free human spirit – the son's effort to vindicate that father's message of sexual difference had to be self-canceling.

Chapter 3

Precocious Incest

First Novels by Louisa May Alcott and Henry James

Half a century ago Pierre la Rose (p. xi) and Katharine Anthony drew attention to the paradox that young Henry James's review of Louisa May Alcott's first serious adult novel, *Moods,* scoffed at her use of the same heroine he himself would build so many novels around: "We are utterly weary of stories about precocious little girls. In the first place, they are in themselves disagreeable and unprofitable objects of study; and in the second, they are always the precursors of a not less unprofitable middle-aged lover" (*Literary Criticism* 1: 189). It seemed odd to la Rose and Anthony that the man who wrote this surly dismissal would in time create a number of precocious girls of his own – Isabel Archer, Verena Tarrant, the governess at Bly, Maisie Farange, Nanda Brookenham. James's first novel would in fact introduce its heroine by twice calling her *precocious* ("Watch and Ward" 238, 241). Even stranger, as Anthony noticed, every one of these girls would fall in love with the older man James claimed to be so weary of. "The mutual influence" of James and Alcott "was perhaps stronger than anyone realizes" (180), Anthony guessed, correctly, even though "influence" in the old sense does not capture the rich network of connections between the two writers. The fuller truth, which this chapter will attempt to glimpse, is that *Moods* assisted young James in defining his response to a large group of novels by women, and thus made it possible for him to absorb their stories and character types in his own narratives. Another way of saying this is that through Alcott's fiction James had full access to the secret fantasy life that helped generate it, and that his fiction records the antagonistic counterstatement of his own imagination.

Some of the basic facts in Alcott's girlhood and youth that contributed to this fantasy life are well known: her familiarity from girlhood on with men who awed her, such as Emerson and Thoreau; the sustained effort of her father, Bronson, to discipline her; Bronson's inability to support his family; this family's poverty and insecurity; the necessity for Louisa to work hard from an early age; and her native rebelliousness. Perhaps a single episode from her journal can suggest the flavor of existence for her. When her parents took in John Brown's daughters to board about a year after his execution, Louisa had to give up writing and turn to house-keeping. Her reaction: "I think disappointment must be good for me, I get so much of it"(*Louisa* 127).

The recent biographies by Martha Saxton, Madelon Bedell, and Sarah Elbert have done a good job of sifting the documentary evidence and discerning the basic links between Alcott's life and writing. Also, the investigations of Leona Rostenburg and Madeleine Stern have made available the gothic thrillers Alcott published under the name of A. M. Barnard. Not everything can be known, but the general picture is clear: The men in Louisa's early years, powerful, dominating, often cold, and remote, endowed her with the dream that if she only worked exceptionally hard, and proved once and for all that she was not the "fiend" (Saxton 162) Bronson Alcott called her, then the stern middle-aged father-lover would relent – would show his faithful girl how ardent his love for her really was.

Readers of *Little Women* will remember that energetic Jo March marries the middle-aged Professor Bhaer.[1] Alcott's other writings are also concerned, as one biographer writes, "with the repeated theme of a romance between a child-woman and an older man; the latter often a guardian, an uncle or an older friend; in short, a displaced father" (Bedell 241–42). This theme, along with the incest fantasy that powered it, was everywhere in nineteenth-century novels by women. *A New-England Tale, The Wide, Wide World, The Curse of Clifton, Beulah, Faith Gartney's Girlhood, Two Men,* and probably at least a hundred more narratives, as James would claim, all told the story of the precocious girl and her middle-aged lover.

For Louisa as writer and reader, however, there were special complications that prevented her easy participation in this narrative tradition. Thoreau, for instance, had sneered at "the nine thousandth tale about Zebulon and Sophronia, and how they loved as none had ever loved before" (*Walden* 105). Alcott was overwhelmed with respect for Thoreau and his opinions. Yet even as she praised his "just content" in her elegy on him ("Thoreau's Flute" 280), she also wrote "Pauline's Passion and Punishment," a steamy tale of discontent. It is not easy to reconcile narratives like this one with the principled severity of Concord's intellectual life.

After *Little Women* made its author famous and she ceased writing gothics, accepting her diminished role as entertainer and preceptor of children, she made a mellow confession of the contradiction within her, which a reporter paraphrased in this manner:

I think my natural ambition is for the lurid style. I indulge in gorgeous fancies and wish that I dared inscribe them upon my pages. . . . How should I dare to interfere with the proper grayness of old Concord? The dear old town has never known a startling hue since the redcoats were there. Far be it from me to inject an inharmonious color into the neutral tint. And my favorite characters! Suppose they went to cavorting at their own sweet will, to the infinite horror of dear Mr. Emerson. . . . To have had Mr. Emerson for an intellectual god all one's life is to be invested with a chain armor of propriety . . . And what would my own good father think of me . . .? (*Behind a Mask* xxvi)

Madeleine Stern relies in part on this very important statement to support her view that the lurid and gorgeous color of the gothic romances Alcott wrote in the 1860s represents a genuine imaginative achievement and, further, that the sexual passion, anger, and vengefulness of her heroines render the narratives as a whole feminist (*Behind a Mask* xix, xxviii).

I believe that Stern is half right. Some of Louisa's thrillers *are* exceptionally well plotted, and also have an unmistakable psychological coherence and validity. The problem is that the secret fantasy the books express is not liberation from male supremacy but bondage made satisfying. Alcott connects color with royalist redcoats, after all, not with rebellion. Her heroines are either submissive girls who grow up to share ecstasy with their stern fathers, or they are sirens and femmes fatales who are obsessed with revenge; either way, men are the one thing on their mind. The shocking thing about Alcott's pseudonymous thrillers is the degree to which they accept male primacy or dominance; they are all in varying degrees politically regressive, even though their author was a radical born and bred, with a strong belief in equality.

"A Marble Woman"

A brief look at the best of Barnard's stories will suggest the depth of Alcott's problem. In 1865 she sent "A Marble Woman; or, The Mysterious Model" to an editor at the Boston story-weekly, *The Flag of Our Union*. The editor recognized the story's high quality and urged Alcott to let him use her name rather than her usual pseudonym. "My friends," he wrote, "think the 'Marble Woman' is just splendid; & *I* think no author of novels need be ashamed to own it for a bantling" (Alcott, *Plots* 16). But it was unthinkable that a woman committed to civil liberties could take credit for a dominance-submission incest fantasy that leads up to the same pleasure as Edith Wharton's narrative of Beatrice Palmato's seduction by her father (Lewis, *Wharton* 544–48).

"A Marble Woman" begins at the usual beginning – weakness and fear. Cecilia has just been left a penniless orphan. Her dying mother appointed Bazil Yorke as the girl's guardian. Yorke is the familiar gothic master, grim, solitary, and dogmatic. He is thirty and Cecilia is eleven. Because Yorke has been "embittered" (143) ever since Cecilia's mother jilted him, he vengefully determines to bring the girl up in isolation from the world and without knowing what it is to love. He even docks her name of its feminine ending. Cecil, as the "castrated" girl is henceforth known, gladly submits.

Five years later Yorke demands that Cecil decide, "now and forever," between himself and a handsome young rival. With "instant and entire willingness" (147) she chooses Yorke, and continues to spend her days and nights with him. Of course she never ceases "to repress all natural emotions" (148). Then it appears that outside the tower-studio in which guardian and ward chisel their marble statues, people are beginning to talk. To prevent scandal and yet to keep Cecil near (for Yorke has begun to love her in spite of himself), he proposes a marriage – in name only, of course. His ward (who has begun to love him) consents. Since the terms of their compact do not permit them to express their growing love, the cold intimacy has the effect of freezing the girl's spirit, transforming her into the frigid marble woman of the title. Only two things can warm her into life, opium (which she renounces after an overdose nearly kills her), and a mysterious older man named Germain.

Germain has been breaking into Cecil's life from the beginning, when his black beard first terrified the orphan. On one occasion he enters Yorke's house, grabs the girl, kisses her "more than once," and calls her "my darling " (149). Cecil is naturally "terrified by this impetuous wooing" (161), but even so she comes to accept Germain. What is odd is that although Yorke is the man she truly loves, it is Germain who makes her marble face flush with color.

The mystery is finally cleared up when Germain, dying, informs Cecil that he is her father and has always loved her "with all the fervor of an undisciplined nature": Germain is the germinator, as Professor Bhaer would be German. This revelation "unlocked her heart, and all its pent-up passion flowed freely" (228). As the biological father dies, the psychological one, Yorke, at last dares to confess *his* love to Cecil. As Sarah Elbert writes, "Her real father's love has empowered her to transform her 'master' into a loving husband" (138). Now that she no longer needs to damp her passion, she freely expresses her love for Yorke. Happily, since they are already wed, their affection and intimacy need not be constrained. *At last* (the title of the concluding chapter), father–husband and daughter–wife may fully enjoy each other.

Two years before Alcott worked out the ingenious details leading up to this satisfying payoff, she became seriously ill while caring for Civil War casualties and spent three weeks in delirium. Of all her delirious "fancies" the most "vivid and enduring" was "the conviction" that she had "married a stout, handsome Spaniard, dressed in black velvet, with very soft hands, and a voice that was continually saying, 'Lie still, my dear!' " She felt "an awful fear of the Spanish spouse who was always coming after me, appearing out of closets, in at windows, or threatening me dreadfully all night long" (*Louisa* 146).

This frightening man was deposited in Alcott's mind by her father's hard discipline and the attractive yet remote figures of Emerson and Thoreau. The Spanish spouse tells Alcott to lie still because that is what these powerful and apparently calm older men had been instructing her to do since infancy. He breaks out of closets or in at windows because Bronson had sought control of his daughter's actions and thoughts. He is stout and sleek, with the portly banker image, because Bronson was stout and sleek and obviously in charge. He wears black because he embodies redcoat-vanquishing Concord. He is Spanish because Spanish means tropical passion combined with unyielding male pride and dominance.

The link between the gothicism of "A Marble Woman" and Alcott's terrified vision of the Spanish spouse is that the former represents a strategy for disarming the latter. Just as the romantic Spaniards in Alcott's thrillers seem to detoxify the oppressive Spaniards of her northern Anglo-Saxon imagination, so "A Marble Woman" seeks to acknowledge the horror of the father-lover and then to explain this as nothing but disguised love. At first Yorke is all grim suppression and Germain is a violent rapist, but in the end Cecil realizes that the embraces of these men need not be resisted. Thus, the story represents an imaginative effort to *defend,* not resist, paternal authority and father–daughter seduction. Of course, this conversion of fear into love was characteristic of the gothic mode, and Alcott surely had the professionalism to understand that she was working some very conventional material. Yet it is equally clear from her delirious fancy that she carried within her the raw sources of gothicism, and that is why "A Marble Woman" is, as her editor wrote, "just splendid." There is only one flaw in the extremely well wrought story. Its secret message – relax, lie still, don't distrust these frightening men – coincides with the command of the suave Spanish husband.

Although it is not known whether James read Alcott's pseudonymous fiction, the novel he would write twenty years later about Boston radicalism is to some extent a sustained criticism of the imagination that produced "A Marble Woman." James's working title for *The Bostonians* was *Verena,* and he intended to focus on the mind of this character, who speaks out for emancipation but dreams of slavery. Verena's déclassée and demoralized mother and her shabby-transcendental father almost look like debased versions of Alcott's own parents. The resemblance between the two fathers, often noted by James's readers, has a taproot reaching all the way to Alcott's delirious fancy of the Spanish husband. This soothing yet sinister man, with his "very soft hands," materializes in Selah Tarrant, whose "long, lean hands" (*Bostonians* 57) quiet his daughter and send her into a trance. (He would rematerialize yet again in Mr. Palmato, whose deft Latinate palm seduces his daughter in Edith Wharton's shocking narrative fragment.) James's trance speaker, a version of Louisa the delirious dreamer, thinks she believes in freedom but is really a closet slave. Whether she submits to Olive Chancellor or Basil Ransom (who bears the same lordly first name as Bazil Yorke), the best Verena can do is exchange one master for another. I am not saying that Louisa May Alcott's life and/or works were James's "source," but rather that his Boston novel is a kind of refutation of Alcott's most deeply rooted fantasy. Somehow, in a way I cannot explain, Henry saw through Louisa and her fictions, and some of the fictions he himself wrote were designed to set hers – and *her* – straight.

Moods

Fortunately, one need not merely speculate on the antagonistic subterranean relationship between Alcott and James. In January 1865, at the beginning of his literary career, James carefully read Alcott's novel *Moods* with the intention of reviewing it. He also gave its author an oral critique. Six years later his own first novel would revive and reinterpret her character types, and even borrow the same key tableau. Among the many particular sources of James's narrative imagination, the novel that Alcott would always love best of all her writings (*Louisa* 116) was one of the most influential.

I think Martha Saxton's biography is entirely correct in arguing that *Moods* holds the central place in Alcott's work, for this book is the bridge between Barnard's thrillers and Alcott's children's stories. Saxton overlooks the great and unrivaled beauty of *Little Women* – its detailed representation of the March sisters' life together at home.[2] But *Moods,* more fervently inspired and much more meticulously revised, was, like many another failure, the author's favorite.

According to Alcott's journal the first draft of *Moods* dates from August 1860: "For four weeks I wrote all day and planned nearly all night, being quite possessed by my work. I was perfectly happy, and seemed to have no wants" (*Louisa* 122). Six months later she rewrote the book in three furious weeks, so absorbed that she could hardly interrupt her work and had difficulty falling asleep. Twice in 1863 she touched the book up, and when she offered it to James Redpath the following winter, it was "a

big thing, thirty chapters long – rather odd, sentimental, & tragical"
(Alcott, *Selected Letters* 103). Redpath rejected the novel, as did James T.
Fields, who had asked to see it. The manuscript might not have seen
print if it had not been for Caroline Dall, who read it and made the crucial
contact with the firm of A. K. Loring and even read proof (*Louisa* 159–
62; journal entries for 23, 24, 27 October 1864 and 1 August 1865, Dall
Papers, MHS). At first, however, Alcott was unwilling to comply with
Loring's demand that she shorten and in other ways alter her novel.
Lying awake in bed one October night in 1864, she thought of a way to
meet his requirements, and for two weeks she "hardly ate, slept, or
stirred, but wrote, wrote, like a thinking machine in full operation."
(Henry James probably revised *his* first "modern novel," "The Story of a
Year," at this time; see ch. 7 ["The Dying Man"].) The novel came out
soon after New Year's Day, and the congratulations and favorable reports began to come in. In her journal the author wrote with proud
humility: "It has always seemed as if 'Moods' grew in spite of me, and
that I had little to do with it except to put into words the thoughts that
would not let me rest until I had" (*Louisa* 161, 163).

The main reason these thoughts would not let Alcott rest is that they
represented her first, and, as it happened, last attempt to integrate her
naturally lurid color with her stern Concord integrity. The novel's Emersonian epigraph – "Life is a train of moods like a string of beads; and as
we pass through them they prove to be many colored lenses, which paint
the world their own hue, and each shows us only what lies in its own
focus" – hints at the enterprise the book represents: It will dare to show
life in full color, not in Concord black and white. Yet the fact that the
authorization for this venture comes from the sage of Concord himself,
even if from his daring essay "Experience," guarantees that the novel will
be safe after all.

The heroine, Sylvia Yule, is an impulsive, wayward, and unstable girl
of seventeen when the novel opens. The chapter introducing her is titled
"Whims," and it is apparently her life alone that is "a train of moods"
(116).³ Alcott attributes her instability to the "adverse temperaments"
(115) she has inherited from her parents, who did not get on with one
another, but it is also clear that Sylvia is driven by the energies of adolescence. When she puts on a boy's linen shirt and half-boots in order to
work in her garden, she shows she is not yet ready to submit to the
decorum of womanhood. Her sprightly tomboyish willfulness clearly
reproduces a basic impulse in her creator, who put almost as much of her
protean self into Sylvia as she would into Jo March. For example, when
Sylvia enters a neighbor's house and borrows a book, it turns out to be
Wilhelm Meister, the same volume Alcott got from her neighbor Emerson
when she was about sixteen (*Louisa* 45). (The title is given in the 1882

revision of *Moods* [32].) At the age of twelve Alcott read Goethe's correspondence with Bettina and was so impressed she herself began writing adulatory letters to Emerson, though without sending any; similarly, Sylvia says she "always envied Bettina" (1882 41). Sylvia has also read *Sartor Resartus* and is as fervid a "hero-worshipper" (1882 66) and Germanophile as her creator, who would sometimes write in a style imitative of Carlyle's rough Nordic wordcraft.

Adam Warwick, the man who becomes Sylvia's Goethe, has "a massive head" with eyes "that seem to pierce through all disguises." He is "the heroic type" (50) she has been dreaming of, tall and masterful and remote, like Jane Eyre's Rochester. Unlike Brontë's hero, however, Warwick is said to have "the sternest integrity" (51), and in the revised version of the novel this integrity takes him into politics, where he advocates such causes as prison reform and women's suffrage (1882 148, 162–63). He boldly advises Sylvia to drop a novel she is skimming and instead read the disreputable Walt Whitman, identified by a reference to "barbaric yawp" (60). Warwick's manner of living, vagrant, solitary, and individualistic, strongly suggests Thoreau's. The difference between Warwick and Bazil Yorke of "A Marble Woman" is that instead of living in the isolated mansion that seems an indispensable part of fantasy fiction, Warwick is a contemporary.

Yet it is equally obvious that Warwick is meant to be a completely attractive hero, with "that genuine manhood, which no art can counterfeit." Sylvia first realizes that her hero worship has been transformed into love after staring at Warwick, "intent upon discovering the secret of the mastery he exerted over all who approached him." When he unexpectedly returns her gaze, she instantly feels "a glad submission to some power, absolute yet tender" (110). This joyful surrender, as Saxton points out (155, 278), is Alcott's idea of love. In both "A Marble Woman" and *Moods* the man's power is as absolute as that of a god, hero, or archetypal father, and the woman feels an instant and ravishing joy in her absolute abandonment to it. In *Jane Eyre* the exercise of tyranny or high-handedness again and again calls up within the heroine a wonderful reciprocal power of resistance. But not in *Moods,* "A Marble Woman," *Beulah,* or *Faith Gartney's Girlhood.* The despairing faith these books express is well summed up by a rhetorical question from another American novel of the 1860s: "Is it ever quite safe to utterly surrender except to the very strong?" (Crane, *Opportunity* 169).

But how could radical northern Louisa, writing and rewriting her novel while caught up in the great war to annihilate slavery, come out in favor of bondage? She could do so in her lurid gothic fantasies by telling herself they were not serious and then publishing them under a false name. Cecil could have Bazil in his tower-studio, but there was no way

Sylvia could have Adam Warwick in mid-nineteenth-century New England: Life was too real and earnest for that. Thus, the condition that allowed Alcott to take her fantasy out of the closet (and it was because she could do so that she was so excited while composing the book) was that she inevitably had to discipline the heroine and deprive her of a happy union. And so, when a series of accidents and entanglements leads Sylvia to believe that Warwick does not care for her after all, the moody girl accepts another man's proposal. Geoffrey Moor, her fiancé, is cultivated, tolerant, understanding, and kind, with a great deal of "the feminine" (1882 146) in him. Sylvia likes him and marries him but of course cannot love him.

Only after it is too late does Sylvia learn that Warwick loves her. The final chapters of the novel are given over to Sylvia's vain attempt to adjust to her error. She strives to ascertain her duty, to choke her passion for Warwick, to make herself love Moor, but nothing works. She loses weight and walks in her sleep, and even though she feels compelled to confess the sorry truth to her husband, who is hurt and angry, her decline cannot be arrested, and she dies.

Saxton writes that "the poignancy of *Moods* derives from Louisa's all-out effort to thrust her unwilling life, kicking and protesting, into a serene, transcendental schema" (280). Arguably, the saddest aspect of this all-out effort is Alcott's deflation of Sylvia in the last few chapters. Originally the girl's great energies and her adventurous boat trip upriver had hinted that her tendency toward hero worship might inspire her with the conception of some heroic action of her own. But the concluding scenes, especially the one in which Sylvia goes to the ominously named Faith for advice, imply that this great potential did not really exist. Faith agrees that Warwick is a mighty man, but insists that ordinary mortals cannot yield to him without "being overcome and possessed" (248). Sylvia is simply not up to him; a "woodbird" (249) must not mate with an eagle. Only those "as strong, sagacious, and steadfast" (248) as Warwick himself may take the risk of coupling with him. Sylvia, apparently one of the little people, had better forget him.

Charlotte Brontë might have chosen to emphasize Warwick's faults or weaknesses in order to make his union with Sylvia workable. But such a solution would not have satisfied Alcott. For her, love is by definition a function of power and powerlessness. Pulling Warwick down from his pedestal would be a self-canceling act – would turn him into somebody one could not love, like Moor, whose first act after the honeymoon is to put on boys' clothes and pretend he is a child again. The ultimate reason, in *Moods* and much of Alcott's other writing, why love is not love unless it is between unequals is very simple: You cannot love anyone but your father, and you cannot love your father.

There is a peculiar ambiguity in Sylvia's relationship with Mr. Yule (Mrs. Yule has been dead for years). In the scene where Mr. Yule pledges, "Friend or lover, remember there is always the old Papa glad to do his best for you in both capacities," and Sylvia replies, "I'll have no lover but 'the old Papa' for a long while yet" (37), it is evident how close father and daughter are. In another scene Sylvia actually mistakes Warwick for Mr. Yule, addresses him as "romantic father" and offers "a daughterly caress" (105). All along, however, Mr. Yule acts "more like an unobtrusive guest than a master in his house," and we are even given the confusing judgment that he lacks the "power to draw and hold" (116) his children, in spite of his daughter's confiding in him. I believe this inconsistent close/ distant relationship is a realistic version of the bizarre relation between Germain and Cecil in "A Marble Woman," where the father never identifies himself yet is in continual ardent pursuit of his daughter. These are two different transcriptions, one in a realistic and the other in a fantasy mode, of Alcott's confusion about her own father's emotional distance. She could never decide whether he was as warm and close as a lover or as cold and distant as an impersonal god. The reason Sylvia cannot leave the boyish Moor for the manly Warwick is that Warwick is a "father," and good little Sylvia cannot love anyone but a father, and it is impossible to marry your father outside a gothic romance, and being grown up is a terrible contradiction that you cannot sort out, and when you write a novel about it everyone jumps on you, and so what do you do but (with the exception of *Work, A Modern Mephistopheles,* and *Diana & Persis*) scribble children's stories for the rest of your life?

"Yes, Sir" and "No, Sir"

After the initial welcome given *Moods,* some disquieting reports began to reach Alcott. Henry James, Sr., jocularly retitled the book *Dumps.* Did he think it was too gloomy? In January she was asked to dine with the James family, and she privately recorded the occasion: "[I] was treated like the Queen of Sheba. Henry Jr. wrote a notice of 'Moods' for the 'North American,' and was very friendly. Being a literary youth he gave me advice, as if he had been eighty and I a girl" (*Louisa* 165). The harsh review by Henry Jr. would not see print for another six months. He would not have *had* to admit his authorship. One must admire his honesty in doing so, and in criticizing her novel to her face. One would suppose that the final sentence in Alcott's journal entry was sarcastic, except for her preceding claim that she had received a royal reception and that Henry Jr. had been "very friendly." Once again, it seems, Louisa forced herself to be satisfied, to grin and bear it as Henry gave an apparently pompous demonstration of the defects of her novel.

Alcott now regretted the revisions she had made for Loring: " 'Moods' is not what I meant to have it," she wrote Moncure Daniel Conway. "I followed bad advice & took out many things which explained my idea & made the characters more natural & consistent. I see my mistake now for I find myself accused of Spiritualism, Free Love, Affinities, & all sorts of horrors." In March she wrote a long reply to a reader who questioned the novel's apparent lesson that "marriage should be founded on some indefinable feeling or attraction not upon respect or esteem." Alcott strongly repudiated this interpretation: "Now if there is any thing I heartily detest it is the theory of Affinities, also Spiritualism & Free Love" (*Selected Letters* 108–9). To her journal she confided, "I seem to have been playing with edge tools without knowing it" (*Louisa* 166).⁴

Henry James's review casually dismissed the accusation that *Moods* illustrated the "doctrine of affinities" (*Literary Criticism* 1: 189), a charge he himself had recently leveled against *Emily Chester*. He generously claimed that there were only two or three novelists more promising than Alcott in the United States, and he hoped for better work from her in the future. Yet the only part of *Moods* James showed any enthusiasm for was the representation of Geoffrey Moor's anger on being told by his wife that she cannot love him, and even so James strongly felt that Moor was not angry enough: He "submits . . . precisely like a morbidly conscientious young girl who is engaged in the formation of her character under the direction of her clergyman" (*Literary Criticism* 1: 193). This passage vividly evokes the conscientious protagonists of Susan Warner, Maria Cummins, Adeline Whitney, and, in England, Charlotte Yonge. It also shows that Alcott's treatment of Moor hit a nerve in James, whose strong identification with this mild and much-wronged man would assume a more definite form in *Watch and Ward,* which vindicates Roger Lawrence against the suspicion that he and his kind were born losers.

James's review aimed its most vigorous sarcasm at Alcott's leading couple, who overshadowed Moor and whom James typed as the "precocious little girl" and the "middle-aged lover" (*Literary Criticism* 1: 189). In attacking this pair, James's prose suddenly came to life:

The other, Mr. Adam Warwick, is one of our oldest and most inveterate foes. He is the inevitable *cavaliere servente* of the precocious little girl; the laconical, satirical, dogmatical lover, of about thirty-five, with the "brown mane," the quiet smile, the "masterful soul," and the "commanding eye." Do not all novel-readers remember a figure, a hundred figures, analogous to this? Can they not, one of his properties being given, – the "quiet smile" for instance, – reconstruct the whole monstrous shape? When the "quiet smile" is suggested, we know what is coming: we foresee the cynical bache-

lor or widower, the amateur of human nature, "Full of strange
oaths, and bearded like the pard," who has travelled all over the
world, lives on a mysterious patrimony, and spends his time in
breaking the hearts and the wills of demure little school-girls, who
answer him with "Yes, sir," and "No, sir." (*Literary Criticism* 1:
190)

This is one of the key passages in James's entire body of work, and it is
right on the mark. James had no trouble seeing that Warwick's freedom
to travel "all over the world" and live "on a mysterious patrimony" is an
indication that he is a juvenile ideal of forceful masculinity, and that this
ideal was poisonous not only because it gave a false picture of men but
because it justified the heroine's demure submission. James would go on
to make a detailed demonstration that Alcott herself was taken in by
Warwick, whose "sternest integrity" (*Moods* 51) was actually a mask for
rudeness, impropriety, and brutality. And Warwick really does browbeat
Sylvia with "the old satirical smile" (*Moods* 192).

James was in an excellent position to see all this. He not only sympa-
thized with Sylvia's wronged husband, but he himself, as Leon Edel
showed in *The Untried Years,* felt unmanned both by his capable and
aggressive older brother, William, and by returning Civil War veterans.
After a miserable year at Harvard Law School, he had conspicuously
failed to find an entry into the world of men. Unlike many young men
his age, he was dependent on his parents. His defensiveness was surely
increased by the fact that he made his debut as a man of letters by
reviewing the fiction of "little women" (*Letters* 1: 58).

Watch and Ward

Watch and Ward is such a strange first novel that James's readers have
generally been at a loss in dealing with it. Robert Emmet Long sums up
the general perplexity in writing that the novel's "abnormal situation" –
a guardian bringing up his ward to be his wife – "is so peculiar that it
would seem difficult to account for" (*Henry James* 11).

The reason for this difficulty is that James has been detached from his
context in American literature of the 1860s. His review of *Moods* led
directly to *Watch and Ward,* which bears an invisible subtitle – *In Defense
of Geoffrey Moor.* What James did in this ungainly and immature work
was to adopt the guardian–ward love story and transform the pleasing
father–daughter incest fantasy intended for women readers into a nice-
guys-finish-first daydream for good old boys. Thus, the character in
James's novel who follows "the good old fashion" (as someone in "A
Marble Woman" puts it) of "making his fair ward his wife" (156) is not

the forceful misanthrope of this and other narratives but a mild, liberal, unassertive man, the type who ordinarily gets left. In superficials James conformed to the conventions of the story: His guardian is twenty-nine at the beginning, and the girl is twelve; he has a mysterious patrimony; he travels to Peru; he is tempted, just like Warwick, to marry a tropical beauty. But in essentials *Watch and Ward* subverted the genre that Louisa and her sisters had made their own.[5]

James achieved this subversion by deromanticizing Roger. "In trifling matters," we are told, "such as the choice of a shoemaker or a dentist, his word carried weight; but no one dreamed of asking his opinion in politics or literature." He yearns to have children, he is starting to go bald, he is a little fat, and he has a pompous manner that makes people snicker. What "genius" he has is only for "common sense" (232).[6] James bravely set out to create a genuine love story with the most prosaic hero imaginable.

James also forswore the use of romantic suspense. Unlike "A Marble Woman" and its many congeners, which generally withhold the complete revelation of the master's warmth until the end, *Watch and Ward* unfolds poor Roger's desire right away. When he first puts his arm around the little orphan's waist, "an irresistible sense of her childish sweetness, of her tender feminine promise, stole softly into his pulses" (238). She is still a child when these very active pulses inspire Roger with the grand design of bringing Nora up to be his wife. James makes it more than clear that bringing up Nora can be Roger's only interest in life. So completely does he live for the girl that he is given the identical advice Warwick gives Moor: "Live for yourself" ("Watch and Ward" 417; *Moods* 1882 146). But Roger is living for himself in the only way possible. How else could this man get a woman except by bringing her up? The novel is saturated with his helpless erotic need, represented with a directness that is neither daring nor decadent but, as Edel suggests, embarrassingly innocent. In this instance, the innocence is connected to James's dislike for the narrative convention requiring the middle-aged lover to impersonate an iceberg.

Another conspicuous difference between Roger and the male leads of *The Wide, Wide World, Beulah,* and *Moods* is that Roger refuses to avail himself of his paternal authority. He sends Nora away to school to grow up apart from his influence, and for the same reason, "to allow her perfect liberty" (421), he lets her go to Europe in company with the woman who rejected him. This determination to respect Nora's independence costs Roger a great deal of anxiety. He sometimes wonders whether he "ought to snub her and scold her and bully her . . . – treat her as Rochester treats Jane Eyre" (326). It is "the old, old story," he worries; "nothing succeeds with women like just too little deference" (333), and, in an alarmingly naive image, he toys with the idea of forcing the girl's affection: "The ground might be gently tickled to receive his own sowing; the petals of the young girl's nature, playfully forced apart, would leave the golden heart of the flower but the more accessible to his own vertical rays" (331). He does not tickle the petals, of course, nor does he try to make Nora feel she owes him her love. Unlike all the other middle-aged lovers who break the hearts and wills of their responsive little wards, Roger alone will not use a father's authority to gain a lover's end. "I wish to leave her free, and take the risk," he decides. "I wish to be loved for myself, as other men are loved" (417). There are moments, in fact, when Roger, rather like some of the popular heroines of the 1850s, seems almost too noble to live. In the novel's most maudlin episode, he lies in bed at death's door while one of his two scheming rivals lays siege to Nora's heart.

The two rivals are James's versions of Warwick, supposedly plausible examples of the men the women's novels falsely idealized as the authoritarian lover. The first, George Fenton, a distant relative of Nora's, now lives in New York but was originally "Southwestern" (330). As with Basil Ransom, the Southerner whom James first conceived of as a Westerner, this geographic origin connotes masculinity. Thus, to Nora's "fancy" Fenton represents (in a rather awkward sentence) "that great collective manhood of which Roger was not" (332). Roger, aware of the inconspicuousness of his own virility, is afraid that Fenton will "be outrageously rough and Western; full of strange oaths and bearded, for aught he knew, like the pard" (329). These lines describe the soldier in Jacques's seven-ages speech in *As You Like It*. James had quoted the identical passage in his review of *Moods*, applying it to the authoritarian middle-aged lover – "the cynical bachelor or widower, the amateur of human nature, 'Full of strange oaths, and bearded like the pard,'[7] who has travelled all over the world." Now, in *Watch and Ward*, James's own aversion to this soldier is attributed to Roger, fearful of the impression the traveled Westerner will make on Nora's susceptible imagination. *Watch and Ward* thus returns to the question that agitated James in his review of Alcott's novel, namely, what kind of man truly appeals to woman's imagination and influences her heart and will?

When Fenton comes for a visit, he makes Roger "feel like a small boy, like an old woman" (330). When he takes his farewell, it appears that he has in fact had the pernicious influence on the ward's fancy that the guardian feared. But in order to follow James's steps at this narrative juncture, it is essential to recur to *Moods*, to the farewell scene James literally rewrote.

Sylvia and Warwick have just met for the first time since her marriage to Moor. The scene is a rocky amphitheater in the mountains, where Warwick, overjoyed to find his love, has thrown down his backpack and rushed to embrace her. Moor, somewhere off in the distance, has been blowing a bugle from time to time to communicate with his bride. Sylvia of course has no choice but to tell Warwick she is married, whereupon the rugged man forces himself to say farewell and at once sets off on his solitary peregrinations:

> With that he left her, never turning till the burden so joyfully cast down had been resumed. . . . He paused on the margin of that granite cup, to him a cup of sorrow, and looked into its depths again. Clouds were trooping eastward, but in that pause the sun glanced full on Warwick's figure, lifting his powerful head into a flood of light, as he waved his hand to Sylvia with a gesture of courage and good cheer. The look, the act, the memories they brought her, made her heart ache with a sharper pang than pity, and filled her eyes with tears of impotent regret, as she turned her head as if to chide the blithe clamor of the horn. When she looked again, the figure and the sunshine were both gone, leaving her alone and in the shadow. (181–82)

In his review Henry James summarized this scene of Warwick's backlighted departure in a highly sarcastic manner:

> Warwick takes himself off, over the crest of the hill, looking very tall and grand against the sun, and leaving his mistress alone in the shadow. In the shadow she passes the rest of her brief existence. She might have lived along happily enough, we conceive, masquerading with her gentle husband in the fashion of old days, if Warwick had not come back, and proffered a visit, – his one natural and his one naughty act.[8] Of course it is all up with Sylvia. (*Literary Criticism* 1: 192)

James clearly caught on to what Alcott had done with the shadow symbol. At first Sylvia's experience is colored by a series of lenslike moods, as in the Emerson quotation, but from now on she lives "In the Twilight" (title of ch. 16) – at least until her death, when she passes "Out of the Shadow" (ch. 21).

In writing *Watch and Ward,* James would conclude Chapter 4 with a version of Alcott's tableau. At the moment Fenton takes his departure, a shadow is thrown across Nora and her responsive imagination:

> As the wagon went over the crest of an adjoining hill he stood up and waved his hat. His tall, gaunt young figure, as it rose dark against the cold November sunset, cast a cooling shadow across the fount of her virgin sympathies. Such was the outline, surely, of the

conquering hero, not of the conquered. Her fancy followed him
forth into the world with a tender impulse of comradeship. (339)

The parallels with Alcott's passage are unmistakable: Fenton disappears
over the crest of a hill; his silhouetted figure rises tall in the setting sun; the
young woman stays behind in the shadow. Nora's girlish imagination –
"the fount of her virgin sympathies" – is captured, apparently, in the
sense that it figuratively trails after him. But there are some noteworthy
differences from the *Moods* passage. There is some doubt ("surely")
whether Fenton is to be "conquering" or "conquered" – whether he is to
prevail over Nora or not. And however "tender" Nora's impulse may be,
it is one of "comradeship" rather than romantic passion, and James's 1878
revision would even delete "tender" (85). All in all, though James's passage transcribes Alcott's in order to suggest Fenton's captivating effect on
Nora's vulnerable imagination, James also hints that this imagination is
still free.

The tall shadow-casting man who is seen against the horizon would
remain a potent image for James. In *The Bostonians,* Verena would feel
that Basil's "tall, watching figure, with the low horizon behind, represented well the importance, the towering eminence he had in her mind"
(385). One of the reasons this novel is so much grimmer than *Watch and
Ward* is that the heroine lacks the power to resist the tall figure. In the
more hopeful first novel, the really imposing silhouette, as Veeder notes
(*Henry James* 110), is Nora's own: "High above the level horizon now,
clearly defined against the empty sky, rose this little commanding figure,
with the added magnitude that objects acquire in this position" (240).

James brings on an even more threatening male presence than Fenton
in the person of Roger's cousin Hubert, a remarkably opportunistic minister. He has apparently "turned parson because parsons enjoy peculiar
advantages in approaching the fair sex." Wittily, we are informed that
"he administered his spiritual medicines in homœopathic doses" (415).
He is an example of "the cynical bachelor" of James's review who enjoys
so much respect and power in women's novels. And when Hubert reen-
ters the story in the third installment at the age of thirty-one, his service
in a "Western pastorate" has left him with "a slightly jaded, overwearied
look, certain to deepen his interest [that is, the interest he inspires] in
female eyes" (416). In every way he is intended to be a realistic version of
the masterful older lover who ruled the hearts and wills of youthful
heroines.

The Wide, Wide World, like *The Scarlet Letter,* illustrates something that
might otherwise be difficult to feature – the minister-hero's romantic appeal in Victorian America. Nora is vulnerable to this appeal, for she develops into "a stately maiden who read the 'Heir of Redcliffe,' and mused

upon the loves of the clergy" (415). It is significant that James chose to mention this spectacularly popular 1853 novel by Charlotte Yonge. Its hero, Sir Guy Morville, combines the highest principles with the strongest and most unruly passions, and in the end he sacrifices his life to save that of his nominal enemy, the priggish Philip. Yonge's novel had been "a favorite" of Louisa May Alcott's, according to Madeleine Stern (*Behind a Mask* xii); there was a copy in the Clemens library signed by Livy (Gribben 2: 792); and James's 1878 revision of *Watch and Ward* would have Nora reading the book for the twentieth time (in the 1871 version the much-reread novel was *The Initials* [327]). The book has caught her susceptible imagination in the same way that Penelope Lapham's would be caught by the self-sacrificial hysteria of *Tears, Idle Tears*. When Nora goes to hear Hubert preach, she sits directly beneath his pulpit and sees his face as "a dazzling focus of light" (422). When she is about to leave for Europe and Hubert advises her not to convert to Catholicism, she gushes, "I'll have no Pope but you" (423). Later, when Hubert makes a histrionic confession of his unfitness for his calling – "I promise you I'm not satisfied, not I! I've room for more . . . I shall maintain I'm a failure!" – Nora is almost ravished by the "medley of mystery and pathos and frankness" (586). But beneath his suave exterior, Hubert is basically one more "bully" (705), particularly in his manipulation of the girl's feelings. James is setting straight the ladies, showing that just as Nora is taken in by this minister, so the authors of *The Wide, Wide World, Faith Gartney's Girlhood,* and *St. Elmo* had been taken in by *their* minister-heroes.

Eventually the time comes when Nora is sufficiently grown up for Roger to propose. "Painfully startled" (595), she cannot accept. Roger is stunned and leaves, and Nora begins to wonder whether she has not made a terrible mistake in refusing him. A friend who considers her ungrateful lets her see a letter Roger had written several years earlier, at a time when Nora was still a schoolgirl: "It will be my own fault if I haven't a perfect wife" (596). Now Nora finally sees the brooding purpose that has hovered over her all these years, and she feels "horribly deluded and injured." Roger should have "told her that she wore a chain" (689). The only way to be free is to run away.

It is at this point in *Watch and Ward* that we see the centrality of the tableau James took from *Moods,* for what Nora does in running away is to demonstrate that Fenton's shadow still darkens her fancy. She hopes this "conquering hero" (339) can be her refuge now and she looks him up in New York. For some of James's reviewers Nora's flight to "her vulgar cousin" was so "unladylike" ("Recent Fiction," *Literary World* 47) that it seriously marred the novel's propriety. But James had to have some such episode in order to complete the exposé of Fenton the "middle-aged lover" and bring the heroine out from under his shadow.[9] Hence, James rather implausibly has Fenton threaten to hold Nora captive until Roger forks over five thousand dollars in ransom. When the brave girl simply calls his bluff and walks out of his office, the cowardly Fenton collapses into a chair. In this way James completes the demonstration he first undertook in his review of *Moods* and other novels by "little women" in 1865. The man who seems so awesome to the feminine imagination is nothing but a weak crook. Unfortunately, as the reviewer for the *Nation* saw, Fenton has an "allegorical thinness," and "the wooden limbs and the strings whereby" he is "jerked" ("Recent Novels," *Nation* 27: 118) are too much in evidence. If few characters James was to create would be as unconvincing as this one, that is partly because the young author was consumed by an antagonistic motive.

In the following scene James unmasks the second rival, Hubert, whom Nora next seeks out for assistance and comfort. Hubert is of course anything but the kind of person others may rely on, and Nora has a sudden vision of his essential hollowness – "all his falsity, all his levity, all his egotism and sophism" (707). Then the real truth comes out: Hubert is engaged to a rich New York Jew. When this person accuses Nora of trying to alienate Hubert's affections, it is clear to the girl that any gentleman who could endure such vulgarity in a wife must be mercenary and worthless. Nora steps out onto the sidewalk. She feels "strangely, almost absurdly, free." The prose strains to emphasize her shadowless state now that she has seen through Roger's competitors: "The sky was blazing blue overhead; the opposite side of the street was all in sun; she hailed the joyous brightness of the day with a kind of answering joy." (The imagery of this climactic moment also emerged directly from James's response to Anne Moncure Crane's 1867 novel, *Opportunity*.) Nora has been liberated into light and open space, and her euphoria even reminds her of the sensations produced by "a dose of ether." Suddenly she sees Roger materialize and approach "down the bright vista of the street." She realizes that this good and mild person who is so unoppressive is "the only man" in the universe "who had a heart" (709). She embraces him, they marry, everything has been unsnarled, and the young male author completes his lecture to dark Louisa and the other women novelists he has taken to task for their shadows.

Commentators on *Watch and Ward* have not detected the book's peculiar literary antecedents and counterthrusts. James's apprentice novel emerged from his strong dislike for *Moods* and the complex tradition of women's fiction Alcott's book summed up for him. Jamesians have tended to see in the novel a reflection of its author's youthful conflicts and fantasies. Edel has stressed young James's obsession with "a 'heroine of the scene' surrounded by suitors who possess traits of the significant figures in his childhood, with himself as the unassertive and self-doubting aspirant. But this time he gives himself the victory" (*Conquest* 44). J. A. Ward has written: "Psychologically . . . Roger wants not to master life, but to combine adult experience – that of a father, a suitor, and a husband – with the security and ease he had known in childhood" (72). These perceptions, shrewd and accurate, should be supplemented by a recognition of the literary heritage behind the book. Leo B. Levy has touched on this: "The guardian–ward motif, familiar in English and French fiction of the romantic as well as the didactic class, is turned [in *Watch and Ward*] into an instrument of comic analysis of fiction of the sentimental kind" (87). More specifically, we may say that what James devised in the novel was an exceptionally adroit solution to the old problem given so much attention in the women's novels he had been reading and reviewing: How does one work out a pleasing incest fantasy without violating decorum? The key to James's solution was the transfer of power and mastery from the paternal lover to the unworthy rivals, a solution designed to render guardian and ward equals and thus to purify their love of all sadomasochistic elements. This merging of James's psyche and personal history with a literary tradition vital to a large population is, I believe, one of the things that rendered him a powerful and important novelist. His mind became to some extent the mind of his place and time.

Of course *Watch and Ward* was too defective to have much power or centrality in itself. The two male rivals are not sufficiently fleshed out to be anything more than counters in an argument, and the argument is pushed too hard. The fact that Roger wins Nora by doing nothing at all, only giving his rivals enough rope to prove their unworthiness, is a sign of the extent to which the novel defends passivity. It was naive for James to assume his nice man would naturally get the girl once the bad men were out of the way. As the *Athenaeum's* reviewer complained, "It seems too much as if the heroine had come to return the hero's love because she had miserably failed in her other ventures" (177).

It is in its treatment of love and freedom, however, that *Watch and Ward* fails most egregiously. In the interval preceding her final reconciliation with Roger, Nora may go sky-high with her euphoric sense of freedom, but she is far from free in a material sense. She has no home of her own, no source of support, no friends in New York, and the purse containing all her cash has been forgotten in Fenton's office. Even worse, she was earlier instructed by Roger that she could not return to his house unless she agreed to marry him. Hence, in spite of all James's imaginative labor, his novel ultimately succumbs to the same confusion as all the other guardian–ward love stories (all except one, Elizabeth Stoddard's *Two Men*): It masks dependency as love. James tried hard to eliminate the coercive pressure of the intolerable middle-aged lover, but when all was said and done the coercion was still there, right at the center and more disguised than ever. That dose of ether in the middle of Nora's euphoria is a telltale sign of this deep rationalization and unconsciousness.

Watch and Ward was a clever move in a game designed by the ladies. In spite of its strongly felt aspect – its vindication of Roger against those who "always speak of him with a little air of amusement" (580), its defense of the Geoffrey Moor type – the book was far removed from James's experience. Even a favorable reviewer had to admit that the novel was "labored to the extent of artificiality" (Review of *Watch and Ward, Library Table* 301). Yet James's virgin novel holds a crucial place in his body of work because it represents his first and last attempt to write a happy love story about the leading couple in American fiction of the 1850s and 1860s, the middle-aged lover and the precocious girl. The step James had to take before he would be able to write his master study of this couple, *The Portrait of a Lady*, was to cease defending them. He had to go back to his review of *Moods*, to its energetic and uncensored statement of aversion toward this couple, before he could move beyond *Watch and Ward*. Only in this way would he enable himself to develop that magnificently sinister paternal lover, Gilbert Osmond, who is so adept at undermining the self-confidence of his youthful wife, Isabel, and at terrorizing his daughter, Pansy. The scene where Osmond begins to woo Isabel by drawing his daughter from her chair "and making her stand between his knees, leaning against him while he passed his arm round her little waist" (*Portrait* 225) is a perfect match, almost, with the early scene in *Watch and Ward* where Roger puts *his* arm around Nora and feels her "tender feminine promise" and starts to dream about marriage. Isabel, gazing at the significant tableau of Osmond and Pansy, sees the holy pair of domestic American fiction; she is as naive as James was when he wrote that early scene in *Watch and Ward*. But now Isabel's author is less naive. He grasps the distinction between dominance-submission and love in women's lives, and he works it out in countless ways. Beneath the surface of *The Portrait*, as beneath the surface of other good realistic novels, lies the author's reluctant renunciation of the hopeful fantasy that destroys its protagonist. James created *The Portrait* by moving backward from a faulty literature to the readers and writers who had generated that literature. His first truly substantial novel was an extension of his criticism.

Life in the Shadow

Finally, what traces did Alcott's encounter with Henry James, Jr., in 1865 leave on *her* fiction? She was undoubtedly stung by his criticism of her most ambitious work, and in time she would thoroughly revise *Moods*, an act that implies she felt it had not yet received proper justice, or perhaps that it had not yet been read in its proper form. This revised version appeared in 1882 – almost simultaneously with *The Portrait of a Lady*. The preface Alcott wrote for the new edition admitted that her original publisher required her to change the book's emphasis from "the mistakes of a moody nature" (v) to the theme of marriage. She claimed that the revision marked a return to her original conception and thus omitted "several" chapters (in fact only two, 1 and 9) and restored some of the "original" ones (vi). By "original" she undoubtedly meant not the August 1860 first draft but the penultimate 1864 version, the one Loring asked her to shorten and revise.

Alcott's broad suggestion that the new edition basically restored the novel to its unbutchered state, only pruning here and there and reversing the ending, is misleading. She had removed fully ten chapters (*Louisa* 161; *Selected Letters* 110) for Loring in 1864. The 1882 version would restore only three of these: 2, 4, and 8. What Alcott's final version of the book represents is an effort at correction as much as resurrection. She wanted to *repair* the faults spotted by the book's critics – chiefly young Henry James.

Thus, Alcott's revisions were to be her final reply to the eighty-year-old youth who lectured her at dinner.[10] His review had pronounced the last part of the novel "very pretty; indeed, if it were not so essentially false, we should call it very fine. As it is, we can only use the expression in its ironical sense" (*Literary Criticism* 1: 193). Now Alcott would attempt to remove "as much fine writing as could be done" (1882 vi). "A literary curiosity" (*Literary Criticism* 1: 190) was James's label for the first chapter, where Warwick scolds a gorgeous Cuban lady named Ottilla because she has inveigled him into an engagement; Alcott dropped the whole chapter and the Latin pantheress with it. (James's bizarre Peruvian episode in *Watch and Ward* demonstrates how a gentleman *ought* to break off with a sensual Latin lover.) The review had glanced with quizzical hauteur (*Literary Criticism* 1: 189) at the scene where Moor mistakes Sylvia for a boy; in the revision Moor would not mistake her gender (1882 18). James's ridicule of Sylvia's extreme susceptibility to shadow-casting Warwick may have prompted Alcott to add a brief conversation between husband and wife in which the unhappy wife shows her moral fiber. Thus, Moor says, "This rarefied air is too much for you," and Sylvia replies, "Yes, mountain-tops are too high for me; I am safer in the valley with you, Geoffrey" (1882 227). The coy symbolism of this answer signals Sylvia's new desire to accommodate herself to her unromantic husband. It also heralds the most startling revision of all: Sylvia does not die. Like Nora in *Watch and Ward*, the revised Sylvia comes to appreciate her gentle husband every bit as much as young Henry James had preached she should.

It is during Moor's European exile that Sylvia begins to mellow and to long for him – "ardently" (1882 333), we are assured. This ardor, supposedly the result of time and distance, may also result from the death of her father, who, in the 1865 version, had continued living. Perhaps Alcott came to understand that Sylvia's attachment to her "romantic father" (105) kept her from caring for Moor. Or perhaps we are seeing the operation of the same law as in "A Marble Woman," where the father's death brings the marble daughter to life. In any case, Sylvia's marriage now begins to flourish, and she goes on to live "a long and happy life, unmarred by the moods that nearly wrecked her youth; for now she had learned to live by principle, not impulse" (1882 359).

But in one essential respect, the new ending does not improve on the old. Alcott does not question Warwick, does not suggest he has any serious weaknesses or faults, and certainly does not permit poor Sylvia to get a sense of them. Back in 1865 Alcott had defended Warwick against those who found him an "impossible character" by arguing that he was "drawn from life" and was perfectly "upright" (Selected Letters 109). Apparently, what James's review said about Warwick's sanctimonious bullying made no impression on Alcott. She even retained a speech whose provincialism had drawn James's fire – Warwick's declaration that "he designs no 'French sentiment nor sin' " (Literary Criticism 1: 192). Instead of ceasing to worship her hero, the amended Sylvia convinces herself more vigorously than ever that she is not worthy of him. The price paid for this victory over self is that Sylvia becomes completely hollow and unbelievable. The ardor she is said to feel for Moor is never convincingly put before us. Also, the comment she makes when she learns of Warwick's death by drowning is unfeeling and entirely too pat: "I could have spared Adam," she says (meaning, oddly, that she could have accepted his survival); "I had given him up and learned to see that it was best" (1882 352). Maybe so, but she is speaking like an automaton.

By melancholy coincidence, the new title of the final chapter – "At Last" – is the same as the last chapter of "A Marble Woman." In the gothic story this expression means that at last Cecil can enjoy the delights of sexual intercourse with Bazil. All the phrase means in the 1882 Moods is that at last Sylvia has become the marble woman.

Worst of all, perhaps, the beautiful Emersonian "motto" (Louisa 122), which had authorized Alcott to undertake her brave and colorful novel in 1860, is not even on the title page of the 1882 version:

. . . a string of beads; and as we pass through them they prove to be many colored lenses, which paint the world their own hue . . .

The shadow had blotted out the colors after all.

Chapter 4

The Chains of Literature

Elizabeth Stoddard and Henry James

Elizabeth Stoddard (1823–1902) was the daughter of the man whose shipyard built the *Acushnet,* the whaling vessel in which Melville sailed. She married a negligible poet, Richard Henry Stoddard, and lived with him in New York for most of her long life, summering at her childhood home on Buzzards Bay. The New York correspondent for the leading newspaper of the Far West, the *Alta California,* Stoddard attended a women's rights convention in 1857 and was impressed by a speech by Lucy Stone.[1] She began writing fiction as well as poetry and sold her first story to the *Atlantic* in 1861. The following year saw the publication of her first novel, *The Morgesons,* in writing which she "endeavored to make a plain transcript of human life . . . without taking on a moral here or an explanation there."[2] We can sense the special underground reputation this novel conferred on Stoddard from a private remark made to Caroline Dall and recorded in her journals: Elizabeth Davis Martin confided that "Mrs. Stodard [*sic*] the author of the 'Morgessons' [*sic*] and her most intimate friend is a person true and passionate but no moral help to her" (5 July 1866, Dall Papers, MHS). Stoddard requires detailed consideration here for two reasons: She wrote the outstanding novel so far discovered by the renewed interest in American women writers of the nineteenth century, and she was the target of the most ferocious, in fact vicious, review Henry James is known to have written.

The Morgesons was published at a time when it almost appeared the South was going to win the Civil War. Even so, the book "attracted more attention than any novel of the season, and was allowed on all sides to show as much genius as power" ("Personal"). Many reviewers made a conscientious effort to do it justice. George Ripley, writing for the *New York Tribune,* was struck by the author's "remorseless habit of stripping the veil from the softest illusions, and cherishing an inexorable sense of reality" (Matlack, "Hawthorne" 286). Twenty-five years later, when *The Morgesons* was brought out in a revised edition together with Stoddard's two other novels, it elicited high praise even from reviewers who admitted their feeling of repulsion (*Independent* 1355). Many of these reviewers, including W. D. Howells, now saw Stoddard as a precursor of the realists.[3] When her three novels were issued for a third time, in 1901, the reviewers once again struggled to express their sense of strange power. Mary Moss was impressed by the sharp local detail, emotional storminess, and penetrating vision. Stoddard "had genius of a high order, but totally undisciplined," Moss summed up; "her books form no link in the chain of literature" (262–63).

This dismal assessment proved to be an accurate forecast of the obscurity into which Stoddard's fiction sank in the first half of the twentieth century. Then, at the end of World War II Gordon S. Haight wrote a paragraph on her in *Literary History of the United States* (Spiller 880), and his tantalizing account of the strange and quasi-modern look of her novels led later scholars to investigate them. James H. Matlack produced two articles on her from his excellent dissertation, one on the real-life connections between *The Morgesons* and Salem history, and the other on Stoddard's career as a newspaper essayist. Richard Foster cogently argued that Stoddard's vitalism, demonic vision, and use of symbolism put her close to D. H. Lawrence. Sybil Weir maintained that *The Morgesons* is major work, an uncompromising feminist story of the maturation of a strong, erotic woman in a world without theistic supports. Recently, Lawrence Buell and Sandra A. Zagarell have declared that Stoddard's was "the most strikingly original voice in the mid-nineteenth-century American novel," after Hawthorne and Melville, and that she "unquestioningly deserves critical recognition" (xi). Susan K. Harris has contrasted her daring treatment of female independence in her first book to the "thematic range" (11) apparent in Susan Warner's *Wide, Wide World* and *Queechy*, Harriet Beecher Stowe's *Minister's Wooing*, and Emma Southworth's *Deserted Wife*.

This chapter carries on what these various critics have initiated by arguing that Stoddard is the one prose writer among the women agonists of the 1860s whose work demands recognition in the late twentieth century. In trying to grasp the nature of her achievement in her first and best novel, it is helpful to keep in mind that it was completed the same year in which "Life in the Iron Mills" by Rebecca Harding Davis appeared, and was published during the year Emily Dickinson apparently reached peak productivity. Independently of one another, these three agonists made a heroic, syntax-wrenching effort to bring to light some things that women writers had been slowly dragging into the open over several decades. What Stoddard did in the *The Morgesons* was to bring woman's fiction to a full – possibly premature – climax, an energetic surge too strongly felt to remain uncensored and too honest to be wholly forgotten. And just as Dickinson's "spasmodic" gait (Higginson, "Emily Dickinson's Letters" 447) had to be regularized for public consumption in the later Gilded Age, so Stoddard's honest portrayal of a young woman's maturation had to be rewritten, in James's and Howells's novels, as the charmingly risky self-assertion of the American girl. There is no doubt *The Morgesons* is flawed. It and the author's later novels are less impressive all in all than the massive output of the male realists, or the work of the best local colorists. But what Howells, James, Jewett, and Freeman did in their fiction appears to be a diminished thing when compared to what Stoddard almost succeeded in doing in one book written in the early 1860s.

In the light of the strange power of *The Morgesons,* it is arresting to note how often the strongest responses to it have been private. The grey eminence of the time, Nathaniel Hawthorne, praised the novel highly, but only in a letter to the author:

> I was particularly impressed with the childhood of the heroine in *The Morgessons* [*sic*], and the whole of the first part of the book. It seemed to me as genuine and lifelike as anything that pen and ink can do. The latter part showed much power, but struck me as neither so new or so true. Pray pardon the frankness of my crude criticism; for what is the use of saying anything, unless we say what we think? There are very few books of which I take the trouble to have an opinion at all, or of which I could retain any memory so long after reading them, as I do of *The Morgesons*. (Matlack, "Hawthorne" 278)

Young Henry James's implacably hostile opinion of this novel also failed to see print:

> [*The Morgesons*] possessed not even the slightest mechanical coherency. It was a long tedious record of incoherent dialogue between persons irresponsible in their sayings and doings even to the verge of insanity. Of narrative, of exposition, of statement, there was not a page in the book. . . . The reader . . . arose with his head full of impressions as lively as they were disagreeable. (Kraft 270–71)

In another act of silence, the review that Edwin Percy Whipple wrote for the *Atlantic* was suppressed by James T. Fields, who evidently felt the novel had "slandered" the Forrester family of Salem (Matlack, "Literary Career" 273). One result of this editorial decision was that the news of Stoddard's remarkable novel probably did not reach Emily Dickinson in her home in Amherst.[4] This missed link seems in retrospect to be almost as lamentable as Stoddard's disappearance from the chain of literature. There has been something as dark, grim, and mysterious in her literary reputation as in the vision her novels articulate. One cannot resist wondering whether Stoddard's disappearance, like Minnie Temple's death, was *required* for James's triumph.

The Morgesons

The Morgesons presents its people in material terms. Grandfather Warren is introduced as "a little, lean, leather-colored man," whose "long polished nails clicked together with a shelly noise, like that which beetles make flying against the ceiling." He displays no grief whatever on his wife's death, only commencing his "habit of chafing his hands."⁵ The schoolmistress at Rosville "had crenulated black hair, large black eyes, a Roman nose, and long white teeth. She bit her nails when annoyed" (40). The heroine, Cassandra, narrating her own story, tells us that she began as "an animal," "robust in health – inattentive, and seeking excitement and exhilaration" (30). She hardly seems capable of thought. Only a few vivid pictures get impressed on her mind and memory. And just as our attention is drawn to her grandfather's and schoolteacher's claws, so our first view of Cassandra exhibits her climbing monkeylike up the knobs of a chest of drawers, so that she can read a book in privacy on the top.

Although the author rarely interprets all the vivid descriptive detail, it gradually becomes clear that Cassandra is quite unlike the usual nineteenth-century maiden. *The Morgesons* is that rare thing, a Victorian novel whose sympathetic heroine is quite devoid of ideality. Cassandra grows up behind the scenes, so to speak, coming to see the pious beliefs and practices of her Calvinistic seaside village as little more than quaint superstitions. After watching her devout aunt Mercy bake the communion bread, Cassandra eats the leftovers that are brought home from church – eats them "reflectively, to test . . . [their] solemnizing powers. I felt none, and when Aunt Mercy boiled the remnants with milk for a pudding, the sacred ideality of the ceremony I had seen at church was destroyed for me" (50).

Other important intimations come to the growing girl, as we see in a tautly rendered conversation with her sister, Veronica, who says:

> "I wish . . . you would pound Mr. Park; he talks too much about the Resurrection. And," she added mysteriously, "he likes mother."
> "Likes mother!" I said aghast.
> "He watches her so when she holds Arthur [the baby]! Why do you stare at me?" (47)

Does Mr. Park's obsession with the apocalypse and unveiling mask an unseemly interest in the physical facts of mothering? Unlike James's innocent protagonists, who experience their thundering carnal revelations only near the end, Stoddard's heroine grows up behind the veil the nineteenth century threw over physical life. In this way she recalls both the Aeschylean Cassandra and Simon Legree's Cassy.

Cassandra is not a literal orphan like many of the heroines of woman's fiction. Her father is the village squire, the family is wealthy and influential, and the Morgeson mansion always remains a central fact for her. Yet Cassandra's mother is so helpless and inarticulate, having been deeply repressed by her own father's Puritanism that, like *The Hidden Hand, The Morgesons* may be read as the daughter's revenge for her mother's silencing. But there are no villains in Stoddard's narrative: Every member of the clan is essentially alone, so that the most confessional conversations serve only to reveal a solitude beyond remedy. When Cassandra asks her father whether he thinks her whole life will be as wasted as her first eighteen years, he can only answer: "You must go in the way ordained, waste or no waste. I have tried to make your life differ from mine at the same age, for you are like me, and I wanted to see the result" (106). Isolation and anomie – the conditions that popular fiction symbolized by the death of the mother – are here firmly rooted *within* mother and home.

Stoddard's first novel thus continues the basic enterprise of woman's fiction, a passionate inquiry into the effect on a heroine of a new and extraordinary kind of homelessness. What gives the novel its stature is that it never seeks rest in the usual refuges, dependency on a man or self-sacrificing godliness. As early as 1856, Stoddard had shown her impatience with popular women novelists who assumed that goodness was "incompatible with the enjoyment of the senses" (Matlack, "*Alta*" 299). *The Morgesons* would address much more fundamental and interesting problems than popular novels of the 1850s: How can the heroine grow up yet keep her independence? How can she find erotic satisfaction without becoming a social reprobate? The answers Stoddard produced to these questions served to define the road nineteenth-century American realism would choose *not* to take.

Cassandra is infinitely bolder than any of Howells's or James's American girls. She is naturally skeptical, laconic, idle, aware of her freedom, and so self-confident she never blinks, no matter how close she comes to the edges. When a popular classmate taunts her about her mother's adolescent troubles, Cassy hits the girl in the face. When a well-born Harvard senior says to her with his nonchalant air, "My acquaintance with you has begun; it will never end. You thought me a boy; I am just your age," she merely replies, " 'Never,' is a long word, Boy Somers" (99). Tall, blonde, with long hair and a deep voice, attracted to the sea, spirited horses, and unruly men, she resembles Capitola Black in breaking nearly every precedent for nineteenth-century heroines. But unlike Southworth's fantasy heroine in *The Hidden Hand,* Cassy has to live in the same tiresome world the reader inhabits – the familiar old world in which "man's life was a vain going to and fro" (148).

The casualness of Cassandra's sensuality is stunning. When she takes up residence with distant relatives in order to attend school, she falls in love with the married man of the house, Charles Morgeson, a rich businessman who runs his house and factory with an iron hand. He has the complexion and personality that were standard for Rochester-like heroes of the 1850s and 1860s, being "swarthy" (109), "imperious, fastidious, and sarcastic" (80). Cassy sometimes sees a devil looking out of his eyes; someone else calls him "a savage, living by his instincts" (108). Attracted to this improvisational recklessness, the heroine becomes aware that "an intangible, silent, magnetic feeling existed between us, changing and developing according to its own mysterious law, remaining intact in spite of the contests between us, of resistance and defiance" (80). Cassy innocently speaks to Charles's wife about this magnetism, and the wife, who lives only for her children and seems personally anesthetized, innocently (or maliciously) mentions it to Charles. Instantly, "he raised his eyes to mine. A blinding, intelligent light flowed from them, which I could not defy. The blood thundered back to my heart" (92).

Cassandra tries unsuccessfully to resist her passion. She openly drifts toward sexual union with Charles, but at the last minute a crazed stallion destroys the chaise in which the two of them are riding. Charles is killed and Cassandra, badly injured, is left with a scar on her face. The episode clearly indicates in its symbolism how imperative it is for Cassandra to hold the reins on her sexuality, or on that of the strong men she likes. The problem of her life is not (as for Edna Pontellier in *The Awakening*) to recognize or express her sexuality, but to learn how to manage it. When she falls in love with an even tougher case, Desmond Somers, the Harvard boy's older brother, her experience with Charles proves to be a great help. Desmond is idle, dissolute, arrogant, and dangerous. He has almost succumbed to an hereditary alcoholism. He is totally bored, with no occupation but to wait for the day he can take possession of an immense inheritance. The Somers family was modeled, as Matlack has shown ("Hawthorne"), after the rich Forrester family of Salem (thinly veiled behind the name Belem). Both Stoddard and Hawthorne disliked this family, and Stoddard's antagonism had an injurious effect on the Belem chapters. Furthermore – and this was to be her chronic problem as a novelist – she did not convincingly realize the events her plot required. Desmond is sent to Spain for a two-year alcoholism-recovery program. He subdues his craving for drink and returns to Cassandra, but his personal reform seems far too convenient. It may have been this segment of the narrative that Hawthorne had in mind when he told Stoddard that "the latter part" struck him "as neither so new or so true."

There is, of course, nothing inherently wrong with Desmond's story. Cassandra's demand that he get hold of himself makes sense; it is the patness with which he succeeds in doing so that makes the skeptical reader feel restive. Fortunately, the novel does a more effective job of representing Cassandra's achieved self-control – her completion (in Sybil Weir's analysis) of the arduous Freudian task "of becoming her own parents" (437). Best of all, Stoddard never asks us to try to believe that her heroine must submit to a rigorous moral vindication before she can go to bed with the man she wants. Susan Warner's heroines must demonstrate what good little girls they are before they can marry; Cassandra must, more sensibly, grow up. In spite of serious flaws, the conception and overall execution of the book remain sound. Author and heroine both earn the speech Cassandra makes to Desmond at the end: "Do you know how I love you? Feel my heart, – it has throbbed with the weight of you" (257).

The Morgesons was thus able to resolve the problem that destroyed the vitality of all the adult novels written by Stoddard's fellow agonists, Adeline Whitney, Rebecca Harding Davis, Louisa May Alcott, and Anne Moncure Crane Seemuller (with the possible exception of the latter writer's third book, *Reginald Archer*). All these authors could not really convince themselves that women had as much a right to happiness as men. The problem never occurred to Stoddard, who simply accepted the likelihood that strong people with strong desires are more likely to find satisfaction than conscientious self-tormentors. The heroine gives voice to the book's basic assumption: "We may determine some things for ourselves, irrespective of consequences" (253). *The Morgesons* is antisentimental, as Mary Moss noticed long ago when she pointed out the novel's difference from "didactic, self-consciously ethical" (261) fiction. To exalt the sentimental tradition, as Jane Tompkins does,[6] is to downgrade Stoddard as well as Hawthorne and Melville.

Veronica, Cassandra's sister and foil, is wonderfully integrated with the novel's prevailing antisentimentality. Virtually everyone who has commented on *The Morgesons* has been fascinated by this beautiful, elusive, useless person. Neither can the Portuguese boy who appears late in the novel take his eyes off her; he sees her as the Virgin. Other characters ask one another how she can grow up, or whether she is human. Veronica has no friends, refuses to look at the ocean, is extremely distant from Cassandra, and near the end admits she has always regarded herself as the "superior" sister, the one with the greater "delicacy of feeling" (246). She has nervous spells and one prophetic dream. Her rhapsodic piano playing entrances everyone. She spends much of her time in her room, which she has decorated so that it resembles "no other place" (140). Mary Moss diagnosed Veronica as "an exalted hysteric or epileptic" (261), but the latter term is inaccurate and the former both vague and reductive. Veronica is the Lady of Shalott, a china doll, a New England eldritch, a sibyl, a sphinx, a madwoman in the attic. Most of all, perhaps, she is Stoddard's version of the angel-child who was incarnated in Stowe's little Eva, Cummins's Rose (in *Mabel Vaughan*), Alcott's Beth, Dickens's little Nell, and a hundred other avatars. Veronica is femininity in the bonds of the ideal, and her family nickname, Verry, is to be associated with the Latin for truth. That the association must be ironic, we see in the brilliant episode near the end in which Veronica vainly tries to postpone the consummation of her marriage:

> "Cassy, will you take these pins out of my hair?" asked Verry, seating herself in an easy chair. "Ben, we will excuse you."
> "How good of you." He strode across the passage, went into her room, and shut the door.
> "There, Verry, I have unbound your hair."
> "But I want to talk."
> I took her hand, and led her out. She stood before her door for a moment silently, and then gave a little knock. No answer came. She knocked again; the same silence as before. At last she was obliged to open it herself, and enter without any bidding. (249)

The writing here has the same taut charge as the last scene, following the wedding, of Howells's *April Hopes*. But Howells could not get nearly as close to the wedding bed as Stoddard could. Her details – Veronica's urge to talk, her "little knock," the fact that her husband forces her to take the initiative of entering – all provide a wealth of insight into this unhappy pair.

In the end, after Veronica's still-youthful husband dies of alcoholism and she gives birth, it requires only one vignette to show what happens to an angel-child compelled to enter animality: "Her eyes go no more in quest of something beyond. A wall of darkness lies before her, which she will not penetrate." As for the baby of this demented Madonna, it is apparently another divine freak, for it "smiles continually, but never cries, never moves" (259).

Considering what *The Morgesons* has to say about ideal femininity as embodied in a childlike, weirdly gifted recluse, it would seem to be a revelation of the first importance that when Thomas Wentworth Higginson finally saw Emily Dickinson in 1870, he was reminded of Stoddard's novels. The first thing he wrote to his wife, who he knew would be eager to hear his impression of the strange poet, was this: "I shan't sit up tonight to write you all about E. D. dearest but if you had read Mrs.

Stoddard's novels you could understand a house where each member runs his or her own selves. Yet I only saw her" (*Letters of Emily Dickinson* 2: 473). I think Haight was right on the mark in suggesting that Higginson had Veronica "in mind" (Spiller 880). To my knowledge, no study of Dickinson has ransacked Higginson's revealing association for all it could tell us about the poet who is supposed to have written over 360 poems the same year Veronica appeared in print. The most intriguing question of all is by its very nature unanswerable: What difference might it have made if Fields had gone ahead and printed Whipple's review of *The Morgesons* in the magazine Dickinson studied so carefully, and what if she had read the novel and seen her own reflection in the character whose "mind fed and grew on pain" (65)? All we can say is this: Thirty years later, when Dickinson was dead and the first selection of her poems was published, Stoddard definitely disapproved. "An eccentric arrangement of words – or ebullition of feeling – do not constitute poetry" (Matlack, "Literary Career" 470) was the now rather stodgy sixty-year-old woman's verdict. Another missed connection.

Hawthorne connected, at least, and it is to his credit that in spite of his old weakness for snow maidens, he liked the earthy vigor of *The Morgesons*. His capacity for woman's fiction had grown since his famous "scribbling women" outburst, provoked by the sales of *The Lamplighter*. When he read Fanny Fern's vengeful *Ruth Hall* in 1855, for instance, he admitted that he

> . . . enjoyed it a good deal. The woman writes as if the devil was in her; and that is the only condition under which a woman ever writes anything worth reading. Generally, women write like emasculated men, and are only to be distinguished from male authors by greater feebleness and folly; but when they throw off the restraints of decency and come before the public stark naked, as it were – then their books are sure to possess character and value.[7]

Hawthorne is at least partly vindicated by the fact that one of the best nineteenth-century novels by an American woman was a frank study of a woman's sexual and social maturation. Of the three reasons given by Matlack for Hawthorne's appreciation of *The Morgesons* – the book reminded him of his early Salem years, he was intrigued by the Forrester connection, and he appreciated the novel's realism ("Hawthorne" 300–302) – the third is by far the most important. Hawthorne positively reveled in the novel's blunt icon breaking, a quality he honored in the sincerest manner of all, by imitating it in his letter to the author. His direct, unpatronizing honesty – "pardon the frankness of my crude criticism; for what is the use of saying anything, unless we say what we think?" – evokes the bloom of his enthusiasm for Stoddard's brilliant crudity.

Of course young Henry James could not appreciate the crudity of *The Morgesons*. The abrupt speeches, the gritty detail, the exact use of colloquialisms all offended him. Stoddard had gone further than Fanny Fern had gone, or than Adeline Whitney or Rebecca Harding Davis would go, in developing a lean, rough, elliptical prose. In fact, Stoddard is sometimes so compact she is "baffling," as Matlack admits ("Hawthorne" 293). Although one of James's earliest works, "The Story of a Year," imitated the jabbing, spasmodic style of the mid-1860s, his prose would in general be remarkable for its smooth elegance, and his later work would be tightly woven, consecutive, polished, with multiple overlapping linkages: James *was* the chain of literature. He could not tolerate writing that sought to eliminate the graceful connective tissue he loved. Neither could he respond to Stoddard's local-color cameos, such as Patience, a finer example of the tough old New England housekeeper than any of Harriet Beecher Stowe's many versions of the type. Most of all, the vigor of Stoddard's attack on sexual prudery, her refusal to idealize any form of weakness, her insubordination before the claims of convention, tradition, and decorum, and not least of all her contemptuous dismissal of well-bred young men as "cubs" (85), mere boys, called up a passionate negation from Boy James, the "angel" of his family.

This negation had the gravest consequences for Stoddard's career and reputation. James's review of her second novel, *Two Men*, was to be so vitriolic, irrational, and poorly argued that it could not be published in the *North American Review*. Once again the woman novelist who wrote about rural New England life with greater penetration than anyone else, even Stowe, could not be safely reviewed in New England. Stoddard was being locked out.

Two Men

Two Men came out in 1865 and was reviewed by both Howells and James. Howells had known Stoddard since before the war. His review in the *Nation* was long, detailed, and generous, but measured in its apportionment of praise and blame. Just as Hawthorne had risen to the truth-telling bluntness of *The Morgesons*, Howells began by making an amusing confession of his own exhilarated response: "Though you are ever so dull a man, you are conscious that hidden springs of epigram have been touched in your nature, and that it is in you for the moment to talk brilliantly. You wish, also, to express yourself violently and recklessly, with an oath or two." The book was unequivocally a "romance," yet it produced "an impression of reality" and its characters, however exceptional, were "veritable American types." Howells regarded the three ex-slaves, Mrs. Lang and her daughters, as "the most successful creations."

He did not mention the sexual liaison between one of these daughters and the white heir of the aristocratic Parke family, an event Stoddard narrated in detail and with a certain defiance. Yet Howells dared to stand by the author: "The book . . . leaves at last an impression . . . of propriety within certain conditions, which must be granted the author as they must be granted to every artist." For all his early and late prudery, Howells had a broad notion of propriety in the second half of the 1860s, the period in which he reported on the early burlesque theater and published Stowe's exposé of Byron's incest in the *Atlantic*. Howells praised the "clear and sharp-cut" style of *Two Men,* but questioned the effectiveness of the book's "intensity."[8] His most damaging – and accurate – criticism was that the three characters who form the novel's triangle are not sufficiently developed.

The unpublishable outpouring by Henry James forms a remarkable contrast to Howells's discriminating review. After a contemptuous backward glance at *The Morgesons,* James assailed *Two Men* for the "violence" (Kraft 267–73) of its style, its disorderliness, absence of facts, and cheap melodrama. The review survives in a manuscript that has a number of deletions and substitutions. The discussion of *Two Men* is contained in one long six-hundred-word paragraph. It would appear that James was quite heated when he wrote it and that he sent it to Charles Eliot Norton without serious revision. It also looks as if Norton set out to tone James down, revising "almost brutally crude" to "curiously crude," but then giving up. According to James Kraft, there is no other evidence of copyediting in the manuscript. Evidently Norton quickly saw that the review could not be printed.

The contradictions within the review are striking. One cannot reconcile James's view that the novel is violently unnatural and empty of facts with his claim that there is too much "natural" and "commonplace" dialogue. Other reviewers saw that Stoddard could be fruitfully compared to Balzac, Hawthorne, or Charlotte and Emily Brontë, but only James, fresh from reviewing Trollope, drew a comparison with this writer. James wrote initially: "Mr. Trollope's flagrant common-place is bad enough; but this distorted common-place is worse." Perhaps James recognized that this comparison was so far-fetched that it gave a mistaken impression of Stoddard's taut dialogue, and he recast the sentence: "Yet this intense and distorted common-place is worse than Mr. Trollope's flagrant common-place." "Intense" fits Stoddard, but now the comparison with Trollope, who was anything but intense, has less to say for it than before. And the combination "intense . . . commonplace" is strained to the point of self-contradiction.

The review is irrational in other ways. It brings forward very few specifics from the novel, and those it does mention it distorts. In attacking the characterization, James wrote that Stoddard is "violent when she says that the same young lady [Philippa] has speckled eyes and feathery hair." A glance at the original passage in the book shows that James's sarcasm here was far from the mark. After Philippa has returned from school, Sarah calls her a cockatrice, and Jason, looking at the girl, finds "himself wondering whether all cockatrices had pale yellow hair that looked as if about to float into the air like the down of flowers. There was something strange in those speckled eyes, though!"[9] What we see here is not the author's strained intensity but Jason's playful reflections on the image of the cockatrice. Also, "feathery hair" was James's phrase, not Stoddard's.

There is a more important respect in which the review commits the same sin it attributes to Two Men. Instead of offering the "facts" he proclaimed to be so important, James indulged in the most solemn fulminations: "We have spoken of her [Stoddard's] imagination. She has exercised it with her back turned upon the truth. Let her face the truth and she may let her imagination rest: as it is, it only brings her into trouble." Only after this little sermon, with over nine-tenths of his space used up, did James finally say something about the story line:

> A middle-aged man who loves a young girl for years in silence, knowing that she loves his own son: who quietly and heroically awaits his wife's death, knowing that she hates the young girl; and who at last when his wife is dead and his son has gone forth from home, casts out his heart at the young girl's feet: all this makes a story quite after the actual taste. (Kraft 272–73)

The all-important word "middle-aged" was added by James afterward. This long-delayed afterthought helps explain why James felt so much blind rage at Two Men. It was the old conjunction of the "precocious little girl" and the "middle-aged lover" that he had objected to so strenuously in his review of Moods and that he claimed to remember from a "hundred" other novels (Literary Criticism 1: 189–90). And as before, the very shadow of the paternal lover again fell on James and the page in front of him: "How tall he looked against the background of the sky" (267), Philippa thinks of Jason. What made Two Men more intolerable to James than Moods was that Stoddard's middle-aged lover is not only stalwart and successful but personally unobjectionable as well, being the opposite of the bullying Warwick. Anyone could see that Alcott was taken in by Warwick, but how could you argue that Stoddard had been bullied by the egalitarian Jason? James's only recourse was to insist that Jason has not even been defined.

The whole point of Stoddard's second novel was that it took a man like Jason to wake Philippa up to her womanhood. In The Morgesons

Stoddard had explored the centrality of sex for women by narrating the life of an unrepressed girl from her own point of view. In *Two Men* she developed the same basic material, but by reversing her strategy: She now told of an unusually tardy maturation by framing the heroine between two foils, the cold and censorious Sarah, who has had to stifle a passion for her cousin Osmond, and the ex-slave Charlotte, who takes a white lover without any reservations. These two opposites, repression and voluptuousness, help sharpen the representation of Philippa's state of mind. Interestingly, James, unlike Howells, had nothing to say about the black characters. One would like to know what he thought about Stoddard's defiant refusal to judge Charlotte for yielding her chastity (160), or the scene in which Jason approves of his son's determination to marry Charlotte. (Two years later, reviewing Rebecca Harding Davis's *Waiting for the Verdict,* James would rather innocently declare that there was no need for Broderip to disclose his fractional black ancestry to his white fiancée [*Literary Criticism* 1: 220].)

Philippa has a fixed attachment to Parke, her guardian's son, which she must overcome before she can grow up. From the day she first takes up residence in the Parke home, she admires the beauty and winning personality of this boy. She falls in love with him, but her love is distorted by an exalted sense of duty to him. In one of her infrequent lofty speeches, she declares that she hopes to offer Parke "the care and watchfulness of slow years, without reward – the patience to endure all weakness, indulgence, selfishness – the bond which begins with a white veil, and ends in a shroud!" (94). A girlfriend perceives that Philippa intends to be a "martyr" (107), and points out that her devotion to Parke will not do him much good if he should ever get tired of it. But Philippa persists, sanctimoniously aspiring to a noble patience: "If our lot is cast with another's, we must bear all the crosses" (131). When Jason at last discovers her attempted immolation of herself and scoffs at it – "what stuff have you in your head about woman's constancy and sacrifice" (223) – he expresses the author's debunking view of the cross of femininity.

In showing how Philippa outgrows this puerile dream, Stoddard did precisely what Howells would do twenty years later in *Indian Summer,* in which an infatuated girl conceives the plan of devoting herself to an apparently disappointed middle-aged man. In *April Hopes,* Howells's most pessimistic novel, the heroine's self-sacrifice has a deep pathology closely connected to the imagery of Philippa's ecstatic speech about the white veil and shroud. (In the 1880s, when Stoddard revised *Two Men,* shortly after the publication of *April Hopes,* she made the shroud "white," like the veil, and in this way called attention to Philippa's morbid fancies about love [*Two Men* (1888) 94].) But *Two Men* remained much more optimistic than Howells's grim novel, finally emphasizing the heroine's strength, sanity, and capacity for growth. In the end Philippa relaxes her fierce virginity. No longer compelled to play providence to her lover, she comes to laugh at the folly of seeking "a particular object to live for" (285). She achieves a healthy equilibrium between self-control and letting go, and she signals her new poise in an interesting way when she finally accepts Jason. She takes from his neck the sling that supports his arm, and putting the sling around her own neck, says "My burden . . . that I love." In itself, this pledge is not much different from her earlier devotion to Parke. But when Jason embraces her with his good arm, she announces that she is ready to yield in a way she never did with Parke: "my protection, that I love better" (288). In view of all the agonized self-assertions and despairing capitulations that had scarred woman's fiction in the preceding decade, Philippa's balancing act would be a remarkable achievement if it were not rendered in such a schematic fashion. As it is, the resolution of *Two Men* seems almost as thin as Desmond's personal reform in *The Morgesons*. Philippa's poised balance between independence and dependency is not worked out on a mundane level, only in symbolic display.

The fact that Jason is twenty years older than Philippa (52), and has been the nominal male authority in the home where she has grown up, shows how closely *Two Men* is linked to narratives like *The Wide, Wide World, Beulah,* "A Marble Woman," and, much later, Edith Wharton's *Summer* (which looks like a skeptical rewriting of *Two Men*). Philippa sees herself "as a young woman, refusing to marry a man much older than herself, with whom she has lived as a relative" (264). Yet all along she has loved a man with whom she has been living as a sister. The fact that the heroine of *Two Men* finally switches her affections from a "brother" to a "father" illustrates the kind of closed domestic circle that Stoddard, like some other nineteenth-century novelists, loved to write about. She herself was very close to her father and her brother Wilson (Matlack, "Literary Career"), and the first edition of *Two Men* even had a dedicatory poem to the latter:

> Who will so well remember what I knew
> As you, whenever comes the day to part?
> We have ascended one wide scale,
> With all emotion in its pale;
> Girl, boy, woman and man, untrue and true,
> Together or apart – with the same heart.

It is striking that the dedicatory note opening a novel whose heroine moves from "brother" to "father" should reaffirm the brother–sister bond in a poem that unmistakably harks back to Heathcliff and Catherine.

Two Men articulated some powerful incestuous attachments, yet Stoddard somehow or other managed to keep this material under control. Perhaps the equality between Philippa and Jason decontaminates the guardian–ward relationship. Unlike James's Nora, Philippa is financially and psychologically independent; aside from her own fancies it is hard to think of something she needs to be protected from. And her sturdy good sense in giving up the dream of devoting her life to another ensures as well that she has mastered the temptation to sacrifice herself.

Another thing that renders Philippa's marriage safe is Jason's proven commitment to "equal rights" (236). His respect for the independence of others bears comparison with that of Ralph Touchett. Also, Jason has all along determined "to exercise no authority" (45) over Philippa, just as Roger refuses to rule Nora in *Watch and Ward*. But while Roger's motive is in part the fear that Nora would not be able to think of him as a husband if she should grow up regarding him as a father, Jason leaves Philippa free without harboring any ulterior motives. He is simply unwilling to discriminate between her and his son: If Sarah will not discipline Parke, then Jason cannot discipline Philippa. In fact, Jason has a strong belief in human equality, setting out on his adult life as a socialist with fervent convictions on "the correct balance between Man and Wealth" (10).

Stoddard makes it evident that Jason's youthful egalitarianism needs to be tested and toughened, and this process begins once he marries the daughter of the leading man in Crest. Abandoning his carpenter's trade, unable to apply his social ideals, Jason enters a long period of suffering from "the impotence of his crude ideas, and his individual isolation" (18). He survives without compromising himself, and in doing so attains the manhood that will make him a suitable mate for Philippa. He manages the Parkes' property but refuses to make any new investments; more important, he repudiates his legal right to his wife's property (77). Although he remains silent much of the time, he is far from beaten. One of the few times he speaks his mind is when he goes on an excursion to a small island with Philippa and a young minister, who causes Jason to scoff at "ethics" (89) and to declare he believes only "in what I feel" (90). Once the excursion is over and the island has become "a distant, different land" (91), Jason becomes reserved once again.[10] Paradoxically, in spite of his disdain for "ethics," there is no character in the novel who has to exercise greater restraint on what he desires, or who follows a higher standard of justice in dealing with others.

After one has read the novel, James's response to the character of Jason seems brittle and hysterical:

Take [Stoddard's] treatment of her hero. What useful or profitable fact has she told us about him? We do not of course speak of facts which we may apply to our moral edification; but of facts which may help us to read the story. Is he a man? Is he a character, a mind, a heart, a soul? You wouldn't suppose it from anything Mrs. Stoddard has said, or has made him say. What is his formula? Is it that like Carlyle's Mirabeau he has swallowed all formulas? A silence like the stage imitation of thunder interrupted by remarks like the stage imitation of flashes of lightning; such to our perceptions are the chief attributes of Jason Auster. (Kraft 272)

Once again, the thunderstorm was located in James, not Jason, about whom there is no mystery at all, even though, as Howells said, he is not fully realized. Jason is a craftsman and democrat trapped in marriage with a proud and privileged woman who does not love him; he falls in love with his own ward, Philippa; no resolution is possible until after his wife dies. The idea of the book is that his long ordeal gives this initially callow idealist the steel he lacks – makes a better man out of him than young Parke, who, indulged from infancy on, takes pleasure where he finds it. Like *The Morgesons*, the novel tests and vindicates a strong ego.

Yet James's summary of the novel's story at the end of his review suggests that in spite of all his protests he understood exactly what was at issue in the book. His final remark shows that he also realized that Stoddard's fundamental mistake was one of execution, not conception – that she had left "the reader" (Kraft 273) to do the work, the detailed imaginative labor, that she herself should have done. In view of the fact that James himself would write a novel five years later in which a guardian tries to give his ward full liberty, and then marries her when she comes of age, it seems that the "reader" may have been none other than James himself. The novel made his imagination go to work, just as *Moods* had done and as Crane's *Opportunity* would do. The significant differences between *Two Men* and *Watch and Ward* – the fact that Roger is rather weak and untried and feels like a boy in comparison with his more manly or worldly rivals, and the correlative fact that the heroine accepts Roger not because she feels any desire for him but because she recognizes that he is "the only man" in the universe with "a heart" ("Watch and Ward" 709) – indicate precisely why Stoddard's novel forced Boy James's imagination, under angry protest, to resume heavy labor. James had to reply to Stoddard's argument that it takes a good strong older man to awaken Philippa's sexuality, and this he did in *Watch and Ward*, which demonstrates that only a nice old boy could be trusted not to exploit the girl.

When James was ready to undertake *The Portrait of a Lady* in 1878, he wrote that he would now at last "rend the veil from the ferocious ambition which has always *couvé* beneath a tranquil exterior" (*Letters* 2: 156). But the veil had already been rent, at the time he read *Two Men* thirteen years earlier. Or perhaps it would be more accurate to say, following Harold Bloom, that the ferocity of imagination was itself created by this novel, and by similar works, and that this ferocity could be released only by the writing of *The Portrait*. *The Morgesons* and *Two Men* angered James because they gave priority to the very things – carnality, egotism, rough egalitarianism – that had been unwelcome in the James household ever since that day in 1844 when Henry James, Sr., had been undone by "some damnèd shape squatting invisible to me within the precincts of the room, and raying out from his fetid personality influences fatal to life" (HJSr, *Literary Remains* 59). Just as the father devoted his life to the philosophical system building that would explain the necessity of suppressing selfish egotism, so the children of the James household were urged never to be content with sensual desires but to convert them into symbol and spirit. Such children could not tolerate novels that insisted symbol and spirit were smokescreens for feelings and bodily needs, and that only those people who were honest, canny, and tough could live well. Stoddard herself was Henry Jr.'s "damnèd shape."

It was just because of Stoddard's vigorous insights that her kind of realism could not prevail during the realistic movement of the 1870s and 1880s. James's strong men – Christopher Newman, Caspar Goodwood, Basil Ransom – would be among his least fully realized characters. Howells would have great difficulty in dealing with egotists like Bartley Hubbard, and he could demonstrate Silas Lapham's rise only by requiring him to sacrifice his fortune rather than risk defrauding a group of British investors. The strong ego was inherently suspect for both James and Howells, whose realism dealt less with free men than with the bondage of unfree women – with Isabel Osmond's torment in an oppressive marriage, Penelope Lapham's struggle to convince herself she need not give up Tom Corey in a lofty self-sacrifice, Verena Tarrant's pathetic submission first to Olive Chancellor and then to Basil Ransom, Imogene Graham's absurd mission of making up to Theodore Colville for the romantic disappointment he suffered in his youth, Alice Pasmer's neurotic slave–master relationship to the young man she marries. James and Howells wrote any number of studies of the vexed struggle for independence and self-realization, and Howells was particularly good at exploring the darker freedom-hating impulses in some New England women. But the case of Stoddard shows that these two writers' triumphs came at a price – the refusal so much as to entertain the possibility of freedom. Male American realism would have its servile streak no less than popular women's fiction of the 1850s. Elizabeth Stoddard, unread, remained the only novelist not in chains.

Chapter 5

Anne Moncure Crane Seemuller

Henry James's Jocasta

Anne Crane was born in Baltimore in 1838, five years before Henry James. During a period beginning in 1864 and ending with her early death in 1872, she became well known for her daring society fiction. Her three novels, published by Boston's quality publisher, pushed the exploration of women's desires and discontents so far and dealt so categorically with the sexual manners of the American leisure class, both in the South and in New York, that Crane acquired a reputation as a scandalous writer. A few weeks after her death, the *Nation* published a uniquely ill-natured obituary note expressing the hope that her immoral influence would cease now that she was dead. The obituarist's wish was gratified. Crane's novels went out of print, and she soon disappeared from the literary record.[1]

But Crane's was an important voice in early American realism, one that had a decisive influence on Henry James. Her 1869 story, "Little Bopeep," was partly about a young woman who "was the very apotheosis of the ordinary" (387). Crane was one of Howells's first admirers,[2] and in *Reginald Archer* she would have one of her most conventional ladies "object . . . to realistic novels, as being too much like life" (237). When the *Galaxy* was started up in 1866 she was solicited for a story (Crane to Church, 22 February 1866, William Conant Church Papers, NYPL) and soon became a regular contributor; the *Atlantic* also approached her, but without success. James wrote long, careful, and severe reviews of her first two novels when he was in his early twenties, and although he disapproved of her work, he was not only challenged by it but his imagination was quickened. Her last novel, *Reginald Archer*, exhibits some arresting parallels with James's own best fiction, particularly "Madame de Mauves" and *The Portrait of a Lady*, which was indebted for both its plot and its heroine's last name to Crane. His links with her are considerably richer and more formative than those with Alcott. After Hawthorne, the one American writer James most persistently sought to rewrite was the one the *Nation* helped sink into oblivion.[3]

Emily Chester

Crane completed *Emily Chester* before the Civil War began but it was not until October 1864, three months in advance of Alcott's *Moods,* that the novel saw print – anonymously. Although it was not aggressively promoted, *Emily Chester* went into its third edition by the end of the year and before long was pirated in England, brought onto the stage, and translated into German. It was the kind of novel educated readers regarded as important and timely. Caroline Dall noted in her diary on 4 October: "Read Emily Chester before I went to bed. I must write a newspaper article on this marriage question." On 21 October Annie Fields wrote in her journal: "Have just finished a remarkable novel written by a Baltimore girl of eighteen – It is entitled Emily Chester – I should as soon think of such a book coming from the moon as from a girl of eighteen years – and Baltimore" (Caroline H. Dall Papers and Annie Adams Fields Papers, MHS). Howard James, Henry's youngest uncle, read the book and was so "strongly affected by it" he urged his nephew to try it. "By all means," wrote twenty-one-year-old Henry on 28 October to a friend, "I want some strong sensation. It will be grand to get one from a non-sensation novel such as E.C." (Harlow 276).

James's clever remark glances at the difference between *Emily Chester* and the British "sensation novels" then sweeping the market. Unlike the brightly colored narratives of Mrs. Henry Wood, Wilkie Collins, Charles Reade, and Mary Elizabeth Braddon, the new American book seemed to be quiet and distinguished. Two years later James recollected the tone of the novel's reception: "It was high time we [Americans] should be having an American novel which sensible people could read ten pages of. . . . Miss Crane's book answered these high conditions" (*Literary Criticism* 1: 596). The novice man of letters had to confront this ambitious and possibly classy production. On 15 October 1864 he wrote the editor of the *North American Review,* Charles Eliot Norton, proposing a critique: "The book seems to me to have gained sufficient notoriety to justify a brief review" (MH-H).[4] James made this proposal blind, relying on what he had heard about the new novel.

When the young man began reading *Emily Chester,* early in November[5] in Northampton, Massachusetts, he found himself seriously challenged. At the time he was taking a "water cure," apparently undergoing daily periods of immersion. He had proposed a short review, but what he sent Norton ran to three thousand words. It was not only longer than almost any other review of an American novel that had appeared in an

American periodical, it was also more detailed, analytic, and argumentative. What troubled the young reviewer was that the novel challenged everything he believed about the nature of feminine sexuality – the wife's redemptive function, the importance of overcoming marital dissatisfaction, the supremacy of spirit over carnal appetite. The book was a hideously distorted reflection of the concerns that would be central in much of his own early fiction.

Emily Chester tells the story of a married woman who falls in love with another man. Earlier novels by American women invariably made the wife who risks adultery a minor character only. In Alone, published about three years before Crane began writing her first novel, Mrs. Read falls in love with Ashlin and is on the point of running off with him when the heroine intervenes; one chapter suffices for this episode (Harland ch. 25). The novelty of Emily Chester lay in making the unhappy wife the heroine. About the same time several other relatively young women writers thought of the same innovation. Aside from the coincidence of Alcott's Moods, Adeline Whitney's The Gayworthys (1865), and Elizabeth Stoddard's Two Men (1865) also stressed the predicament of a woman with a distaste for her husband. This predicament, James wrote, "suggested something aside from the beaten track of Anglo-Saxon fiction, and promised to deal with really great passions" (Literary Criticism 1: 595). His own "Tragedy of Error" had dressed the subject up in Gallic dress. Yet at this moment in the mid-1860s the story of the wife tempted by adultery became a very American story, and in the early 1870s it even began to dominate the daily newspapers, now much more open in reporting sensational crimes and trials. In 1870 the New York Tribune gave extensive day-to-day coverage of the McFarland crime-of-passion case (see note 17, this chapter), and a few years later even the staid Boston Daily Advertiser printed transcripts of the Beecher-Tilton testimony. By the mid-1870s, when Annie Howells had a novel serialized about an unhappily married woman who loves another man, the story had grown somewhat shopworn, according to W. D. Howells, who wished his sister had chosen a "fresher" subject (Selected Letters 2: 73).

Of all the novels dealing with the disaffected wife between 1864 and 1875, Anne Crane's Emily Chester was the most relentless and daring. The young unmarried Southerner came closer to writing a New World Madame Bovary than anyone else before Kate Chopin, but she paid a price: Shuddering allusions to "affinities" by her contemporaries were probably pointed at her at least as much as at Goethe. One reason Howells urged his sister not to have "Reuben Dale" published in book form was the fear that "her literary career" might be "retarded" (Selected Letters 2: 124). This was prudent advice.[6] Howells himself had been burned in 1869 when he brought out Stowe's revelations about Byron's incest in the *Atlantic,* and by the mid-seventies the lesson of Crane's career was plain: Your voice would be silenced if you wrote too recklessly about women and marriage.

The heroine of *Emily Chester* is presented as a complicated and exceptional woman, born to conflict. Her father is a well-to-do Yankee Calvinist, her deceased mother descended from "one of the conspicuous old Southern families" (14). A maternal ancestor signed the Declaration of Independence, as did Crane's own maternal great-grandfather, Thomas Stone (his signature is three down from that of John Hancock). All this involves pride of pedigree rather less than it reveals a long-nurtured capacity for revolution. Emily should be ranked with other American heroines – Hester Prynne, Southworth's Capitola, Howells's Kitty Ellison – whose inheritance of a struggle for general political liberty leads to a specifically female kind of fight. Also, like Alcott's Sylvia, Emily has been inspired by the heroic spectacle of Goethe, and she is eager to enter a course of full self-development. And finally, she is a kind of indigene: "Certainly no red Indian, just from his native woods, could have a more supreme disregard for any cramping conventionality" (14) than Emily has.

"Cramp" proves to be a key word. Like most other heroines of woman's fiction, Emily, abruptly orphaned, learns that she has inherited much less than she had expected. She struggles to support herself but (like Evans's Beulah Benton) begins to succumb to illness, overwork, solitude. An old friend, Max *Cramp*ton, finds her at the point of death, pressures her into marrying him, and then takes her to Europe on a convalescent honeymoon. Emily reveres Max, who is "some ten or fifteen years" (2) older than she, but she is also repelled by his ugliness and forceful Germanic will. Married, she feels a repulsion for him, which in time develops into an aversion so powerful her matrimonial bond comes to resemble "the old torture, binding a dead body to a living one" (333). The author would use the same image in *Reginald Archer,* where the heroine, married to a rake, feels like "those Roman criminals bound to decaying corpses" (345). Unlike this later rake, however, Max is for the most part a decent and understanding person. His cramping effect on the heroine is presented as a mystery not even the author claims to understand.

Emily's torture is aggravated by her ambiguous friendship with Frederick Hastings, a man quite different from her husband. Frederick is graceful, artistic, "harmonious," with "an intuitive, womanlike perception of character" (25). He has a remarkable influence over what is called "the supersensuous portion" (285) of Emily's being. She definitely likes him, yet we are repeatedly assured that she does not truly love him and that her heart is not involved. There is "a constitutional affinity" (329) between the pair – yet the woman finds the man "constitutionally insufficient" (136). Emily herself calls this ambiguous attraction "a mystery in nature, which even I, its centre, have no words to define, have no control over beyond the weakest endurance" (330). In spite of her effort to endure, she gives way, slowly and inevitably, and the main action of the novel turns out to be her long-drawn-out death. Frederick inadvertently torments her by striving to be near her. Her husband torments her, also unintentionally, by refusing to intervene. The two well-meaning men destroy the helpless wife: "They seemed to divide between them all the gifts that Heaven can bestow upon a human being; together, they would have formed a man of ideal perfection; apart, they were each of them terribly lacking in several things needful" (51). Emily is said (solecistically) to be "literally torn asunder" (285) by them. She becomes whiter and weaker and sterner and holier and then she dies.

Superficially, Crane's first novel would appear to have a conventional Victorian morality. The heroine resolves to do her duty by her husband, steadfastly denies her desire for the second man, devotes herself to others. The author reminds us that no one is able to "purify and redeem this world" as well as "some women" (216), exhibits Emily patronizing the urban poor, and throws in a brief homily in defense of Sunday schools. But just as in Susan Warner's fiction, this religious content is accompanied by a strangely emphatic carnality. As the scandalized young James observed, the real message of *Emily Chester* seems to be that the body is stronger than the soul. From its opening lines, in fact, Crane's novel makes us aware of the physicality of its people:

> A man and a woman.
> As the story I have to tell relates chiefly to the lives of these two, and as their peculiar physiques exercised a singularly potent influence upon it, I shall give you a minute description of what these mute figures looked like. (1)

The same emphasis shows up in the description of Emily, who is "fluent, luxurious, elegant; peculiarly open to outward influences, upon whom the claims of the body were large and imperative" (13–14). One suspects that Crane had read the 1855 or 1856 *Leaves of Grass* and resolved to be the novelist of the body as well as the novelist of the soul. Certainly, like Whitman, she drew on Transcendentalist sources in order to recreate a flowing and "luxurious" kind of life. The "supersensuous" attraction Emily feels for Frederick and her mysterious repulsion from Max are somehow sensual as well as spiritual. Crane's "supersensuous" inverts the usual meaning, which might be illustrated by Henry James, Sr.'s, own rigorous usage: "Remember then that the incomparable worth of the Bible lies . . . in . . . what it does for the intellect in gradually divorcing it from sense, and wedding it to supersensuous truth."[7]

Emily Chester's brave Goethean epigraph declares: "It is in her monstrosities that Nature discloses to us her secrets." The monstrosities in question must be Emily's own irrational magnetisms, which are monstrous for the obvious reasons: They violate the laws of society and are beyond rational understanding or control. Yet they are, if one alters one's perspective, completely natural, physical, and it is only because our view is blinkered by absolutes that they seem to be dark and chthonic.

"I hope you will not regret it if . . . conscience should compel me to be 'severe,' " James advised Norton on 11 November 1864 (MH-H). In writing his review of *Emily Chester,* he assumed a familiar persona – the doughty controversialist who unhappily recognizes in the volume laid before him certain unmistakable signs of modern deviance that all right-thinking men will join in condemning. Assuming the anonymous author to be a woman, James wielded his scalpel like an acerbic octogenarian, just as when, a couple of months later, he explained the faults of *Moods* to its author. But James overdid his performance in reviewing Crane. His painstaking and triumphant logic, high moral reprobation, and snooty wit all betray the hand of a very young man.

James dogmatically classified *Emily Chester* as "a story of character" – a category he would find useless two decades later in "The Art of Fiction." He noted that the three main characters formed a familiar triad, "a husband, a wife, and a lover," and he considered all three stereotyped and weakly imagined. The wife, James announced, was meant to be "very perfect," an intention he found "laudable"[8] but "very perilous." The basic flaw in the author's conception of Emily was that she was too much of a martyr:

When anything particularly disagreeable happens, she becomes very pale and calm and statuesque. Although in the ordinary affairs of life she is sufficiently cheerful and voluble, whenever anything occurs a little out of the usual way she seems to remember the stake and the torture, and straightway becomes silent and cold and classical.

This hostile passage points ahead to one of James's own female characters from his middle years, Olive Chancellor, who goes stiff and averts her eyes when she meets Basil Ransom. In the light of young James's strange plea – "Heaven preserve us from any more radical specimens of this perfection!" – we may wonder whether the specter of Olive Chancellor was already lying in wait. What enrages Olive, however, is precisely the usual things of life.[9]

In commenting on Max, James reverted to a familiar category:

We have a strong impression of having met him before. He is the repetition of a type that has of late years obtained great favor with lady novelists: the ugly, rich, middle-aged lover, with stern brows and white teeth; reticent and yet ardent; indolent and yet muscular, full of satire and common-sense. Max is partly a German, as such men often are, in novels.

This comes very close to James's vitriolic characterization of Alcott's Warwick in *Moods*. In some ways the reviewer's perceptions were right on the mark: We recall the father–lover in "A Marble Woman" who is named Germain and the middle-aged Germanic Professor Bhaer in *Little Women* (still to be written). What was characteristic of James was his continuing obsession with the "ugly" and "middle-aged" qualities of the type, an emphasis that reappeared in his review of Stoddard's *Two Men*.

James took his contempt for the middle-aged lover further than most contemporary reviewers did. He called Max "essentially a woman's man; one of those impossible heroes, whom lady novelists concoct half out of their own erratic fancies and half out of those of other lady novelists." This view was a good deal more strident and sweeping than the opinion expressed by the *Saturday Review* in its notice, which identified Max as "a familiar character in young ladies' novels, . . . one of the most thoroughly unpleasant of all the regular types of impossible people. He is the man with the irresistible will."[10] The vehemence with which James articulated this widespread view of women's heroes eventually led to his critical portrayals of Euphemia Cleve and Isabel Archer, who both fall for ugly middle-aged men. His narratives about these women, like his earliest reviews, sought to correct the "erratic fancies" of women novelists.

The last part of James's review exhibits a revealing inconsistency in its treatment of Max. As James considers Emily's alienated affections, Max is abruptly transformed from a Rochester-like tyrant into "a kind and virtuous husband." Suddenly it appears that Emily has not tried hard enough "to discern the subtle halo" he wears. Indeed, even though he has compelled her to marry him " 'through his divine right of the stronger,' " James now feels quite certain that Max's motives are not at all "brutal" but aim "to serve, cherish, and protect." There is a flat contradiction here between the reviewer's deep sympathy for a girl in subjection to a strong paternalistic man and a deep loyalty to male supremacy in marriage. This split, which helped generate much popular fiction of the 1850s, would reappear in *The Bostonians*, which variously regards Basil as brutal and noble.

Interestingly, the reviewer who would one day be regarded as a psychological novelist par excellence directed his most withering scorn at *Emily Chester*'s "would-be psychological mode."[11] He claimed to find the book dull and boring because of its unconventional interiority – its many episodes involving an exchange of glances, a quick reading of a face, a stern outer bearing masking a terrible unease. Perhaps James had met too many stoic sufferers in women's fiction to put up with one more: Emily "goes down into her grave after a life of acute misery without ever having 'let on,' as the phrase is, that there has been anything particular the matter with her." The identical criticism that would often be leveled against James he now brought against Crane, who juxtaposed three characters and then, "during three hundred and fifty close pages," invited the reader "to watch the moral operations of this romantic trio. What a chance for dulness is here!" *Emily Chester* was a clumsy instance of the sort of narrative James would learn to write so much more adroitly.

There was another and more important reason why James attacked the novel for being "psychological." What this term meant for James was an undue emphasis on "temperament, nature, constitution, instincts . . .; upon . . . physical rather than . . . moral sense." The young reviewer believed that this emphasis was dangerous and he earnestly opposed it, meticulously documenting his case, quoting key passages, even giving page numbers. He ridiculed a passage on animal magnetism and expressed great contempt for the notion that the heroine's " 'nature had no correspondence' " with the " 'human law' " (matrimony) that bound her. He gave a tendentious expression of the novel's basic idea: "in proportion as a person is finely organized, in so far is he apt to be the slave of his instincts, – the subject of unaccountable attractions and repulsions, loathings and yearnings." Such an idea is "immoral," James suggested, because it violates the well-known rule that, whereas "beasts and idiots act from their instincts; educated men and women . . . act from their reason . . . and their affections." Thus it is Emily's duty "to conquer a peace." She should have been able, given her basic respect for Max, to adjust her feelings and enter "a career of comfortable resignation." But as the book stands, she is "a profoundly vicious person."

There is a determinedly innocent obtuseness in this denunciation. "We do not understand [Emily's] predicament," James wrote. "It is our belief that there is no serious middle state between friendship and love." Showing the same moral ferocity as Strether's stern critic, Mrs. Pocock, he would have absolutely nothing to do with the idea that Anne Crane tried, awkwardly, to dramatize – that there are several kinds of human love and that some of them can have a destructive effect on ordinary social institutions. James could only fulminate that any woman who was drawn to a man without being able to plead "the excuse of loving well, must be curtly and sternly dismissed." His brittle prescription that Emily "conquer a peace" shows that he could not allow the author her subject.[12]

James may have recollected Crane fourteen years later in questioning Hawthorne's "extreme predilection for a small number of vague ideas which are represented by such terms as 'sphere' and 'sympathies.' Hawthorne makes too liberal a use of these two substantives; it is the solitary defect of his style; and it counts as a defect partly because the words in question are a sort of specialty with certain writers immeasurably inferior to himself" (*Hawthorne* 119–20). Writing *The Portrait* the following year, James embodied temperamental psychology in the flighty, undignified Countess Gemini.

The denunciatory tone of James's review approaches that of Rebecca Harding Davis in her conservative 1869 essay, "Men's Rights," which insisted that no wife must "brood over possible new elective affinities for herself" and bemoaned "the most salient and apparent change in women, in the last few years . . . [,] the growth in impurity" (224, 214). Daugherty has shown that James's review reflects the moral idealism he approvingly found in Edmond Schérer, a French critic he reviewed in 1865. "Nous avons tant mis de physiologie dans notre psychologie," Schérer had written, "que nous sommes en danger de confondre l'amour avec les appétits ou les plaisirs" (Daugherty 5). What gave this passage such great authority for James (in addition to the cultural changes that caused Davis to become such an alarmist) was its partial agreement with his father's teachings. Few things were clearer and more distinct for the senior James than the vast gulf between his animal and spiritual sides. His morbid, agonistic metaphysics was partly designed to justify the difficult task of forever spurning the former. His son's condemnation of Emily's sexuality at the beginning of his literary career recalls the father's early encounter with a fetid squatting shape in a room in Windsor. The fact that young James met a whole sequence of temperamental and faithless heroines in women's novels merely solidified his impression that the female imagination was extremely subversive. That is partly why his own first truly ambitious effort in fiction would be both a critique of the American girl's callow imagination and a didactic representation of her determination, once she sees her error, nobly to do justice to the bad marriage she has foolishly contracted.

The ferocity of James's assault on Emily Chester has concealed the extent of his debt to this character. " 'If I were to marry, I should die, I should suffocate!' she exclaimed, passionately. 'I have lived a free life too long, not to revolt from the very shadow of a chain! . . . It is the aim of my existence to become a self-contained, self-sufficing woman, depending on myself for happiness" (*Emily Chester* 44, 45). James did not forget that the fate reserved for this presumptuous speaker was a suffocating marriage to a willful Europeanized American. *The Portrait* was to be, among other things, a corrective rewriting of the fiction of the forgotten Anne Crane. There is strong additional evidence of this surprising fact in James's tantalizing review of her second novel.

Opportunity

Opportunity was published in 1867. Like Stoddard's *Two Men* (1865), it was a study of two opposing male types, corresponding, as the author herself pointed out, to Esau and Jacob – the same brotherly pair that forms the basis of Edel's analysis of William and Henry James's relationship. Crane's Esau, named Douglas, is a deliberate, self-confident, self-contained man rather like Christopher Newman. The Jacob character, called Grahame, is a graceful, lazy, somewhat vapid and innocently selfish man who attracts and destroys women without ever quite realizing his effect on them. Grahame is obviously another version of Frederick, the sympathetic man in Crane's first novel, with this crucial difference: The author has become more conscious of the weak and self-indulgent side of this sort of person.

James judged this second version of the Jacob type to be exceptionally well conceived and executed, "a capital specimen of what is called, in the language of the day, a 'swell' – wonderfully, wofully handsome, elegant, fastidious, languidly selfish, lazy, cynical, idle, a charmer of women" (*Literary Criticism* 1: 597).[13] This type, the light man, would be a leading figure in James's repertory of characters, reappearing in Hubert Lawrence in *Watch and Ward*, Morris Townsend in *Washington Square*, Sir Claude in *What Maisie Knew*, Vanderbank in *The Awkward Age*, and the Prince in *The Golden Bowl*. A sort of male siren, an *homme fatal* in James's imagination, the character's charm would have a confusing or destructive effect on women. In 1873, when James looked back on the stories he had written before "A Passionate Pilgrim," the one he felt proudest of was "A Light Man" (*Letters* 1: 357). This story, which originally appeared in the *Galaxy*, Crane's chief outlet, may well have been crystallized by her characterization of Grahame. What is interesting, as Feinstein first pointed out, is that James's "Light Man" focuses on a masculine relationship that is "transparently homosexual" (233).

Even more interesting is that the character in *Opportunity* who made the deepest impression on James was the girl Grahame attracts, the strikingly named heroine, Harvey Berney. Harvey is a bulldog of an adolescent, brilliant, abrupt, incisive, high-minded, half genius and half tomboy. The lady-characters do not regard her as an adult, but Grahame finds he is strangely drawn to her. She persistently ignores him, however, and when he finally asks what she objects to in him, she lets him have it:

"Your Sultanic ways, for one thing" . . .
The man's eyes grew larger.
"If I unconsciously possess such, I scarcely think you have any

reason to complain of them," he remarked after a moment. "It must be something more than that."

"You are lazy, self-conceited, and worthless," the clear young voice rang out. (131)

There are few conversations in the book as keen as this one, partly because the girl falls in love with Grahame and sets herself the conventional task of reforming him: " 'I know you better than any one else; I have read you more thoroughly,' she answered hurriedly. 'You have wilfully thrown away time, talents, and opportunity. . . . And to think what you might have been!' " (131). Her love for Grahame does not prosper, nor does that, later on, for Douglas, and in time her eyes take on a "starved, craving, dying look" (294).

James did not care for the speech – a "shrewish blowing-up" – in which Harvey objects to Grahame's "Sultanic ways," or for the one that makes a "puerile" appeal to his "better nature." "Too young to talk as she does," she is "simply pert and pedantic." In making such remarks, James was joining the attack on an aspect of women's fiction that had drawn the ire of numerous male reviewers – the girlish presumption that led so many righteous young heroines to set straight some older and more worldly person. Oliver Bunce, the tart editor of *Lippincott's Magazine*, bitterly denounced these presumptuous maidens: "The thing least to be endured with patience in a novel is a heroine scarcely out of pinafores, . . . running about and disposing of grave and vexed questions with a flippant assurance deserving of nothing so much as boxed ears" (160).

The fascinating thing in James's response to *Opportunity* is that, in spite of his disapproval of Harvey, he found himself abandoning the standard masculine judgment and sympathizing with, in fact being deeply stirred by, Harvey's freshness:

> Harvey is meant to have a mind of her own, to be a fit companion for a man of sense, to be a strong and free young girl. She thinks and lives and acts, she has her face to the sun. Many thanks to the author for what she would fain have done; she has at least enlisted the imagination on the side of freedom and real grace.

It is unusual to find such enthusiasm in the pages of the *Nation*, which generally spoke of current fiction in more scornful accents. But James was truly excited by *Opportunity*, and even when he regained the regulation aloofness –

> Miss Crane's figures strike us as perfectly vague and thin, and we find that in order to give any account of her book at all we have

been obliged to press our own little stock of imagination into the
service and to force it to do extra work[14] –

he made it clear for the second time that his imagination had been
touched. These passages, all the more striking because of James's pervad-
ing disapproval, offer prima facie evidence that his reading of *Opportunity*
made a very strong impression on him. If, in addition, we recall that the
germ of *The Portrait of a Lady* was an image of a "presumptuous" girl
(*Literary Criticism* 2: 1077), and that James claimed he had been nursing
this image for some time before beginning to build a novel around it,
perhaps in 1876 (the first year he mentioned the book in letters), we have
every justification for asking whether *Opportunity* may have given his
imagination a decisive fillip.

Daugherty's thorough survey of James's book reviews and literary
essays helps explain why Harvey caught James's imagination. The young
reviewer was generally quick to respond to "the rebellious or suffering
heroine – a stock figure in the mid-nineteenth-century novel," and he
loved Hetty Sorrel, Maggie Tulliver, Lady Glencora in Trollope's *Can
You Forgive Her?*, the heroine of the same author's *Linda Tressel*, Cynthia
in Gaskell's *Wives and Daughters,* and Kate Gaunt in Charles Reade's
Griffith Gaunt. At the same time, as Daugherty shows, the youthful
James disliked those authors, such as Trollope or Flaubert, whose leading
characters never rose superior to their circumstances. The young man
was "profoundly anti-deterministic" and "disliked characters who were
too much affected by the 'accidents' of life" (21–24, 13, 17–18). The
characters in whom James took the greatest sympathetic interest were
young women engaged in resisting some consciously felt oppression –
and of these Harvey Berney, however poorly realized, was the single
most conspicuous American example.

But in spite of this enthusiastic response, James in the end pronounced
Harvey a typically infatuated American girl. In the concluding section of
the novel the heroine, having outgrown Grahame, falls in love with
Douglas, the solid Esau-like brother. Douglas loves Harvey in return and
there are no real impediments to their union, but they do not marry.
James vigorously objected to this unhappy ending: "We protest we don't
see what obstacle there is to their union." In James's account, Harvey
renounces Douglas so that he can marry Rose Carvel, who has a prior but
slight claim on him. James assailed Harvey for this renunciation: "Here,
alas! is the objection to these high-toned, free-thinking heroines, in
whose favor, for Harvey's sake, we just now entered our voice. At the
crucial moment they are certain to do something utterly pedantic and
unnatural and insupportable."

In uttering this dismissal, James rebounded to his old disapproval of "free-thinking" American girls who are full of "theories." Both of these terms evoked strong opprobrium in the James household. Henry, Sr., not only believed that all humans were far too opinionated but was certain that woman, already man's rational inferior, inevitably made a fool of herself when she tried to think. Henry Jr.'s reviews of Crane's and other American women's novels evoke a vast undifferentiated body of crazy female speculation, which, in his concluding remarks on *Emily Chester,* he glanced at with a shudder:

> We infinitely prefer the old-fashioned love-stories, in which no love but heart-love was recognized, to these modern teachings of a vagrant passion which has neither a name nor a habitation. We are not particularly fond of any kind of sentimentality; but Heaven defend us from the sentimentality which soars above all our old superstitions, and allies itself with anything so rational as a theory. (*Literary Criticism* 1: 594–95)

It is partly because of the distasteful connotations of "theory" in James's mind that when Isabel Osmond wonders whether she "married on a factitious theory," her "cheek tingled" and she "quickly" came up with another explanation. Theories were something for women to blush about, especially those that substituted idle fancies for true passion or teetered on the edge of adultery and free love. The two extremely important paragraphs describing Isabel's mind in Chapter 6 are not only organized around the topic of her "many theories" but take a consistently apologetic tone. Her thoughts are "a tangle of vague outlines," "inflated," "dogmatic" (*Portrait* 374, 41–43). Theories were so characteristic a product of the American girl that James even made the word the family name of two New England-raised sisters in one of his sensational potboilers, "Georgina's Reasons." His dismissal of Harvey's "pedantic" renunciation is an outstanding example of his prejudice against the views of bright American girls, a prejudice that would generate his best and worst fiction.

The odd wrinkle, however, is that James was wrong about Harvey – she did not, in fact, renounce Douglas. She had been led to believe that he was *already* engaged to Rose, and meanwhile, because Douglas is not aware that Harvey is misinformed, he fails to declare his sentiments. (While writing the novel, Crane brought out a story, "My Courtship," in which the man is too diffident to propose.) A combination of male timidity and false rumors forestalls the happy issue James expected. In other words, the heroine's "unnatural and insupportable" renunciation existed only in the eye of the reader – a reader, moreover, who would all but specialize in unnatural and often very high-minded renunciations.

Eight years after reviewing *Opportunity* James would have Claire de Cintré abruptly abandon her fiancé in favor of a convent – only to double back thirty years later and criticize his narrative for not sufficiently explaining her motives for withdrawal (*Literary Criticism* 2: 1068–69).

It would seem, then, that James brought a lifelong obsession of his own to his reading of Crane's second novel. His mistake was not a casual error but a product of his own deep preoccupations. The confession that he found it necessary to press his "own little stock of imagination into the service" takes on a strange reverberation. Crane *spoke* to James, but precisely because she challenged his unretractable pledges and stirred up his deepest worries, he could not spare the attention to listen carefully. Instead, he found his narrative powers fired by her clumsy, dissatisfying novel, lost interest in what was on the page, and began reimagining the book for himself.

Reginald Archer

It is at the cost of certain others, at the best, of certain obscured, hindered, sacrificed growths, that the happiest examples of any rich human efflorescence have hitherto managed to bask in the light. (Henry James, "The Speech of American Women," *French Writers and American Women Essays* 35)

Others have pointed out that James's preface to *The Portrait of a Lady* reveals very little about the origins of this novel, and much of what it does say is misleading. As a historian of himself and his works, James was circumspect, elusive, and always willing, as he told a nephew in another context, to drop from the record, "for worry-saving, certain stitches" (Edel, *Untried Years* 139). He wrote the preface in 1906 (H. Parker 500), three decades after first beginning work on *The Portrait,* and he inevitably forgot a great deal. He also boasted. The precedents he cited for his first novel with a claim to greatness were themselves all great: He wrapped himself in Turgenev's mantle and adduced some memorable female characters created by Shakespeare and George Eliot – Juliet, Hetty Sorrel, Maggie Tulliver, Rosamond Vincy, Gwendolen Harleth.

This assortment of names from Eliot is surprising. Gwendolen obviously belongs here, being the ardent, unconventional, and self-injuring heroine of *Daniel Deronda,* which had a tremendous influence on *The Portrait,* but it is not immediately apparent what the other three Eliot characters have in common with Isabel. It is odd that James singled out the ultrafeminine foils of *Adam Bede* and *Middlemarch* and did not even mention Dinah Morris or Dorothea Brooke, the independent-minded heroines who seem much more closely affiliated with his own heroine.

But the strangest thing James had to say about the characters he names is that "they are typical, none the less, of a class difficult, in the individual case, to make a centre of interest" (*Literary Criticism* 2: 1077).

Even allowing for the possibility that James may have been thinking of the childish lightness of these characters,[15] it is hard to see how he could have been more wrong. The only class they all belong to is that of the single young woman at the point in her life when she moves out into the world. Most novels had for decades been based on the premise that this class was inherently fascinating. The central young woman had virtually been a genre feature, and it was taken for granted, and rightly, that readers were ready and willing to take an interest in her. The best excuse for James's statement is that it justifies his preface's big point – that his great stroke in composing *The Portrait* was to secure the reader's interest by exploiting the heroine's *own* sense of her life. And yet here, too, James, caught up in his late absorption with point of view, conveyed a misleading impression of what American novels were like around 1880. Charlotte Porter made the point in 1885 that most serial novels did what James claimed to have invented: "The transfer of the author's attention from the story about his characters to the representation of the life within them has revealed the individuality of the heroine, and developed an altogether new estimate of woman's moral value" (812). There is no question *The Portrait* was far better written than most other serial novels of the time, but the author's prefatory huffing and puffing three decades later should not be taken at face value.

Allon White, commenting on James's treatment of sexual intimacy, points out that his "fiction is haunted by the anxiety that its narrative preoccupations may be seen as vulgar" (135). Some such anxiety haunts the preface to *The Portrait*. James delivered his haughty *obiter dicta* that young ladies are intrinsically uninteresting precisely in order to establish a firm line between himself and the tradition of vulgar female narrative that lay behind him. It was on this line that he had built his career. "We are utterly weary of stories about precocious little girls" (*Literary Criticism* 1: 189) he wrote in 1865 – and then went on to write about precocious girls.

So we must be cautious in receiving James's disclosures about the early history of *The Portrait*. He tells us that he began with the image of a heroine, a "presumptuous" girl "affronting her destiny," and that some time later he apparently "waked up one morning in possession of" the other characters. These are the two stages he gives for the novel's growth. He has little to say about the second stage, except that he wonders about his motives for giving Henrietta such broad comic development. As for the first stage, he remembers beginning with "the sense of a single character, the character and aspect of a particular engaging young woman." He implies that he can say more about this "dim first move" toward the novel but he prefers not to: His "acquisition" of this image was made "after a fashion not here to be retraced." All he will say is that he had possessed the image "for a long time."[16]

Minnie Temple died in March 1870. A letter James wrote in October 1876 first speaks of his plans for *The Portrait,* and another from July 1878 is the first to mention any actual writing (*Letters* 2: 72, 179). These dates are consistent with the received view that James's remarks in his preface refer to his cousin Minnie. A letter of 28 December 1880 confirms that he was thinking of her when he created Isabel (*Letters* 2: 324). And yet it says absolutely nothing to trace the fictive person back to the real one. The pressing questions are what James took from Minnie, and what he chose not to take, and why, especially since there are good reasons to believe that she and Isabel were quite dissimilar. James's nephew had the impression that Minnie was "more authentically revealed" by the letters in *Notes of a Son and Brother* than by *The Portrait* or *The Wings of the Dove* (*Letters of William James* 1: 36). Minnie's own 15 August 1869 letter to James (which he did not reproduce in his memoirs) made it clear more than once that unlike two of her sisters she was disgusted with the idea of marrying an older man (LeClair, "Henry James and Minny Temple" 44–45). To ask why the author transformed his cousin into a woman who fell for a forty-year-old man, almost twice her age, may seem naive and impossible to resolve, yet we must grope for some explanation if we are to understand that dark fork, that "dim first move," where life swerved into literary narrative through James's far from disinterested mediumship.

What happened, I believe, is that Minnie became assimilated in James's novel-saturated mind with the heroines of fiction, especially those created by the agonists. Like most of these characters, Minnie was an unusually self-reliant orphan possessed of her own stock of ideas. Her effect on James was to detoxify the freethinking heroine he was inclined to disapprove of. Simultaneously the novels he had read, in combination with his father's dogmas, convinced him that if his cousin had not died she would have made a conspicuously foolish mistake – perhaps marrying someone like Osmond. These speculations are worked out in Chapter 6, which shows how Minnie liberated, within definite limits, James's imagination. My argument in this chapter is that one particular agonist, Anne Moncure Crane, inadvertently played the decisive part in showing him how Minnie could be made the heroine of a novel. The writer's first heroine, Emily Chester, showed James exactly how a wife should *not* act once she learns she cannot love her husband. The second heroine, Harvey, gave James an invigorating glimpse of the presumptuous girl's great literary potential, if rightly developed. And Crane's third and last heroine, Christie Macalaster Archer, along with the novel built around her, gave James even more: his plot, his crucial last name, and scores of touches and developments. Published one year after Minnie's death stimulated James's passionate rumination on his cousin's image, *Reginald Archer* enabled him to work out the second stage of his dim early work on *The Portrait*.

Around the time Crane completed her second novel, she renewed acquaintance with Augustus Seemuller, according to one source a "neighbor and playmate and admirer in her childhood" ("Mrs. Anne Moncure Crane Seemuller"). He had dropped from view as a result of the Civil War and his travels in Europe. In 1869 Crane married Seemuller and moved to New York. She evidently drew on her new experiences and observations there in writing the daring *Reginald Archer*, for when reproached for the book she reportedly said, "Since I have lived in New York, I have learned of such fearful things, that had I not written this book, the very stones would have cried out against me!" (Boyle 356). The remark is characteristic of Seemuller (as I must now call her), who invoked biblical allusions precisely when she was at her most risqué.

Reginald Archer was announced 18 March 1871 in the *New York Tribune* ("Books of the Week"), and some of the comment it attracted in the following weeks was highly scandalized. The *Nation*'s reviewer considered it beyond the pale:

> The character of Mrs. Seemuller's hero, the incidents recorded of him, the sort of intimate knowledge of his vileness which she displays, do not, we confess, make her book one which we should be glad to see generally read; and a certain intensity and force there is in it only deepens our objections to it. (326)

The reviewer for the Boston publication *Literary World* was less censorious, even while characterizing the title hero as

> . . .a professional seducer, handsome as Antinous, intelligent, good-humored. . . . His life is devoted to the conquest of female virtue. . . . We should be sorry to believe that her [Seemuller's] pictures of our "best society" are true ones; but we must acknowledge the skill with which they are drawn. . . . "Reginald Archer" is well worth reading. ("Minor Book Notices" 172)

The *Daily Picayune* (New Orleans) and the *Southern Magazine* (Baltimore) also conceded the book's literary skill but still regretted that it had been written. Sorosis, a prominent women's club in New York City, had a "spirited debate" on the question, "Is the moral intention of 'Reginald Archer' a sufficient justification of the book?" and in the end the members universally condemned the author's choice of "topic." She was "defended from any charge of intentional immorality, as her wish to do good was fully recognized; but the book itself was stigmatized in the strongest terms" ("Last Meeting").

James was living in Cambridge with his parents in the spring of 1871. Since few of his letters survive from this time, there is less documentation than usual on what he read and thought. It can be assumed that he noticed the *Nation*'s scandalized comment on a novel whose author's previous productions he himself had heavily censured. James was a regular reader of this magazine; the author of *Emily Chester* was the one novelist whose full output he had critiqued in order of publication; he and she had made their debut simultaneously. Now she had kicked up her biggest storm yet with her daring treatment of sexual irregularities in leisure American society, and the book had been brought out by the same Boston firm that published James's father's books (and that would in time publish James's own).[17] Surely he paid attention to this noisy new arrival.

What he found was something he could in most respects better – and in others could never equal. Like Seemuller's first novel, *Reginald Archer* focused on the agony of a woman who contracts an unwise marriage. Christie Macalaster is a rich heiress from California who has "grown up entirely apart from the world and ordinary social existence. Her ideas of human nature and life were gathered from poetry, and novels of the better sort; and what relation they bore to facts may be imagined" (66). Just as James would thrust Isabel, another well-read innocent, into a society more complex than the one she was used to, Seemuller moves Christie and her money to the Eastern seaboard, where she meets Reginald. This rake and fortune hunter, who decides in cold blood to marry the heiress, easily fascinates her. He is concerned that "Christie lacks style fearfully," but he feels sure he "can train her to it" (80), just as Osmond is certain Isabel will agree to sacrifice all her very bad ideas. Reginald's good brother, Tom, also loves Christie and tries to warn her of her danger, but she indignantly spurns his advice to take legal steps to secure her inheritance.

The novel hinges on Christie's decision to marry Reginald. Her feeling of respect for him strongly evokes Isabel's admiration for Osmond: "She had erected a noble temple within her heart to his homage: she still maintained the splendid edifice; she chanted the service, and kept the sacred fire burning" (200). During the two-month honeymoon, however, Christie changes from a "merry girl" to "an indefinably altered woman" (202). Although she does not yet fully realize it, her husband has begun to disclose his evil nature:

His manner towards Christie was formed upon a finely-graduated scale, – from the lover he had necessarily appeared, to the cool, courteous, and absolutely unrestrained husband he intended to be.

The change was so adroitly managed, that Christie, feeling the effect in every fibre of her being, could scarcely define or analyze the cause. It was like an almost imperceptible but constant lowering of the temperature. (194)

Similarly, Isabel feels the shadows gather "as if Osmond deliberately, almost malignantly, had put the lights out one by one" (372).

One of James's artful tricks in *The Portrait* is to deny us immediate access to Isabel's mind after her marriage, so that we wonder for several chapters whether our premonitions have come true. Seemuller was less systematic, but she gave close attention to the subtle external signs of Christie's disillusionment. The young wife's eyes register great anxiety. Without complaining or making scenes, she becomes more reserved and elegant and thus acquires the presence of a "somewhat conventional lady" (213). Tom, at dinner, studies her face in an effort to discern how much she knows about her husband, just as some of James's bachelors – Goodwood, Ralph, Longmore in "Madame de Mauves" – study the faces of pure wives. "Tom," a fellow dinner guest teases him, alluding to a popular book, "you must be having a 'revery of a bachelor' " (216). "Madame de Mauves," one could argue, is an extended bachelor's reverie.

Seemuller's chief interest in *Reginald Archer* would be similar to James's in the last third of *The Portrait,* namely, the wife's groping sense of her husband's calculated self-disclosure and her pained attempt to reach an honorable adjustment. Seemuller summed up Christie's predicament in a way that makes evident its resemblance to Isabel's:

Utterly ignorant of evil, of falsity, of the world and its tenets, of every thing but her own pure nature, and necessarily judging all things by it, she had to work through these barriers to a recognition of facts which an experienced woman would have seen and understood at a glance. (194)

Christie soon realizes "that her marriage was a dreadful mistake," but she also continues to suppose "that it had been an unwitting one on his part as on hers" (226). A Mrs. Lester maliciously tells her that Reginald had taken a certain woman for a mistress before marrying, and Christie frigidly answers, "I cannot possibly discuss my husband and his affairs with you or any one else" (245). She resolves "to be an honest, loving wife, to stand clear before her own conscience" (255). Isabel is also isolated in her misery by her sense of the impropriety of discussing Osmond with others and by her determination to do justice to her marriage vows.

Near the end of *Reginald Archer,* Christie descends into a cloudy half-world and becomes unable to think or act:

For the past month or two, she had lived, as it were, in a thick, black cloud of doubt. . . . Turn which way she would, dark shadows rose, which she could no more reduce to fixed form than she could overcome them or drive them away. It was the intangibility of that which oppressed her which paralyzed her. (341)

When she receives a poison pen letter revealing that her husband is having an affair with Mrs. Van Arsdale, Christie's "fears and doubts . . . become certainties" (343) – just as Isabel is freed from "a mesh of fine threads" (*Portrait* 472) by the knowledge of Pansy's parentage. And just as Isabel goes to Ralph, Christie runs "to the one man whom she knew to be absolutely pure, faithful, and honest" (344).

At this point, however, there is a divergence between Christie's and Isabel's ordeal that bespeaks James's contempt for Seemuller's moral sloppiness. The man Christie flees to is not, like Ralph, an invalid or blood relative but the plain and stalwart Tom, a businessman like Goodwood who has all along had to suppress his love for her: Tom feels a "throb of joy" (348) when she walks into his office. That Christie loves him back – loves the man she goes to in refuge from her unfaithful husband – would seem to be a blot on her own fidelity. The means by which Seemuller seeks to deflect the inevitable suspicion that Christie is no better than her husband is to stress her moral helplessness: "If [Tom] deceived her, then indeed all would be lost" (344). She asks him to remember his "promise to be my brother when I needed you" and then breaks down in tears: "You are all I have in the world now" (348). Good Tom, choking his throb of joy, forces himself to remember, "even at that moment, that she was another man's wife" (349). Thus, in her ultimate crisis, Seemuller's heroine is spared the burden of moral responsibility, which is neatly transferred from her shoulders to those of a strong man. Concluding *The Portrait*, James would have nothing to do with such cheap moral evasions. His own stalwart businessman offers to shield Isabel from the world – "If you only trust me, how little you will be disappointed!" (518) – only to make it all the clearer that a woman of Isabel's strength and stature cannot possibly hand over the direction of her life to a male savior. This moral was pointed by James's conspicuous mention of Wimpole Street in his last scene – Wimpole Street being Elizabeth Barrett's residence at the time of her celebrated escape to Italy with Robert Browning. Like James's early reviews, Isabel's final act was a critique and a correction of the moral weakness of all those women writers who trusted, ultimately, in male protection.

What James did not understand was that Seemuller had another kind of strength. When Mrs. Conrad advises Christie to take lovers of her own after catching on that everyone else does this, the unhappy wife is briefly tempted: "Her own nature . . . made the same subtle suggestions" (261). The Baltimore editor and critic William Hand Browne was shocked that "such a woman as she is represented to be" would "wrestle with such a temptation as this" (115). But that is the point about Seemuller: she enthroned Christ and Eros side by side. When the lovely, lubricious, and interestingly named Mrs. Van Arsdale, confronted by her outraged husband, defends herself by claiming that she only did what he did, the author hastens to point out that the fallen woman has "unconsciously used" (358) Christ's argument in defense of the woman taken in adultery. In the end, after Van Arsdale moves in with a wealthy lover, Seemuller very nearly invites us to envy her: "She has gained that freedom of action, that license to gratify every impulse and passion of her nature, which the world grants men at their birth, but which a woman can only gain by breaking every social tie" (377). The novel's ramshackle moral scaffolding is part and parcel of its supple, stretching psychological truthfulness. Together these two qualities stimulated James's strenuous effort to create a nobler heroine. *His* wife would follow "a very straight path" (519).

Human sexuality is so scrupulously barricaded off in most of James's narratives that it can be confronted only through earthshaking melodrama, and even so it oozes out all over. James paid a price for making moral firmness so salient a part of his fiction: He never created a male sinner to compare with Reginald Archer. Osmond is richly imagined, his depravity and hard vanity being one of James's finest achievements, but it is not easy to see Osmond as an attractive sex object, to imagine Madame Merle ever wanting to go to bed with him. Much later, with Gloriani, James evidently sought to create a glamorously sexual man, but the intention seems more conspicuous than the achievement. Gloriani is pretty much a conjuring trick compared to Reginald, who is one of the outstanding Don Juans in nineteenth-century American fiction (not that that necessarily says much). As an easygoing immoralist, Reginald could not care less whether Christie remains faithful to him: "I am afraid, for the future, we [men] have got to give freedom, as well as take it; that liberty, equality, and fraternity are going to become feminine as well as masculine nouns" (329–30). Completely without principle, he is also without spite or fear. It is characteristic that he should feel a friendly respect for the brother who works so hard to control his throbs of joy. Witty, theatrical, and shrewdly self-critical, Reginald carries out even to the point of death his corrupt aim of transforming himself into a "glorious work of art" (361). He faces his jealous murderer in the grand style, and although he dies painfully he remains a sly and cheerful grandstander to the end. "I am dying like a dog, Tom, but a dog that has had his day" (371). James's room in the house of fiction could have used a dog like this.[18]

The moral integrity James imposed on women's fiction served to

endow his version of their heroines with the steel of personal accountabil-
ity. But the thing, above all, that made *The Portrait* superior to Seemuller's third novel and all other agonist fiction (*The Morgesons* excepted)
was the artistry with which James told the story he took from them.
James *realized* their characters; he imagined what they would say and do
with rich abundance; he convincingly *gave* the scenes that brought them
to life. His presentation, chapter by chapter, of Isabel's story shows an
unparalleled mastery of dramatic narrative. Browne identified the fundamental weakness of Seemuller's third novel when he admitted that her
"strength does not lie" in "the dramatic method" but in "what we may
call the scientific or analytical method" (113). Her novels often seem to be
summaries and explanations of some prior narrative: Seemuller wrote
fiction like a critic. She knew there was a great novel in the loveless
marriage, but she could not get it out. She had taste, insight,[19] a sense of
life, and a link with a continuously unfolding narrative tradition and with
the dreams of readers, but she could not flesh out people and scenes. The
story she tried to tell, twice, in *Emily Chester* and *Reginald Archer,* would
not take definitive shape until a young male critic read her botched efforts
and saw his opportunity – a critic who read like a novelist. "Invention,"
Tintner rightly says, "was never one of James's strong points; development and conversion were" (*Book World* 125). What James did with
Reginald Archer and the other two novels was to reimagine them, just as
he admitted in his review of the fittingly named *Opportunity* – the one
and only time he ever thanked an author for her useful hints.

   One of James's greatest gifts was for making things look real that
weren't. His problem in the first phase of his career was that he lacked
material, his experience of life being formal, truncated, and derivative.
His first truly impressive novel had to derive from a group of tormented
narratives that lacked the serene artistry of classic fiction. It was by
strenuously resisting what these female novels had to say about the sexuality of American women that James developed the power to create his
great novel about an innocent American woman. And it was because he
forged *The Portrait* from the very books that tarnished his grand myth of
American innocence that he was so anxious and uncandid about his relationship with all the vulgar female agonists, and so scrupulously careful
to forget them, Anne Crane Seemuller in particular. William, the lean,
strong, older brother, had to fight it out one way or another with the
powerful fathers. Henry also had to distance himself from them, but
never in direct confrontation. For him, the sweaty battle was not with
Laius but Jocasta – the obscene, somewhat older writing woman he
loved and loathed. Simultaneously his progenitress and offered mate, she
gave birth to his imagination by threatening to engulf it.

A Matter of No Significance

On 10 December 1872, two and a half years after Minnie Temple's death and four years before James's earliest mention of his plans for *The Portrait of a Lady*, Anne Seemuller died, of an "old affection of the liver."[20] James knew she died because he read it in the *Nation* for 30 January 1873:

> Mrs. A. M. C. Seemuller, whose death in a German town where she has been residing for the benefit of her health has just been announced, is perhaps better known by her maiden name of Anne Moncure Crane, and still better by her title of "Author of 'Emily Chester.' "

The anonymous writer went on to identify Seemuller as one of a group of women writers active in the early 1860s:

> A dozen years ago, three or four American young women made a sudden reputation for themselves by writing a novel apiece, and of these Miss Crane was one. The author of 'Rutledge' [Miriam Harris] was another; another was the author of 'The Amber Gods' [Harriet Prescott]; but Miss Crane's first book was more widely read than those of either of the other ladies. It will not now be recollected very well by many people, as its success was in reality essentially an ephemeral success, and the reputation it procured for its author fleeting.

Evidently, the writer of this strange death notice wished to remind everyone how important it was that the author of *Emily Chester* be forgotten:

> And this it is worth while to point out, because its example was not without influence on many of its author's young countrywomen, and there was at once a rise in the market value of the young heroine who is wavering between two gentlemen, for one of whom she feels "an affinity," and to the other of whom she is bound by common or statute law. . . . It, in short, brought to the knowledge of the average school-girl Goethe's "Elective Affinities," or rather a pale shadow of that work, and so was popular for a time. "Nature is to be studied in her monstrosities" was its characteristic motto, and it may be supposed to have done the school-girls vast good.

The obituarist remembered reading the eight-year-old novel surprisingly well and put in circulation a story designed to illustrate its juvenility:

> It was, indeed, the work of a writer who, at the time of writing, was hardly more than a school-girl herself, and who had that excuse for the crudity of her book. It is told of the novel that the author

was one day with a party of young ladies, her companions, one of whom proposed that they should form a literary club, each member of which should in turn write something to be read to the others, and that, acting on this suggestion, "Emily Chester" was written, although the proposed club was never organized.

What a silly, infatuated girl the author was!

Mrs. Seemuller's subsequent productions, whether short stories for the magazines or longer ones, have attracted little attention, and required little; but if they showed no marked capacity, they showed, too, that the somewhat unfortunate plot of "Emily Chester" was a matter of no significance.

For the unknown writer of this shockingly nasty death notice, Seemuller was a monster of such power and proportions that it was necessary, publicly, to drive a stake through her heart. It was essential that this novelist never rise again.

What better authorization would James have needed for his slightly risky enterprise of appropriating and rewriting Seemuller's novels? She was dead and buried, her two later books were forgotten, and the famous first one was fading so rapidly that its final edition appeared the same year as the *Nation* essay, 1873. Who would ever know? It would be a civilized and responsible act to turn her shapeless and immoral narratives into a novel of rounded perfection.

Chapter 6

Minnie Temple's Death and the Birth of Henry James's Imagination

*You are both right & wrong about Minny Temple. I had her in mind
& there is in the heroine a considerable infusion of my impression of
her remarkable nature. But the thing is not a portrait. Poor Minny
was essentially* incomplete *& I have attempted to make my young
woman more rounded, more finished. In truth everyone, in life, is
incomplete, & it is the mark of art that in reproducing them one feels
the desire to fill them out, to justify them, as it were.*

Henry James to Grace Norton (28 December
1880, MH-H)

*I am enclosing the copy of a wonderful letter from Harry James[1] –
which you may return any time (I have the original – so do not worry
about it[)]. M.T. is Mary Temple – my great great friend a very
remarkable person,* ~~& the character~~ *[sic]. He used her personality in
"The Portrait of a Lady," tho' her circumstances were in every way
different[.]*

Helena de Kay Gilder to Mary Hallock Foote
(11 November 1914, Gilder Papers)

A Plain-Spoken Young Woman

To say that Mary ("Minnie," as her nickname was commonly spelled)
Temple was a tremendously important presence in James's imaginative
life is to say nothing new. Yet almost everything remains to be said on
the subject of what Minnie meant for James. This couple presents us with
a classic instance of woman-as-muse and man-as-inspired-writer. Criticism and biography and feminist revisionism have yet to take up the
challenge of close critical scrutiny here. What is going on when a man is
inspired to do his best work to date by an ardently worshipped image of a
woman? Quentin Anderson's claim that "Minny Temple became the
priestess of 'father's ideas' " (133) in James's imagination comes close to
the truth yet remains walled away from it. James's fictions may have
sought to *make* Minnie over into some such priestess, but the original and

decisive fact is that in herself she was the father's antagonist or even nemesis rather than his priestess, and that it was her wholesale opposition to everything the father stood for that gave her such tremendous value for the son. Even more important, the evidence strongly hints that after Minnie's death at the age of twenty-four on 8 March 1870, she became assimilated in James's imagination with the type of woman he had earlier reacted against so strongly in his reviews of women agonists, and also in some of his first stories. Minnie brought everything together for James – his boyhood fantasy about the orphan life, the independent but doomed agonist heroine, a dominant tradition of women's fiction, and the young author's own muffled questioning of his family and his father's ideas.

The key to understanding what Minnie meant in James's imaginative life, however, is to get some sense of the differences between what she was and what James made of her. Unless we catch a glimpse of the historical reality before James's imagination transformed it, we cannot understand what that imagination was up to. While there is obviously no way to get a complete picture of Minnie, we can learn something about her from the letters she and others wrote. There happen to be two particularly good sources of information that have only recently come to light.

Thirty-five years ago Leon Edel suggested that James "doctored" (*Untried Years* 313) the letters written by Minnie excerpted in *Notes of a Son and Brother,* and this shrewd guess has proved correct. In 1985 I discovered what appear to be accurate copies of Minnie's original twenty-three letters to John Chipman Gray, a young law teacher at Harvard. Not only do the fair copies (available at the Houghton Library) provide a tremendous amount of new information about Minnie, but the differences between these copies and James's edited versions offer an unparalleled insight into his fiction making.

Second, there are modern typescripts (made by Rosamond Gilder) of eight letters written in the 1860s by Minnie to her close friend Helena de Kay (later Gilder). These letters have not been made public as yet. One of them was penned in the James parlor in Newport in 1863 and describes William's and Henry's behavior in the present tense.[2]

Minnie's other surviving letters are a note dated 19 November 1869 to her sister Ellen describing a recent visit to the Jameses in Cambridge; two sheets of a 10 February 1870 letter to William; an undated fragment that I believe was sent to William on 15 January 1870; and three letters to Henry James himself. The letters to Henry, omitted from his memoirs, have been made available by Robert C. LeClair; those to William will be found in my article "New Light on William James and Minny Temple."

In addition to these thirty-seven letters of Minnie's, we see her reflected in the letters of others – the Jameses, Gray, Helena de Kay, Janet Halleck Drake de Kay (Helena's mother), and others. All these documents convey a surprisingly coherent picture of a remarkable young mind, whose "gay clearness" – James's good phrase (*Notes of a Son* 489) – continually probed for the truth of things.

The relationship between Henry and Minnie was so well established that after learning of her death he wrote: "As I look back upon the past, from the time I was old enough to feel and perceive, her friendship seems literally to fill it" (*Letters* 1: 219). Yet *A Small Boy and Others* throws no light on their friendship as children, even though James must have been well acquainted with Minnie before she and her five brothers and sisters were orphaned by the death of their parents in 1854. One would especially like to know how Henry conducted himself with Minnie in adolescence and early adulthood. Without access to all of the available evidence, slender as it is, Leon Edel proposed that in 1865 Henry behaved in this fashion: "To sit back and observe his cousin, to worship her from afar, to give her signs of devotion at the real right moment, this seems to have been the love stratagem of Henry – as it was of a number of his early young fictional heroes" (*Untried Years* 234). But there is scant documentary evidence for this scenic reconstruction, which rests not on letters but on a few early stories of James in which the male lead worships from afar and waits for the "real right moment." The problem with this method of restoration is its circularity: We merely create a separate reality if we use the early stories to extract James's attitude toward Minnie (and other American Dianas) and then draw on these supposed attitudes – awe, perplexity, fear – to disclose the real content of the stories.

But we are not interested here in any separate reality; our aim, rather, is to follow the path a remarkable imagination once picked out. If we are to locate James in society and history, we must do what no Jamesian, strange to say, has ever done – scrutinize Minnie's own letters to see what *they* can tell us about her. Only after such an investigation can we hope to understand the use James made of her.

In reading Minnie's letters to Gray, we should not forget James's cautionary statement that they were "essentially not love-letters" (*Notes of a Son* 484). The Houghton copies contain a good deal of information that James suppressed in editing Minnie's correspondence, and they prove that he had good reason for urging caution: Gray took a romantic interest in others, a Miss Adams at one time and perhaps a Miss Greenough at another, and Minnie was the third party, a confidante. Disregarding James's warning, Edel termed the letters "love-letters" (*Untried Years* 317) and thus overlooked their unusual nature – an intimate but nonromantic exchange across the barrier of gender. We must keep in mind what Minnie herself sometimes pointed out – her illness often made it unwise for her to speak to others, even in a whisper, and the exchange of letters was a substitute for society and talk. In addition, as she sometimes intimated, the "hindrances"

(7 July 1869)³ of temperament and gender made her infrequent meetings with Gray rather dissatisfying compared to their long-distance exchanges of thought.

One fact to be gleaned about Minnie from her letters is that she was unconventional to the point of indecorousness. In her teens she took pride in her reputation for "insanity" (Rosamond Gilder's typescript, MT to Helena de Kay, 12 July 1862, Gilder Papers). Once, after just arriving in New York, she made "a first call" on a new acquaintance without taking the time to dress properly (21 November 1869). Elsewhere she threatened to write Gray as often as she pleased:

> I know quite well that I do not owe you a letter, & that the custom is for maidens to mete out strictly letter for letter – but if you don't mind it, I don't, & if you *do* mind that kind of thing, you had better learn not to at once, if you propose to be a friend of mine, or else have your feelings from time to time severely shocked. (9 May 1869)

Her sisters were much tamer in comparison: "If by chance I say anything or ask a question that lies at all near my heart, Kitty & Elly both tell me that I am 'queer' & that 'they wouldn't be me for anything' " (29 August 1869). Once she lightly proposed to study the law and "convert myself into a perfect Myra Blackstone" (12 December 1869), referring under this composite name to the pioneering woman lawyer, Myra Bradwell, editor of an Illinois law review. Elsewhere, she daringly invited Gray to disguise his gender and accompany her on a vacation: "Won't you dress yourself up like an old woman, & take me to Lenox with you?" (29 July 1869). The playful transvestism of these two propositions posed a joking challenge (like Penelope Lapham's humor) to the strict nineteenth-century separation of the sexes. James struck both suggestions from the record in *Notes of a Son and Brother*.

Minnie's vacation proposal shows another side of her that James consistently edited out of the letters – her teasing directness. William James later wrote that she had a "coquettish impulse" (letter to HJ, 24 August 1872), and this phrase seems perfectly apt if one understands by it the sort of playfulness that likes to challenge or provoke. She warned Gray not to be too censorious of other men's strict fiancées: "You may 'catch a tartar' yet" (27 January 1869). Elsewhere she probed for his meaning in calling her "Pyramid" (7 January 1869), teased him about his moustache, and questioned a declaration of his about "*no* sentiment" (3 February 1869). In her letter of 27 June 1869, she half-jokingly complained of the difficulty of knowing a man who seemed to wear such various masks as Gray. Judging by her next and very interesting letter, which for some reason James chose not to reprint, Gray was stung by what Minnie called her "nonsense" (7 July 1869). She once twitted him for working so hard, accusing him of designing to present himself as a more substantial suitor. Because James consistently pruned out much of Minnie's personal banter, *Notes of a Son and Brother* finally conveys a one-sided and misleading image of her. Among those who have been misled is Edel himself, who sums up the letters to Gray as "the communications of a serious young lady" (*Untried Years* 317). But the real woman probably had much less starch than the edited person we dimly see in James's memoirs – or than the very serious Isabel Archer, who, as Alice Wellington Rollins pointed out in 1884, does not have "a particle of humor."

Looking back over forty years later, James tended to stress Minnie's unassertive sympathy: "She liked nothing in the world so much as to see others fairly exhibited; not as they might best please her by being, but as they might most fully reveal themselves, their stuff and their truth" (*Notes of a Son* 461). This view no doubt reflects Minnie's encouraging support of James, but it is not consistent with her treatment of others or her view of herself. At the age of seventeen she "quite surprised not to say disgusted" a young man named Dance by telling him he was "the most affected creature I have ever seen" (Rosamond Gilder's typescript, letter to Helena de Kay, 1 January 1863, Gilder Papers). Later that year, when Minnie and her friend Helena de Kay were studying literature under George P. Bradford at Newport, Helena's brother wondered, "How is the little man who pretends to teach you and is bullied by you and Minnie?" (quoted in Rosamond Gilder 29). At twenty-four she confessed to Gray that she had "a tendency to take more than I give of sympathy & interest" (30 December 1869), and he, miffed by her ridicule of his work and his seriousness, definitely agreed. He considered her "a long way off" (30 November 1869) from him in spirit, and bluntly wrote, "Verily you are a plain-spoken young woman" (7 July 1869). One need not accept Gray's complaint that she had "narrow sympathies" (7 July 1869), or was "intellectually, so unsympathetic" (12 December 1869) – but neither should one take James's entirely opposite claim at face value. We get a more balanced sense of her character by noting her response to Gray's apparent plea for "a start on the way of righteousness." Minnie's no-nonsense rebuff makes it clear she would have nothing to do with the standard role of female monitoring angel that Gray wanted her to play: "I think you know that way better than I do. The only thing that I can say is – Don't stop saying your prayers – & God bless you" (7 January 1869).

In *The Portrait of a Lady* Isabel had been so excited by the Civil War that she was moved "almost indiscriminately" (28) by the valor of the men on either side. Minnie was both more partisan and better informed. "How discouraging the war news is!" she wrote the day the Federals were defeated in the Second Battle of Bull Run. "I can't bear it, we have had such wretched fate of late." She eagerly wished for black emancipation, both "for its own merits" and as a means of "crushing" the rebellion. When on 25 August 1862 the *New York Tribune* published Abraham Lincoln's declaration that his object was to save the union and not to destroy slavery, she was "highly disgusted" with "the President's letter." It was "very very weak and I don't at all like the way he looks at Slavery" (Rosamond Gilder's typescript, letter to Helena de Kay, 30 August 1862, Gilder Papers). Several years after Appomattox a much-publicized boat race between Harvard and an English crew "stirred up all the old feeling within me, which has been slumbering since the war" (29 August 1869).

Preeminent among Minnie's values and beliefs was some sense of personal integrity: "the absolute value of the individual – the absolute necessity of uncompromising & unfaltering truth" (30 December 1869). She once asked Gray if he remembered "my old hobby of the 'remote possibility' of the best thing, being better than a clear certainty of the second best? Well, I believe it more than ever, every day I live" (29 August 1869). Her letters exhibit many traces of this "pet theory" (7 January 1869), and one of William's letters to Henry commenting on her determination to be "true to her own instincts" (5 December 1869) suggests that this phrase was well known to the Jameses and that they made fun of it among themselves. Writing to Henry in Europe, she characteristically extolled the sort of courage that trusts one's own private intuitions: "I think the best comes thro' a blind hanging on to some conviction, never mind what, that God has put deepest into our souls, and the comforting love of a few chosen friends, which comes to us 'all along of "said" hanging-on' " (LeClair, "Henry James" 46). In this instance she was advising Henry himself, who had recently dispatched some despairing letters from Florence. One person she greatly admired for her "*self-reliance*" (21 November 1869) was Fanny Dixwell, who was known to Henry and the other Jameses.

Inconsistently, Minnie also considered the "selfishness" of her life to be "detestable" and frequently wished she could devote herself "to God's service" (29 August 1869). Her letters show how hard she struggled to reconcile self-reliance with the obligation "to be unselfish, to live for other people, to mould our lives as much as possible on the model of Christ's all-embracing humanity" (12 December 1869). At times, sensing that the answer to her uncertainty lay in orthodox Christianity, she wished to be convinced of "the old beliefs" (2 April 1869) – especially the doctrine of Christ's atonement. She went to hear the preaching of Phillips Brooks (Gray's minister), since he seemed to unite progressivism with orthodoxy, but even he could not finally resolve her doubts.

Minnie's running internal debate between self-trust and selfless devo-

tion reached an intense climax during a depressed period in late January
1870, when she had a month and a half to live. Lying awake one night,
she had a sudden insight into the kind of repose that Christianity
promised – a halt to her "conscious battle between right & wrong." She
joined "intellectually . . . the long line of Christians" who had found
comfort in "unconsciousness of self, love & trust."[4] She had never been
persuaded of Henry James, Sr.'s, doctrines, but now she wondered "if
the good gentleman had all along got hold of the higher truth" (25
January 1870). Apparently he had not, for a couple of days later her
"momentary vision of Redemption from thinking & striving" had "vanished away again," and in place of it was her old stubborn rejection of all
spurious promises of transcendence: "So back swings the universe to the
old place – Paganism – natural Religion,[5] or whatever you call the belief
whose watch word is 'God and our own Soul' – And who shall say there
is not comfort in it – One at least feels that here one breathes one's native
air – welcome back the old *human* feeling, with its beautiful pride, and its
striving – its despair, its mystery, and its faith" (27 January postscript to
25 January 1870). What makes this independence of spirit all the more
unforgettable is that Minnie may have known by now that time was
running out for her.

A perceptive reader of George Eliot, Minnie was curious about the
inconsistency between the self-abnegating heroines and the author's own
self-assertiveness:

> The creature interests me, personally, & I feel a desire to know
> something about her life – how far her lofty moral sentiments have
> served her practically – for instance in her dealings with Lewes – I
> see that she understands the character of a *generous* woman, that is,
> of a woman who believes in generosity, & who must be that or
> nothing, & who feels keenly, notwithstanding, how hard it is practi-
> cally to follow it out, & how, (looking at it from the point of view
> of comfort as far as this world goes,) it "pays" not at all[.] (24 April
> 1869)

In this passage Minnie's skepticism asserts itself in a remarkable way
against a massive cultural pressure. If Rebecca Harding Davis had possessed more of this power of resistance, "A Story of To-Day" and *Waiting for the Verdict* might have been stronger narratives.

On the question of whether marriage is good for women, which
Rebecca Harding Davis in particular tried to work out, Minnie felt it was
safer to remain single. "I am aware that if all other women felt the eternal
significance of matrimony to the extent that I do, that hardly any of them
would get married at all, & the human race would come to a stand-still."
She conceded that her views on the subject might be "fanatical and im-

practicable" but characteristically held firm: "We must be true to ourselves mustn't we?" (29 August 1869).[6]

The marriage that displeased Minnie most of all was that of her sister Elly to Dr. Christopher Temple Emmet, a man twenty-eight years her senior. One of the reasons Minnie was shocked by the news of their engagement in the summer of 1869 was that Elly was the second Temple sister to marry a father figure: Kitty, wedded shortly before, was twenty-two years younger than *her* husband (who was Temple Emmet's brother). To Gray Minnie wrote that "the irretrievableness" of Elly's step was "very depressing" (29 August 1869). Letters to Henry James himself make it clear that Minnie felt disgust at the idea of taking a much older, "bald-headed" husband: "I have quite determined that the line must be drawn *here*" (15 August 1869). Judging from some of the surviving letters written by Minnie's brother, Bob, and by Mary and Henry James, the entire clan shared Minnie's disfavor.[7] One wonders how the various relatives felt when they read *The Portrait of a Lady* twelve years later and saw that Henry had used Elly's unpopular marriage to a much older man as the basis for Isabel's perverse choice of the middle-aged Gilbert Osmond. Did any of the James relatives notice that the character James based on Minnie was made to choose the very type of bridegroom the independent-minded cousin said she would not?

Minnie's single most noteworthy aspect in the minds of others may have been a kind of natural eminence. In Henry's view she was "ever the heroine of the scene" (*Notes of a Son* 462), and for William she remained a bright standard of comparison for other young women. For her brother, Bob, a ne'er-do-well whose instability is fully communicated in his few surviving letters, Minnie was "the best one of the family" (letter to HJ, 17[?] September 1869). But it is essential to see that Minnie was not universally admired and loved. Her sisters frowned on her restless questioning, and John Gray accused her of not taking a real interest in his ideas and pursuits. Her best friend's mother saw her as a dangerous influence:

> You are doing a wrong and dangerous thing in allowing your friendship for Minnie to become an engrossing passion. Do not surrender your *self* your convictions of Truth and Justice – piety and honour to any one – much less to a young and undeveloped and perhaps mistaken person of your own age. (Rosamond Gilder's typescript, Janet Halleck Drake de Kay to Helena de Kay [March or April 1863], Gilder Papers)

The point is this: The person we see in Minnie's letters was not the sort who charmed all she met. There was a forceful, challenging, and conspicuously dramatic quality in her that drew some of her contemporaries and repelled others.

Another reason why Minnie commanded attention is that she represented in heightened form some of the social tendencies of her time. Over half of her extant letters were written in 1869, a year that had a special tone of challenging newness. When Helena de Kay ended a letter by asking to be remembered to a friend, and "her sister & mother," she added: "(The mother sh'd have come first but then what's the use of living in 69 if we cant do such things.)" (letter to Mary Hallock, 28 September [1869], Gilder Papers).

A year after Minnie's death an editorial appeared in a Boston magazine, *The Literary World,* that reveals how close contemporary women's writing was to her own prickly individualism. The anonymous editorialist was struck by

> . . . the pessimism which so largely prevails among female writers. If they write a novel, the lover is faithless, and the maiden dies broken-hearted. If they write a poem, its burden is buried hopes. This is true of the majority. There are other female writers who make up their lack of humor with desperate cynicism, and seem to strive to illustrate that whatever is, is not right. It is odd, but we believe it is true, that the sex, which men in their books have eulogized as the synonyme [sic] of gentle goodness, in its own literary expression identifies itself with bitterness and sarcasm.[8]

The perception of this probably masculine writer was to some extent blocked by certain contemporary stereotypes about modern women, and also by a preference for an already moldy code of feminine decorum. Minnie, for instance, was neither bitter nor sarcastic, and yet this writer might have seen her as such. But if we can correct for the editorialist's astigmatism, we at once see from his little sketch that Minnie was a young woman of her time insofar as she dared to say *no* in ways that were unthinkable to the preceding generation, or the other sex. Her sort of unbudgeable integrity actually made some men (but not Henry) bitter or sarcastic themselves.

A Free Orphan of One's Own

What did confrontational Minnie make of Henry James's parents, brothers, and sister, and what did they make of her? If we keep in mind that her deepest beliefs were completely out of line with what the James father taught about "woman" and human self-transcendence, we stumble upon an awkward fact that has hitherto escaped notice. With the significant exception of Henry Jr. (for Wilkie and Bob there is no evidence), the James family disapproved of their orphaned kinswoman.

Minnie's letters cite Henry James, Sr.'s, ideas in a way that shows how large he loomed in her life. In 1863, grieving over the death of her brother, who was killed in battle, she wrote: "Uncle Henry says that no human-being can stand for a life time without almost superhuman strength the spontaneous *worship*" that her brother had attracted. It appears that her forceful and original uncle was a major complication in her adolescence. When he told her "it was my *duty* to go" back to school "and urged me to overcome my *feeling* by my sense of *Right,*" she finally complied, not "from any *real* feeling that it was right in itself" but because, following her brother's death, she "could not bear *controversy* or *opposition* just now, and because I wanted to do as he thought best" (Rosamond Gilder's typescript, letter to Helena de Kay, 12 or 13 May 1863, Gilder Papers).

"I agree with you perfectly about Uncle Henry," Minnie wrote Gray several years later. "I should think he would be very irritating to the legal mind – He is not at all satisfactory even to mine" (7 January 1869). This privately expressed dislike differs considerably from the usual public response to Henry Sr. – enjoyment of his quaint heartiness, amusement at his intensity and obscurity. Minnie evidently tried to take him at his word, unlike some others, and as her reference to the legal mind implies, she was annoyed by his evasiveness. What is particularly intriguing is the confrontation between Minnie and her uncle Henry in which she appears to have told him off. This quarrel, which has not drawn comment of any kind, apparently took place a few months before her death. The only documentary evidence for it is her 25 January 1870 letter to Gray – the letter telling of her momentary acquisition of some sort of Christian faith and her later abandonment of it. This brief moment of faith had made Henry Sr.'s notions seem momentarily more plausible:

It throws a light upon Uncle Henry's talk, which has seemed to me hitherto neither reasonable nor consoling – When I was in Cambridge, it so far disgusted me, that I fear I manifested plainly unto him that that [*sic*] it seemed to me not only highly unpractical, but ignoble & shirking – & [I] knew all the time that he ~~hate~~ [*sic*] disliked me for what he called my *pride* & *conceit* – & I have felt that his views didn't touch my case a bit – didn't give me the least comfort or practical help & seemed to me wanting in earnestness & strength – Now it occurs to me, what if the good gentleman had all along got hold of the higher truth, the purer spirituality? (25 January 1870)

Her strong language hints that she detected the morbidity and self-hatred that shaped Uncle Henry's system of salvation. Certainly she herself had a much stronger, healthier, and more open character than this man who regarded the "sense of selfhood" as nothing less than "the curse of mankind" (*Literary Remains* 62). Two days later, when Minnie returned to her old sense of things ("Paganism – natural Religion" [27 January postscript to 25 January 1870] she no doubt also returned to her low valuation of Henry Sr.'s ideas.

Minnie's hot rejection of Henry Sr.'s ideas gives an unrivaled insight into the birth of Henry Jr.'s imagination, especially since her feeling that his father's ideas were impractical, unreasonable, and not consoling seems to have been her mature view, based on years of experience. One cannot know whether the talk that disgusted her was a formal lecture, a casual conversation, or a private admonition directed at her alone. Whatever form this talk may have taken, Minnie evidently felt so provoked that she expressed her feelings, and these feelings verged so closely on contempt that she felt some compunction afterward. One thing is very clear: Her defense of what *he* chose to call her "*pride & conceit*" tells us that the senior James attempted in some way to get her to question her assertive individuality and self-trust. She evidently fought back in a direct and personal way, showing him "plainly" that she considered his ideas "ignoble & shirking." These were very insulting terms in an age of lingering gentlemanly chivalry – and yet, as I have tried to show in Chapter 2, they do capture the evasiveness and self-hatred that mark Henry Sr.'s intellectual history.

It would seem, then, that the James father got a kind of comeuppance from the outspoken niece who would later be memorialized in his son's *Portrait of a Lady*. In establishing the setting for this confrontation – "When I was in Cambridge" – Minnie was apparently referring to the week-long November 1869 visit to the James family that she had already mentioned in earlier letters to Gray. (In *Notes of a Son and Brother* James's rewriting of the phrase – "When I was with him" [510] – made the location in space and time much less definite.) Henry himself was in Italy, and none of the extant accounts the Jameses sent him of Minnie's November visit mentions her debate with the father.[9] Indeed, some of these letters imply that the visit had gone more smoothly than her earlier visits. Minnie herself wrote Helena that she "had a most delightful visit at Cambridge" (Rosamond Gilder's typescript, November [1869], Gilder Papers). The evidence is contradictory, yet it appears that in her trenchant candor Minnie gave a sharp, Zen-master's slap in the face to a decidedly pompous theoretician on "woman" and marriage. The ladies he lectured generally showed more gratitude. Was he stung by her? In

Minnie's account of his feelings, the first word, "hate," is crossed out and replaced with "dislike." Of course, there is no way of determining whether this change represents Minnie's second thoughts or those of the copyist, in this case Alice H. James (William James's widow).

The first volume of Edel's biography of Henry James astutely demonstrates that the novelist's father was both patronized and protected by his wife and children. While we do not finally know how the philosopher reacted to Minnie's criticism of his "talk," his family often regarded her with real hostility. One of Alice James's few surviving letters has this to say about her cousin:

> We had a little visit a short time since from Minny on her way to Conway from New Rochelle where she had been staying at the Emmetts[sic]. She is not nearly as interesting as she used to be, she is so much influenced by the last person she has been with and taken a fancy to that one never knows where to find her. She was looking very pretty and her manner is certainly perfectly fascinating. (6 August [1867], Strouse 115)

That the frigid cattiness of this passage was typical of Alice's treatment of her cousin, we see from a letter written by Minnie to her own sister Elly: "Alice did not snub me as much as usual – She began by doing it, but I asked her to stop, wh. she consented to do" (19 November 1869). Apart from these two letters there is no other documentary evidence whatever for Alice's dislike of Minnie, this in spite of the certain implication in the second letter that the dislike endured for years. In other words, some of the strong family antagonisms within the James clan have – ineffectively, in this instance – been censored out of the record.

One of the reasons Alice expressed her nasty–nice view of Minnie to William (there is a neat contrast here with Minnie's own direct confrontations) is that for a time William seems to have shared his sister's antagonism. Soon after Minnie's November 1869 visit to Cambridge, William sent Henry a letter that both acknowledged his aversion and resolutely put it behind him:

> M. Temple was here for a week a fortnight since. She was delightful in all respects, and although very thin, very cheerful. I am conscious of having done her a good deal of injustice for some years past, in nourishing a sort of unsympathetic hostility to her. She is after all a most honest little phenomenon, and there is a true respectability in the courage with which she keeps "true to her own instincts" – I mean it has a certain religious side with her. Moreover she is more devoid of "meanness," of anything petty in her

character than any one I know, perhaps either male or female. *Je tiens à* telling you this, as I recollect last winter abusing her to you rather virulently. (5 December 1869)

The record for the previous winter (1868–69) sheds no light whatever on William's aversion to Minnie. Did this aversion have something to do with the strong sexual preference he revealed in his 1869 response to Mill's *Subjection of Women* – his dogmatic confidence that the average American man rightly prefers a dependent wife (review of Bushnell, 562–63)? In any case, the letter to Henry definitely registers a change of mind that has come about as a result of Minnie's visit. William now admires his cousin, and the qualities he likes in her – forthrightness, staunchness, lack of "meanness" – happen to be the traits his devious family often lacked. The passage is nothing less than a confession: The writer wants it understood that he has finally outgrown his constitutional antipathy to their cousin. (After the visit, Minnie wrote Elly that William had been "nicer than ever" [19 November 1869].) The reason William directed his confession to Henry was that Henry had been Minnie's sole champion in the James family, the only one up to now to appreciate her.

There is something else of great importance that we learn from William's letter. Even though he had disliked Minnie "for some years past," and made no secret of this dislike, *not one previous extant letter* by any of the Jameses so much as mentions his hostility. The only prior reference is to be found in a revealing letter Minnie sent six years earlier: "Willy James is the same strange youth as ever, stranger if possible, but good as ever. He is not *cross* to me, but I think he has rather *renounced* me, in the depths of his heart, as a *bad* thing" (Rosamond Gilder's typescript, letter to Helena de Kay, 3 April 1863, Gilder Papers). Given that this hostility does not appear in six years of James family correspondence, one suspects that the documentation has been selectively preserved. Surely, one of the letter burners was Henry Jr. himself. His memoir, *Notes of a Son and Brother,* never so much as hints that William had "rather *renounced*" Minnie. The reason, I would guess, why Henry did not burn his brother's 5 December letter was that it extolled Minnie so warmly and thus confirmed the wisdom of Henry's own partisanship.[10]

Then there is the James mother, also (like Minnie) named Mary. There are several hints that Mary disliked Minnie and was worried about Henry's fondness for her. In the summer of 1869, when Henry took a walking tour in Switzerland, his family took temporary lodgings in Pomfret, Connecticut, where they saw a great deal of Lizzie Boott. A letter from Mary to Henry praised Lizzie's refined cultivation to the disparagement of Minnie's raw energy: "What a striking instance [Lizzie] is of what a careful and thorough education can accomplish. . . . Look at

Minny Temple in contrast with her – Minny has all her tastes and capabilities naturally in a higher degree; and look at the difference." The implication here is that Minnie was unsteady, undisciplined, and not particularly cultivated. Mary did not bother to specify these faults because they had been frequently talked over in the family. Also, Mary wished to be tactful and thus followed up this passage with a report she felt her son might welcome, enthusiastic as he was about his cousin: "Minny writes that she gets up at 6 o'clk every morn-g and takes a lesson in drawing – Perhaps she is beginning to work out her own salvation" (24 July [1869]). Judging from the tone of Mary's other surviving letters, I would say that the second sentence was not meant to be ironic or humorous: She really meant that drawing lessons and early and regular rising represented the first steps in some kind of salvation. The passage expresses her habit of cool strictness toward unworthy outsiders, the same attitude that is apparent in Mary's acerbic comments about the wives of her two youngest sons. Minnie could obviously never be part of the inner circle Mary guarded.

There can be no doubt that Henry's feelings for his cousin were consistently warmer than those of his father, mother, sister, and older brother. In 1863 he traveled from Cambridge to Newport "for a day or two *expressly* to see *me,*" wrote Minnie to her bosom friend. When he asked her for "a short description . . . *body and mind*" of this friend (Helena de Kay), Minnie "told him *loads*" – and then wrote Helena to ask, "How could I help talking about *you* to any one so *dear* as Harry?" (Rosamond Gilder's typescript, 3 April 1863, Gilder Papers). The gap between James's confidentiality and his family's aloofness helps explain his peculiar gratefulness in the letter he wrote his mother after receiving her unexpected announcement of Minnie's death. Instead of recalling the flare-up between Minnie and Henry Sr. during the November visit, Mary's letter had diplomatically dwelled on "the pleasantness of that last visit." Henry's gratitude overflowed: "Dear bright little Minny – God bless you dear Mother, for the words" (*Letters* 1: 219, 221). These four words, twice quoted by Henry from his mother's letter (which does not survive), hardly represent a glowing testimonial to a remarkable person. The reason they called forth such an exaggerated response from Henry is that in the context of the James family the tepid phrase represented a major concession: Permission was granted to think well of "little" Minnie.

In spite of the selective destruction of letters and other forms of documentation, then, we can still discern the James family's deep instinctual aversion to their orphaned relative and her "*pride & conceit.*" Without some sort of recognition of this muffled enmity, it seems to me that the basic shape and direction of James's imaginative career cannot be discerned with any real acuity. When "powerless-feeling Harry" (as William called him in a letter home; [G. Allen 308]) sided with Minnie against his family, and then took her image as the basis for his first major heroine, Isabel Archer, he was making a bid for freedom, self-assertion, imaginative achievement. Minnie simultaneously enabled James to distance himself from his oppressive father-philosopher and to write about the sort of person his father preached should not exist – the independent woman without family who affronted the world. Minnie Temple became Henry James's heroine, and in so doing brought his imagination to life; and one reason she was able to do so was that she fulfilled the requirements of the personal orphan champion he had long been fantasizing.

For the amazing thing is that James's imagination had needed Minnie since early boyhood. According to *A Small Boy and Others*, James's first "conception of true richness" was that he and his brothers and sister "should be sent separately off among cold or even cruel aliens in order to be there thrillingly homesick" (15). This charming fantasy, with its mix of fear and fascination, was no doubt stimulated by the many Victorian novels that thrust a solitary child into a cold, cruel world – *Oliver Twist*, *Nicholas Nickleby*, *The Old Curiosity Shop*, *The Wide, Wide World*, *The Lamplighter*, and hundreds of others. Yet the terms in which young Henry liked to imagine parentlessness are revealing and particularly appropriate to himself: "It was my habit . . . to attribute to orphans *as* orphans a circumstantial charm, a setting necessarily more delightful than our father'd and mother'd one" (*Small Boy* 120–21).

Just how thoroughly fathered and mothered little Henry really was has been well established elsewhere. His father often remained at home instead of going off to work like other men; the mother was strong and supervisory; the family was notoriously close; and because his mother's sister lived with them after 1855, he had three parents instead of two. As an old man writing his memoirs, James would look back on his rich family life with celebratory piety, yet the boy's orphan fantasy informs us that there was another side to this closely enveloping home life: The boy felt so smothered that he liked to dream of a parentless and dangerously free existence somewhere else. This boyhood daydream was connected with James's later absorption in motherless or mother-abandoned heroines – Daisy Miller, Isabel Archer, Verena Tarrant, Fleda Vetch, Maisie Farange, Nanda Brookenham, and others – and it may have influenced his decision to settle in Europe, among "cold or even cruel aliens," before his parents died.

Not only was there to be an unbroken continuity between James's early fantasy, his admiration for Minnie, and the books he later read and wrote, but he was actually present as an eleven-year-old boy at the scene of Minnie's orphaning.[11] Fantastically, his own father played a conspicuously unpleasant part in this scene.

In the summer of 1854, at a time when Minnie Temple's father was at the point of death, some members of the James clan decided that it would be wise to keep the very ill mother from returning to his bedside, a course she "passionately rejected." The man summoned to enforce this decision was Henry James, Sr., her brother. The scene took place at Rhinebeck, New York, on Augustus James's spectacular Hudson River estate, Linwood. Henry Jr.'s memoirs would later recount the event but without being able to explain why his father was selected for this mission, or why he took his second son with him. What the son chiefly remembered was that he waited outside the house while his father went in to do what had to be done, and that after a time Mrs. Temple's cry – "the wail of her protest and her grief" – was carried out beyond the verandah. Hearing this vivid testimony to his father's coercive patriarchal authority – his "resources of high control" – the boy went "creeping off to the edge of the eminence" above the river, where, as he reported or imagined sixty years later, he felt "the great bright harmonies of air and space becoming one with my rather proud assurance and confidence" (*Small Boy* 183).

This must have been an unforgettable initiation into death and separation and iron discipline and vast serene vistas for the eleven-year-old bystander. Surely that sense of "proud assurance and confidence" did not represent the sum of his feelings. It is understandable that the small boy crept away from the brutal scene, but why did the aged memoirist treat it so superficially? Ten years earlier, in *The Wings of the Dove*, Susan Stringham finds Milly Theale poised on the edge of another great valley, apparently enjoying an uplifted sense of possession. Then Stringham and we discover that Milly has been worrying about the results of a medical examination in New York. Apparent exhilaration masking cryptic terror: The passage mimics the structure of the brief memory in *A Small Boy*, except that the autobiography labors to cover up what the work of fiction discloses. What is fascinating is that James created the more honest version of his early experience by attributing it to a character modeled after the *daughter* of the woman whose wails originally sent *him* to the precipice.

Did James ever realize that both the dying Mrs. Temple and her dying daughter, Minnie, had to undergo a harsh ordeal as a result of Henry Sr.'s intervention? Just as he effectively kept the dying mother away from her dying husband, so some twenty-five years later he would tell the dying daughter that she must give up her "*pride & conceit.*" In either case a person fighting for her life was told she must renounce.[12] The difference is that Minnie was able to resist the dark old man who taught dying women that "the primal curse of man is personal consciousness" ("Spiritualism New and Old" 361). Even near the end, when the theologian's doctrines received support from a sudden vision of Christian peace and trust, Minnie held out and reaffirmed her own intuitive "Paganism."

It would have been as impossible for Henry Jr. to stand up to his philosopher-father as it would have been for Catherine Sloper in *Washington Square* to try to refute the doctor. But Minnie Temple, a free orphan notwithstanding her fatal illness, stood relatively firm in the face of her uncle's crusade against the individual human will – *and Henry loved her for it*. Everything came together for him in her. She was not only the sort of person – restless, intellectual, female – his father's doctrines could not tolerate, but she was the free orphan the good and loyal son had always dreamed of being.

Yet it was not easy to resolve the conflict between his loyalty to Minnie and to his father. We can see just how extreme the dilemma was for Henry, and how intimately it was related to his fiction, in his 8 March 1870 letter to William. (That he wrote the letter from England the same day that Minnie died in New York is only one more fateful coincidence in this strange story.) The first part of the letter seems almost rebelliously independent. Henry ridiculed Englishwomen for their cut-and-dried nature – their dowdiness and lack of "moral spontaneity." He compared them unfavorably to free American types, naming Minnie Temple and Clover Hooper (who would marry Henry Adams), and he grew quite enthusiastic over the Americans' "alertness, their cleverness & self-assistance." He was charmed by the "graceful ease & laxity & freedom" of an American friend, Mrs. Winslow, in spite of all "her little vulgarities." In expressing these views, Henry was challenging his family's, and especially his father's, deep-seated repudiation of modern female independence. The fascinating thing about this letter is that its concluding remarks seek to wipe out the covert defiance and return the errant writer to the family fold: "À propos – I retract all those brutalities about the Engländerinnen. They are the mellow mothers & daughters of a mighty race." This recantation served to reaffirm the father's (and brother's) view: Women are not supposed to be strong themselves but to make strong men. What brought about this reversal? The immediately preceding passage surely provides the answer:

> Among the things I have recently read is Father's *Marriage* paper in the *Atlantic* – with great enjoyment of its manner & approval of its matter. I see he is becoming one of our prominent magazinists. . . . Whose are the three female papers on Woman [in the *Nation*]? They are "so very clever."[13]

Henry's high regard for his father's reactionary views on "Woman" and marriage, together with the *Nation's* antifeminist series of articles reporting a women's suffrage convention in Cleveland, forced the young writer to disown his own stated preference for independent women.

It was clearly going to be no easy task for Henry James to free himself of his family's views, or to trust his own intuitions. There was no way to reconcile his father's theories with Minnie's undeniably attractive force. James could manage this contradiction only by withdrawing (as in childhood) into the world of fiction, departing the material world, where ideas stood for clashing choice and action, and entering an alternative universe – narrative. James continued to adhere to his father's conservative doctrines, but the image that inspired his narrative imagination was the young, free, confrontational woman who was anathema to the father. The paradox is that James wrote about the free young life precisely because he himself was neither free nor strong, nor perhaps quite alive. This paradox not only helps explain why *The Portrait of a Lady* ultimately turns against freedom and strength, but also hints at the vampiristic nature of James's imagination.

Or is the better term necrophiliac? For the moment this imagination was born was the moment James opened his mother's letter containing the startling news that Minnie no longer lived. Minnie's death brought James to life by putting her identity wholly at the disposal of what may be called his monstrousness.

Removed from Her Own Heroic Treatment

Leon Edel has written well about the remarkable pair of letters James wrote his mother and older brother (not father, interestingly) after learning Minnie was dead – his repetitions, his uncharacteristically effusive outpourings, his recirclings around her image, his inability to stop writing (*Untried Years* 323–33).[14] In these letters we observe a mind invigorated to the point of giddiness and racing around a wild loop. James was of course suffering real grief over the death of a close friend, yet grief cannot account for what is most anomalous and disturbing in his passionate letters – the note of scarcely ashamed pleasure. His feeling was no ordinary *schadenfreude:* "The more I think of her the more perfectly satisfied I am to have her translated from this changing realm of fact to the steady realm of thought. There she may bloom into a beauty more radiant than our dull eyes will avail to contemplate" (to WJ, 29 March [1870]). The voice we hear in this sentence is not that of a bereaved friend but of an already sportive imagination. The passage shadows forth Minnie's destined apotheosis in Henry's future fiction.

The indecency of James's letters is so blatant that it is tempting not to take him literally. When we read that he was glad to think of Minnie "as unchained from suffering and embalmed forever in all our souls & lives,"¹⁵ we want to assume that the initial phrase expresses a benign satisfaction that her physical suffering has ended. But the context is Minnie's "absolutely defiant reality,"¹⁶ and elsewhere in the same letter there are hints that James was thinking of her *spiritual* suffering, her chronic unhappiness and dissatisfaction. He was glad all *that* was at an end. As he wrote his mother:

> On the dramatic fitness – as one may call it – of her early death it seems almost idle to dwell. No one who ever knew her can have failed to look at her future as a sadly insoluble problem – & we almost all had imagination enough to say, to murmur at least, that life – poor narrow life – contained no place for her. How all her conduct & character seem to have pointed to this conclusion – how profoundly inconsequential, in her history, continued life would have been! (26 March [1870])

This idea – that Minnie was so alive she was better off dead, that continued life would have brought only agony or anguish – became one of those fixed formulas that James repeated again and again for the rest of his life. He expressed it a few days later in letters to William and his friend Grace Norton: Minnie had been "a divinely restless spirit – essentially one of the 'irreconcilables;' and if she had lived to great age, I think it would have been as the victim and plaything of her constant generous dreams and dissatisfactions" (*Letters* 1: 231). Twice in his memoirs he expressed his certainty that if she had lived she would have found "the mystifications of life . . . much in excess of its contentments" (*Notes of a Son* 491).

This way of justifying Minnie's death compares most unfavorably with Emerson's response to the tragic drowning of another talented American woman, Margaret Fuller, three decades earlier:

> It is a bitter satire on our social order, just at present, the number of bad cases. Margaret Fuller having attained the highest & broadest culture that any American woman has possessed, came home with an Italian gentleman whom she had married, & their infant son, & perished by shipwreck on the rocks of Fire Island, off New York; and her friends said, "Well, on the whole, it was not so lamentable, & perhaps it was the best thing that could happen to her. For, had she lived, what could she have done?" (*Emerson in His Journals* 444)

The bitter satire applies to James also, I think, and to the many critics who have told us that Isabel grows up precisely by abandoning a callow Emersonian optimism – and that James is thus vastly superior to the naive Transcendentalist allegedly unendowed with a sense of tragedy.

The relief James found in Minnie's death strikes me, without qualification, as inhumane and sinister. The plain and brutal fact is that she wanted to live (*Notes of a Son* 515). James's contentment took no account of her own decided preference: There is a flat opposition between what pleased him and what she herself would have chosen. Her extinction as a willing and acting person did not solve what he saw as her problem (inevitable dissatisfaction with life) nearly so well as it solved his own. The most challenging person he knew had now become a manipulable object and could therefore no longer defy his father's views or do something unspeakable. Now she was Henry's to rethink, and as the evidence overwhelmingly indicates, he devoted enormous imaginative energy to this pleasing task. And inevitably, whenever he rethought her, he changed her, converted her into someone different or even opposite. The evidence lies in his letters, his fiction, and his final rewriting of her own letters to Gray.

One of the most fascinating conversions to observe is that of strength to weakness. James had "always looked forward . . . to the day when I should have regained my natural lead and our friendship on my part, at least might become more active & masculine."[17] Thus it comes as no surprise that in the months preceding Minnie's death he was to some extent animated and inspired by the image of her forced passivity: "I now become sensible how her image softened and sweetened by suffering & sitting patient & yet expectant, so far away from the great world with which so many of her old dreams & impulses were associated, has operated in my mind as a gentle incentive to action & enterprise" (to MJ, 26 March [1870]). About two months after writing this sickly passage, in which a fatal illness sweetens Minnie, making her more approachable, James used her imagined conversion to gentle suffering as the basis for one of his weakest stories, "Travelling Companions."[18] With this work James's fancied travels with Minnie in Italy materialized into two characters, a weak dandy who slowly acquires strength of character and a stereotyped strong-minded woman who undergoes an emotional collapse when her father dies. The conclusion has the same sick saccharinity as James's comments about "softened and sweetened" Minnie: The heroine's sudden infirmity serves somehow to strengthen the man, and they end up happily wedded. The trouble with this narrative is that the process of conversion went too far, fatally compromising Minnie's power and thus destroying the basis for any interest in her. "Travelling Companions" succinctly reveals one of James's dilemmas as a writer about women: how to create a heroine strong enough to be interesting and weak enough to be certifiably feminine.

Another trait of Minnie's that James had to convert to its opposite was her restlessness, or what he and others thought of as such. The grimly serious young woman who could not relax was one of the principal American stereotypes in the 1860s and 1870s; she shows up in dozens of novels and articles of the period. James was nervous about Minnie's closeness to type, and in writing his memoirs he insisted on her essential difference: To stress her "restless young mind, one felt from the first, was to place her, by a perversion of the truth, under the shadow of female 'earnestness' – for which she was much too unliteral and too ironic" (*Notes of a Son* 78).

At the same time that James had to keep Minnie uncontaminated by a type he and his family considered vulgar, he was driven to admit that she was "ever so restlessly . . . 'psychologic' " and to wonder (once again) "how her restlessness of spirit . . . was to be assuaged or 'met' by the common lot" (*Notes of a Son* 79, 462). But because the common lot to which she seemed destined was the one thing from which, in James's view, she had to be kept distinct, her restlessness had to be transmuted to repose (another way of saying she had to die). This transformation is painfully clear in Henry's 29 March 1870 letter to William. The beginning of the letter concedes the "vast amount of truth . . . in all the common-places that she used to provoke – that she was restless – that she was helpless – that she was unpractical." Near the end of the letter, however, Minnie has been worked over into something quite different and much more acceptable: "Among all my thoughts & conceptions I am sure I shall never have one of greater sereneness & purity: her image will preside in my intellect, in fact, as a sort of measure and standard of brightness and repose." But repose is the *opposite* of restlessness.

Precisely the same transformation works itself out in *The Portrait of a Lady*, which turns a spirited American girl into an unusually reserved lady. This realistic novel, like James's rethinking of Minnie, represents among other things a sustained denial of reality.

That the problem of Minnie's vulgarity weighed on James's mind can be seen in his shockingly thorough rewriting of her letters in *Notes of a Son and Brother*. He consistently dropped the humorous catchphrases she used in quotation marks – "& no mistake," "let me down easy." Plain words or expressions got replaced by more flavored ones: Where Minnie called the weather "fine," James substituted "splendid" or "grand." Where she wrote, "the only thing that I can say," James substituted proper diction: "The only advice I can give you." Minnie's straightforward remarks about George Eliot – "Do you like her too? I don't remember ever hearing you speak of her" – were modulated to this: "But I don't remember ever to have heard *you* speak of her" (Habegger, "James's Rewriting"). This highly mannered rewriting added an abruptly haughty invidiousness to Minnie's prose, turning the writer into a different kind of person, more cultivated and on edge.

In dealing with Minnie's forwardness, restlessness, and uncultivated diction, James betrayed an unmistakable desire to transform her into someone new and improved. In one respect, however, it appears that James's reading of her blamed her for a trait she probably did not have, namely, a supposed penchant for theorizing. From the vantage of old age, he attributed to her a vague "enthusiasm of humanity" – the same thing that animated some of his foolish reformers in *The Bostonians*. Minnie became the "amateur priestess of rash speculation" for him, and he would recall with pity how she could "range in her groping, her naturally immature and unlighted way from end to end of the scale" (*Notes of a Son* 79, 78, 462). The pity James expressed for her reckless speculativeness appears to be a mild version of his father's scorn for the "absurd, abominable opinionativeness" (*Literary Remains* 62) of mankind, especially that half Henry Sr. regarded as weaker in intellect. Henry Jr.'s sense of Minnie also betrays the lurking stereotype of the undisciplined and ill-prepared female theorist who ventures into realms of thought that are too demanding for her. This image materializes in Chapter 6 of *The Portrait of a Lady*, which informs us that Isabel has a bloated collection of untested theories. James's Minnie and Isabel exemplify the old notion of woman as a cave of winds, her thoughts blown about by "a dozen capricious forces" (*Portrait* 28).

But this emphasis on rash theory did a serious injustice to the young woman we can reconstruct from Minnie Temple's surviving letters, which prove that she was not nearly so lofty, theoretical, or serious as Isabel Archer. Minnie's postadolescent opinions tended to be essentially down to earth, often rather negative or skeptical, expressing her unshakable sense of things. In her confrontation with Henry James, Sr., she set the needs of "my case" against his highly allegorical and constrictive preachments. There was little of the Jameses' own morbidity in Minnie, who at times appears to be anything but "restlessly . . . 'psychologic' " in her letters. One of the things she enjoyed in her correspondence with Gray was "that delightful immunity I have enjoyed so much with you, from sickening introspection, analysis of myself & yourself, exhausting & nauseating subjectivity, with which most of my other friends see fit to deluge me" (30 November 1869). (This passage, written shortly after Minnie returned from the Jameses in Cambridge, may hint at the nature of her conversations with William.) It is true that Minnie engaged in a good deal of religious speculation, when she would succumb to what she called "the old questioning spirit, the demon of the 'Why, Whence, & Whither' " (25 January 1870). But in every instance the upshot would be that she shrugged off the other world in favor of this one.

The transformations through which James put Minnie belong to various categories and served different purposes. Some changes, as in his editing of her letters, were cosmetic, intended to present her in a better light; some amounted to apparently unconscious distortions that reflected James's own psychological needs; and some represented a deliberate appropriation of Minnie for the purposes of narrative fiction. In many instances, however, it is impossible to say which of these three motives is dominant. One cannot, in other words, establish a clear demarcation between James's experience of Minnie Temple and his creation of Isabel Archer, and the consequences of this blurring are far-reaching and call into question in a fundamental way the usual assumption that we can separate a writer's fiction from his or her experience.

Thus the very terms in which James grieved for, yet celebrated, Minnie's dying anticipated some sort of issue in narrative: "She was at any rate the helpless victim & toy of her own intelligence – so that there is positive relief in thinking of her being removed from her own heroic treatment & placed in kinder hands" (HJ to WJ, 29 March [1870], MH-H). This sentence speaks of Minnie not as one who lived and died, one who can be thought of in some intuitive sense as a creature or a being in nature, but as the *author of herself,* writer and heroine together. Her mistake, that of the too ambitious artist, was to dream of too heroic a treatment of herself. But there is no tragedy, nothing has been wasted, Minnie is not *really* dead, James's sentence says, for the uncompleted manuscript has now been transferred to a more indulgent writer. She is in her cousin's hands, and he will rewrite and complete the narrative, and in good time the perfected edition of *Minnie* will be published.

The reason why James was so exhilarated by his cousin's death is that the youthful writer saw her as an unfinished manuscript he could turn into a masterpiece. After receiving the sad–happy news of her death he realized that the heroine of this ambitious fragment bore *all* the distinguishing marks of the major character type in American fiction of the 1860s: She was parentless, she was outspokenly fond of her liberty, she was intelligent, earnest, at risk in the world, and she was doomed. Of course James had not known she was doomed until he learned of her death, and then, as his letters home indicate, he discovered with overwhelming excitement that *he* had known a true agonist heroine.

The image of Minnie thus became assimilated in James's mind with a body of fiction. On the one hand she detoxified women's novels for him, so that he no longer felt the stiff resentment he reveals in his first short stories[19] and reviews, but on the other hand, what he felt about the modern heroine led him to depreciate Minnie – to emphasize her theories, to make Minnie–Isabel decide to marry a middle-aged man, to put her in the agonist's story of the unhappily married wife. Three years before Minnie died, James complained in his review of Anne Moncure Crane's *Opportunity* that, however attractive all these young independent heroines might be, they inevitably did something stupid before the end, something "utterly pedantic and unnatural and insupportable" (*Literary Criticism* 1: 599), which destroyed one's sympathetic interest. Here once again we can sense why Minnie's death relieved her cousin: The character he now saw as a true heroic type could no longer make her fatal mistake. And again we sense why he would insist for the rest of his life that she was fortunate to die young.

So it was that James came into possession of his most important character, the restlessly searching young woman who struggles against a smothering ambience. Minnie's death resolved the young man's personal contradictions by turning them into the stuff of a professional career. She enabled him simultaneously to distance himself from an oppressive father-philosopher and to establish a productive relation with the agonists' treatment of womanhood in fetters. And just as there was no longer any danger that Minnie could displease the young writer, neither was there much chance that he would now be troubled by the agonists. Elizabeth Stoddard had written her third and last novel, the tottering *Temple House* (1867). Louisa May Alcott, burned by the poor reception of *Moods* in 1865 and overwhelmed by the success of *Little Women* in 1868, had turned into a writer of children's fiction. Adeline Whitney, slipping from the level of *Faith Gartney's Girlhood* (1863) and *The Gayworthys* (1865), had declined into a vigilant preceptor of adolescent girls who might be tempted to think there was some fun to be gotten out of life. Anne Moncure Crane Seemuller, now married and living in New York, would bring out her third and last novel, the scandalous *Reginald Archer,* one year after Minnie Temple's death, and would then move to Germany and die there in 1872 at the age of thirty-four. Only Rebecca Harding Davis of all the agonists would continue to grind out adult fiction – novels so clumsy and earnest that there was no need for anyone to pay attention to them. The agonists were a lost generation and Minnie Temple was dead and Henry James, Jr., was left in charge of all the independent heroines who had delighted and worried him.

Chapter 7

The Fatherless Heroine and the Filial Son

Deep Background for The Portrait of a Lady

Among the many ways of summing up Isabel Osmond's earlier life there is one that goes like this:

The late Mr. Archer, indulgent and affectionate, provided his favorite daughter with numerous advantages, the chief of which was not to bring her up too strictly. But he was somewhat irresponsible, and once, when Isabel was in her eleventh year (thirteenth in the serial version), he left her in Switzerland with a French maid, who then ran off with a Russian. A sturdy adventurer even then, the girl was quite certain she had no cause to worry or feel deserted.

Now in her early twenties, her father having died, Isabel has grown up to be a remarkably independent young woman who seems ready and eager to take on the world. For the time being, however, she has secluded herself in a remote room of the same house where her father died. She is undergoing a harsh Prussian discipline, forcing her mind "to advance, to halt, to retreat."[1] Mostly retreat, it would seem, for while "the large number of those to whom he owed money" (26) feel that Mr. Archer got what he deserved in his early, unhappy death, Isabel naively worships the "handsome, much-loved father. . . . It was a great good fortune to have been his daughter; Isabel was even proud of her parentage" (26).

At Gardencourt Isabel is lively and alert and appears to have outlived her bereavement, but she is still wearing black – "more than a year" (15) after Mr. Archer's death. (Later, after her child dies, she discards her mourning within six months [343].) When Ralph Touchett makes a joke about her adoption by his mother, he seems to touch a nerve and the young woman briefly loses her composure: " 'Adopted me?' The girl stared, and her blush came back to her, together with a momentary look of pain, which gave her interlocutor some alarm. He had under-estimated the effect of his words. . . . 'Oh, no; she has not adopted me,' she said. 'I am not a candidate for adoption' " (15). Obviously, she must have it understood that she will remain in charge of her life. But what does that momentary look of pain signify?

Months later, visiting Gilbert Osmond's apartments on Bellosguardo for the first time, Isabel is fascinated by his obedient, porcelain-like daughter. Pansy is fifteen years old and physically mature (309) but somehow remains a little girl. Isabel is twenty-two. Osmond is forty. They are all sitting together. Suddenly, the devoted father does something: He has Pansy get up "out of her chair, . . . making her stand between his knees, leaning against him while he passed his arm round her little waist. The child fixed her eyes on Isabel with a still, disinterested gaze, which seemed void of an intention, but conscious of an attraction" (225). The silent display has no heat or pressure, only a cool, still limpidity: A childish grown-up is required, in the presence of a stranger, to stand between her father's knees, her waist encircled by his arm, her mind emptied of all volition or interest and containing only a passive responsiveness. The eyes of the child-woman are wide open, but she does not seem to be fully awake. We wonder what cruel operation has been performed on her to make her so perfectly responsive to another's will. Is the will that has shaped her engaged in another project at this very moment? Could Osmond be using Pansy to reach Isabel in some sinister fashion?

It seems so, for when we next observe father and daughter in this scene, standing now but still entwined, the heroine has begun to mimic the feelings that presumably possess the serene daughter:

> Mr. Osmond stood there . . . with his hands in the pockets of his jacket, and his daughter, who had now locked her arm into one of his own, clinging to him and looking up, while her eyes moved from his own face to Isabel's. Isabel waited, with a certain unuttered contentedness, to have her movements directed. (227)

Again, though there is not the slightest hint of applied force, the father appears to be in total control. He does not even have to use his hands. Pansy seemingly takes the initiative of clinging, locking to him, and mysteriously, Isabel has begun to want to do the same, in spite of her insistence not too long ago that she was not a candidate for adoption. She too would like to be a passive daughter, and she feels a novel embarrassment about her undirected independence: "I am rather ashamed of my plans; I make a new one every day" (231). Something tells her she is not at all the right sort of woman.

The courtship begins. Since we have already witnessed the scene where Madame Merle offers Isabel to Osmond, we are anxious to know how the young woman will regard him. We soon find out, in Chapter 26:

She liked to think of him. She had carried away an image from her visit to his hill-top which her subsequent knowledge of him did nothing to efface and which happened to take her fancy particularly – the image of a quiet, clever, sensitive, distinguished man, strolling on a moss-grown terrace above the sweet Val d'Arno, and holding by the hand a little girl whose sympathetic docility gave a new aspect to childhood. The picture was not brilliant, but she liked its lowness of tone, and the atmosphere of summer twilight that pervaded it. It seemed to tell a story – a story of the sort that touched her most easily; to speak of a serious choice . . . ; of a lonely, studious life in a lovely land; of an old sorrow . . . ; a feeling of pride . . . ; a care for beauty and perfection . . . a quaint, half-anxious, half-helpless fatherhood. (242)

The young woman's fancy has been taken captive by a resonant and compelling image. She is not in love yet, does not know what it feels like to desire another person. She has simply seen – been shown – a picture she cannot get out of her mind, a picture of a father and his daughter. She likes to think about this picture, to return to it in the way in which one savors a pleasing daydream or rereads a favorite passage in a novel. She has found – or been handed – a kind of fetish, one that seems "to tell a story." The phrases lightly sketching in this story have the hyped-up organ tones of a certain kind of fiction – "lonely, studious life," "old sorrow." Vague in plot, the story nevertheless evokes a strong emotional response and carries a special and distinguished aura. A choice dream has magically come to life before the eyes of the free American girl. She is not in the dream, of course, for the simple reason that she is not distinguished. She is not like the refined man and the docile girl. *He* would never abandon her in her eleventh year. *She* would never be restless. They do not change their plans every day. How comforting just to finger the quiet picture they make.

But why is the father so sad, "half-anxious, half-helpless"? Is there something he needs that the fond dreamer might be able to contribute? Is there a way for the dreamer to get into the dream? "I should like to see you when you are tired and satiated," Osmond says to her. "I shall prefer you in that state" (269).

Isabel and the Masterful Guardian

After surveying the contemporary comment on James's fiction, Linda J. Taylor observes that *The Portrait* "made him famous all across the [American] continent. . . . It was James's most widely reviewed work and created a peak in his reputation" (xv). The most detailed record of a reader's

contemporary response to the novel is in Constance Fenimore Woolson's
12 February 1882 letter to the author. By turns fulsome and resentful, this
letter gave special attention to the spectacle of Osmond and Pansy and to
Isabel's responsive fancy. Noting how Osmond poses with "his little
daughter, in her short white frock," Woolson lavished praise on James's
rendition of Isabel's capitivated imagination: "And then the impression
summed up in chapter 26 – page 242 – how perfectly one understands
the effect – sees what she saw, feels what she felt. It was precisely the sort
of picture to win an Isabel. And it almost seemed to me as if you were the
only man who has ever divined it" (HJ, *Letters* 3: 534). This obliquely
confessional passage, with its rather coy substitution of the impersonal
"one" for "I," shows how profoundly James's exhibition of Isabel's fantasy life could speak to a contemporary woman reader. James had not
invented, he had "divined," this fantasy life, and Woolson became almost
abject in registering her shock of recognition.

James's reply, if he wrote one, has been destroyed. His one surviving
comment on the effect that Osmond and his daughter have on Isabel's
imagination is to be found in his 1914 memoir, *Notes of a Son and Brother,*
where he acknowledges that he himself had been inspired by the picture
of two friends, Francis Boott and his daughter Lizzie, in their Florentine
villa:

> A not other than lonely and bereft American, addicted to the arts
> and endowed for them, housed to an effect of long expatriation in a
> massive old Florentine villa with a treasured and tended little daugh-
> ter by his side, *that* was the germ which for reasons beyond my
> sounding the case of Frank Boott had been appointed to plant deep
> down in my vision of things. (*Notes of a Son* 481–82)

Like the preface to *The Portrait,* this passage appears to reveal a private
source of inspiration, but in fact the door James opens merely discloses
another door that remains closed. The Bootts furnished James with his
image – fine. But why did the image make such an impression on him?
"For reasons beyond my sounding." James, as long-ago dreamer-up of
The Portrait, here seems almost as helplessly responsive as Isabel is. He
liked to dwell on a certain vision, and he had (or has) no idea why. His
use of the passive voice – "had been appointed" – even hints that some
external agency had been directing his imagination, much as Osmond
directs the heroine's.

One explanation why the father–daughter image gripped Isabel, and
James, *and* Woolson, is that it was a resonant *public* image of the time,
especially for novel readers. Isabel was the heroine of a thousand novels,
the independent orphan-heroine in search of the sorrowing father-lover.
Neither the momentary look of pain nor the image that seems to tell a

story was original with *The Portrait*. Both belonged to a type of heroine and to a nineteenth-century story formula containing her. Osmond is the paternal lover who already has a daughter – like Mr. Lloyd in Catharine Sedgwick's *New-England Tale* (1822) or Rochester in *Jane Eyre* (1847). Isabel is the girl who suddenly finds herself in an unprotected state, who is forced to take care of herself after her father dies or in some other way deserts her, and who often finds consolation in the end by marrying this same poor lost father. But there are differences, chiefly because Isabel is a metaheroine as well as a heroine. That is, *The Portrait* tells the traditional orphan-heroine's story, but it also is concerned to enclose, sum up, assess this story. W. D. Howells pointed out in his perceptive 1882 essay on James that unlike George Eliot's Dorothea Brooke, who has "grand aims," Isabel has "beautiful dreams" ("Henry James, Jr." 26), and this distinction hints at the critical nature of James's narrative, which is *about* the treacherous feminine imagination that had created a vast Anglo-American tradition of fiction.

In the American 1850s, when James grew to be a passionate reader, the heroine of almost all the most popular novels was a girl, frequently a little girl, whose sudden homelessness required her to look after herself. She inevitably matured with amazing rapidity, learning how to provide her own livelihood, acquiring leverage over those who were older and more powerful, and resolving terrible moral dilemmas all by herself and even settling one or two riddles of the ages as she went. But she often fell secretly in love with the man of the house where she happened to be residing, or with the preceptor who kindly supervised her education, or with a strong, older, manly, unmarried minister or doctor, and in the end she married this masterly guardian. Most of the novels do not seem to be conscious of the contradiction between the juvenile dependency her final union implies and her preceding hard-won independence.

The younger and more anxious generation of American women novelists who tried to work out the contradictions of this fiction all focused on the tormented relationship between a remarkably original and self-reliant girl and a strong, older man. In James's reviews of the agonists' novels, however, it was precisely their treatment of this material that aroused his youthful ire. His unpublished notice of *Two Men* sarcastically observed that its romance between a girl and a "middle-aged man" was "quite after the actual taste." With *Emily Chester,* he noted that Max Crampton "is the repetition of a type that has of late years obtained great favor with lady novelists: the ugly, rich, middle-aged lover." With *Moods* the young man's disdain overflowed: "We are utterly weary of stories about precocious little girls. . . . They are always the precursors of a . . . middle-aged lover." James had a deep hatred for this quiet, understated tyrant, who "spends this time in breaking the hearts and the wills of demure little school-girls" (*Literary Criticism* 1: 617, 590, 189, 190), and he could not understand why so many heroines and women novelists let themselves be browbeaten by him. Other reviewers frequently objected to heroes of the Rochester type, but James seems to have felt a special animus, as if he had seen a particularly chilling example of disguised paternalistic oppression from very close up, or had himself struggled against it.

What James attempted in his first published long narrative, *Watch and Ward* (1871), was to purify this disturbing story about the precocious girl and her middle-aged lover. The novel begins when the irresponsible Mr. Lambert shoots himself, in this way abandoning both his debts and his little girl, Nora – much as Mr. Archer has abandoned Isabel, first in Switzerland and then by dying. Kind Roger Lawrence, who lives on a patrimony and travels to Peru if not all over the world (as James had accused the middle-aged lover of doing) pities the miserably orphaned child and tries to comfort her:

> "Do you remember my taking you last night in my arms?" It was his fancy that, for an answer, she faintly blushed. He laid his hand on her head and smoothed away her thick disordered hair. She submitted to his consoling touch with a plaintive docility. He put his arm round her waist. An irresistible sense of her childish sweetness, of her tender feminine promise, stole softly into his pulses. ("Watch and Ward" 238)

How suggestive the passage is, especially if we look ahead to Osmond's use of Pansy's waist, or to the way Isabel looks to him for comfort after losing her own father. Is little twelve-year-old Nora in the same danger that Isabel and Pansy will be? *Of course not*, the whole narrative insists. Roger is decent and liberal, *kind, kind, kind*, as the stage version of Christopher Newman would proclaim himself to be. Roger gives Nora perfect freedom to choose, and if he hopes all the while that she will choose to satisfy *his* pulses by eventually marrying him, he staunchly refuses to force her choice.

But *Watch and Ward* was in most respects a failure. It could not be published as a book until James's later novels created a market, and its representation of life violated some of James's most vigorously expressed convictions. Five years earlier, reviewing Adeline Whitney's *The Gayworthys*, he had showed great indignation at those narratives (such as Thackeray's *Henry Esmond*) that grounded erotic love in attachments originating in childhood: "If we desire to learn the various circumstances under which love-making may be conducted, let us not repair to the nursery and the school-room. . . . The age for Daphnis and Chloe has passed. Passion and sentiment must always be more or less intelligent not to shock the public taste" (*Literary Criticism* 1: 637). It was James's objective in *Watch and Ward* to produce a fully conscious – "intelligent" – representation of nursery lovemaking, yet in spite of the fact that the novel concerns the adult's feeling for the child more than the child's for the adult, it finally conveys the same sense of perverse innocence as the fiction James had criticized. Roger glides with suspicious ease from Nora's "childish sweetness" to her "tender feminine promise." Then there is his Humbert Humbert-like question about "last night in my arms." These and other glaring ambiguities in the novel derive from the problematic nature of the task James had set himself, that is, providing a refined version of the vulgar guardian–ward romance. Instead of expressing his own strong anger at the middle-aged lover, James was somewhat foolishly seeking to rehabilitate him.

For James, the logical step after the pretty-pretty *Watch and Ward* was to provide his next orphan-heroine with both a puerile love for a father figure and an independent source of income and *then* see what she would do. That James took this step in *The Portrait,* however, does not mean he was merely continuing his earlier, misguided enterprise of purifying women's fiction. It would have been captious for him to continue hammering away at the women's genre, even if that was where the vitality and much of the market lay, and it would have been opportunistic to override his own masculine sense of the servility in much feminine fiction. The decisive turn of mind that eventuated in *The Portrait* was a final impatience with the agonists. If all the precociously independent heroines would insist on falling for a middle-aged monster, all right then, his own heroine would do so with a vengeance. And if it was not possible to renovate the old masterly lover, then he should be made as quiet and sinister and poisonous as possible.

Hence James worked out his most ambitious novel to date precisely by developing – not eliminating – the falsities in the genre to which it belonged. He refused to take at face value either the benevolent distinction of the middle-aged lover or the heroine's proclaimed love of liberty. Let her sense of freedom weigh on her so heavily that she begins to dream of confinement, of daughterly surrender.[2] Restore the purse that Nora loses at the end of *Watch and Ward,* or better, have some unexpected inheritance be the very thing that causes her true nature to declare itself, so that a hidden internal bondage subverts her gloriously untrammeled ideal. And shouldn't there be a generous friend who naively believes in the heroine's independence (for James had been this person while reading Crane's *Opportunity* and while writing *Watch and Ward*), someone whose hopefulness only ensures her self-entrapment?

It is because *The Portrait* emerged from a *denial* of the agonist premise that the heroine truly wishes to be free that the novel picked up and revised so many agonist hallmarks, from Crane's three novels in particular. Her first heroine, Emily Chester, had roundly declared: "If I were to marry, I should die, I should suffocate! . . . I have lived a free life too long, not to revolt from the very shadow of a chain! . . . It is the aim of my existence to become a self-contained, self-sufficing woman, depending on myself for happiness" (*Emily Chester* 44–45). Isabel Archer says the same thing, the difference being that her creator nudges the reader toward a recognition of the spread-eagle oratory. James's implication is that her noble resolution not to marry is stagy and unfelt: " 'I like my liberty too much. If there is a thing in the world that I am fond of,' Isabel went on, with a slight recurrence of . . . grandeur . . . 'it is my personal independence' " (139). At twenty-two Isabel is older than Harvey in *Opportunity* and the other precocious heroines, yet she retains her adolescent callowness. "Her thoughts were a tangle of vague outlines" (42) in the first edition, and in the serial "her head was full of premature convictions and unproportioned images" ("Portrait" 46: 741).

In reviewing *Emily Chester,* James showed strong disdain for the heroine's calm stateliness. The author, he believed, had wished to create a "perfect" woman who would be "high-toned, high-spirited, high-souled," and he could not help belittling the heroine's pretensions: "When anything particularly disagreeable happens, she becomes very pale and calm and statuesque" (*Literary Criticism* 1: 589). Isabel would be much the same. She insists on holding her head high long after her marriage has failed, has an a priori "nobleness of imagination," and feels "an unquenchable desire to think well of herself." Her wish to be always in the right represents her author's reinterpretation of Emily's perfection, and indeed of a whole line of women's heroines. The grandeur is generic; what James adds is the skeptical perspective that calls attention to the absurdity of Isabel's claim of superiority. In Chapter 34, where Ralph criticizes her fiancé, in the process giving Isabel her most disagreeable moment to date, she rebuffs him by taking a "heroic line" (300) and sustaining an air of "careful calmness" (304). The dignified composure slips from time to time, but it fools her into thinking she is being rather magnanimous to her poor misguided cousin. In the end, Ralph is chilled by his failure to make contact with her, and *she* feels exalted. This, one of James's finest scenes, reflects his canny sense of the noble nickle-plated mask worn by so many women's heroines of the time.

This scene exhibits another of Isabel's aspects that James took from *Emily Chester* and its congeners – the imperviousness of a theoretical emotion. One reason James detested Crane's first novel was that he regarded the heroine's passion as wholly unreal, something cooked up for the sake of "a theory" and then passed off as honest feeling. This view distorts Emily's attraction to Frederick and disgust for Max, but it applies beautifully to Isabel. There is so much infatuated nonsense in her system, as when she tells Warburton she cannot marry him because to do so would be to try to escape her fate, that it is hard to believe she could possibly reconnect with her spontaneous feelings. (Of course, the point is that she can do so only at the cost of terrible pain brought on by her own blindness.) She has just enough insight into herself to fear she has lost "the natural and reasonable emotions of life" (98), but she quickly dismisses this thought. Similarly, in Chapter 42, when she wonders whether she married "on a factitious theory" (374), she blushes and tries to forget the shocking truth. The theory-thick approach to life, which James detected in the agonists, is shown to be an all but inescapable slough.

Then there is Isabel's need for a master, a need harking back to the precocious girl who says (in James's review of Alcott's *Moods*) "Yes, sir" and "No, sir" to the middle-aged lover. In *The American* (1877) Christopher Newman's naive dream of freeing the perfect European woman from her ancient entanglements had been frustrated by her preference for the discipline of convent walls. *The Portrait,* in one sense a spin-off, had as its original working title *The Americana.*³ Its protagonist, the "perfect" American heroine who loudly announces her freedom, would finally choose a similar form of confinement for herself, and again the walls would be palace walls and convent walls. But there are differences: *The Portrait*'s convent is not so much a female refuge from worldly pressures as an indoctrination center that does the work of willful tyrants, in Pansy's case transforming an irregularly conceived child into a model girl-woman. Behind those walls Pansy has been "impregnated with the idea of submission, which was due to any one who took the tone of authority" (205). "Impregnated" – the word tells us that *The Portrait*'s convent offers a far less effective retreat from the world than the one Claire de Cintré chooses. Pansy's tampered-with mind is now "void of an intention" but "conscious of an attraction" as her daddy poses with her. The fact that Isabel's far more lively mind is captivated by this appallingly tractable daughter sums up James's muted lesson: Even the freest American woman dreams of submission to a dominating master.

It is well to remember that during the months James's plans for *The Portrait* became sufficiently firm to be mentioned in letters to Howells at the *Atlantic,* James admitted to his brother, William, that *Daniel Deronda* was "a great *exposé* of the female mind."⁴ Juliet McMaster is one of several readers who argue that Isabel is drawn to the opposite of freedom – "death, and immobility, and suffering" (50). Sandra K. Fischer follows R. W. Stallman, William Bysshe Stein, and others in arguing that Isabel is repressed and prefers enclosed security to passion: "What Caspar shows Isabel at the end in a flash of illumination is that vulgar street – what she might call the base or common passions – and it confirms her in her terror" (52). These reactions originate in the daughter's abandonment. Because Isabel feels much more deserted by her father than she realizes, she is dangerously responsive to the studied self-portrait of the mutually dependent father and daughter. Freedom and fatherlessness have split the heroine into two disconnected halves – a partly factitious determination to be her own master and a dark fascination with images of dominance and submission. That is why she abruptly begins to imitate a fifteen-year-old girl's devotion to a forty-year-old father's every whim, and then takes him as her preceptor. "You know everything, and I know nothing" (270).

Thus, embedded in the first thirty-five chapters of *The Portrait* is a certain grim thesis about the cause of the subjection of women. Although not an exposé in tone of "the female mind," these chapters are emphatically an exposé in substance, as Woolson recognized. According to the preface, written in 1906, the compositional problems that exercised James involved questions of substance much less than questions of presentation – especially the difficulty of getting the reader to sympathize with the "mere slim shade of an intelligent but presumptuous girl" (*Literary Criticism* 2: 1077). His basic problem was not how to build a lengthy narrative around a young woman's development. There were already thousands of such narratives, and readers loved them. The real difficulty was how to keep the reader sympathetic to a heroine *intentionally* endowed with the kind of instability that leads to grave self-betrayals. James addressed this problem with all his adroitness and in the process produced a work of fiction as long on beauty as it is short on moral candor.[5] In the end he produced a diminished picture of human freedom: Isabel's treacherous servility leads to a very conservative sort of responsibility, which finds freedom only in the acceptance of traditional forms.

Reading *Daniel Deronda* several months before he first mentioned his own ambitious new novel, James was put off by the moralizing commentary – "the defects of later growth, of the author's style."[6] Constantius, the character closest to James in his sparkling "Daniel Deronda: A Conversation," feels that George Eliot's novel showed "a want of tact" in making "moral reflections" and setting forth " 'views' upon life" (*Literary Criticism* 1: 986). In both its moral reflections and its story content, James's novel was to be the antithesis of its discursive feminine forebears and rivals. Not just tactful, it was to be a deliberately *un*forthcoming narrative, one that carefully veils its "views."

Isabel and Minnie Temple

But *The Portrait of a Lady* emerged from more than James's critical response to an Anglo-American tradition of women's fiction. James created the novel by fusing his reading with elements of his personal life – his close friendship with his remarkable cousin Minnie Temple, his tremendous respect for his father and his philosophy of marriage, and his own curious feeling of impotence.

Most commentators seem disposed to assume that Isabel more or less reproduces Minnie. In December 1880 James's friend Grace Norton, having read only the first two numbers of the serial, wondered whether Isabel was a portrait of the cousin. James's reply constitutes his one surviving comment on the closeness of his representation:

> You are both right & wrong about Minnie Temple. I had her in mind & there is in the heroine a considerable infusion of my impression of her remarkable nature. But the thing is not a portrait. Poor Minny was essentially *incomplete* & I have attempted to make my young woman more rounded, more finished.

One might assume from this that Minnie was incomplete because she died young, or was ill and confined, or was prevented from traveling to Italy, or some such thing, and that in his novel James imagined what her life might have been if allowed to go on in altered circumstances. James may have meant this, but he also meant something quite different and more grandiose, as his next sentence hints. "In truth every one, in life, is incomplete, & it is the mark of art that in reproducing them one feels the desire to fill them out, to justify them, as it were."[7] The claim here is that Minnie was incomplete not just because of her personal history but because of a defect endemic to all humanity. By the same token, James's desire to reproduce her, to fill her out, had nothing to do with his peculiar nature and relationship with her. Instead, he was simply enacting an impulse characteristic of artists in general, the impulse not to create an imaginary person but rather to perfect, and thus "justify," an actual one. Yet even as James wrote this shocking word, which would be perfectly in character for the meddling scientist who seeks to perfect his wife in Hawthorne's tale "The Birthmark," James backed away from his haughty and transcendent claim, adding the mitigating phrase "as it were."

If we compare James's heroine to what we can reconstruct of his cousin, it becomes clear that he had cause to feel uneasy about his highhanded art. Isabel embodies a drastic reinterpretation of Minnie's character from a definite point of view. Although no author, no matter how realistic, has an obligation to reproduce his models accurately, the alterations he chooses to make can be extremely revealing about the nature of his imaginative work.

Minnie's "pet theory" (fair copy, MT to John Chipman Gray, 7 January 1869, MH-H) was that one should always hold out for a chance at the best, no matter how remote, rather than settle for second best. James in Chapter 6 describes Isabel's version of this high integrity as one of her "many theories" (41):

> The girl had a certain nobleness of imagination which rendered her a good many services and played her a great many tricks. She spent half her time in thinking of beauty, and bravery, and magnanimity. . . . She had an infinite hope that she should never do anything wrong. . . . she had seen very little of the evil of the world, but she had seen women who lied and who tried to hurt each other. Seeing such things had quickened her high spirit; it seemed right to scorn them. Of course the danger of a high spirit is the danger of inconsistency. . . . Isabel . . . flattered herself that such contradictions would never be observed in her own conduct. (42–43)

This passage is heavily premonitory, looking forward to Isabel's long and painful effort to maintain a noble, impassive front after her marriage goes bad. But there is no evidence of any kind that Minnie got in trouble by applying her favorite theory, or that she ever had cause to modify or regret it. "I believe it more than ever, every day I live" (fair copy, MT to Gray, 29 August 1869, MH-H), she wrote six months before her death at the age of twenty-four. Less than two months from the end, she was able to dismiss the fevered religious conversion induced in her by Henry Sr.'s denunciation of her "*pride & conceit*" (fair copy, MT to Gray, 25 January 1870 and 27 January postscript, MH-H). When James endowed Isabel with an untested need always to think well of herself, he was effectively deflating his cousin's rigorous integrity. He was saying that this firm self-reliance was a schoolgirlish pose, that it could not possibly survive intact, and should not.

There is a very interesting difference between the real woman's known opinions and Isabel's "many theories." Minnie's characteristic mode of thought seems to have been practical and antitheoretical. She resisted Henry Sr.'s indoctrination because it "didn't touch my case a bit – didn't give me the least comfort or practical help" (fair copy, MT to Gray, 25 January 1870, MH-H). Her tragic mentality, her refusal to accept any sort of "happy Rest this side of Eternity" (ibid., postscript of 27 January 1870, MH-H), was far removed from Isabel's "fixed determination to regard the world as a place of brightness, of free expansion, of irresistible action" (42). James transformed a person who had a down-to-earth openness toward experience and a proven independence of thought into a character who tended to lose touch with her feelings, to dwell on a complicated self-image involving noble and picturesque attitudes.

The easy, comradely tone of Minnie's letters to Gray marks a key difference in the two women's male friendships. Minnie was on close terms with several highly masculine men, William James and Oliver Wendell Holmes, Jr., among them. Although these friendships were at times tense and involved, they were considerably less stiff and more reciprocal than Isabel's relationships with Goodwood and Lord Warburton, whose romantic pursuit (to some extent required by the novel form itself) puts her on the defensive. In old age Gray looked back on his acquaintance with Minnie in these terms (as reported by Alice H. James): "I . . . was never in love with her. 'I liked better to write to her than to see her.' She was the only *just* woman I have ever known. Her friendship is one of the things in my life which I best like to remember" (AHJ to HJ, 17 May 1913, MH-H). In "completing" Minnie, James retained that prickliness that caused Gray to prefer to communicate with her in letters rather than face to face. Similarly, young men are "afraid" of Isabel, believing "that some special preparation was required for talking with her" (28). But James eliminated Minnie's capacity for dealing with forceful men on a basis of relaxed equality.

Surviving documents have nothing to say about Minnie's memories of and feelings for her father, who died in 1854, when she was eight. But she remembered her mother (who died later that year) with warm feelings, recalling in her teens that the face of a brother killed at Chancellorsville had a "*sweet heavenly* smile . . . which always made me think of heaven and Mama" (Rosamond Gilder's typescript, MT to Helena de Kay, 12 or 13 May 1863, Gilder Papers). Isabel's mother, however, is not mentioned, her father being the parent she fondly remembers.

When Minnie attended a young ladies' academy in 1862 and 1863, she shared a room with Helena de Kay, and the two girls became extremely close friends.[8] During vacations they engaged in the intense "school-girl correspondence" (*Morgesons* 122) that was all but an established institution. Minnie's surviving letters are lavish in their expression of affection. "And now what is my own darling doing tonight?" begins one, and further on: "Good Night my Blessing. I will try and do without your dear, *motherly* care tonight, but it will be very hard" (Rosamond Gilder's typescript, 3 April 1863, Gilder Papers). Another says, "I am afraid you need a little 'titeru' which I will also have in readiness for you upon your arrival" (Rosamond Gilder's typescript, 12 July 1862, Gilder Papers). Following a rebellion of some kind by the pupils in the spring 1863 term, Margaret Robertson, one of the two sisters in charge of the institution, sent letters to both Helena's mother and Henry James, Sr., with whom Minnie was to spend spring break. Mrs. de Kay promptly wrote her daughter, advising that Minnie's character was still unsettled and her influence should be resisted. The schoolmistress's letter to the Jameses was read by Minnie during her Newport visit. Judging by her report to Helena, this letter warned that the two girls were so close they did each

other "a *great deal* of harm," encouraging each other to "forget . . . the
rest of the human race." Minnie's blunt response: "Ha! ha! ha! – I don't
agree with her."[9] Nineteen-year-old Henry James was at home then; a
letter written decades later to Helena confirms that he was aware of "your
young, your younger intimacy" with Minnie (*Letters*, ed. Lubbock, 2:
417). The relationship between Isabel Archer and *her* longtime best
friend, Henrietta, lacks this intimate and juvenile character. Isabel seems
to have lost much of her affection for her friend, being chiefly concerned
to resist her intrusive advice and criticism. It is as if James has put into
effect the teacher's wishes and separated Minnie from a bad feminine
influence, weakening the sororal relationship along with the maternal
and fraternal ones. In the end Isabel's closest bond is with her male
cousin.

Divorce as a topic is strangely absent from Isabel's life and mind, and
yet it showed up in an interesting way in Minnie's. In 1869 one of her
friends, Ella Dietz Clymer, apparently attempted without success to get
out of an unwise early marriage. Minnie alluded to this effort in a letter to
her lawyer friend Gray: "By the way I don't know whether she has been
divorced from that man or not. I have heard it contradicted" (fair copy, 9
May 1869, MH-H). Evidently, divorce was a respectable enough option
that Minnie could comfortably bring it up with Gray (though not with
Clymer herself). In Isabel's world, however, legal divorce seems to be
either unmentionable or inconceivable. Curiously, one of Henrietta's
American friends traveling in Europe happens to be named *Climber*. There
will be proposals of marriage, Henrietta warns Isabel: "Annie Climber was
asked three times in Italy – poor plain little Annie" (143). It is fascinating
that James reached back to Minnie's circle for the name of such a minor
character. The real Clymer was known for her beauty and was an active
and prominent feminist. In 1868 she played a decisive role in organizing
the most important early women's club in America, Sorosis, and at the
time James wrote *The Portrait*, she was nearing the peak of her acting career
on the London stage.[10] Did James's respelling of her last name represent a
snide judgment of a prominent public woman who apparently refused
(unlike Isabel) to accept a bad marriage?

Minnie's views on marriage were definitely advanced for her time.
Even the well-seasoned Mary Chesnut had been scandalized in 1864 to
learn that the author of *Adam Bede* was living with George Henry Lewes
(*Mary Chesnut's Civil War* 543), but five years later the unmarried Minnie
not only took this awkward fact for granted but wondered in a letter (to
Gray, not James) how George Eliot's "lofty moral sentiments have
served her practically – for instance in her dealings with Lewes" (fair
copy, 24 April 1869, MH-H). Also, she doubted whether others would
enter matrimony if they felt as she did about the institution,[11] thus differ-

ing radically with her spiritual adviser, Uncle Henry, who made marriage a means of salvation. When her sister Kitty got engaged to a man over twenty years her senior, James's letter of congratulation slyly asked how Minnie "in that deep inscrutable soul of hers contemplates your promotion. It is a rare chance for Minny's cogitations – heaven bless her! If she could drop me a line I should be very glad to have her views" (Edel, *Untried Years* 252). This sounds as if he sniffed Minnie's disapproval. After a second sister, Elly, got engaged to a man almost thirty years her elder, James no longer had cause to feel uncertain as to Minnie's judgment. "I must confess my imagination had taken higher flights in the way of a spouse for Elly," she wrote him, using an image he would later attribute to Ralph Touchett. As for her own future, she was categorical: "I have quite determined that the line must be drawn *here*." Unlike her sisters, she was resolved never to "become the prey of a bald-headed Emmet" (MT to HJ, 15 August 1869, MH-H).

Minnie could not have foreseen that she would become the prey of her slightly older cousin. She had vigorously resisted that cousin's father, who advised her to renounce, but the heroine based on her has a secret dream of servitude that confirms the father's opinion: Women are made to serve. Whereas Minnie was skeptical about indissoluble bonds, Isabel refuses to leave the tyrannical husband who hates her. James "completed" Minnie by having the mature Isabel reject the real woman's free-spiritedness.

The single most telling alteration James performed on Minnie was to make her dream of and then marry a middle-aged husband. Osmond is not bald (his "hair, still dense, but prematurely grizzled, had been cropped close" [199]), but he is almost twice Isabel's age, as Kitty's and Elly's husbands were. As the central event of his most ambitious novel yet, James required the character modeled on his cousin to do the one thing she emphatically told him she would not. If one couples this use of her with James's repeated claim that Minnie was fortunate to die young, that life would have proved treacherous to someone so spirited, one can sense how *The Portrait* secretly questions her strength and judgment. The novel says that she and other women who affront traditional constraints are weaker and more foolish than they suppose and that in the end, like the freethinking heroine of Anne Moncure Crane's *Opportunity*, they are bound to do something "utterly pedantic and unnatural and insupportable" (*Literary Criticism* 1: 599). James's scheme for "justifying" Minnie reveals a deeply rooted insistence on her folly.

In the end Isabel understands that Osmond has used her as he would "a dull un-reverenced tool" (484). Ralph says she has been "ground in the very mill of the conventional" (506). But what about James's use of Minnie? In writing *The Portrait,* was he justifying, not her, but his own mysterious and powerful need to take over her life? The remarkably uninhibited letters he wrote his mother and older brother after learning of Minnie's death bespeak a desire to transform her into a text all his own. This possessive urge was so strong and tenacious it would seem to be a founding motive in James's life and art. In 1913, when he excerpted Minnie's 1869–70 correspondence for *Notes of a Son,* he ascribed to her a passage composed by himself and thus committed a fraud that is the converse of plagiarism:

> This climate [in New York] is trying, to be sure, but such as it is I've got to take my chance in it, as there is *no one I care enough for,* or who cares enough for me, *to take charge of me* to Italy, or to the south anywhere. I don't believe any climate, however good, would be of the least use to me with *people I don't care for.* (Habegger, "Henry James's Rewriting" 166–67, 176; italics mine)

With this fabrication James drastically compromised Minnie's independence of character and the closeness of her relations with her sister Kitty, with whom she had been living in 1869. The arrogance of this alteration of fact is shocking: Not only would Minnie's survivors have been pained by the claim, twice repeated, that she did not "care for" her people, but James's high-handed destruction of the letters effectively prevented anyone from clearing up the bad feelings. (The only reason we can detect the fraud is that William James's widow and daughter meticulously copied Minnie's letters before sending the originals on to James.)

What is particularly disturbing is that the transformations we can observe in this fabrication are identical to the alterations James performed on Minnie in order to create *The Portrait.* James built the novel precisely by pretending that Minnie was far less capable of taking care of herself, and far more alienated from friends and family, than she in fact was. He took charge of her, transformed her into a witness against her own will and history, and then said he was only completing and justifying her.

Yet James kept faith with Minnie by reproducing her stern sense of justice. Gray (who became an authority on property law) remembered her as "the only *just* woman" he had ever known. No reader of *The Portrait* has been more attentive to Isabel's passion for dealing justly with others than has Joseph Wiesenfarth, who shows how she resolves competing claims during her married years. Wiesenfarth gives a fine exposition of her tough honorableness, yet leaves out something that seems crucial – Minnie's awareness of what would "touch my case," what was owing to herself. In fabricating his heroine, James required Minnie's passion for being just to others to crush her other more anarchic, freedom-loving impulses. He "justified" his cousin by demonstrating how a determination to be noble and just would in time refine away the crudity – and with it the independence.

If one tries to determine what James's immediate family and more distant relatives thought about his use of this remarkable cousin, one is in for a surprise. Even though James's letters home had billed the novel as his biggest and best yet, stimulating William to inquire as early as 1878 about the "great novel" (*Letters* 2: 179), there is not one surviving letter from any of the family expressing an opinion about *The Portrait*. I can find only two faint hints. James's 30 January 1881 letter to his father informs us that Henry Sr. was critical of the Isabel–Henrietta friendship: "Thank you for your little criticism on the 'Portrait.' Yes, it appears unnatural, certainly, that Isabel should fraternize with Henrietta, but it wouldn't if I explained it" (*Letters* 2: 337). One is reminded of the teacher's disapproval of Minnie and Helena's bond. Then there is a tantalizingly incomplete report in a letter Alice H. James sent William soon after *The Portrait*'s appearance as a book:

> The night [Josiah] Royce called he talked delightfully of novels, very much disgusted with Howells's definition of the future novelist. He said some admirable things of Harry – the best *hostile* criticism I ever heard of him and when through he concluded with, "I don't know what Prof. James thinks of his brother's writings, but I should judge his opinion would be much like mine." (17 December 1882, MH-H)

Equally suggestive is the unexplained and never-patched-up quarrel between Henry James and Minnie's sister Elly, who resented his appropriation of Minnie's letters in *Notes of a Son* and whose surrounding "depths of illiteracy" (*Letters* 4: 707) he in return haughtily denounced. If we try to read James through Elly's eyes – Elly who briefly moved to California in 1869 with her elderly bridegroom – we cannot help lingering over James's supercilious account of Isabel's sisters, particularly Edith, who unwillingly spends her life in "various military stations, chiefly in the unfashionable West" (23). I predict that if Elly's letters of 1881–82 ever turn up, they will be found to be highly critical of James's use of her sister in creating *The Portrait*.

The Dying Man

What should James's betrayal of Minnie Temple mean to us as readers and interpreters of *The Portrait of a Lady?* To answer this question, we must strive to plumb the soul of the heroine's possessive cousin. I mean not only Minnie's cousin Henry but Isabel's cousin Ralph, the spectator and secret arranger of her life. This strange man, who bears a special, nonerotic love for her and dies slowly from a lingering illness during the four years the novel covers, surely reflects in some devious way the author's own private state.[12] Just as surely, the differences between James and Ralph illuminate James's own act of appropriating Minnie.

The chapter in which Isabel's engagement is made public contains the first announcement of "the now apparently complete loss" (295) of Ralph's health. Isabel sees that "he was dying" (296), and the blunt phrase wipes out the studied ambiguity that has up to this point veiled his fate. This is a big revelation – but strange to say, both James and Isabel appear to forget it. Only four chapters later the following exchange takes place between Lord Warburton and Isabel after Ralph arrives in Rome:

> "I sometimes think he is dying," Lord Warburton said.
> Isabel started up.
> "I will go to him now!" (335)

This curious and ineffective repetition identifies one of the novel's most Victorian features, Ralph's prolonged death, which is characterized less by the realistic treatment of tuberculosis than by the solemn drapery of significance. Each announcement that Ralph is dying follows upon a fresh sign of Isabel's tragic capitulation. The linkage is this: As the heroine goes down, the observant male cousin who lives through her suffers mortally. His slow decline conveys the ponderous sense of the operations of Nemesis that we get in other Victorian novels, in Crane's *Emily Chester* in particular. But the decline also tells us something about James himself.

Three decades after writing *The Portrait,* James admitted that in composing his second novel based on Minnie's image, *The Wings of the Dove,* he had felt uneasy about the "idea of making one's protagonist 'sick.' " He decided he could avoid the taint of morbid interest by imputing to the dying heroine "the unsurpassable activity of passionate, of inspired resistance." A writer, he wisely argued, "essentially *can't* be concerned with the act of dying. Let him deal with the sickest of the sick, it is still by the act of living that they appeal to him." This said, James recollected his various "accessory invalids," naming Ralph Touchett but only to insist that he was an anomaly. Rather than contributing a sense of morbidity, he was "a positive good mark, a direct aid to pleasantness and vividness." James could not explain why sick Ralph was not morbid when sick Milly so easily could have been, but he emphatically denied that the difference had anything to do with "his fact of sex" (*Literary Criticism* 2: 1288).

In fact, Ralph is a version of a sickly and specifically male type that was so important for James he could not detect its morbidity. The type appears in two of his earliest short stories in which a badly wounded Civil War veteran, hanging between life and death, dies after discovering that the young woman he thought was pledged to him has accepted another man's proposal. In "The Story of a Year" (1865), published when

James was only twenty-one, John Ford, brave and generous, persuades Lizzie Crowe to keep their engagement secret as he goes off to battle, in this way leaving her free. Unfortunately, the noble man does not suspect that Lizzie, as James tells us with surprising directness, is a "poor misinformed creature" (*Tales* 1: 26). She soon falls in love with a second handsome man and accepts his proposal. When John, now gravely injured, learns of the vain and easily swayed girl's faithlessness, he goes into a rapid decline and dies. In the second story, "A Most Extraordinary Case" (1868), the protagonist is once again a desperately unwell young man who has had little experience of women's ways. Ferdinand Mason is not engaged to Caroline Hofmann, but he feels that they share an unspoken compact: He "extracted from her words a delicate assurance that he could afford to wait" (*Tales* 1: 250) before eventually proposing. Caroline, however, is put before us as a hard and self-sufficing woman, one who lacks the refined consideration the officer imputes to her. In the end the news that she has become engaged to someone else destroys Ferdinand's will to live, and he too suffers a relapse and dies. In each of these sickly narratives an unwell man feels let down by a woman who proves to be less affectionate, refined, and trustworthy than he had counted on. The stories are stiffly accusatory, not of the man who fails to act out a passionate and inspired resistance, but of the woman who disappoints him.

These early and unsuccessful stories are important because they introduce the material James would rework in *The Portrait,* where Ralph is seen to be "dying" the moment Isabel's engagement becomes known. As Leon Edel has pointed out, Isabel is a complicated, more sympathetic version of James's early killer-Dianas. After turning down Lord Warburton, Isabel wonders, with reason, "whether she were not a cold, hard girl" (95). She lets Caspar Goodwood understand that if he should hear of her engagement, he may "venture to doubt it" (140), and he does. She gives him permission to try her again in two years, and he does this too. Warburton is not an officer, but he is associated with the Dying Gladiator when Isabel dismisses him in Chapter 28. In her dealings with Ralph, Warburton, and Goodwood, Isabel makes the same moves as James's early hard, heartless heroines. Behind James's critical treatment of her stand these early resentful narratives, and behind Ralph lie John Ford and Ferdinand Mason. What James did over a period of fifteen years with these two dying characters was to peel away the factitious elements and embody them in accessory figures. The jilted-suitor aspect became Goodwood; the dying-soldier aspect turned into Warburton the Dying Gladiator. What remained was the sickly spectatorial dependency on a heroine, and this, the heart of the matter, evolved into Ralph. If Isabel's manly suitors often seem wooden and unfelt, that is because their segments of the original material were outside the orbit of James's knowledge, interests, and experience. The only part that was inside was what went into the richly imagined Ralph.

Sickly dependency on an observed heroine with a stirring life of her own: This material, closely related to James's identity problems as an adolescent and to the women's novels he was reading, generated Ralph and Isabel. The first volume of Leon Edel's biography, published in 1953, interprets this material in a way I believe to be partly mistaken. According to Edel, the dying-officer stories inform us that James adored Minnie in a distant, even humiliated, way and that this worship reflected a more general view that women were dangerous and unfathomable Dianas:

> Henry in reality wanted only to worship Minny from a quiet and discreet – and we might add safe – distance. . . . To sit back and observe his cousin, to worship her from afar, to give her signs of devotion at the real right moment, this seems to have been the love stratagem of Henry – as it was of a number of his early young fictional heroes. . . . *True love is best by silence known.* And such silence can have in it a component of fear. . . . Henry James feared women and worshipped them and hesitated to express his feelings lest he be turned away. (*Untried Years* 234)

Much of this seems dubious: the claim that James's attitudes toward Minnie were representative of his attitudes toward women in general; the assumption that his early fictional heroes tell us in some transparent way about his own real-life feelings; the omission of all reference to contemporary thought and fiction about women. I know of no firm biographical evidence that James was fearful of women, although his memoirs show plainly that he was intimidated by the taunts, tricks, and superior capacities of boys and men. Above all, what does it mean to say that James "loved" Minnie, especially since he himself denied the imputation in a letter home? Any sound interpretation of his feelings for and appropriation of Minnie must somehow take into account the homoeroticism that erupted in him in the 1890s, a subject rightly emphasized in Edel's later volumes.

In order to thread one's way through the difficulties (and the gaps in the record), we need to distinguish between James's direct and spontaneous feelings for Minnie and his representation of those feelings when absent from her – especially when writing about her to William or for other male readers. On the first point, the evidence suggests that even though he was almost three years older than Minnie he was so close and affectionate he seems rather kittenish. The same early letter (to which Edel was not given access) that speaks of William as having "rather *renounced* me, in the depths of his heart, as a *bad* thing" declares that "Harry is as *lovely* as ever, verily the *goodness* of that boy passeth human comprehension" (Rosamond Gilder's typescript, MT to Helena de Kay, 3 April 1863, Gilder Papers). One would suppose that if anyone chose to debunk Minnie "as a *bad* thing" it would have been Willy, not Harry, who, here and in other letters, looks, from her perspective, like a sweet, affectionate – and unfathomable – comrade. But even though her slightly patronizing report, written in the present tense from the James's parlor in Newport, would seem to make cousin Harry's betrayal of her more mystifying than ever, the passage provides the crucial information needed to solve the mystery.

The fact is, *William* disliked Minnie, at least as early as 1863 and as late as the winter of 1868–69, and he was not the only one. James's father, mother, and sister also felt a persistent hostility toward her. Minnie's letter of 1863 was written from enemy territory, so to speak. Henry Jr. was the only member of his family who felt and showed any real warmth for her. The fundamental reason he betrayed his defiantly independent cousin was to reaffirm his loyalty to the strongly patriarchal values of his family, particularly as expressed by his father and older brother.

There is room here for only the briefest sketch of James's complicated situation. One reason for his closeness to his orphaned cousin was that she fulfilled his early and tremendously important orphan fantasy, in which he and his brothers and sister were "sent separately off among cold or even cruel aliens in order to be there thrillingly homesick" (*Small Boy* 15). Another reason is that he lived on extremely uneasy terms with the aggressive male world of his time. Deeply "feminine," James projected himself onto his strong cousin, as onto certain heroines of fiction, but simultaneously remained in thrall to William and Henry James, Sr., two extremely vigorous and forceful men who not only insisted on reactionary views of female emancipation but specifically disapproved of Minnie's self-assertiveness. In 1870 Henry Jr. let his family know three times that he agreed with Henry Sr.'s views, as if it was crucial to stand with the family on this matter. James was divided between a warm attachment to Minnie and the necessity (extremely pressing during the Civil War) of proving himself to be a man. It was because of his determined loyalty to the world of men that he represented his early dying soldiers (and later on Ralph) as in terrible jeopardy from heartless Dianas. James *had* to betray Minnie and his own affection: The only way to win respect in the world of the fathers was to take captive the Amazon who had challenged them. James "completed" Minnie in order to make her – *and himself* – acceptable to the patriarchy.

My point is that James's career as a fiction writer began not with any sort of direct transcription of his experience but with just the opposite – a remarkably polished effort to put his own experience totally out of the question. The early fiction sets in operation a severe and dignified program of transformation. As Maqbool Aziz, Richard Brodhead, Michael Anesko, and others have pointed out, James hungered from the beginning of his career to be "just *literary*" (*Notes of a Son* 294).[13] That is one reason why the early dying-soldier stories have such a conspicuous conservative rhetoric. Writing in clear opposition to the current trends in women's fiction, James wanted to demonstrate that things would unravel if women renounced their sacred pledges. Both "The Story of a Year" and "A Most Extraordinary Case" declare that the modern American woman's abandonment of her redemptive mission – her refusal to be affectionate, faithful, refined – will destroy the man who trusts her, especially if he is a traditional man still loyal to the claims of honor in war and polite society. James began as the agonists' antagonist.

Going to particulars, "The Story of a Year" strongly reacts to Rebecca Harding Davis's *Atlantic* serial of 1861–62, "A Story of To-Day," whose title James probably adapted, and Crane's *Emily Chester* (1864). In the former narrative the heroine abandons her philanthropic devotion in favor of romantic love; in the latter she develops an irresistible physical repugnance for her husband and a strange "supersensuous" attraction to another man. Each work treats the heroine's change of heart with notable sympathy, and James's story indirectly rebukes both. In reviewing *Emily Chester* he expressed the same outrage at the title character's psychological infidelity that his own story shows for Lizzie Crowe's fickleness. The review denounced Emily's helpless preference for another man over her husband, and strenuously argued that morality, not magnetic psychology, was what fiction must attend to. James went so far as to call the book immoral because it failed to say that the heroine had an obligation to "conquer a peace." Any wife, in fiction or out, "who indulges in a foolish passion, without even the excuse of loving well, must be curtly and sternly dismissed" (*Literary Criticism* 1: 592). In line with such preachments, James led the reader of his own story to dismiss Lizzie Crowe as curtly and sternly as possible: Her vacant-mindedness must not be tolerated. In the scene where she forgets her wounded fiancé and allows her fancy to run after handsome Mr. Bruce, the narrator magisterially assures us that her "intellect was unequal to the stern logic of human events" (*Tales* 1: 42).

"The Story of a Year" was published in March 1865 in the *Atlantic*. A letter from James to Thomas Sergeant Perry implies that the narrative had been written by the previous March, seven months before the publication of *Emily Chester*. But there is reason to believe James revised and shortened his story in November 1864, at the same time he confronted Crane's novel. He had originally called his work a "modern novel" and a "novelette" (Harlow 273), categories that suggest it would not have fit into a single issue of the *Atlantic*. Furthermore, his 28 October 1864 letter commenting on this magazine's notice of acceptance grumbles, in an ambiguous phrase, that "it is so little" (Harlow 275). (For a reproduction of the letter, see Anesko, frontispiece.) The mysterious phrase probably refers, not to the size of James's payment, as has been suggested, but to the *Atlantic's* length requirements. Fields regularly tried to squeeze short fiction into a single issue.

The likelihood that James was asked to shorten his first signed narrative is all the more significant because of the coincidental dates. On 15 October James had written Charles Eliot Norton proposing to review *Emily Chester,* but the letter was unaccountably held up. A memorandum in Norton's meticulous hand on the back of the sheet reads, "Recd. Octr 29th. Ansd. 30th" (MH-H). James, meanwhile, was waiting for the reply. His 28 October letter to Perry reveals that he had not yet begun reading the book. Thus, events conspired so that he read and reviewed *Emily Chester* at the same time he took his own "modern novel" in hand for condensation. James's first American narrative probably reflects his hostile response to an agonist novel dealing with a woman's magnetic disorders. His career as a fiction writer may have begun in a literal attempt to chasten and correct a currently influential account, by a woman, of women's experience. And just as James's review showed strong sympathy for Emily's husband, so the story resentfully declared that it is not the faithless woman who will die, as in Crane's novel, but the abandoned man.

The second story, "A Most Extraordinary Case," constitutes a connecting link between "The Story of a Year" and *The Portrait.* (The same goes for the better known "Madame de Mauves.") Caroline Hofmann is more ambiguous than Lizzie, so that it is hard to know whether she or her idealizing admirer is more at fault. For much of the story she almost appears to be James's second portrait of a noble, civilized lady (the first being Adela Moore of "A Day of Days").[14] We cannot help wondering whether the dying man's conviction that he and Caroline share a delicate pact is a delusion. But then comes the scene where Caroline descends to the Hudson River and sings German lieder, simultaneously imitating the Lorelei, who lured mariners to their death, and wearying Ferdinand to the point of exhaustion. At the party, where she and some other American girls further wear out the hero, it appears that Caroline actively contributes to his death. A bystander points the moral: "Was there ever anything like the avidity of these dreadful girls?" (*Tales* 1: 259). In the original version one of the lethal defeminized girls was named Miss McCarthy, but when James reworked the narrative in 1884–85 for *Stories Revived,* he renamed her Miss Masters, a change that underscores her dominating masculinity. But the Diana-like heroine remains less blatant.

James's impulse to punish women's restless heroines was becoming less obtrusive. At times the outrage would moderate into a project of rehabilitation: *The Portrait* shows how a rather thoughtless girl turns into a noble lady precisely by enduring the miserable marriage that Crane's and Alcott's heroines could not stand. The uncanny thing is that James announced this general project in the text of "A Most Extraordinary Case." The doctor says of Caroline Hofmann: "She looks as if she had come out of an American novel. I don't know that that's great praise; but, at all events, I make her come out of it." Ferdinand's prescient response: "You're bound in honour, then . . . to put her into another" (*Tales* 1: 234).

James entered the craft of fiction as a severe and precocious professional whose narratives bore a critical relation to existing literary modes and tastes. He was impregnated with extremely idealistic notions of propriety and morality: Some things were absolutely sacred. He was correspondingly alienated, and would remain so until his fifties, from much of his own experience, and thus his fiction was devoted to noble ideas that, taken as a point of observation or judgment, made life look rather cheap. His impulse was not to reproduce or reflect life but to neutralize, devulgarize, dignify it – to "justify" it. The disjunction between his art and his life baffles any naive project of recovering that life from his fictional narratives. It is not that the life is not there, in every finely turned phrase, but that it is so meticulously and thoroughly worked up, like timber transformed into inlaid veneer.

And so we return again to *The Portrait,* to see where its beautifully finished and varnished surface reveals the original twisted grain. The place to look is in James's two portraits of gentlemen, Ralph Touchett and Gilbert Osmond.

James and Ralph: Reverence Centered Wholly upon His Father

The great paradox in James's imaginative development is that he broke through to his most important material by inventing people whose lives are empty. Ralph is set before us so richly and beautifully because he captures his creator's distance from life. Many readers feel that Ralph's generosity, truthfulness, tolerance, and lack of dogmatism reflect James's own best qualities. Yet it is obvious that Ralph is not a simple self-portrait. His shabby attire, vagrant humor, idleness, and stalled career suffice to rule out any straightforward equivalence. More important, Ralph's hopes for Isabel are far more naive than are those of the author, who sees Isabel as folly-ridden. The key difference is that, where James believed Minnie was fortunately prevented by her death from wading into some tragic downfall, Ralph acts to increase Isabel's power of self-expression. In doing so, he is animated by a particular mental image: "I had a sort of vision of your future. . . . I amused myself with planning out a kind of destiny for you. . . . You seemed to me to be soaring far up in the blue – to be sailing in the bright light, over the heads of men" (301). Ralph's private daydream is based on light and shadow, like Isabel's favorite picture of the refined father and his still daughter. But where Ralph likes to think of Isabel aloft and in brightness, she herself prefers "the atmosphere of summer twilight" (242). Tragically, Ralph founds his life on *his* pictured daydream, just as Isabel relies on her own, and when she inevitably disappoints his dream he declares, "It hurts me . . . as if I had fallen myself!" (302).

Readers coming fresh to James might sensibly conclude that Ralph's error is to try to live someone else's life rather than his own. But James was not the kind of man to dramatize such plain truths. He himself not only lived in the "constant hum of borrowed experience" (*Notes of a Son* 413), but Ralph's sun-lit vision of Isabel exactly recapitulates the imagery James himself was fond of in his twenties. In 1867 he had loved Crane's heroine in *Opportunity* for being "a strong and free young girl" who "has her face to the sun." He had criticized Alcott because she let the heroine of *Moods* succumb to "the shadow" (*Literary Criticism* 1: 598, 192). His own first novel, written a few years later, told of a heroine whose fancy was temporarily darkened by the "cooling shadow" of unworthy suitors but who finally emerged into airy light: "The sky was blazing blue overhead; the opposite side of the street was all in sun; she hailed the joyous brightness of the day with a kind of answering joy" ("Watch and Ward" 339, 709). Nine years later, writing *The Portrait,* James assigned light and dark the same basic values – but without the hope. Isabel meets her eventual master in a cool, poorly windowed apartment, is treacherously stirred by Osmond's attractive picture of a life conducted in "the shadows just lengthening" (308), and then slowly realizes that she has been led into "the house of darkness, the house of dumbness, the house of suffocation" (375). Pansy is already a flower of the shade. Following Osmond's orders, she waits for the shadow to reach a certain line before stepping into the bright sun-lit garden (277–78).

It would seem, then, that Ralph embodies a vital phase of the author's own developing imagination. The passionate cultivation of a glowing picture of Isabel reproduces James's own early quest for a female champion. But there is this difference: Ralph is impaired, only half a man. He lacks his maker's deep suspicion of female independence, suspicion that counteracted James's identification with female heroism and bright Minnie Temple, and thus saved him from being Ralph Touchett. Behind this suspicion stood Henry Sr.'s conservative doctrine on sexual difference – doctrine Henry Jr. endorsed three times the year Minnie died.

The key fact about Ralph is that Isabel is only his second passion, the first being his father, Daniel Touchett. "Such slender faculty of reverence

as [Ralph] possessed," James announces, "centred wholly upon his father" (50). The son admires Mr. Touchett as "a man of genius" and
"enjoy[s] . . . the opportunity of observing him" (31). Father and son are
"close companions," so much so that the latter has long hoped and taken
"for granted" that he will be the first to die. If Ralph is "steeped in
melancholy" when Isabel enters his life, his outlook lying "under the
shadow of a deeper cloud" (51–52), it is not because of his invalidism. He
is depressed because his father's illness took a fatal turn for the worse the
preceding spring. The loving son dreads the inevitable separation.

   This passionate filial attachment merits our closest scrutiny. Although
James was not one to represent ideally positive characters, Daniel Touchett comes very close to being the perfect father. He combines a penetrating shrewdness with an amiable and reassuring mildness, in this way
exhibiting Adam Verver's union of power and love. Daniel's "genial
acuteness" (63) – elsewhere "veiled acuteness" (159) – is such that he anticipates Warburton's misadventure with Isabel and Isabel's own susceptibility to "the fortune-hunters" (162). He himself has acquired a fortune in
banking, a beautiful English country house, and what would appear to be
(within the novel) some sharp insights into class and character in England. His skepticism about upper-class "radicalism" (a term so vague
one cannot say what issues are involved) is clearly intended to be seen as
shrewd. As for his own political sympathies, Daniel is fundamentally
conservative, amused by the way people take up "progressive ideas" (62)
and indifferent to proposed reforms so long as he can retain his accumula-
tions: "You see they want to disestablish everything; but I'm a pretty big
landowner here, and I don't want to be disestablished" (61). All this, yet
Daniel remains the epitome of kindness and pleasant blandness, a man of
self-made wealth and power who seems to have been declawed. James
even claims that his "feeling about his own position in the world was
quite of the democratic sort" (31).

   Not only is Daniel Touchett a godlike Daddy Warbucks fantasy figure, but Ralph's devotion also seems too good to be true. Would a son
who has "no great fancy" (31) for the bank his father runs, who takes no
more interest in it "than in the state of Patagonia" (298), love to study the
old man's mental operations? Ralph's conspicuous neglect of Mr. Touchett's great achievement does not seem consistent with James's insistence on the closeness of their bond. During his eighteen months in a
subordinate position at the bank, Ralph was fonder of "walking about"
than working at his "high stool" (31); it was while so employed that he
first showed symptoms of his fatal disease. After his father's death, he not
only lets the firm drift into some kind of trouble but ignores his mother's
advice "to see what they were doing at the bank" (342). Exhibiting no
uneasiness at all over this unconvincing father-and-son business, James

innocently asks us to believe that the son lives chiefly to nurse his aged father and cherishes a secret dream of dying with him.

Ralph's filial attachment is one of those segments of Jamesian narrative in which an extremely correct and depleted version of human behavior gets substituted for the real and living thing. It is like what James saw in *Emily Chester*, theory masquerading as feeling – except that James is tame where Crane is wild.

Most curious of all in a novel absolutely devoid of happy family life is that Ralph's filial attachment is one of *three* intense father–child bonds. In handling Isabel's and Pansy's worship of *their* fathers, James wants us to see through the daughter's devotion. With Ralph, however, the authorial detachment appears to collapse.

What we are dealing with here is James's unconscious projection onto Ralph, with James exposing more than he intended of the obligatory or slavish aspect of his relationship with his father. Mr. Touchett's bank corresponds to Henry Sr.'s philosophy, which Henry Jr. for the most part avoided even while continuing to regard his father as a great, not-to-be-questioned thinker, especially on "woman" and marriage. Given such attitudes, it makes sense that James was unable to detect the hollowness of Ralph's primal passion, and it also makes sense that James exhibited this passion as a rival of Ralph's great spectatorial interest in his lively American cousin. Ralph's turn from his dying father to his cousin effectively translates the dialectic of James's own mind, caught between an allegiance to the paternal doctrine on women and marriage and a private absorption in untamed heroines.

The centrality of this opposition explains why Ralph takes such a dreadful risk in delivering his father's money to Isabel, and why the revelations of Isabel's mistake repeatedly get yoked to Ralph's "dying." Mr. Touchett held the money. Isabel has been given his substance. She grows rich the instant the banker-father dies. Her empowerment, that is to say, derives from his extinction, and the vital transfer has been engineered by none other than the supposedly loyal son. This is why Ralph must die: He has recklessly handed over the patriarch's vital stuff to a girl who cannot help squandering it, and the fathers are not to be appeased.

Ralph is the scapegoat, made to pay the supreme price for exercising the author's suppressed impulse toward freedom and hope. Hence Ralph's best intentions only serve to usher Isabel into the old father–daughter marriage after all. Pansy resists such a marriage (to Warburton) and gets punished. Ralph, intending to free Isabel once and for all, inadvertently sells her into slavery and is punished even more. One of the novel's grimmest moments comes when Ralph realizes that his desperate final strategy for drawing Isabel out of Osmond's reach is to be successful only in the short term. She tells Ralph she does not "think anything is over" between

her husband and herself. " 'Are you going back to him?' Ralph stam-
mered" (507). Her return to Rome demonstrates that she believes in
Ralph's ideal of freedom less than in her husband's defense of the insoluble
bond: "I take our marriage seriously. . . . I am not aware that we are
divorced or separated; for me we are indissolubly united. You are nearer to
me than any human creature, and I am nearer to you. . . . I think we
should accept the consequences of our actions" (471). Whether spoken
sincerely or not, this speech expresses the position the novel works out. If
Isabel is to make the right choice at the end, to follow the "very straight
path" (519) and thus become the "consistently wise" (88) woman James
actually steps in to tell us she becomes, she must oppose Ralph's plan and
return to her husband.

The whole opposition between Ralph and Osmond is one of the rich-
est and best-worked-out elements in *The Portrait*. Their antagonistic relationship is given with far more mastery than Ralph's unconvincing bond
with his father. Ralph could not care less about establishing an identity
before others, but Osmond, who depends on the illusionist's art for his
place in the world, cares about little else. Whereas Ralph has Harvard,
Oxford, a big banking house, and an early Tudor mansion to back him
up, Osmond takes his derivation from an affected mother who wished to
be known as the American Corinne. (The first – Italian – Corinne was
the lyre-playing improvisational poet in the novel-travelogue by Madame de Staël.) Ralph has so much tradition he is bored by it, but
Osmond, having nothing, turns into a complete snob, an emperor without a country. The former is a son of a self-made financier and landed
proprietor whereas the latter is a tyrant who enshrines himself in bric-a-
brac and old medals, talks of being the Pope of Rome, and exhibits a
perfect daughter and wife to the public. Osmond detests Ralph: "But that
long jackanapes, the son – is he about the place?" (212). This contemptuous and antiquated word (its only other use in James, as far as I know, is
in connection with the "crazy" Costa Rican envoy in *Roderick Hudson*
[222]) catches Osmond's feeling that Ralph is too foolish, shapeless, and
witless to stake out a dignified position in society. Osmond is wrong
about Ralph, but Ralph, who in this connection as in others does enjoy an
aristocratic advantage over Osmond, easily sees through the "sterile dilet-
tante" (303). Ralph's insight into Osmond's act is so lucid and un-
mediated that he cannot imagine Isabel's inability to detect the sham. He
even knows "by instinct, in advance" (408) how Osmond will punish
Isabel for Warburton's withdrawal.

Judging by the written comment on *The Portrait*, it would seem that
no reader has ever doubted the truth of Ralph's insight into Osmond
(certainly I do not). But there is a remarkable anomaly in the whole rich
antagonism between the two men: It lacks all semblance of a *narrative*

basis. Each character is *already* equipped with a complete opinion of the other, and one of them, Ralph, evidently sees through the other with the author's eyes. The text, however, brings the two characters together only once, at St. Peter's, where Ralph gets a shock on seeing Osmond with Isabel:

> On perceiving the gentleman from Florence, Ralph Touchett exhib-
> ited symptoms of surprise which might not perhaps have seemed
> flattering to Mr. Osmond. It must be added, however, that these
> manifestations were momentary, and Ralph was presently able to
> say to his cousin, with due jocularity, that she would soon have all
> her friends about her. His greeting to Mr. Osmond was apparently
> frank; that is, the two men shook hands and looked at each other.
> (258)

James's manner here is so bland that he scarcely indicates the settled enmity. In revision, he did two interesting things with the passage. He made the irony heavier, so that instead of merely showing surprise Ralph now appears "to take the case as not committing him to joy" (*Portrait*, ed. Bamberg, 252). And James deleted the last sentence, thus doing away with the solitary contact between the two chief male architects of Isabel's fate. In combination with the many other revisions that stress Ralph's fear and hatred of Osmond (see, for example, the Ralph–Warburton conversation that ends volume 1), the New York Edition thus enhances the paradoxical situation of the first edition: an implacable opposition between two characters who never collide.

Is it a lapse that two central and mutually antagonistic characters should fail to meet in a novel as well plotted and dramatic as *The Portrait*? Perhaps not, though it is certainly a striking omission and one that begs for comment. The tension of Isabel's life would not be dissipated, nor the story materially altered, if James had allowed Ralph and Osmond at least to cross swords. *The Portrait* is not like *The Ambassadors*, where Madame de Vionnet and Mrs. Newsome *must* deal with one another chiefly through Strether and other envoys, or else the novel will not work. Osmond's scenes with Warburton and Goodwood are extremely effective. Why is it that he cannot have a scene with Ralph?

The answer, I believe, goes back to Ralph's improbable primal passion for his father and to Henry Jr.'s loyalty to Henry Sr. Faithful Ralph must not face Osmond because Osmond represents the dark side of his and his author's male parent. They, along with the late Mr. Archer, share a number of characteristics with each other – and with Henry James, Sr. They are all divorced from American life, have no niche in society, and are adulated by their children. Although the novel strongly insists on the difference between Mr. Touchett and Osmond, this difference almost vanishes if we try the experiment of regarding the two parents from the point of view of their fond children. Doing this, we see that the two children have a similar filial bond. Ralph idolizes the acuity of his father's "genius," which is never authenticated for us, just as Pansy feels that Osmond "knows everything" (325). Both children love to study and gratify their fathers. Both are in theory grown up yet their maturity is ambiguous and we see them chiefly at home fondly tending the parent. Osmond's mocking question as to whether the "jackanapes" – followed by "the son" in apposition – is still "about the place" focuses exactly on this grotesque immaturity. We know Ralph by his first name, as sons and heroines are known, but Osmond goes by his last like other men. Just as James exaggerates Ralph's closeness to Mr. Touchett, he exaggerates the separation from Osmond, and the reason is simple: Ralph must not learn the truth about his father. But it is precisely because Osmond *is* the father that Ralph already knows him so mysteriously well.

Of course the novel insists that the Daniel–Ralph relationship is loving and the Gilbert–Pansy one cruel and vicious. But we may safely question Henry Jr.'s ability to make this distinction. He too worshiped his philosopher-father and found it difficult to tell the difference between paternal love and authoritarianism. Even while he remorselessly exposed the emptiness, isolation, cruel will, and magic arts behind Osmond's quiet parental facade, James showed no awareness that Ralph's own filial adoration is suspect. Even while emphasizing Pansy's subjection, the filial author did not question Ralph's fondness for tending his empire-building father and his dream of dying with him. If we ask what kind of novelist could possibly ask us to accept this idyllic father–son bond, the answer is irresistible: He must have been a Pansy.

James sensed that behind the benign mask the philosopher of marriage was some kind of male Medusa. The only way a faithful son could gaze at that face was through fiction – the magical reflecting surface that turns a familiar object into something safely alien. The face that flashed on the mirror was Osmond's. The creative power that fused *The Portrait* came, precisely, from James's indirect engagement with his father's authoritarianism – the authoritarianism that had sent Alice to spend a winter with an antifeminist physician specializing in women's troubles just as Osmond sends Pansy back to the convent. At one and the same time Osmond is the great evil presence and the spokesman for the most solemn and ultimate truths. He and Isabel *are* "indissolubly united." She *does* have too many ideas ("theories" is the author's word), and she grows conspicuously more elegant, thoughtful, honest, and responsible by entering and then choosing to reenter the house of bondage.[15]

Predicated on Henry Sr.'s dogmas about women and marriage, *The Portrait* is the artifact of a brilliant but uneasy pansy. The conclusion, structured in such a way as to show Isabel rejecting passionate love and reaffirming her marriage vows, endorses Henry Sr.'s much repeated revelation: "Love is a great reality to experience, but is so little an *end* of human life, that I have no regard for it save as ministering to marriage" (HJSr to Julia A. Kellogg, 9 September 1871, MH-H). Separation or divorce might make sense to practical Henrietta, but Isabel belongs to a higher order and thus swears allegiance to the sacred bondage that constituted Henry Sr.'s basic message to the modern world:

> The law is . . . just, and even good, though it slay me. Yes, death at its hands were better than life at the risk of its dishonor at my hands. So I abide by my marriage bond. I see very well that the bond ought to be loosened in the case of other people. . . . But as ˙for me I will abide in my chains. (HJSr "Morality vs. Brute Instinct")[16]

Why does the novel's one date happen to be 1876, the centennial year of American national independence? When patriotic Isabel calls Henrietta an "emanation of the great democracy" (79), or when we read that "the national banner had floated immediately over" (152) Madame Merle's birthplace, the Brooklyn navy yard, James seems to be inviting us to estimate the value of independence in terms of what it means for American women. Isabel's talk about liberty has a great deal of empty posturing in it. Madame Merle is all the worse for having the "breezy freedom" (152) of the American flag. Mrs. Touchett dries up from following "her own theory" of what makes "a good wife" (156). *The Portrait* is a countercentennial novel. It consistently shows that the sort of liberty that takes shape in institutional reform – the emancipation of women in particular – is worthless. The freedom that interests James is the internal kind, where the manacles do not get taken off the hands but the spirit – somehow – spreads its wings.[17]

James betrayed Minnie Temple in *The Portrait* not because he feared or resented her. He was extremely fond of her, not only wishing her well but entering deeply into her experience, as Ralph does with Isabel. But James had been vigorously instructed by his father not to believe in Minnie's or anyone else's free intrepidity, and he himself was often passive and absorbed life at secondhand. It was just because of this spectatorial orientation that he both adored his cousin and discounted her love of liberty and the high integrity of her "pet theory." When she died, he became convinced in a moment of electrifying power that *he* had known a genuine agonist heroine, one whose brilliant potential must have come to nothing, and he began thinking his way toward *The Portrait*. He figured out how to combine the precocious girl and middle-aged lover from women's fiction with his own heartless Diana and dying soldier.

Yet the energizing insight that gave his imagination a once-in-a-lifetime impetus was based on a final refusal to imagine that his cousin could have survived on her own terms. James was able to write his greatest novel to date precisely by ascribing to Minnie his own private defeat, stabbing her image with the paternal steel that had been driven deep into his own soul. *The Portrait* is the book of a supreme artist in deep and unconscious subjection. That is why, in betraying Minnie Temple, James also betrayed himself. In taking over her image and then transforming her into someone so different, he transformed himself, as keeper of her flame, into the manipulative middle-aged guardian–lover he detested.

Chapter 8

The Return of the Father in
The Bostonians

Indications

As James takes us through *The Bostonians,* he favors us from time to time with unequivocal declarations about the inner nature of his fictive people. These disclosures present themselves as absolutely unquestionable judgments or analyses – revealed truths guaranteed by the author. "In reality," we are told, "Olive was distinguished and discriminating, and Adeline was the dupe of confusions in which the worse was apt to be mistaken for the better" (194). In Basil's "false pride," James informs us, "there was a thread of moral tinsel, as there was in the Southern idea of chivalry" (320). Assessing Verena's devotion to Olive, he says that "at least a portion of her nature turned with eagerness" (138) to the older woman's guidance, in this way implying that the magnetism is real yet somehow not wholehearted. In such passages James steps forward, very briefly, as god of the novel, displaying an omniscience that is able to discriminate among the threads that make up his characters.[1]

Inevitably, authorial intrusions or comments have great specific gravity. They stand out, make special claims to veracity and importance, play a leading role in guiding our understanding and interpretation. Less obviously, the *manner* in which a novel's creator breaks into his or her creation discloses some powerful secrets about its hidden constitutive principles. James speaks out in *The Bostonians* far more often than in his other narratives, and yet, contrary to the impression his more sweeping authorial pronouncements convey, he does not display a steady, unruffled, all-surveying mastery. It is not just that James prefers the artful insinuation to the flat Trollopian declaration: It is that his authority in this book, both insistent and muted, is inherently peculiar.

Again and again James does *not* speak openly and freely in his authorial commentary. Here is how he summarizes and then comments on Olive's extravagant suspicions of Henry Burrage:

He was weakly pretentious, softly original, cultivated eccentricity, patronised progress, liked to have mysteries, sudden appointments to keep, anonymous persons to visit, the air of leading a double life, of being devoted to a girl whom people didn't know. . . . Such were the images that proceeded from Olive's rich moral consciousness. (169–70)

Olive, now anything but distinguished and discriminating, projects a malignant image onto a gentle, cultivated, and inoffensive young man and seeks to poison Verena's mind against him. There is real sternness in James's final sarcasm, yet his form of speech – "such were the images" – merely indicates his detachment. He does the same thing in connection with Olive's fervid sense of the future: "I know not what may have been the reality of Miss Chancellor's other premonitions" (80). These apparent withholdings of judgment have in fact misled some readers.

Another peculiar aspect of James's commentary is that it is often confined to parentheses. Verena's mother "knew, in advance, just the air she should take (or she fancied she knew it – Mrs. Tarrant's airs were not always what she supposed), just the *nuance* (she had also an impression she knew a little French)[2] of her tone" (107). Here, as he presents a character's pathetically transparent affectations, the narrator seems unable to repress his scorn. There is a similar effect in James's parenthetic comment on the mother's pretentious analysis, before Verena, of Olive's "motive and temperament (Mrs. Tarrant, with the most imperfect idea of the meaning of the term, was always talking about people's temperament)" (105). Such comments lead us to dismiss Mrs. Tarrant without finding out what her air is (assumed or actual), what she understands by temperament, or what the perfect meaning is. The parenthetic comments on Verena and Basil are generally less haughty. At times the godlike narrator seems to shrink (ironically) before Basil's fierce "conviction . . . that civilisation itself would be in danger if it should fall into the power of a herd of vociferating women (I am but the reporter of his angry *formulae*)" (50). Assuming this kind of simple reportorial guise, James often professes his detachment in the mildest way conceivable: Verena "guessed Miss Chancellor didn't like this handsome joker (it was so that Basil Ransom struck her)" (91).

In passages such as these, the parenthetic commentary reduces itself to a kind of stylized (but elegant) nineteenth-century hand pointing in from the margin. Indeed, a margin, two margins, are exactly what parentheses shape. They mark off a small space separated from the regular narrative, a space in which the author can appear to step in and speak. Just as gods are said to descend in glowing sheaths, James enters in parentheses. His unabashed, nonparenthetic revelations show that he *can* descend in force and forthrightly explain and judge his characters. In his initial statement of intentions in the serial version of the novel, he even spoke of "the events I have undertaken in some degree to *explain*" (*Century* 29: 530; italics mine). But James clearly felt more comfortable in his noncommittal, bracketed interventions, and so, in revision, "explain" became "set forth" (5).

Quotation marks that frame questionable diction are the other form of punctuation facilitating James's intrusions. In his description of the rundown Marmion lodging house, he puts quotation marks around *register, boy, guest* (repetitiously, as the usage had been tagged on page 103), and *retiring* – "the vile habit of 'retiring' with the cocks and hens" (347, 349). Once again it is the Tarrants' speech that calls down the author's special reprobation, as when Selah sees "considerable many" (75) patients or pronounces the potatoes or the newspapers "fine" (100). The quotation marks enclosing Selah's *going in, selling off, on the spot,* and *open letter* all signal this character's slippery vulgarity: "If Mrs. Farrinder could be induced to write an 'open letter' about Verena, that would do more than anything else" (102–4). Most of the usages James tags in this manner are, loosely, Americanisms, and they range from commercial euphemism to familiar colloquialism. James uses quotation marks once again as a marginal hand, an intrusion that indicates rather than explains. They provide no information about the condemned usages – we are expected to know better already – but they do tell us a great deal about the cultivated mind that condemns. A modern reader might feel that if any one word in the sentence cited above belonged in quotation marks, it would not be *on the spot,* which seems standard and unavoidable, but *induced.* Quotation marks reveal James's universe of correct, nonvulgar diction, his vaguely transatlantic perspective on American speech along with his disdain for the publicity industry, the institutionalization of pretension. The quotation marks are a kind of punctuated sneer: Their substance is negligible and yet they convey an extremely strong attitude, and in this respect they perfectly exemplify the authorial presence in *The Bostonians.*

From this perspective, the words James uses without quotation marks become equally revealing. In *The Portrait of a Lady* it is the repellent Gilbert Osmond who says, "I know plenty of dingy people; I don't want to know any more" (209), but in *The Bostonians* it is James who divides the children playing in Washington Square into "the little curled and feathered people who drove their hoops under the eyes of French nursemaids" and "the dingier types from the south side" (315). The two other instances of *dingy* – "Miss Birdseye's rather faded and dingy human collection" (57) and her "dingy, loosely-habited air" (212) – are given through Basil's perspective. But the view they register is amply confirmed by James's own representation of Miss Birdseye, with her "dirty, democratic little hand" (27). *Dingy* fits right in with all the punctuated sneers; both look *de haut en bas.*[3]

James sometimes tagged his characters' language with quotation marks *and* parenthetic comment, as if to make his own superior detachment crystal clear. When Verena accepts Basil's invitation to take a seat in Olive's parlor, Olive, definitely annoyed, reflects that the girl's compliance is "a signal sign of the absence of that 'home-culture' (it was so that Miss Chancellor expressed the missing quality) which she never supposed the girl possessed" (89). James wants us to despise the quoted phrase, which recalls Mrs. Farrinder's earlier "sweet *home-women*" (35; italics hers): Such language represents for James a debasement of culture, manners, privacy. But what about "signal sign," a redundancy that evidently slips by without notice in all the energetic semaphoring? James displays a different sort of anxiety about Basil's use of a condemned usage: "The 'party,' as he would have said (I cannot pretend that his speech was too heroic for that), . . . had reopened the affair" (209). For James as for the *Oxford English Dictionary, party* was "shoppy, vulgar, or joc., the proper word being *person*" (3rd ed., Shorter). What makes the parenthetic comment especially revealing is its admission that Basil is supposed to be heroic, and that there is a disharmony between his heroism and his realistic speech limitations. This message alerts us to one of James's many shifts in composing the second half of the novel, namely, his reconstruction of Basil's heroic qualities.[4]

When he revised the *Century Magazine*'s serial text of *The Bostonians,* James removed quotation marks from many words and in so doing made the novel a bit less sarcastic.[5] In the serial Basil's envious survey of Olive's plush, cozy parlor concludes with this sentence: "Such a mood, however, could only be momentary, for he was conscious at bottom of a bigger stomach than all the 'culture' of Charles street could fill" (*Century* 29: 535). David Howard, responding to this sentence in the book version, which lacks the quotation marks, reads into it James's "sardonic handling" (66) of Basil. I believe the serial makes obvious what the book version says with less emphasis. James was sneering at Boston's upholstered refinement and rather admiring Basil's desire for a higher and less comfortable kind of distinction. We have already seen how James lifts his eyebrows at "home-culture." That is what Olive's parlor puts on display for Basil, who "had always heard Boston was a city of culture, and now there was culture in Miss Chancellor's tables and sofas, in the books that were everywhere, on little shelves like brackets (as if a book were a statuette), in the photographs and watercolours that covered the walls, in the curtains that were festooned rather stiffly in the doorways" (16). Quotes around *culture* draw special attention to the spuriousness of something Basil first admires and then (like the self-expatriated author) spurns.

Among the strangest of James's minimalist intrusions are those hinting that he *could* tell a bundle if he only chose to. In the scene at the Tarrants', where Olive tries to believe that Verena responds to the Harvard boys out of a rich, gracious nature, and not because she is "in the smallest degree a flirt," James breaks in to disclose the possibility of an absolutely true judgment:

> Olive may have been right, but it shall be confided to the reader that in reality she never knew, by any sense of her own, whether Verena were a flirt or not. This young lady could not possibly have told her (even if she herself knew, which she didn't), and Olive, destitute of the quality, had no means of taking the measure in another of the subtle feminine desire to please. (119–20).

This curious passage may imply that Verena is a flirt, but it conspicuously refrains from making a decisive statement on the matter. What James really confides is that Olive and Verena, for different reasons, are *not* capable of knowing something about their sex's behavior – knowing "in reality." His apparently offhand reference to "the subtle feminine desire to please" flashes at us the powerful claim that *he* understands the feminine breast better than these female characters do.

In passages like this, or the following one, where James claims a supreme insight into his characters even while withholding it from his readers, he inadvertently discloses a strange nervousness about his sovereignty over these characters:

> But this pale girl, with her light-green eyes, her pointed features and nervous manner, was visibly morbid; it was as plain as day that she was morbid. Poor Ransom announced this fact to himself as if he had made a great discovery; but in reality he had never been so "Boeotian" as at that moment. It proved nothing of any importance, with regard to Miss Chancellor, to say that she was morbid; any sufficient account of her would lie very much to the rear of that. Why was she morbid, and why was her morbidness typical? Ransom might have exulted if he had gone back far enough to explain that mystery. (11)

James scoffs at Basil's crude provincial categories and evokes the deeper insights the reader anticipates. This looks at first like standard expository rhetoric – leaving interesting matters temporarily unresolved, sharpening our discernment through contradiction, ridicule. But these explanations do not touch the passage's real oddities. James is unaccountably precipitate in coming down on Basil, who has only just met Olive and is still groping for some working formulation of her. If we are to belittle Basil's failure to go "back" very far in explaining Olive, why does James himself remain so vague? Who is she supposed to be typical *of* – New England spinsters, suffragists, Bostonians? James never says, or indicates, and neither does the novel unfold this mystery, or rather twin mysteries – why she is morbid, why her morbidity is typical. Also, James takes for granted that the Boeotian word is the right one, and he employs it in a later authorial aside: Olive "was intelligent enough not to have needed to be morbid, even for purposes of self-defense" (152).

The transcendent knowledge and cultivation the author-narrator so conspicuously claims in *The Bostonians* turns out to be a very anomalous thing indeed. James assumes a supreme godlike gaze, but in practice his relation to his three main characters (and Miss Birdseye) seems as shifting and uncertain as any ordinary human relationship. What exactly *does* he think of Basil's courtly notion of the difference between the sexes?

> He had a certain sentimental, provincial respect for women which even prevented him from attempting to give a name to it in his own thoughts. He was addicted with the ladies to the old forms of address and of gallantry; he held that they were delicate, agreeable creatures, whom Providence had placed under the protection of the bearded sex; and it was not merely a humorous idea with him that whatever might be the defects of Southern gentlemen, they were at any rate remarkable for their chivalry. He was a man who still, in a slangy age, could pronounce that word with a perfectly serious face. (192)

In spite of James's amusement at the dated gallantry, the final sentence still manages to convey a strong feeling of respect. Whatever Basil's faults, the passage hints, he has at least managed to resist the vulgar familiarity that threatens to do away with what little privacy, dignity, and personal distinction still survive in Gilded Age America.

The problem of how to understand Basil becomes especially acute if we take a second look at James's categorical statement about the "thread of moral tinsel" in this character's "Southern idea of chivalry." Basil has been agonizing over Verena's success with Mrs. Burrage's well-heeled circle. He feels a deep contempt for "the stupid, gregarious, gullible public" and he regards Verena's talk as "fluent, pretty, third-rate palaver," and yet he is impressed that the way to wealth is now open to her. Then comes this abrupt authorial comment: "I shall perhaps expose our young man to the contempt of superior minds if I say that all this seemed to him an insuperable impediment to his making up to Verena" (320).

Who is the object of James's scorn? I would say he is sneering not at Basil but at those readers who feel they are above the old rule of honor requiring a man to be able to support his bride. James's alteration in tone comes very close to Olive's sudden defiant challenges. It transforms Basil from a reactionary fool into a noble holdout, and makes his lonely act of renunciation seem all the finer in that the public at large is too depraved to respect it – the stupid, gregarious, gullible public to which the contemporary reader evidently belongs. But the real oddity here is not that the author has suddenly made common cause with "the poor fellow" (334) he so often ridicules, but that this partisanship is so ambiguously stated as to be more or less masked.

What then, moving to the heart of the problem, are we to make of this (in every sense) challenging passage?

> This boldness did not prevent him from thinking that women were essentially inferior to men, and infinitely tiresome when they declined to accept the lot which men had made for them. He had the most definite notions about their place in nature, in society, and was perfectly easy in his mind as to whether it excluded them from any proper homage. The chivalrous man paid that tax with alacrity. He admitted their rights; these consisted in a standing claim to the generosity and tenderness of the stronger race. The exercise of such feelings was full of advantage for both sexes, and they flowed most freely, of course, when women were gracious and grateful. It may be said that he had a higher conception of politeness than most of the persons who desired the advent of female law-makers. When I have added that he hated to see women eager and argumentative, and thought that their softness and docility were the inspiration, the opportunity (the highest) of man, I shall have sketched a state of mind *which will doubtless strike many readers as painfully crude*." (193; italics mine)

Philip Page quotes part of this in a perceptive article and rightly points out that the narrator seems "extremely conscious of his readers, even to the extent of being uncertain and suspicious of their reactions" (378). James's tone initially implies that of course he does not stand behind Basil's benighted opinions on women; he is only reporting them. The Mississippian's "definite notions about their place in nature, in society," have a foolishly rigid look. But then James tactfully brings up the fact ("it may be said") that Basil has a "higher conception of politeness" than do the suffragists, as if to hint that we should weigh his reactionary views against their bad manners. Is not James taking sides – *switching* sides? To say that the suffragists are pushing for "the advent of female law-makers" distorts their goals; to claim that they ignore the importance of social refinement is to repeat a common antisuffragist bromide. Coming from one who valued manners as much as James, this would have been a heavy charge. I think he stands behind Basil more than the prevailing narrative tone admits. The italicized sentence is making another sarcastic dig at the reader's "superior" liberalism. But why does an author who allows himself to "go behind"[6] his characters fall silent at the moment of truth, and instead of speaking out turn to *us* with a gesture of muffled defiance?

Faced with such anomalies, James's critics have until recently settled for some easy resolution (the irony cuts both ways, the difficulties force the reader to participate in creating the novel) that shore up the old myth that James is totally in charge. The haughty author of *The Bostonians* clearly wants us to accept this myth. In many respects, however, his novel is absolutely out of control, and he is improvising far more desperately than Verena, even introducing radical changes as he goes. His uncertain voice, his ambiguous appeasement/defiance of the reader, the contradiction between his calm overview and his brittle, nervous, punctuated sneers all warn us that in some way the authorial identity is gravely at risk.

In the last two chapters, in fact, this identity undergoes an ultimate kind of collapse: It merges with one of the characters. Would the doors in the Music Hall's balconies remind a man who has not been to Europe, and does not have a firsthand sense of "Roman vastness," of the "*vomitoria*" (429) in the Colosseum? Would a former Mississippi planter be so ignorant of the uses of tobacco that he could not name "something" in the policeman's "mouth which made a protuberance in his cheek" (432)? Most telling of all is Basil's final reflection on Verena's mother, who "heave[s] herself into the arms of Mrs. Burrage, who, he was sure, would, within the minute, loom upon her attractively through her tears, and supply her with a reminiscence, destined to be valuable, of aristocratic support and clever composure" (449). This sardonic passage (its reference to tears anticipates the final sentence and nudges us not to take Verena's pain too tragically) silently attributes to Basil the *author's* own very insistent view of Mrs. Tarrant. But something has injured James's detachment. He has forgotten that Basil has seen Mrs. Tarrant only once, briefly, at Miss Birdseye's long-ago gathering, and that she was only one of many strangers and did not display her sad social climbing. Furthermore, the clever, waspish tone is all wrong for Basil, though it is right for James, who has all along given tremendous scornful emphasis to the woman's unadmitted snobbery. Without seeming to know it, the author is identifying with "the poor fellow" who triumphantly defies the congregated reformers of Boston and forcefully wrenches away their rising star.

Basil Ransom as Intended Hero

When Philip Rahv in 1945 and Lionel Trilling in 1953 brought *The Bostonians* back into print and official critical approval, they rested their case to a great extent on some large claims for Basil Ransom as conservative hero challenging a culture of triumphant vulgarity and intrusiveness.[7] Irving Howe's 1956 introduction to the Modern Library edition continued to regard the novel as a masterpiece of culture criticism but astutely called into question Rahv's and Trilling's reckless praise of Basil. Howe noted the withering irony James sometimes directs at this character's provincial overreaching – "he had read Comte, he had read everything" – and he demolished the idea that Basil has a career as political essayist thanks to placing a single article with something called the *Rational Review*, "a journal of which the title," Howe neatly wrote, "sufficiently suggests both its circulation and influence" (xxv, xxvi). But there was an important question Howe finessed: What exactly does the novel say about the subjection of women? His essay has been extraordinarily successful in persuading canny readers not to worry about this and to regard *The Bostonians* as essentially ironic, to feel that they can understand and enjoy the novel without having to take Basil too seriously. "He is in no clear way James's spokesman," writes Howard (66).

The downplaying of Basil's spokesmanship, along with the ingenious detection of the most delicious ironies in James's handling of him, has for thirty years been a fundamental condition allowing liberal-minded readers to admire James's most reactionary book. The evidence of his partisanship within the novel, or of his disdain outside it for female suffrage and the female intellect and imagination,[8] does not seem to make a difference; Basil *must* be read ironically. And we are not without excuse, as the book is not only inconsistent and disingenuous but additionally attempts a difficult balancing act unprecedented in James's oeuvre.

Obviously Basil is opinionated, rigid, brutal. James tells us so over and over. *The Bostonians* goes much further than any of James's earlier or later realistic novels in drawing our attention to its hero's negative traits. James's letters make clear that he meant to break new ground in this respect – "to mark a new era in my career." He had extremely high hopes for the book. A few months before beginning it, he professed to Howells that he was "a failure! – comparatively." His characters had up to then showed "too damnably much" of "a certain 'gloss' " (*Letters* 3: 21, 28). The implication is that his next ambitious work would strip away the varnish, and in particular would give the hero a more naturalistic treatment.[9] But James's great difficulty, in some ways unforeseen, was to prevent Basil's very grave flaws in character from impairing that likeable dignity a traditional hero required.

Basil is definitely meant to be the one figure whose fortunes we follow with most interest. "We are so anxious," R. D. Gooder rightly claims, "for Ransom to win the struggle" (xxviii) with Olive – "we," I take it, referring to the unresisting reader the novel tries to create. And Basil does have virtues, the striking, martial ones: He is bold and resolute; he has a high ambition and a searching vision of his country that approximates that of his alienated, less doctrinaire creator; he adheres to a noble standard regardless of the corruption that mires others; he is honest in his pursuit of Verena, not stooping to the level of furtive manipulation we see in Olive (buying the girl behind her back, not telling her of the Burrages' "magnificent offer" [313], pretending to share "everything" [299]). And as the novel's final chapters make particularly clear, Basil often sees with James's eyes, especially when he scorns the causes trumpeted by the popular press or responds to color, charm, theatricality. In spite of his rough-hewn tastes, he has a latent Jamesian feeling for art: "Basil Ransom had seen very few pictures, there were none in Mississippi; but he had a vision at times of something that would be more refined than the real world" (359). The novel wants us, in spite of everything, to *like* this man – to wish his career and courtship well, to sense real distinction in his opinions, to take him seriously as a conservative intellectual.¹⁰ James attacks Basil superficially but backs him up on deeper levels: his antidemocratic notions find corroboration in the spectacle of all the tawdry reformers, and his belief that Verena does not really care for the emancipation of women is confirmed by her own heart. The reality James fabricates says that Basil is right.

The concluding chapters definitely build up Basil's dignity. Howe's ridicule notwithstanding, the *Rational Review* article is meant to be taken seriously. "Rational" culture criticism had been James's own high standard from the beginning. "It is just these vague random utterances and all this counterfeit criticism," he wrote in a review of Rebecca Harding Davis, and sounding exactly like Basil, "that make the rational critic the more confident of his own duties" (*Literary Criticism* 1: 224). There were no twentieth-century "little" magazines of restricted circulation in America in the 1870s. To be a *review* was to be something substantial – the *Edinburgh Review*, the *Saturday Review* (London), the *North American Review*. It was a coup for James's father to get his article on Swedenborg's ontology into the *North American*, and the same journal not only gave Henry Jr. his first assignments as a critic but held to its high standards by declining a couple of his productions. Like the real journals, Basil's *Review* seems to be very well endowed. In a detail that has been universally overlooked, the journal's editor has paid for Basil's article in advance, and this tangible expression of enthusiasm is so sizable that Basil is able to take a full month off work. Payment in advance was *not* the rule; the exception made for Basil spells out just how big his break really is. In touching up *The Bostonians* for book publication, James gave added emphasis to the advance payment. In the serial Verena simply tells Olive of "the letter that editor wrote him about a contribution" (*Century* 31: 209), but the book gives her an additional phrase – "and his paying for it right off" (378). It is the first step in what may be a noteworthy career. Basil faces struggle and deprivation, but he at least has a chance to support himself in an intellectually debased society without selling his intellectual honor. The phrase Basil uses – "makes an era in my life" (368) – even appeared in James's own letter about his plans for *The Bostonians*.

I am talking about intentions. Whether James succeeded in *realizing* Basil's literary promise, either intrinsically or in relation to the publishing industry and the reading public, is of course another question. I would say that the novel fails, dismally, in its presentation of Basil's career – his effort to establish himself in public life. The inconsistencies are overwhelming. We are told he used to speak at vague "political meetings" (58) in the South during Reconstruction, but in New York he seems absolutely out of the political scene, *doing* nothing, knowing no one. During a summer in Mississippi, as we are informed (without apparent irony), he "mastered" the German language because of its "large literature of jurisprudence" (16), yet now, in New York, where Basil frequents a saloon whose regulars speak German, we are told that "their colloquial tongue was unknown to him" (190). He is obsessed with social and political questions and even dreams of making nationally important orations, but goes "for weeks" (203) without looking at a newspaper. He fought in the Civil War, yet his life "had not been rich in episode" (201). We must distrust James's basic account of his hero, if only because of the significant pattern running through these inconsistencies – the habit of attributing to Basil a high degree of involvement in human affairs only at a distance or in some former time. There is a very strange blockage here: James does not, cannot, imagine Basil as doing but only as having done.

There is another, much more serious, contradiction that illustrates this general failure. In Chapter 21 James makes it clear that his young lawyer has virtually no clients and is getting nowhere in his profession. Basically, what he does is to sit by himself and read and write, or sit and smoke in a beer cellar. But in Chapter 35, about half a year later, he arrives at Marmion hugely relieved to get away from his "long grind in New York, without a vacation." Now it seems his work has entailed much hurried activity – "daily movement up and down the long, straight, maddening city" (347). He says, apparently speaking truthfully, "I haven't had a holiday for more than two years" (365). The least one can say about this contradiction (has no one noticed it?) is that James has done a wretched job of imagining Basil's life as a struggling young professional. How can a narrative so uneven and uncontrolled sustain *any* reading, let alone an ironic one? James's basic invention of Basil's career is too threadbare for a decent representational illusion.[11] Hence the confusion over the *Rational*

Review – a confusion that uncannily reproduces James's own hyperbolic and unjustified hopes for his novel.

It is precisely because Basil is one of James's trickiest people, never doing or being what his author claims, that we *have* to go outside the novel in order to get hold of him. *The Bostonians* is the mutant in James's oeuvre in many respects, and not least in that if we are to read it well we must strive, *independently,* to read its author – his conscious intentions and opinions, the influences on him, the darkened regions of his soul. Basil is troublesome because he is James's tall, dominating, shadow-casting man.[12] He not only throws other characters into a strangely powerless state (Verena "felt that his tall, watching figure, with the low horizon behind, represented well the importance, the towering eminence he had in her mind" [385]) but he darkens the imagination of his own creator. Basil is a projection of James's peculiar conservatism, and even more of the external power that forced that conservatism on him and rendered his embrace of it simultaneously compulsive and factitious. In Basil, James made one of many attempts, culminating in the apparition lurking in "The Jolly Corner," to show, to face, aggressive male power. One way to understand what he was doing with Basil, and what Basil did with him, is to regard the author's imagination *from the outside* and consider the three eminent public men who shaped his conception of the Southern conservative: Senator Lucius Q. C. Lamar of Mississippi, Thomas Carlyle, and Henry James, Sr.

Lamar and Carlyle

We know Basil is partly modeled on Senator Lamar because James admitted it. Lamar was known for his charm, oratory, learning, and political suavity. During the Civil War he was sent to Europe as the South's special envoy. Mary Chesnut, whose private journal offers an unsurpassed inside view of the Confederate leadership, wrote in 1862 that he was "the most original and the cleverest of our men" (*Mary Chesnut's Civil War* 309). In 1877 Lamar became the first Confederate of high rank to enter the U.S. Senate. He was one of the backroom pols who put Rutherford B. Hayes into the White House on condition that Federal troops be withdrawn from the South, thus ending Reconstruction. Courtly, conciliatory, and shrewd, Lamar won numerous friends in the North. In 1888 he was appointed to the Supreme Court by Grover Cleveland.[13]

James met Senator Lamar in Washington in 1882 and was evidently charmed out of his usual reserves. The letter to John Hay that acknowledges Lamar's influence seems surprisingly disarmed:

I am immensely touched & gratified by your friendly note anent the
Bostonians & the noble Lamar. It was a kind thought in you that led
you to repeat to me his appreciative judgment of my rather reckless
attempt to represent a youthful Southron. It makes me believe for a
moment that that attempt is less futile than it has seemed to me on
seeing the story in print; & I am delighted, at any rate, that the
benevolent Senator should have recognized in it some intelligence
of intention, some happy divination. He himself, for that matter is
in it a little, for I met him once or twice in Washington & he is one
of the few very [*sic*] Mississippians with whom I have had the
pleasure of conversing. Basil Ransom is made up of wandering airs
& chance impressions, & I fear that as the story goes on he doesn't
become as solid as he ought to be. He remains a rather vague &
artificial creation, & so far as he looks at all real, is only fait de chic,
as the French say. But if you ever get a chance, without betraying to
Lamar that you betrayed him, do whisper to him that it gave me
very great pleasure to know that in the figure of B. R. he did
recognize something human & Mississippian. His word is a reward.
(Monteiro 97)

One cannot take everything at face value in this gracious letter, written at a time when James was coming to terms with the hostile reception
of the serialized *Bostonians* and the bankruptcy of the firm that was supposed to publish the book version in America. Still, it seems inconceivable that he could have confessed making use of "the noble Lamar" if
Basil had been intended as a provincial crank. Did Lamar sincerely approve of the representation of the "youthful Southron," or was he once
again exercising his diplomacy? Whichever, the telling fact is that the
author approved of the model's interpretation and manner of reading,
which, as refracted through James's letter, did not seek to register the
novel's achieved mastery (like so many post-1945 essays) but instead
penetrated to "some intelligence of intention, some happy divination."
James's phrases in effect concede that the narrative is not quite right and
that Lamar has known how to compensate for this. And then there is
James's remarkable – and probably truthful – confession that Basil "is
made up of wandering airs & chance impressions."

Only a few of these airs may have been Lamar's. James did not hesitate
to paint real people (Elizabeth Peabody), but the senator was bearded and
considerably older and more experienced than Basil. Both men, however, combined courtly manners and personal distinction with an unrelenting drive. Both saw political orations as the great lever, and what
Basil dreamed of, Lamar delivered. His celebrated eulogy of Charles
Sumner, the abolitionist and Radical Republican, downplayed sectional

antagonisms and praised "the deeds of heroism and devotion done on both sides" (Burger & Bettersworth 119), just as Basil does when he and Verena visit Memorial Hall. Also, the rape of Verena from the Music Hall definitely resembles what Lamar did to Radical Reconstruction and black civil rights.

As near as one can judge, however, there is less of the senator in *The Bostonians* than there is of the one nineteenth-century intellectual Basil regards as having got things right: "He was an immense admirer of the late Thomas Carlyle, and was very suspicious of the encroachments of modern democracy" (190). When Verena ringingly assures Basil that "this is an age of conscience," he answers by quoting his master: "That's a part of your cant. It's an age of unspeakable shams, as Carlyle says" (334). Like the Scotsman, Basil is a contemptuous outlander who scorns modern liberal reforms.

In E. L. Godkin's view, Carlyle had "furnished the pro-slavery school of philosophers at the South with . . . the arguments by which they sought to show that slavery is the divinely ordained condition of the laborer" ("Thomas Carlyle" 194). Basil has had to give up slavery, but he is still "sick of all the modern cant about freedom and had no sympathy with those who wanted an extension of it. What was needed for the good of the world was that people should make a better use of the liberty they possessed." Even "the spread of education" is "a gigantic farce – people stuffing their heads with a lot of empty catchwords that prevented them from doing their work quietly and honestly" (327).

But Basil does more than give voice to Carlylean doctrine; he *is* a transatlantic Carlyle, narrow, cruel, backward-looking, explosive, and brilliant in thought and style – brilliant especially as a critic of democratic limpness. The disdain, the contemptuous laughter, the completely self-assured bluntness in announcing to Verena that she has no idea who she is, the right-stuff brutality in resolving to prevent her from speaking out, "to strike her dumb" (320), all proclaim that Basil has the true Carlylean spirit. With a first name that means *royal,* he is a reincarnation of that lordlike no-nonsense strong man who, in Carlyle's books, periodically saves a degenerate Anglo-Saxon civilization by forcibly setting it straight. Basil's speeches (unlike Verena's, which *do* lack conviction) shake with berserker fury: "The masculine character, the ability to dare and endure, to know and yet not fear reality . . . – that is what I want to preserve, or rather, as I may say, to recover; and I must tell you that I don't in the least care what becomes of you ladies while I make the attempt" (334). Basil's one significant achievement in the novel, preventing someone whose words are empty from speaking, seems the quintessential Carlylean act.

Yet in handling its Carlylean materials the novel is once again notably two-faced. Following Basil's speech on masculine daring, James comments: "The poor fellow delivered himself of these narrow notions" (334). This seems to settle the matter, and it would if the author were in control of his voice. But Basil's narrow notions assail the same items – "hollow phrases and false delicacy and exaggerated solicitudes and coddled sensibilities" (333) – that the novel's general representation of modern reformers asks us to regard with contempt. The paradox in this situation is that James feels a sneaking admiration for someone who broadcasts an uncompromising scorn of sneaks. In this respect as in so many others, the author-narrator of *The Bostonians* definitely seems more bullied than bullying. He is apparently laboring under someone's shadow.

In fact, Carlyle helped preside over the conception and composition of *The Bostonians*. Dates are crucial here. It was in early April, 1883, that James recorded in his notebooks his original plan for the novel, and it was apparently between mid-August, 1884, and mid-April, 1885, that he wrote it. His planning coincided with his reading (and reviewing) of Carlyle and Emerson's correspondence,[14] and his writing began while he was absorbed in the last two volumes of James Anthony Froude's life-in-letters of Carlyle. That the Scotsman's grim spirit hovered over these two stages of the production of *The Bostonians* is very suggestive, especially if we recall James's contemporaneous comment that Emerson did not have enough "contempt" (*Literary Criticism* 1: 243) for the mediocre Concord folk.

James's private comments about Carlyle regard him with the same doubleness that *The Bostonians* regards Basil. Writing to Grace Norton in November 1884, James felt that "decidedly Carlyle was a brute, a man of a jealous, grudging, sinister, contemptuous, ungenerous, most invidious soul." Fully "nine-tenths" of his "contempt – the brutal mockery he poured over all human things" – struck James as "perfectly barren and verbose." But that leaves one-tenth, and there James was overwhelmed with admiration: "What a genius, painter, humourist, what a literary figure, what a faculty of expression. These things *put him in the front rank,* though not in the highest place in it, I think; for I am convinced that he will be a curiosity for future people rather than a teacher" (*Letters* 3: 55; italics mine). Rather than comment on Carlyle's views, James allows the expressive, aesthetic genius[15] to cancel some of the brutality. An earlier letter to Violet Paget similarly insists on Carlyle's rank as artist – "as a painter . . . one of the very first of all" (*Letters* 3: 51).

This way of salvaging the cranky Sage of Chelsea came to James, I believe, from his father, who told Annie Fields in 1863 that Carlyle "is an artist, a wilful artist, and no reasoner. He has only genius" (M. Howe 73). The lecture-essay in which the senior James summed up his views and reminiscences of Carlyle may have been his single most popular work. Caroline Dall considered this "the finest *lecture* I ever heard" (journal entry for 19 January 1865, Dall Papers, MHS). William James wrote Henry that "Father read his paper on Carlyle yesterday at the Radical Club very successfully" (8 December 1872, MH-H). In 1881 it appeared in the *Atlantic* as "Some Personal Recollections of Carlyle," and after Henry Sr.'s death it was collected by William in *The Literary Remains of the Late Henry James*. Henry Jr. must have known this essay and its leading idea that Carlyle was not a thinker but one who had, like Basil, "an immense eye for color, an immense genius for scenic effect" ("Some Personal Recollections" 600).

Henry Jr.'s own response to Carlyle substitutes an emphasis on the picturesque for any direct confrontation with controversial political ideas. The identical evasion shows up in his initial inspiration for *The Bostonians:* "Daudet's *Évangéliste* has given me the idea of this thing. If I could only do something with that *pictorial* quality" (*Complete Notebooks* 19–20). But not only was the material too troublesome to be dealt with this superficially, James's own analytic approach to character was irreconcilable with his determination to be pictorial. The father's essay on Carlyle shows a similar split. In spite of Henry Sr.'s civilized claims, the real interest of his paper lies in the spectacle of cruel genius – the many anecdotes of savage explosions in which Carlyle absolutely buries someone.

The basic evasion in everything the two Henry Jameses had to say about Carlyle is easy to spot. They *loved* his ferocious assault on popular optimistic liberalism far more than they admitted. Henry Sr. himself was even seen as "something of a Carlyle in his mannerisms and trenchant style, which never comes out in full force except when he comes in contact with something that calls forth that inexpressible disgust he feels toward everything that is a *sham*" ("Word about H. J."). Like Carlyle, the Jameses felt such a strong aversion to the sentimentalizing of the downtrodden that his scorn for reformers had an inevitable appeal, along with his utter repudiation of human equality. Of course, Henry Sr. often appeared to look forward to a day of perfect equality. He supported the North in the Civil War and even attended a freedmen's benefit afterward.[16] His well-known Fourth of July oration, "The Social Significance of Our Institutions," attacked class oppression, as did his many apotheoses of the free-and-easy American horsecar: "Whenever I get my stupid sconce above water for a half an hour, some of the reigning idols, Plato or Emerson or Washington, is [*sic*] sure to plump himself down upon it, and submerge me. . . . The people in the horse-cars never do this. . . . They talk so heartily of household expenses and weather & raising chickens that it is sweet to be near them."[17] Yet this could only have been written by one whose class position was separate and distinct, who hobnobbed with humbler folk for obscure reasons all his own. In practice, the senior James seems to have avoided "common people," especially at hotels, as a letter of his wife's inadvertently reveals: "It was about half full of respectable common people who behaved very well, but were not re-munerative as companions – It was utterly doleful in this respect to me, I felt utterly dreary – Father of course was in his room all day & in the evening too" (to Alice James, 18 July [1872?], MH-H). Father believed in social equality as a truth of reason, not experience. Carlyle fascinated precisely because he openly repudiated this metaphysical dodge. As Henry Sr. put it, Carlyle "had no conception of human brotherhood or equality as the profoundest truth of science . . . but only as an emotional or sentimental experience of happily endowed natures" (*Literary Remains* 445).

The Bostonians expresses Carlyle's position as interpreted by Henry Sr. Verena's belief in equality turns out to be merely the untested emotional or sentimental experience of a happily endowed nature, and those who profess political equality – Miss Birdseye, Matthias Pardon, Selah and Mrs. Tarrant, Olive Chancellor – either delude themselves or others. The same letter to Grace Norton that condemned Carlyle's brutality also happens to contain one of James's declarations against extending the franchise: "I don't think all the world has a right to" marriage "*any more than I think all the world has a right to vote*" (*Letters* 3: 54; italics mine). The Sage of Chelsea's famous contempt was more attractive than James con-fessed. It is precisely this kind of duplicity that governs *The Bostonians,* where James obsessively disowns his novel's contemptuous hero.

The parallels in the two Henry Jameses' response to Carlyle bring us to a matter of fundamental importance in any attempt to confront *The Bostonians,* that is, the powerful and mysterious presence in this text of the author's own father.

Taking His Charge Too Much to Heart

Henry James, Sr., died 18 December 1882. Within four months his sec-ond son had worked up the plans for his next novel. Rightly sensing a connection between these events, Leon Edel has attributed the "uncon-trollable prolixity" of *The Bostonians* to "the disappearance of the home in Quincy Street, . . . probably the single deepest emotion" from which the novel sprang (*Henry James: A Life* 311, 313). This explanation of James's loss of control is vaguely correct yet misses the remarkable facts the bare chronology hints at.

First of all, there *had* been a painful ambiguity in the father's dying. The *New York Post* and *New York Tribune* both reported the cause of death as anemia of the brain (Obituary and "Henry James"). This report undoubtedly reflected an inside view, probably communicated by Aunt Kate.[18] Alice James herself wanted a doctor to undertake an "examination of the brain to discover if there was any disease there" (AHJ to WJ, 19 December addition to 18 December 1882, MH-H), but was dissuaded. The best available picture of her dying father's erratic behavior is to be found in Alice H. James's many letters to her husband, William, then in London. On 14 December, for instance, she reported that "the doctor says he will not speak of food to him [Henry Sr.] again. However, he eat, [*sic*] (asked for) two baked apples yesterday. Every other day he is excitable. This was his weak day." Three days later "he asked Alice for water, the only thing that had passed his lips for 24 hours, and as he took it he said 'What vile-tasting stuff, and what a vile world!' " (AHJ to WJ, 17 December 1882, MH-H). It is by no means clear the elder James had a fatal disease; one doctor thought he did not. He probably hastened his death, perhaps even killed himself by self-starvation, not just to rejoin his beloved Mary, but also out of disgust with the vile world and his own carnal appetites. His passing may have been the ultimate – and voluntary – expression of the "genuine self-contempt" (HJSr to Julia A. Kellogg, 19 December 1864, MH-H) that he considered the one true sign of spirituality.

Everything Henry Jr. had to say about this terrible death, as about the death of his mother the previous winter, breathes a hushed and correct piety. He had eulogized her as the perfect wife and mother, fulfilled by devotion to family. He wrote of his bereaved father as "rather seriously unwell" and professed he would "remain near him for the present" (HJ to Dall, 10 February 1882, Dall Papers, MHS), much as Ralph selflessly cares for old Mr. Touchett. Seven years earlier Henry Jr. had censured a writer who drew attention to his father's lameness (Henry Sr.'s own handicap): To disclose a parent's weakness hardly reflected "the mascu-line way of looking at things" (*Literary Criticism* 1: 279). This is the same stoic privacy we see in Basil Ransom, who knows how to "hold his tongue" (190) concerning his ancestors and womenfolk. Outside the fam-ily, James was stiffly eulogistic about his father: "the most generous, most comprehensive, most beneficent of men" (HJ to Dall, 5 February 1883, Dall Papers, MHS). Inside, he showed an exemplary correctness even when admitting Henry Sr. had ended his life of his own will. Writing to Bob: "You may imagine how we miss father – how we feel his personal absence. But since the night I arrived I have heard everything about his end, and I am glad he has given up a life of which he was so weary" (Maher 148).

But this picture represented a decorous adjustment of reality. Henry Jr. had crossed the Atlantic to see his father (as Ralph had sought a last interview with Mr. Touchett), but the father could not or would not wait, evidently preferring to die. By the time the son reached Cambridge, three days later, the James family home had gone to pieces. Alice had "turned against Aunt Kate again, worse than before," and Katherine Loring, the inseparable friend, treated the aunt with equal rudeness. Before long Miss Loring would be taking domestic liberties in the house, "arranging the papers on the table or pulling a stray chair in place." When William's wife dropped into Quincy Street the day after Henry's return, he was, by Aunt Kate's report, "sick upstairs with the worst headache he ever had." It was "rheumatic"; a Dr. Beach called twice that day. Several days later Henry was "recovering from his headache but he looked very ill and was sitting in an attitude of despondency" (AHJ to WJ, 22 December 1882, 6 January 1883, 27 December 1882, MH-H).

Alice H. reveals what Henry Jr. would not, namely, his overwhelming feelings of loss, confusion, responsibility. What touched her most of all was his pathetic concern for his sister as he talked of "her future and the extraordinary tie between her and Katherine. Then Aunt Kate came in and he dropped the subject, naturally. He takes his charge too much to heart" (AHJ to WJ, 27 December 1882, MH-H). This perceptively catches the nature of Henry Jr.'s far too proper effort, trying to hold together the home so wisely and lovingly created by the perfect parents even as it fell into dissension and queerness.

There were other reasons for guilt. James's last novel, *The Portrait of a Lady*, had memorialized the young woman, Minnie Temple, who defied Henry Sr. to his face. Acting now as executor, Henry Jr. moved so aggressively to alter Henry Sr.'s will that he incurred a sharp accusation from William: "For us absolutely to ignore that element in father's will [regarding former disbursements to Wilkie] would be to cast rather a dishonourable slur on *him*, would it not?" (WJ to HJ, 22 January 1883, MH-H). And then there was the worst slur of all on a father whose transcendent genius was simply not to be questioned: Henry Jr.'s intellectual neglect of the philosophical ideas Henry Sr. had spent his life developing and preaching. William, even more overcome by guilt, not only edited his father's papers but years later developed a pragmatic philosophy partly designed to justify religious faith.[19] "I must now make amends," wrote William three weeks after his father passed away, "for my rather hard non-receptivity of his doctrines as he urged them so absolutely during his life, by trying to get a little more public justice done them now. . . . Father's cry was the single one that religion is real. The thing is so to 'voice' it that other ears shall hear, – no easy task, but a worthy one, which in some shape I shall attempt" (typescript, 9 January 1883, MH-H). When William carried out the first part of this assignment in the summer of 1884 by preparing *The Literary Remains of the Late Henry James*, he "seemed to sink into an intimacy with Father, which I had never before enjoyed. I trust he takes cognizance of it, somewhere" (WJ to Katharine Prince, 24

December [1884], Colby). He also sank into "a fever," and when his wife rejoined him following his summer's labor, she "found him rather used up" (AHJ to Katharine Prince, 3 October 1884, Colby).

William's solemn dedication was sent to Henry, who once again followed his older brother's lead. He engaged in no public breast-beating, but he joined the project of seeking public justice. He took the charge to heart. His next novel would seek to vindicate the one department of the father's thought the son understood, sexual difference and the "marriage sentiment." The novel would show that this sentiment was stronger and more natural than the spirit of feminism (which entered into Alice and Katherine Loring's troubling bond), and it would take up the father's battle with those privacy-invading radical journalists who had hounded and exposed him. *The Bostonians* was born from a profound and complicated desire for compensatory restitution.

A Very Considerable Mystery

Behind this pious undertaking lay Henry Jr.'s longstanding and strangely misplaced sympathy with his father's views on sexual difference. In Chapter 2 of this study I have attempted to sketch the drama of Henry Sr.'s evolving views – his radical advocacy in 1848 of a Fourierist version of free love, his conservative reaction as he became an apologist for marriage seen as a kind of purgatory, his insistence after 1852 that woman belonged to a different order from man and that she voluntarily enslaved herself to him for the sake of his ultimate social and spiritual redemption. Here I can merely refer to the intricate, force-inspired, and disingenuous aspects of the father's thinking about human sexuality, and to the son's anxieties about the father's apparent victimization by free-love journalistic scoundrels, and most important, to the son's thrice-stated 1870 endorsement of his father's ideas on marriage.

Taking this preliminary history for granted, the challenge we then face is to carry through a history-saturated reading of James's novel. Where does the book express the father's marriage doctrines, and with what alterations? In what ways is the text itself a thick continuation of the father's and son's tangled involvement in a certain idea of sexual difference? It is not enough to argue, as earlier, that various elements – the authorial commentary, the contemptuous representation of the reformers, the plot – back up Basil's concept of female destiny. Without assuming that James was the doctrinaire theorist his father was, we must now also try to show that he identified his father's views with Basil's, and, as commenting author, stepped into the novel to endorse them.

It is in Chapter 38, at Marmion, that Basil delivers his most carefully considered statement of the part he thinks women should play in society.

Verena has just asked him why she was given her talent for public speaking if she is not to speak out, and Basil jokingly answers: "The dining-table itself shall be our platform, and you shall mount on top of that" (389). Then, abandoning this offensive flippancy, he comes up with an answer to her good question. His speech constitutes his one earnest defense of his view of women's social function:

> "We shall find plenty of room for your facility; it will lubricate our whole existence. Believe me, Miss Tarrant, these things will take care of themselves. You won't sing in the Music Hall, but you will sing to me; you will sing to everyone who knows you and approaches you. Your gift is indestructible; don't talk as if I either wanted to wipe it out or should be able to make it a particle less divine. I want to give it another direction, certainly; but I don't want to stop your activity. Your gift is the gift of expression, and there is nothing I can do for you that will make you less expressive. It won't gush out at a fixed hour and on a fixed day, but it will irrigate, it will fertilise, it will brilliantly adorn your conversation. Think how delightful it will be when your influence becomes really social. Your facility, as you call it, will simply make you, in conversation, the most charming woman in America." (390)

This was the curtain speech ending the eleventh installment of the serial. It was probably James rather than his editor at the *Century* who chose this form of emphasis; a cryptic notebook entry proves that James planned the "divisions of installments" (*Complete Notebooks* 31) from fall 1884 on. But even without this conspicuous placement, the speech has an earnest eloquence that asks for special attention. The oddities of diction and imagery – "gush," "irrigate," "fertilise," "lubricate" – recall the James family's language, as when Mary urged Henry Jr. to get married: "Your social life, the life of your affections must need the moisture and sunshine" (Feinstein 343). And the speech's basic point – the high civilizing function of social charm – was one of Henry James's fundamental concerns, showing up in dozens of his narratives. This idea was derived in part from his father's doctrine that marriage is the institution in which woman achieves the social redemption of man.

The key detail is James's introduction to the speech, which explicitly vouches for its truth in a manner absolutely without parallel in his entire fictional output: "There was more reason, however, as well as more appreciation of a very considerable mystery, in what he went on to say" (390). The comparative, "more reason," refers to Basil's offhand dining-table remark. What Basil will now say evidently merits our serious consideration. And how striking that James should bring forward those two big guns, reason and mystery, which so often serve to defend fervent religious convictions. Even though James addresses the matter with his customary light touch rather than with his father's argumentativeness and high unction, he is clearly instructing us to regard Basil's speech as right and profound.[20] There is reason in what he will say, and there is revelation, an insight into the great mystery of social life. Woman makes her charming influence felt, not by entering the political arena, but by remaining confined within the home. We recall James's earlier declarations that Basil "had a *higher* conception of politeness" than the suffragists, or that he regarded woman's "softness and docility" as "the inspiration, the opportunity (the *highest*) of man" (193; italics mine). Basil does not defend the paternal idea in its pure form – marriage as a form of bondage in which woman is given to man so that her selflessly affectionate nature can lead him from the selfish to the social. Instead Basil expresses a secularized version: Marriage confines woman in order to produce brilliant social conversation and general refinement.[21] The passage shows as nothing else in James's fiction what he made of his father's marriage doctrine. It simultaneously reveals a major continuity and a major shift, and in doing so it tells us something tremendously important about James's lifelong emphasis on refinement – that for him this great good thing depends on, perhaps even justifies, a prior forcible enslavement.

Basil's speech sets forth one of Henry Sr.'s basic paradoxes, how pain is converted to the higher good. At the bottom (in every sense) of that paradox lies the word "fertilise," a much earthier word in the 1880s than now, when a variety of chemical agents have replaced manure. For Henry Sr., the use of sewage in European agriculture became a powerful symbol of how the base makes possible the spiritual ("Some Personal Recollections" 607). This idea was a familiar one in the James household, and when Henry Jr. sought to express the value of his first trip to Italy in 1869, he wrote: "Let it lie warm and nutritive at the base of my mind, manuring and enriching its roots" (*Letters* 1: 208). James was undergoing treatment for constipation when he wrote this.

Manuring, for James, had a curious affiliation with the idea of social refinement. Twenty years after *The Bostonians,* he wrote an essay, "The Speech of American Women," dedicated to the proposition that the basis of civilization is "the vocal sounds with which a woman affects the ear of man." James argued that the great civilized truth taught by Europe – "the number of common figures and common lives required . . . to fertilize the ground for the single type of the gentleman" – was just as true "for the type of the lady." Unfortunately, there was "no fertilization of the social ground" in America, where women had not learned how to produce "colloquial comfort." There would have to be fear and pain before there could be any civilizing womanly refinement. As it is, "the soil has undergone, for the plant of the fine individual life, none of the preparation of the grinding, the trampling, the packing into it of other lives, lives resigned to a mere subsidiary and contributive function" (*French Writers* 38, 35, 40). Basil could not have said it better.

Thus, there is a sacred terror at the heart of *The Bostonians* (and this is another reason the novel is hard to read well), a terror closely related to the mystery at the heart of the Jameses' various considerations of Carlyle (the man's a brute, what a genius!) and to the senior James's argument that true liberty is to be found only in self-denial. It is the classic stricture of conservatism, the ancient, fearful argument that an extension of liberty will turn out to be the end of liberty. Henry Jr. had only recently worked out this argument in *The Portrait of a Lady*, where the hopeful American girl, freed from restraint by the Touchett legacy, ends up ground in the mill of the conventional – and thus turns into a finer person than before. In this respect *The Portrait* confirmed the senior James's argument that selfhood is wicked, that one must transcend one's self by passing from the selfish to the social. In *The Bostonians* the good son went further, offering a more challenging defense of the paternal mystery and aiming it at the sloppy, liberalizing modern world that ignored the father's wise instruction. And the particular mystery James tried to work out was that Basil, the former slaveholder all "superior" Northern readers would look down on, is better for Verena than her supposed liberator, Olive Chancellor. The book would vindicate the father by showing that Basil's slavery is freedom and Olive's freedom, slavery. Henry Jr. was taking the charge to heart.

The stunning irony is that as far as James the private man was concerned, his father's teachings simultaneously *lost* their personal appeal and relevance. His letters to Grace Norton, which try to get her to cease urging him to marry, show his personal feelings on the matter. On 3 November 1884 (soon after he had begun *The Bostonians*) he declared: "Singleness consorts much better with my whole view of existence (of my own and *of that of the human race*), my habits, occupations, prospects, tastes, means, situation 'in Europe,' and absence of desire to have children." He pays lip service to the paternal (and conventional) notion that marriage is "the highest human state" (*Letters* 3: 54), yet the phrase I have italicized hints at his real feeling. Several years earlier he had told Norton that if he married "I should pretend to think just a little better of life than I really do" (Edel, *Conquest of London* 358). Evidently, his own independent sense of life was painfully remote from the "very considerable mystery" his new novel had committed him to defend.

Basil and the Dead Father

To ransom is to redeem, and redemption was the father's great theme. Basil Ransom not only voices and enacts Henry Sr.'s marriage doctrine, he carries the dead man's spirit as well, battling for old, strict, painful truths. When Emerson looked at one of Henry Sr.'s books, he felt "that you have not shed your last coat of presbyterianism, but that a certain catachetical & legendary Jove glances at me sometimes, in your page" (letter of 25 February 1850, MH-H). When Henry Jr. read his father's 1870 essay on marriage, "The Woman Thou Gavest with Me," he made a similar comment, but from a perspective opposed to Emerson's: "I am very glad to see some one not Dr. Bushnell & all that genus insist upon the distinction of sexes." This very awkward sentence distinguishes "some one," the senior James, from a Congregational theologian and his "genus." The father is *not* Bushnell – but he deserves praise for doing what Bushnell does.[22] The verb "insist" aptly expresses Henry Sr.'s mode of tireless argumentation – and Basil's. Both the real and the invented man insist upon the distinction of sexes. Each is dug in, for the duration, in a war the others are forgetting. When Basil dreams of publishing his iconoclastic "lucubrations" at his "own expense" (197), he is thinking of a life similar to Henry Sr.'s.

Although not identical with Henry James, Sr., Basil does embody the good son's vision of his paterfamilias, and because of this the solid differences between hero and father are as instructive as the differences that fade away under inspection. As an instance of the latter, Basil's ridicule of the spread of education seems opposed at first to the practice of Henry Sr., who sent his younger sons, Wilkie and Bob, to Frank Sanborn's radical coeducational school in Concord, where they sat next to John Brown's daughter. But many of the schools the father selected for his children were strict and old-fashioned, and he was apparently opposed to providing young women with advanced education. There is no evidence he considered sending Alice off to school. When Wilkie and Bob left for Concord, the father's chief (though jocular) concern was the tempting presence, causing "bewilderment" (Maher 16), of female classmates. "Distinction of sexes" remained primary.

Another apparent difference is that Basil seems much more highly sexed than the author's father, especially as represented in *A Small Boy and Others*. The former has a variety actress as mistress; the latter was devoutly uxorious. But Henry Sr. frequently hinted that he had a checkered past, and in any case few nineteenth-century writers were more obsessed with the idea of carnal attraction. Whether he defended the idea (as in his early translation of a Fourierist free-love pamphlet) or attacked it (almost everywhere else) it continually rose to the surface of his thought, even in the avuncular letters he sent the various young ladies who sought his spiritual counsel. To Julia A. Kellogg, for instance, he announced that "under the advent of a true society among men, all the appetites and passions of our nature will be free of reproach . . . and secure of ample satisfaction" (25 January 1864, MH-H). In another letter to this correspondent he insisted that "the whole truth of paternity is spiritual not physical" and drew a fascinating distinction between the parts the sexes play in conception: "All we know of the phenomena of generation, scientifically, is confined to what the mother contributes to the process. We know, scientifically, absolutely nothing of how the male sperm quickens the ovum in the womb of the female. The process of quickening or life-giving is spiritual, and therefore exceeds our microscopic wisdom" (31 August [no year], MH-H).[23]

This bizarre contrast between the spirituality of paternity and the physicality of motherhood has no real parallel in Basil. The Southerner's vision, it is true, often highlights the physical presence of Verena, whose "flat young chest" (58) develops into "loveliness" (336) of figure. But such emphases derive from Basil's asserted maleness. By comparison, Henry Sr.'s sense of sexual difference seems tortuous and oddly precious. In 1865, after Caroline Dall had dined with the James family, the men held a debate about the gender of her "intellect." The sons, some of them at least, argued that this strong-minded feminist had a masculine mind; the father insisted that she was after all "remarkably feminine" (HJSr to Caroline Dall, 13 January [1865] Dall Papers, MHS).[24] According to Dall's private journal, the elder James asked the somewhat miffed woman, both by letter and in person, for her "*own judgment* on the subject!!" Her record of this episode offers a brilliant sidelight on the curiousness of the James father's obsession:

> "Fussy & futile distinction of sex" – he once said of "Absolute James" – Humph! thought I – quite fussy & futile here but I laughed & told him what I thought.
> Lizzie Merriam came in while he was here. . . . I began in a joke – to tell her what Mr. James had come for. "Oh, don't speak! let me guess! May I?" she exclaimed, clasping her hands. "Feminine, *strongest* feminine!" (journal entry for 13 January 1865, Dall Papers, MHS)

In the cryptic first paragraph, Dall is endorsing another man's opinion of "Absolute" Henry James, Sr., and his "fussy & futile" obsession with gender difference. Lizzie Merriam's friendly parody confirms just how notorious the obsession had become.

The same journal entry has a report, unmatched for vivid intimacy, on the James father's response to the strongly assertive Dall. Henry Sr. here repeats what he told his wife after first meeting Dall, confessing now to Dall herself:

> "I have had a curious experience," said he[,] "we had a little talk – I think *she* was on her guard – " I *know* I was. "She said little, did not assert herself, but I *felt* her *predominance*, wanted her ap-

proval, found myself growing diplomatic in order to obtain it. I was conscious of a sort of dread, wh. I never feel for a man.["]
" – so I am now," continued he quite innocently . . .
    It was the funniest thing I ever knew. It never seemed to me for a moment that he was talking about me – & when I told [Charles G.] Ames tonight, he fairly rolled on the floor in convulsions of laughter. (journal entry for 13 January 1865, Dall Papers, MHS)

Henry Sr.'s open confession of "a sort of dread" stimulated by Dall's gender struck her and Ames as innocent, weird, comical. This parade of candor and unguardedness would be utterly out of character for Basil, but it seems perfectly appropriate for Matthias Pardon, in Long's phrase a "poor excuse for a man" ("Society" 110), with his babyish ways and eager servicing of the more aggressive ladies and his dedication to revealing all that is hidden. This effeminate reporter, so despised by his author, tells us an important truth about the author's father and the author's defensiveness about his father. If that father would not be properly guarded and mind the usual social barriers, then the son would do the guarding. Basil is a retroactive dignifying of Henry Sr., an enhancing of his manhood and crusading indomitability. His more anomalous and embarrassing qualities are projected onto the contemptible Pardon, conceived of as the embodiment of American journalism and its impudent invasion of privacy. Henry Sr. had taken advantage of Carlyle's hospitality in putting together his "abusive" and popular lecture on him (M. Howe 79), and had himself been spectacularly invaded by *Woodhull & Claflin's Weekly* in 1874. As Dall's marvelous anecdote reveals, he had a profoundly exhibitionistic side, which sought, precisely, to expose his own social guardedness. The only way good son Henry could deal with this compulsion was to project it onto the hideous radical press. The utterly fascinating result: The effeminate character who gets ridiculed by the son in an act of filial loyalty actually enacts the father's own neurotic assault on privacy.

    Henry Jr.'s embarrassment over his parent cannot be emphasized too much, especially since this embarrassment produced a deep feeling of incapacity (Edel, *Untried Years* 51–52). As a boy, living in New York, he was terribly uneasy about his father's lack of professional identity; now, writing *The Bostonians,* he could not produce Basil's professional life in New York. It is partly because of the compensatory element in Basil that the novel ends up defending oppressive force in a manner that is simultaneously extreme and disingenuous. One obvious difference between Basil and Henry – the former a Southern slaveowner and the latter a Northern Unionist – is definitely more apparent than real. The fact is that hero and father both believe, *still,* in slavery – the forceful possession of one person by another. That woman was given to man in marriage was a truth Henry Sr. took literally, just as he sometimes asserted an authority over his children that was extreme even in his time. Maher's biography of Wilkie and Bob reveals an extraordinary number of letters (from their siblings and mother as well as their father) exhorting, requiring, even conjuring the children to steel themselves to some onerous duty or other in the name of honorable masculinity. Bob, the lifelong drifter who went on alcoholic binges, shows the underside of the James family's mighty assertion of will. Compulsion, by oneself or others, was the key to life, and Henry Sr.'s prose bristles with words like "bondage," "chains," "perforce." His brilliant antagonist, Stephen Pearl Andrews, spotted the resemblance between his theory of marriage and Southern chattel slavery.[25] There is no paradox at all in the fact that Henry Sr.'s spirit returned to life in his son's characterization of an ex-Mississippi planter who takes his wife by "muscular force" (448).

The elder James's style, particularly brilliant in invective, reminded his son William of "the rich vascular temperament of the old English masters, rather than that of an American of to-day" (HJSr, *Literary Remains* 9). Similarly, Basil Ransom, with his fondness for antiquated terms of abuse, "seemed at moments to be inhabited by some transmitted spirit of a robust but narrow ancestor, some broad-faced wig-wearer or swordbearer, with a more primitive conception of manhood than our modern temperament appears to require" (190). (Is this how Mrs. Tarrant should have used the word "temperament"?) But the primitive sense of manhood came from the nineteenth century, not the seventeenth, and the ancestor was the author's, not the hero's. It was true enough, though, that Henry Sr.'s modern temperament *was* in flagrant disharmony with his atavistic and absolute conception of himself.

Elizabeth Peabody Revived

The simplest way to sum up the rich contradictoriness of *The Bostonians* is to say that the novel itself is inhabited, possessed, by the author's undead father, and that the waspish, sarcastic voice that surfaces throughout the book represents the son's own token resistance and helpless skepticism. Basil's and Olive's struggle for possession of a gifted young person reflects a sinister and archaic takeover on a more fundamental level: The novel's themes recapitulate its own ontogeny and the Jameses' phylogeny. As Lionel Trilling observed, there is a large-scale invasion of "malign, archaic influences" (114). But it was not some witch-ridden realm, as Trilling would have it, that threatened the writer; it was the old world of male supremacy. If James flung his sarcasms at Basil from time to time, it was to strive, vainly, to distance himself from the mind of his novel, which had a life of its own that was thoroughly repulsive to Harry's gentler, more humane side. But the spell could not be broken, and James wrote on, an unwilling medium, until he finally reached the nasty end of a novel few readers seem to have followed. *The Bostonians* was James's ultimate ghost story. The one who got snatched was the author himself.

This happened to James, not simply because of his profound and complicated feelings about his recently deceased father, but also because at the time he meditated and composed *The Bostonians* he was, in dozens of ways, living in the middle and late 1860s. He was extensively revising his earliest tales, "revamping & almost rewriting" (HJ to Grace Norton, 24 January [1885], MH-H) them for republication in the aptly titled *Stories Revived.* He revamped the name of a trance speaker he heard in 1863, Cora L. V. Hatch,²⁶ when he invented Ada T. P. Foat in Chapter 10 of *The Bostonians.* As Howard Kerr has cogently demonstrated, the book further revives a number of "magnetic romances" and antireform satires of the 1850s and 1860s: Orestes Brownson's *Spirit-Rapper,* Fred Folio's *Lucy Boston; or, Women's Rights and Spiritualism, Illustrating the Follies and Delusions of the Nineteenth Century,* and, of course (as Marius Bewley showed long ago), Hawthorne's *Blithedale Romance.* As if James had never written *The Portrait of a Lady,* he suddenly relapsed to his old suspicion of overmastering, masculinized young ladies: Miss McCarthy of "A Most Extraordinary Case" (1868) he now renamed Miss Masters; Miss Blunt of "A Landscape-Painter" (1866) became Miss Quarterman. Public events of the post–Civil War quinquennium, controversies over books, *The Nation*'s hardening attitude toward female suffrage in the late 1860s all came to life again in *The Bostonians.* In 1868, for instance, James himself had started an outcry in this journal against the novel, *What Answer?,* which opens with a young woman's graduation speech on slavery ("one night of oppression and despair") and was in fact written by the celebrated speaker who has been claimed as a model for Verena, Anna Dickinson.²⁷ James evidently recollected this book in writing *The Bostonians,* where one of Verena's speeches is said to have "the value of a pretty essay, committed to memory and delivered by a bright girl at an 'academy' " (268).

James's mind was so vulnerably open to the past that he even lost control of his pen. In a curious mistake first noted by Edel, the letter James wrote in February 1884 about his plans for a novel the following year (*The Princess Casamassima*) three times says 1865 rather than the intended 1885. For Edel, this error reflects "the extent to which in his inner mind that year had an emotional importance for him." William's departure in particular made 1865 seem "ever after an *annus mirabilis*" (*Untried Years* 226). But Edel's emphasis on fraternal rivalry seems unwarranted here. For reasons probably originating in the death of Henry

James, Sr., his bereaved second son was revisiting, reviving, the past on a massive scale. Although James dreamed that his forthcoming novel would "mark a new era in my career" (writing this the month before his pen wiped out two decades), his immersion in the past meant that *The Bostonians* would be "essentially a backward look at one phase of American life along lines already established by other writers" (Kerr 219).

James's obsession with a two-decades-old past opened a door through which his father's ghost reentered the world and rechained his son. This ghost haunted the author's voice, the Carlylean hero's defense of marriage, and the whole demonstration that the sentiment of sex is stronger than suffrage. Most of all, the ghost determined the presentation of Miss Birdseye.

Many commentators have argued that James basically treats the aging reformer in a kindly manner. This interpretation arises from her "altered characterization" (Heaton's apt phrase) in the later chapters and from James's own protestations of innocence in his letters to William. But the Miss Birdseye of Chapter 4 is undoubtedly the sloppiest of James's many sloppy women. Her life is an ongoing dissolve of causes, refugees, new truths, and falling articles of clothing. The harsh string of adjectives introducing her – "confused, entangled, inconsequent, discursive" (27) – draws attention to her lack of connectedness and sequence. Her thoughts reflect a permanent state of confusion – "wondering most of all what had been her idea in convoking these people" (31–32) – and the hand forever groping at the back of her head for her falling cap is the image and emblem of her half-conscious quest for presence of mind. There are few objective deviations in her passage through the novel: She is weakheadedness shading into senility, and she dies as she has lived, deluded, supposing that Verena has converted Basil. Chapter 4 constitutes James's most concerted assault on female empty-headedness since his presentation of Lizzie Crowe in "The Story of a Year" (1865) – Lizzie, whose "intellect was unequal to the stern logic of human events" (*Tales* 1: 42). Birdseye and Crowe: both birdbrained.

James's tone with Miss Birdseye becomes more temperate after Chapter 4, partly in response to William's criticism and partly because Basil's chivalry dominates the later scenes in which she appears. But chivalry, as Basil understands, is for one's enemies, not friends. Beneath the apparent warmth lies a settled coolness, a contempt for a profoundly thoughtless person. In her later appearances, Miss Birdseye continues to be remarkably unintelligent even as she is sentimentalized as an "innocent old dear" (221).

One reason James produced this essentially hostile portrait of an aging New England reformer is that he hated the failure to discriminate. Miss Birdseye is obviously one of those on whom everything is lost, and her inability to distinguish has a close connection, for James, to her quarrel with societal segregation, her impulse to bring down the high and elevate the lowly. The finicky phrase with which James describes her offered handshake – "a delicate, dirty, democratic little hand" (27) – hints at the author's disgust with those who want to level downward. Evidently, there is something even worse than ignoring class and that is preferring the wrong one, especially when Miss Birdseye judges the down-and-out by more lenient standards than she applies to those who are more privileged. Thus, we are told that her "animosity to flourishing evils lived in the happiest (though the most illicit) union with the mania for finding excuses" (109). The wit here is very fine, unlike the moral sympathy. Commenting on her preference for what he calls "the dingier types" (315), James makes an extremely crude attribution of motive:

> Whenever money was given her she gave it away to a negro or a refugee. No woman could be less invidious, but on the whole she preferred these two classes of the human race. Since the Civil War much of her occupation was gone; for before that her best hours had been spent *in fancying* that she was helping some Southern slave to escape. It would have been a nice question whether, in her heart of hearts, *for the sake of this excitement,* she did not sometimes wish the blacks back in bondage. (28; italics mine)

How unfair for someone as remote as James from the tragedy of black subjection to make such claims about the abolitionists' private motives.[28]

When the first installment of *The Bostonians* appeared in February 1885, some of its readers saw at once that Miss Birdseye was modeled on the well-known New England reformer Elizabeth Peabody. In a harsh letter that has disappeared, William called this representation of a living, respected person "really a pretty bad business." James heatedly denied the accusation. He admitted taking the detail of the slipping glasses from Peabody but insisted that in all other respects Miss Birdseye had "evolved entirely from my moral consciousness" (*Letters* 3: 69, 68).

Nobody who has considered the matter doubts that James was lying – that he refused to admit an obvious pillorying.[29] But there remain some hard questions to be asked about the episode, especially as regards James's motives. He must have realized that some of his Boston readers would recognize his hostile portrait. Did he mean to give offense? If his portrait of Matthias Pardon was intended to assault or "*bafouer*" (*Complete Notebooks* 19) a phase of American life, why not that of Peabody? Yet to produce a transparent portrait was to stoop to Pardon's level – to "pour . . . contumely on their private life, on their personal appearance, with the best conscience in the world" (123). The irony, as Howard hints (69), is that this outraged sentence describes James's own performance more accu-

rately than it describes Pardon's bland journalistic intrusions. The news-
paperman may show a low undiscriminating curiosity, but it is the novelist who pours the high proud scorn, though whether with the best
conscience in the world it is hard to say.

The way that others, especially Henry Sr., regarded Peabody helps
explain why Henry Jr. was out for her blood, and even more why he
permitted himself to take a cheap public shot at her. On 8 May 1875,
several months before he sailed to Europe, the *Boston Times* ran a long
satirical poem that made fun of Peabody along with several other members of a well-known Boston discussion circle, one to which the senior
James had read three papers. The poem, called "The Radical Club" after
the organization itself, was written pseudonymously by the Southern
humorist Katherine McDowell. The first two lines of stanza twenty-one
refer to Peabody:

> The Kindergarten mother clucked an answer to his brother,
> And her curls kept bobbing quaintly from the queer head dress
>   she wore;
> And another *magnus corpus,* with a figure like a porpus,
> In wonder did absorb us, as she viewed our numbers o'er,
> And talked about the "Oversoul" and other mystic lore,
>   Nameless here, forever more.
>   ([McDowell], "Radical Club")[30]

Compared to James's rough handling of Peabody, this seems fairly good-
natured, yet the poem ruffled some feathers. A rejoinder appeared the
following year that reproved the author's poor taste, especially in lam-
pooning Peabody:

> Touch her not: each hair is sacred
> On that gray and honored head;
> Let the "head-dress" shame the critic:
> Babes will weep when she is dead.
> Blessed "Kindergarten mother,"
>   Twas well said.   (*Radical Club*)

The pious veneration that is evident in this defense reveals the iconic
stature Peabody acquired in Boston during the 1870s, the decade in
which James severed many connections with the city. His hostile portrait
harks back to a more divisive time in the previous decade (that time warp
again) when Peabody made a number of enemies among Boston's leading intellectuals. Annie Fields, for instance, considered one of her lectures
"slobbery" in 1865. Two years later Fields was offended that Peabody
should press her to attend another lecture "*for a very particular reason*" and
then reveal afterward that the motive was to get the paper published in

the *Atlantic*. The next year there was a private gathering in which Emerson "talked openly of the untruthfulness of the Peabodys" (journal entries for 20 October 1865, January 1867, and 19 October 1868, Fields Papers, MHS). In addition to being an often maladroit schemer, Peabody was famously absentminded, had numerous enthusiasms, and accepted the claims of spiritualism. Yet she was often effective as well as kindly, and her letters reveal a self-possessed, even rather flat-footed, mind; she did not wander. As late as 1885, according to Jane Marsh Parker, Peabody "held to her thread no matter what its length; never dropped a stitch; and her sequences were so simple and clear that following her was seldom baffling or fatiguing" (*Letters of Elizabeth Palmer Peabody* 396). This testimonial to her mental soundness was probably meant to counteract the self-replicating legend of her forgetfulness.

The senior Henry James appears to have been the fiercest of Peabody's detractors in the latter 1860s. The letters he wrote her in 1863 about Wilkie's injuries (Maher ch. 2) show how close the two originally were. But in the spring of 1866, when Henry Jr. was living at home, Peabody sent Caroline Dall a letter that seems to have made some deadly accusations – "the gravest charges," according to Dall's journal. Henry Sr. became her champion, offering sympathy and support, questioning Peabody's "good-breeding," even delivering a personal reproach. After the episode blew over, James wrote Dall that "Elizabeth P. I fancy is now very reticent and decorous in your direction. She seemed to me sorry that she had pushed matters as far as she did."[31]

Obscure as the episode remains, it seems to have established Henry Sr.'s idea of Peabody once and for all. Writing in 1868 to his old friend, Garth Wilkinson, he gave a sketch of her that reads like an early version of Miss Birdseye:

> Elizabeth Peabody is a very odd personage in every point of view, as you must have observed; but her judgment in my estimation is her feeblest part. She is enthusiastic for every thing exceptional, and has a contempt for the common place which will condemn her to dark-corners to all eternity, if she dont look out betimes. She is a sensationalist of a pronounced pattern, and you cannot rely in the least upon her observation of facts, whether physical or moral. (29 September 1868, MH-H)

The feeble judgment, the contempt for the common, the enthusiasm for the exceptional, the inability to observe – these were to be the leading traits of Miss Birdseye. Even more striking than this parallel is Henry Sr.'s arrogant, even minatory, tone. He is evidently privy to the ultimate metaphysical status this foolish enthusiast is preparing for herself if she "dont" mend her ways. These inquisitorial attitudes helped make possible Henry Jr.'s harsh treatment of Peabody. In fact, one could say that the judgment brandished by the stern father was executed by the son. And for the many twentieth-century critics who accept *The Bostonians'* claim to authority, the old reforming ninny *has* been condemned to dark corners.

The key evidence of this father-to-son transmission is a first-person report by Edward Emerson of something Henry Sr. once said about Peabody in front of his children. Edward was having dinner with the Jameses when William returned from Boston with a story about an elderly woman who urged him to attend some lectures on art anatomy by William Rimmer. Recalling the occasion decades later, Edward pointedly named the woman Jane Smith and characterized her as "an eager reformer, absolutely self-forgetful, but . . . with superabundant faith in the virtue of each new prophet." Suddenly, Edward writes, "Mr. James broke in with violence" on William's story:

> "The man's a fraud! It's impossible he should be anything else if Jane Smith believes in him! . . . Wh-wh-why! J-Jane Smith – she's one of the most d-d-dissolute old creatures that walks the earth!" etc. Here the family shouted with joy . . . at the Jamesian felicity of the adjective. For they saw, in memory, the gray hair falling down under the bonnet askew, the spectacles slipping down with resulting upturned radiant face, the nondescript garments and general dissolving effect, symbolizing the loose reasoning and the charity falling all abroad – yes, in a sense a dissolute personality.[32] (Edward Emerson 156–57)

Edward's recollection of this violent and humorous Carlylean denunciation, recorded decades after the event, may have been influenced by the legend that gathered around Peabody or even by *The Bostonians'* own notorious lampoon of her. But the key word, "dissolute," with or without the stammering, is surely authentic, a remnant of the James father's speech at home straight from the 1860s. This chance remnant identifies the source of the basic image in Henry Jr.'s presentation of Miss Birdseye, who is dissolute in both the moral and the physical senses of the word: She enjoys illegitimate pleasures ["the happiest (though the most illicit) union" (109)], and she is a solid going into solution. Even her face looks

> . . . as if it had been soaked, blurred, and made vague by exposure to some slow dissolvent [*sic*]. The long practice of philanthropy had not given accent to her features; it had rubbed out their transitions, their meanings. The waves of sympathy, of enthusiasm, had wrought upon them in the same way in which the waves of time

finally modify the surface of old marble busts, gradually washing away their sharpness, their details. (26–27)

The witty polish of this sketch, or rather bust, suggests that James had been meditating on his study in philanthropic dissoluteness for a long time. Consistent to the end, in spite of his apparent tenderness, he finally washed away the last trace of Miss Birdseye, who, in Doctor Prance's words, "just melted away, towards eight o'clock" (401). She dissolved, but the father's word was etched in stone.

It was because Henry Sr.'s spirit haunted *The Bostonians* that the novel assailed the foolish woman who would not "look out," and it was because Henry Jr. was living in the past, safely lapped in the old family fold as he wrote, that he did not realize just how partisan and savage his lampoon was. He was not only caught off guard by the outcry against it, but he felt it was singularly unfair of William to join the attack and was wounded by his harsh criticism: "Still," James snapped back, "I didn't expect the charge to come from you" (*Letters* 3: 68).

Verena's Singular Hollowness of Character

Of course *The Bostonians* is more than a ghost-written novel. As we now attempt to understand exactly what it says about "woman," and Verena in particular, it will be essential not to conflate Henry Jr.'s perspective with that of his father. The feral names given the two minor feminists, for instance – Catching, the Harvard library cataloguer who is "wrapped up in the cause" (240), and Croucher, whose 56th Street residence forms the "principal centre" (290) of the movement in New York – remind us of the son's suspicion of mastering women. "Croucher" happens to have the same consonantal pattern as the key word in James's interesting phrase, "the encroachments of modern democracy" (190). This malign female animalism, which enters deeply into James's conception of Olive, seems alien to his father's vision of women. For Henry Sr. in 1844, the "fetid," "squatting" (*Literary Remains* 59) presence was definitely male, but for Henry Jr. the evil usurping squatter was often female.

One of the reasons why it can be so difficult to see what James is saying about women in the novel is that he tends to obscure it underneath a certain programmatic tenderness. It is this sort of tenderness that he brings to play on Miss Birdseye near the end, and which he mentioned in a letter warning William not to judge too hastily: "The later apparition and death of Miss B. is the prettiest thing in the book" (*Letters* 3: 71). The same thread of pretty tinsel runs through James's treatment of Verena. This very important figure was originally intended as the novel's heroine and point-of-view character. She still furnished his "provisional" title (typed copy, HJ to

Richard Watson Gilder, 31 July 1884, Gilder Papers) even after he had written the first two installments (*Complete Notebooks* 31). Her warmest, most attentive interpreter may be Howard (72–80), who sees her as analogous to Huckleberry Finn, that other untutored genius of sweetness. But however marvelous Verena may be as a conception – the innocent, improvising offspring of a tacky American bohemian – James could not quite realize his intentions with her. Something went seriously wrong.

On the surface the commenting author protests that he feels a supreme homage for his heroine, whose unworthy mother

> . . . was only vaguely aware of the fact that she had at her side the sweetest flower of character (as one might say) that had ever bloomed on earth. She was proud of Verena's brightness, and of her special talent; but the commonness of her own surface was a non-conductor of the girl's quality. Therefore she thought that it would add to her success in life to know a few high-flyers, if only to put them to shame; as if anything could add to Verena's success, as if it were not supreme success simply to have been made as she was made. (106)

James makes some large claims for Verena here yet unmistakably hedges his praise. The parenthetic equivocation, "as one might say," following "the sweetest flower of character" registers the author's uneasiness with his insipid phrase (his, not Mrs. Tarrant's). Then there are the two "as if" clauses near the end, which put the assertion that Verena's nature is virtually perfect into the subjunctive mood. Clearly, the author does not feel what he asks the reader to feel.

It is not that James is orchestrating any great subtlety here, but rather that his reserve masks itself as warm appreciation and yet unmasks itself after all. The reserve is of course justified; Verena *does* seem rather lightweight, as when she secretly admires Mrs. Luna (107). After Basil decides in Chapter 8 that the girl does not really believe in the political ideas she expresses, only liking to please parents and other audiences, the author breaks in with this comment: "I know not whether Ransom was aware of the bearings of this interpretation, which attributed to Miss Tarrant a singular hollowness of character" (61). James's implication here seems to be that Basil is only being Boeotian once again, that Verena has real solidity. Only later, looking back, can we see how misleading the comment is. The fact is that James's plan for the novel absolutely requires Verena to have a singular hollowness of character – and also requires the author to conceal this grave defect. His love for her, like Basil's (but this too must be covered up), is inseparable from contempt for her intellect.

The Central Park and Marmion episodes fully corroborate Basil's opinion of Verena. Her charming performance *does* reflect a sweet-natured eagerness to please others. She has a *very* weak hold on the ideas she spouts, and she cannot function unless someone directs her. Soon after telling us that "the deepest feeling in Ransom's bosom in relation to her was the conviction that she was made for love" (330), James brings on a nursery maid and two children so that he can confirm the Southerner's intuition: Verena looks "with a *quickened* eye at the children (she adored children)" (331; italics mine). When Basil serenely announces to her that he knows far better than she what she is about, she is affected as with the force of revelation: "These words . . . had sunk into her soul and worked and *fermented* there" (italics mine). She comes to see herself exactly as Basil sees her, and not only that but she "liked herself better" (384). Has Basil simply overborne her? Well, "it was in her nature . . . to like being overborne" (328). The dependent girl feels "more free" walking with "a remarkable young man who would take beautiful care of her" (324).

It is essential to see that Verena is not the only one who finds freedom in yielding freedom. The author too, after first raising his eyebrows at Basil's cynical opinion of her, ends up confirming it by using *his own* prerogative of omniscience to expose *her* inner nature to view. Once again we see how extraordinary Basil's control proves to be: In many respects the novel unfolds from *his* deepest, most private convictions. This is one of the reasons the book attacks the public exposure of the private.

Many readings of *The Bostonians* go subtly astray, I believe, by seeing Verena's capitulation to Basil (or earlier, to Olive) as resulting from an individual weakness. In fact, she lets herself be wrenched away from the Music Hall because her *generic* feminine nature has come into operation. Verena's mentality has little to do with her antecedents, her environment, or even her experience, but derives almost entirely from her gender: She is what she is because she has been more richly endowed than the other female characters with beauty and feminine grace. It is femininity that determines her behavior, and this femininity has two related components, a weak capacity for thought and an emotional disposition to yield to others – "give herself away, turn herself inside out" (380).

On the first point, it seems evident that the novel belittles women's capacity for thinking well, and thus backs up Basil's (and Henry Sr.'s) conviction that women "have no business to be reasonable" (216). (Henry Sr.: "Learning and wisdom do not become her" ["Woman and the 'Woman's Movement' " 279].) The speech Basil prevents Verena from giving is called "A Woman's Reason," a title that harks back to Anna Dickinson's 1869 lecture, "Nothing Unreasonable" (reported in the *New York Tribune* on 29 May). Verena's title has a lamentable irony in view of the medley of unfelt imagery her two earlier talks consist of: "Good gentlemen all, if I could make you believe how much brighter and fairer and sweeter the garden of life would be for you, if you would only let us help you to keep it in order! You would like so much better to walk there, and you would find grass and trees and flowers that would make you think you were in Eden" (267). That the rising young star of the women's movement can do no better than this tells us exactly how hollow James felt the cause of "the 'emancipation' of woman" (HJ to Grace Norton, 8 June 1879, MH-H) to be. Once again, the quotation marks, like his father's in "Woman and the 'Woman's Movement,' " express contempt.

Olive has a better mind than Verena, but James presents her, too, as fundamentally irrational. "Her manner of repairing her inconsistency was altogether feminine: she wished to extract a certainty at the same time that she wished to deprecate a pledge" (137). Olive's pet idea, "the historic unhappiness of women" (163) – an emphasis that leaves practical Mrs. Farrinder cold – has nothing to do with any possible program of action. When Verena tries to question this devoutly held idea, pointing out that there have been many notoriously evil women, Olive disposes of the objection with a neat sophistry: "If the influence of women in the past accounted for every act of virtue that men had happened to achieve, it only made the matter balance properly that the influence of men should explain the casual irregularities of the other sex" (176). This is the sort of thinking the *Rational Review* presumably exists to combat. Olive's reasoning is not only false, but her clenched hold on a fixed idea injures the cause of freedom itself. James turns her exalted response to Mrs. Farrinder's counsel into a revelation of this inner self-betrayal: "It was one thing to choose for herself, but now the great representative of the enfranchisement of their sex (from every form of bondage) had chosen for her" (36). There is a sinister loop here: Olive's intense focus on the painful subjection of the female "organism" (182) actually increases the subjection rather than correcting or preventing it. More than a martyr, Olive is the vampire of herself. She recalls William James's agonizing subjectivity. Unlike the two other major characters, she is a brilliant creation, no doubt about it – an extraordinary study in pathology. The trouble is, she is clearly meant to say something negative about feminism and about women, and she continues to be interpreted in this way.[33]

James's other women in *The Bostonians* are either foolishly self-deceiving, like Miss Birdseye and Mrs. Tarrant, or manipulatively bent on some private agenda, like Mrs. Farrinder, Mrs. Luna, and Mrs. Burrage. Mrs. Tarrant, always trailing after her husband in his various campaigns on the radical fringe, seems chronically unable to focus on her secret dream, recapturing a respectable position in society.

The glaring contradiction in James's attitude to Verena is that he tries to admire her precisely for having more of the very quality (irrational femininity) that renders the other women contemptible or oppressively manipulative. Verena is supposed to be a supreme success in being made as she is made, and yet she cannot begin to glimpse her own nature until a strong man pulls back the curtains. Inevitably, a writer who preferred finely conscious protagonists ran into trouble with such a fatally incapacitated heroine.

The whole contradiction came together in a wretchedly tangled sentence in which James attempted to separate his sympathy for Basil's masculine force from his inevitable contempt for Verena's supineness. Significantly, the sentence immediately follows the all-important speech where Basil justifies women's subordinate domestic role – the same speech James touts for its "reason" and "very considerable mystery" and that originally ended the eleventh installment:

> It is to be feared, indeed, that Verena was easily satisfied (convinced, I mean, not that she ought to succumb to him, but that there were lovely, neglected, almost unsuspected truths on his side); and there is further evidence on the same head in the fact that after the first once or twice she found nothing to say to him (much as she was always saying to herself), about the cruel effect her apostasy would have upon Olive. (390)

How many readers would continue with an installment that opened like this? The initial parenthesis records a classic double take in which James recoils from the chasm that has opened in his narrative. He *must* not admit that Verena is *that* weak-minded, and so he strains to cobble up a distinction between her yielding to Basil's lovely truths and her succumbing to the force of his argument. James's struggle *against* clarity largely accounts for the sentence's clumsy, insincere clutter.

Likable Dr. Prance is an exception to James's women, as she both knows what she is doing and shows no deviousness. But James emphasizes that she has not only unsexed herself by entering a male profession, she is also a closet antisuffragist. She apparently has "as many rights as she had time for" (48). She thinks that women who want to get ahead, or rather "have a better time" (42), should work more and talk less. At Marmion, she feels oppressed by the seriousness of the female reformers, who cause her to take an even dimmer view of their movement: " 'Well,' said Doctor Prance, with a small sigh, 'I am afraid I have moved back, if anything!' " (354). Her flat, inexpressive speech (see Zuckert 41–42) reflects the blinkered humanity of one who has "no general ideas" (377) and likes to hole up in her workplace-apartment, a very meager stall compared to the home the "sentiment of sex" generates.

The second aspect of Verena's femininity is her pleasure in pleasing others, especially those in command. An authorial disclosure explains what the Central Park episode makes sufficiently obvious: "A force she had never felt before was pushing her to please herself" (386). The force is sexual attraction, but it would be wrong to understand this as some sort of hormonal female drive. What Verena feels is a nineteenth-century *sentiment,* a term difficult to gauge with any real precision. Basil's quarrel with "the muddled sentiment" (338) of the day illustrates the usage. The point to note is that James did not say muddled *beliefs* or *opinions.* These are ideas, but sentiments, uniting ideas with feelings, are far more basic and powerful (and conservatives, like T. S. Eliot, often yearn for them). One might think of sentiments as feelings that are virtually detached from any particular stimuli, innate feelings, feelings with a hold pedal. Like ideas, however, sentiments were felt to have an obligatory quality. They could be right or wrong, as ideas can be. You would be justified in setting straight a wrong sentiment. But because sentiment was partly nonrational, you would not be able to correct it solely by argument. You might have to use force.

When Olive finally concedes that she is up against the real force, she sees that Verena's devotion to the cause "had been a kind of hothouse loyalty, the mere contagion of example, and a sentiment springing up from within had easily breathed a chill upon it" (410). (In *The Portrait* Isabel's theories and independence "had been absorbed in a more primitive sentiment – a sentiment which answered all questions, satisfied all needs, solved all difficulties. It simplified the future at a stroke, it came down from above, like the light of the stars, and it needed no explanation" [1881 ed., 308–9].) Verena's story, as James conceived it, is not about the victimizing of a weak person but about the painful replacement of muddled sentiment with something very different that the age foolishly wanted to extirpate – "the sentiment of sex." Thus, Verena's end was not meant to be tragic but *natural,* even wholesome, in spite of the tears. For the Jameses, enforced pain was an unavoidable and healthy part of all human scenarios, individual and racial.

Most modern readers resist the novel's rhetoric of force. They read the language of spells (167, 385) as a sign that Basil treats Verena no better than Olive does, and interpret the fact that these two successive patrons each conceal the girl's features by throwing a cloak over her head as proof (P. Page 378) that Basil and Olive equally repress her identity. Many readers wish to conclude that these two dominating characters are equally oppressive and that James stands equidistant from them, because this reading decontaminates the novel's implied ideology. But this solution obliterates too much of the evidence. When James confided to his notebook that he wanted to focus on "the situation of women, the decline of the sentiment of sex, the agitation on their behalf" (*Complete Notebooks* 20), he was using *agitation* and *decline* with their usual negative connotations. Four years earlier he had praised Mrs. Orr (*Letters* 3: 241) for her conservative essay, "The Future of English Women," which predicted that "the one fatal result of female emancipation is this, that in its full and final attainment not only the power of love in women, but for either sex its possibility, will have passed away" (1030). The love story of Basil and Verena was designed to illustrate a countermovement to this disastrous modern tendency.

Yet we have every justification for resisting James, if only because he himself apparently had no experience of the sentiment of sex, relying as he did on what his father, brother, and others had to say about it. The "marriage sentiment," Henry Sr. had preached, was "the only sentiment worth living for, for it alone emancipates one from the bondage of his organization, and conjoins him spiritually with the divine" (HJSr to Julia A. Kellogg, 9 September 1871, MH-H). (When Basil asks Verena if she would make "any sacrifice for affection" [232], he is touching on one of Henry Sr.'s favorite ideas.) This was the sort of thing Henry Jr. long suspected he ought to believe and that he found in Orr's essay, which claimed that love caused men and women to "become to each other the carnal revelation of everything towards which their being was consciously or unconsciously aspiring" ("Future" 1031). Back in 1869, when William attacked John Stuart Mill's *Subjection of Women* for reflecting a "sentimental ideal" of equal friendship between the sexes, and thus overlooking the fact that "the representative American [man]" wishes for "a dependent being" as a wife, Henry thought that the review was "very well and fluently written."[34] Thirteen years later, conceiving of *The Bostonians,* James would have his heroine give up another kind of sentimental ideal, sororal union,[35] after listening to her heart, and William loved it, once he got over his dismay at the treatment of Peabody. He found the latter two-thirds of the novel "simply sweet. There isn't a hair wrong in Verena, you've made her neither too little nor too much – but absolutely *liebenswürdig.* . . . – her discovery of the truth on the Central Park day . . . [is] inimitably given" (Matthiessen 328). This response, ignoring the ironies post–World War II readers have looked for, specifically approves of the book's insistence on an exaggerated asymmetry in male and female sexual response.

In fact, like father and brother before him, James was practicing a strategy of control, an ongoing assertion of male authority over the emotional nature of women. In creating his sweet flower of femininity who abandons political independence once she finds she is in love, Henry Jr. was signing on to one of his father's most vigorously pursued enterprises – setting women straight as to their real nature. At a time when Minnie Temple was fighting for breath, the James father told her she had too much "*pride & conceit.*" He confirmed Annie Fields's belief

that women are not supposed to get up and speak. He had the nerve to
spell out for the New England Women's Club the exact nature and scope
of "woman."[36] He explained to his many women disciples that they
would dishonor themselves if they tried to get personal satisfaction. One
lesson Henry Jr. learned from this earnest paternal endeavor was that it is
right for woman to listen to man to find out who she is.

Leon Edel believes that the James father was dominated by his rigid
and commonplace wife, to the degree that Henry Jr. became virtually
obsessed in his fiction with the figure of the viciously overmastering
woman (Edel, *Henry James: A Life* 11–16). Mary did indeed assume
control of household affairs, as her family and lame husband demanded
much attention, especially when looking for and moving into summer
quarters. There is even a letter in which Henry Sr., recovering from an
illness, jokes that he must sign off for fear of a wifely "broomsticking"
(to Julia A. Kellogg, 8 November [no year], MH-H). But the preponder-
ance of evidence indicates that he enjoyed a commanding relationship
over his wife. She gave up her Christian orthodoxy in marrying him,
accepted and defended his ideas, read less and less on her own, and
remained silent in those famous family arguments where her husband's
voice boomed loudest.[37]

Particularly when expressing his opinions on womanhood and marriage, the senior James appears to have been a formidable indoctrinator,
for both his second son and his female disciples. His correspondence with
Julia A. Kellogg reveals the sort of authority he assumed. Ending an early
letter in the series that sets forth his teachings, he donned the autocrat's
mantle: "There! Enough for one day. Think well before you answer,
unless your answer be one of sweet spontaneous accord, which will
require no delay."[38] When, inevitably, Kellogg began to question and
criticize, her guru turned wrathful and dictatorial:

> You may go on to entertain what opinions of me you conceive to
> be congruous with the facts of the case; but please withhold the
> knowledge of them from me. . . . I can't permit you to impose any
> of your specific judgments of my conduct upon my own under-
> standing, under the menace of a forfeiture of your friendship unless
> I acknowledge its truth. (17 September [no year], MH-H)

While the cause of this quarrel remains obscure, the letter that apparently
patched it up has an intriguing reference to Kellogg's uneasiness over his
"speculations about woman." In this letter Henry Sr. repeated his usual
doctrines on the subject and then concluded that there was no real difference between his disciple and himself: "So we are hopelessly at one" (7
January [no year], MH-H). Such documents back up Feinstein's emphasis on William's difficult fight for individuation from his father. They

speak volumes about the sort of authority good son Henry had to somehow come to terms with – a philosopher-father who had solved the
riddles of the ages and who either could not tolerate aggressive dissent or
would blandly ignore it. The difficulties in freeing oneself from such a
person can be endless.[39]

Hence, just as Basil reincarnates the spirit of the forceful mentor,
Verena turns out to be the perfect receptacle for his teaching. Her answer,
one of sweet (though delayed) accord, proves her to be the ideal proté-
gée, with none of Kellogg's independence of thought. Verena is the
apotheosis of nonrational feminine sentiment, and her inmost nature
softly receives the penetrating, Ransoming doctrine. (Ransoming her to
death, Huck Finn might say.) The collapse of her interest in her own civil
liberties – a collapse unthinkable in Kellogg or Minnie Temple or Caroline Dall or Frances Macdaniel or numerous other women in the Jameses'
orbit – serves to confirm one of Henry Sr.'s most fervent convictions.
Assuming (as did Bushnell) that women would eventually get the vote,
Henry Sr. nonetheless reiterated to Kellogg: "I told you at the same time
that women wouldn't avail themselves of it [the suffrage] when it was
granted" (7 January [no year], MH-H). *The Bostonians* says the same
thing: It is not in female nature to care about personal freedom.

The most fascinating aspect of James's application of this thesis to
Verena is that it more than once forces him to falsify and censor his report
of her growing up. If we recall Pansy Osmond's final compliance with her
father's wishes, we see at once that *her* servility is perfectly in character, for
she has been brainwashed and intimidated by her father and Roman Catholic discipline. But Verena has enjoyed an unusually unconstrained girlhood, possesses a lively assertive spirit ("Well, I must say, . . . I prefer free
unions" [84]), and loves excitement and activity. It is all wrong that she
should so completely renounce thought for sentiment. Torn as she is
between Olive's and Basil's views, she is never once shown comparing
them, *thinking* about them, trying to work the conflict out. Her only
arguments are token protests, followed by silence. For a girl with her free-
and-easy background and fondness for being heard, this silent acquies-
cence does not ring true. Even worse is James's smarmy concentration on
her affections: "She loved, she was in love – she felt it in every throb of her
being" (384). I think one would have to spend many hours culling the so-
called sentimental novels written by women in the 1850s and 1860s to find
a sentence as bad as this one, with its pointless repetition ("loved, . . . in
love") and worn-out cliché ("throb"). This uncharacteristically tepid writing tells us that Verena truly does have "a singular hollowness of
character" – but in a sense any author would be embarrassed to admit.
Hence the novel's oft-noted defect, namely, that the conflict is worked out
externally, through melodrama, and not within the heroine.

It is not just that James's material took revenge on him but that he himself actively suppressed the essential stage of Verena's mental maturation – the moment that establishes her mental independence from her parents. From her first appearance, James emphasizes the tremendous disparity between her and them, along with her childishly unconscious acceptance of their standards. She depends on her father's guiding hands and takes him and her mother on trust: "No authority appealing really to her imagination had fixed the place of mesmeric healers in the scale of fashion" (76). Clearly, as Verena enters the world and interprets it and acquires her own social imagination, she will *have* to develop a critical sense of the people who produced her. This must be a major and dramatic phase of her growth, and James definitely prepares for it. When she makes one of her brief return visits home, we learn that she is growing "rather weary" (105) of her mother's pertinacious theorizing about Olive. When she is reproached for not bringing Olive along, Verena begins to squirm: "She guessed Miss Chancellor didn't think much of that personage [her mother], true as it was that the girl had discerned this angular fact" (107). It would seem that Verena is entering on Maisie's line of development in *What Maisie Knew*, a line beginning in concealment and wary observation and painfully forced comparisons. But then, in Chapter 20, James summarily dismisses the whole development in one brief parenthesis: "(she judged her mother now, a little, for the first time)" (168). And that is all there is. James may claim that under Olive's tutelage, Verena "expanded, developed, on the most liberal scale" (167), but she is only "fait de chic," like Basil. From Chapter 20 on, James wholly finesses the development his opening chapters both prepare for and require. Eleven years later, composing the beautiful *What Maisie Knew*, James not only focused on the heroine's passionate processes of thought, but showed that Maisie finally becomes free, as Sir Claude realizes, precisely by confronting her parents' and stepparents' moral dinginess. But in writing *Verena*, as he originally called it, James had to back away, and so the book became *The Bostonians*. What is Verena's judgment of her mother? What does she think about the father whose hands she originally had to feel on her head before she could speak? These are pressing questions, both psychologically and dramatically, but James keeps silent.

Some of the reasons for his silence are obvious. Because his heroine was constructed to illustrate the preeminence of sentiment over thought in the female mind, James could not risk letting her begin to think independently. He had to throttle this vital tendency from the start, when she breaks away from home. He also had to prevent his book from growing even larger than the originally projected six installments. But James's silence also had a private cause, for he was doing to his heroine exactly what his father's ghost was doing to *him*. The far too faithful writer had been sucked back into the old mid-1860s family circle, still presided over by the forceful philosopher of marriage. His father's hands were on his head, the two Henry Jameses were once again hopelessly at one, and it remained unthinkable that the younger could for one second heed those rascally journalists' claims about the great father's secret dinginess. The father's spirit had to be vindicated – meaning the heroine's spirit had to be made vacuous.

For James, just as for Verena or Isabel Archer or Pansy Osmond, there was an absolute prohibition against any real confrontation with the male parent's bohemian irregularity. Changing one consonant turns "Tarrant" into "parent." Not until after James had experienced his theater debacle was the prohibition lifted. In the latter 1890s the man who had been his family's "angel" entered his belated adolescence.[40] Finally he separated from the man Caroline Dall and others called "Absolute James," and he did so precisely by telling the story of Maisie Farange the far-ranger, the traveling *ange,* so fortunately deserted by her parents.

History

James moved on, but *The Bostonians* remains. Like other realistic novels, its claim to importance has to rest not on what it says about its maker but on what it tells us about the generalized lives of men and women of its time, their passions, their inner history and culture. But it is precisely in its handling of the men and women of its time that the book is so misleading, so gravely and insidiously wrong. There is a major historical irony in the fact that this loose, baggy, but *still* repressed monster[41] has guided many readers in their interpretation of American life and thought in the Gilded Age.

James's emphasis on Basil's solitary opposition to the women's movement reverses the actual power relations of nineteenth-century men and women. At the Music Hall or the Wednesday Club gathering, Basil stands conspicuously tall and alone against a very foolish crowd. Even the policeman supports the women's movement by urging Basil to listen to Verena: "Now I wouldn't lose the lecture if I was you. I guess it will do you good" (433). Is it probable that one of Boston's finest would deliver such advice? The reason James makes this silly mistake (apart from his ignorance about American life) is that he must establish Basil as the man who takes on a feminized age. Such is James's authority (or Basil's authority over James) that many readers have innocently accepted the notion that American culture and history had in some way become women's work, thus managing to forget that law, politics, industry, commerce, and finance were run almost exclusively by some men. Presented as a desperate challenger, Basil is actually a kind of boss. He is not about to yield power and does not deserve a minority outsider's pathos, except in relation to the South's defeat.

Similarly, the novel conveys false images of journalism and the women's movement, which James represents as being hand in glove. There is not room here to document his many inaccuracies and distortions, but there is an easy way to illustrate the essential falsity of the novel's version of the history of American reform. In 1875 the free-love magazine, *Woodhull & Claflin's Weekly*, printed a technical exposition of what Fourier called his "passional series" (Cridge 2–3). In content this article was identical with what Henry James, Sr., caused to be published in his 1848 translation of Hennequin. The difference was that the senior James had been backed by the society of American Fourierists, whose leaders included Parke Godwin (later William Cullen Bryant's son-in-law and editor of the New York *Evening Post*) and George Ripley (afterward literary editor of the *New York Tribune*). A generation later the same radical ideas were relegated to the scandalous fringe. *No one* in a respected position stood up for them. This altered packaging and reception sum up the sort of changes that took place in American life between the elder Henry's *Love in the Phalanstery* and the younger Henry's *Bostonians*, and it also shows how dubious is this novel's historical thesis that reform movements in the United States became corrupt and vulgarized *after* the Civil War.

It is true that the novel develops this view with great effectiveness. There is bloated Mrs. Tarrant, who has fallen away from the simple decency of the Greenstreets (and who seeks to recapture the greenness by giving her daughter a name suggesting verdancy). There is Miss Birdseye, the only character who still recalls "the heroic age of New England life – the age of plain living and high thinking, of pure ideals and earnest effort, of moral passion and noble experiment" (179); when she dies it is definitely all over. James's powerfully drawn picture of large-scale cultural and moral decline takes in the rise of privacy-invading journalism, the replacement of Tremont Temple with the Colosseum-like Music Hall, the degeneration of reform lectures into fashionable entertainment. But his critique derives from a censored vision of antebellum reformers.

The character of Selah Tarrant epitomizes the novel's insidious lack of veracity and what I consider to be James's failure as realist and historian. Selah surely stands as one of the book's most memorable portraits, summing up the age's vulgarity, opportunism, moral hypocrisy. Yet he tells us much less about the Gilded Age than about the decades preceding the Civil War – the Oneida-Cayuga experiment, the rise of spiritualism and mesmerism, and the antebellum fascination with magnetic influence. The surprising fact is that magnetic Selah resurrects Henry Sr.'s own buried life from before the Civil War. At the time the James father translated

Hennequin's free-love pamphlet, the label of choice for the Fourierists was "Associationists." This term underwent a degradation of meaning as Fourierism lost appeal and became identified with that mythical assault on the sanctity of the family that has energized more than one conservative American backlash. The word entered *The Bostonians* weighted with this decades-old accumulation: "Selah was quite enthusiastic at one time about Mrs. Foat, and it was his wife's belief that he had been 'associated' with her (that was Selah's expression in referring to such episodes) at Cayuga" (72–73). This effectively dismisses the question of marriage reform, as does Olive's prim repudiation: "She didn't like the 'atmosphere' of circles in which such institutions [as marriage] were called into question" (84). Yet the author's honored father, the proponent of the "very considerable mystery" the novel defends, was *the* most prominent American Associationist of his time to call the institution into question.

Like the slip of the pen in which Charles of Oneida became "young man Henry" (*Literary Criticism* 1: 567), Selah is a classic instance of the return of the repressed. An inadvertent travesty of the father's alienated radicalism, he smuggles in the forbidden history the novel as a whole works to cover up. Even Selah's itch to get into the newspapers, one of his most vulgar traits, reflects a secret truth about the author's father. Of course there are differences: The former aims at self-promotion, the latter bombarded the press with blasts of abstruse controversy. Still, the accusation leveled at Verena's father ("he would gladly have sacrificed . . . the innermost sanctities of home" [101]) has a straightforward application to the novelist's own father, who drew public attention again and again to his effort to vanquish his own animality. When *Woodhull & Claflin's* published his private letter admitting his sexual dissatisfaction with his wife, he did not maintain a dignified silence but instead sent two rejoinders to the magazine. His essay on Carlyle made an insensitive and surely embarrassing allusion to his different feelings as a parent for his successful and his failing children, "those whom an unkind nature . . . consigns to comparative indigence and ignominy" ("Some Personal Recollections" 609). He often claimed that it was wrong to favor one's own children over others', and this belief, however modified in practice, was closely allied with his commitment to social, not private, bliss. He even insisted in "Spiritualism New and Old" that it was necessary to "hate" (362) one's family. Built into the father's tortuous system was a prejudice *against* the innermost sanctities of home. The problem with the troubled son's projection of all this onto sleazy Selah is that it saddles us with a misleading image of the *public* world of post–Civil War America.

The Bostonians is a conservative novel gilded, plastered in fact, with conservative guilt. It may in some respects prove to be a typical Gilded Age product, but it does not report on this age with much reliability. The

author combined an antidemocratic, antireform bias with a nervous refusal to know his father's real character and history or to express fully his
own private mind. His supercilious voice registers a helpless effort to
ward off the spirit of this invasive parent.

Even more, the book's deep self-hatred represents a permutation of
the father's own self-eviscerating nature. Because Henry Sr. had been
divided against himself, Henry Jr.'s attack on the radicals his father abandoned inevitably turned into an attack on the father's own badly compromised love of liberty. It was slavery-equals-freedom all over again. The
sickening irony is that even though most contemporary readers had
strong reservations about the book, some very influential twentieth-
century readers have proclaimed the truthfulness of what it says about
American life, and these readers have often seen *themselves* as liberal or
even radical lovers of freedom. The spirit of intimidation, betrayal, and
forgetfulness continues to reinvade us.

But James escaped this noxious cloud, ten years later, and so can we. We
should take a lesson from the penetrating sanity of a review of *The Bostonians* published in 1886 by the Boston *Woman's Journal*, a magazine sponsored by the National Woman Suffrage Association. The author, identified as L.T.A., was eager to see the representation in fiction of changing
"conditions of life," but she was disappointed by James's novel, which was
"evidently intended as a tremendous satire on the whole 'woman question.' " Her use of quotation marks reflected her perception that the book
was exceedingly vague in its picture of "the great 'cause' for which all are
laboring." On the novel's basic inaccuracy, she was categorical: "Mr.
James is by no means true to nature, and merely conveys the idea which he
assumes the leaders of the 'woman movement' to hold." L.T.A. felt "disgust" for Olive's "bitter, unnatural antipathy towards marriage and men"
and was certain that this "morbid, abnormal, disagreeable enthusiast"
belonged "neither to Boston nor any other city." She and Verena were
"the most impossible personages in modern fiction" – though "the vulgar
and voluble Mrs. Luna is, we fear, by no means a rare person." L.T.A.
understood that Basil was meant as a likable hero, but "in that last
wretched scene his absurd selfishness and obstinacy" were deplorable. In
the end she pitied Olive's "humiliation" as strongly as she felt "contempt
for Verena's weakness." The novel would have been more accurately
called *The Cranks,* or "some less vulgar title which would express that
idea." (*Crank* had come into vogue a few years earlier during the trial of
President Garfield's assassin.)

This sensitive and sensible critique was written by Lucia True Ames,[42]
an active suffragist who was thirty years old at the time and still single (she
enters biographical dictionaries under her later married name, Mead). She
lectured women's groups on literature and contemporary American soci-

ety, choosing among her texts Emerson, Carlyle, and James Bryce. Her father and grandfather had been active in the antislavery cause, as had Mrs. Tarrant's people, but unlike this character Lucia Ames went on to become president of the Massachusetts Woman Suffrage Association. She later joined the National Association for the Advancement of Colored People and the American Civil Liberties Union. She was considered a "forceful speaker," unlike Olive, and she was "logical and concise in her arguments," unlike Verena. She opposed American entry into World War I, unlike the aging James, who was caught up in England's war fever. She died in 1936 in a New York subway rush.

Without knowing anything about the private history of *The Bostonians,* Lucia Ames was in exactly the right position to spot the book's shallowness, confusion, and misrepresentation of American life. Not only that, but she herself was part of the reality the novel has managed to cover up. The cause of freedom was as solid and embattled as it has always been. James's pictures of vulgar democratic laxity, of the moral decline of reform, of Verena the empty performer, tell us next to nothing about Lucia Ames or her world. The posthumous collaboration of Henry James, Sr., with his son has bequeathed to twentieth-century readers a prejudicial image of our most farsighted American political forebears. There is a great suppression of memory here.

Chapter 9

Conclusion

This book has attempted to trace James's development by exploring the opposition in his work between feminism and patriarchy. My strategy has been to situate James against certain women writers – against because they form the backdrop, the ground, of his resistance. I have in effect followed the interpretive program outlined by Marilyn Butler in her useful essay, "Against Tradition: The Case for a Particularized Historical Method," though I have gone beyond Butler's program insofar as I have reached for the desires and purposes behind genres and sign systems and have caused my inquiry to terminate in acts of historical evaluation.[1] In particular, I have argued that because James's fiction embodies a covert act of force directed against women, we should not accept his mastery on the terms his texts tend to impose. We cannot read him well unless we resist his authority.

It is still not well understood how revolutionary our current questioning of the "canon" is going to prove.[2] To challenge James's authority as a writer about women is to do more than amplify voices that have been hidden or stifled. It is to turn the amplification of suppressed voices (the chief task of civil liberty) into one of the leading principles of aesthetic judgment. It is to raise and press the question of free speech, evaluating novels not solely as artful constructions but according to whether they enlarge or restrict the *principle* of expression. *The Portrait of a Lady* and *The Bostonians* seem to me to be opposed on several levels to free speech. Isabel and Verena, whose speech is initially so infatuated, get hushed just like the actual women (Minnie Temple, Anne Crane, Louisa May Alcott, Elizabeth Peabody, Anna Dickinson) whose voices were appropriated by James. Even more insidiously, these two novels suppressed much of what *James himself* thought. They represent a sustained act of silencing in addition to being supremely expressive in other respects. That is why I have tried to reconstitute their obscured literary history. But my goal is not just to read James with more historical precision and political canniness. It is also to read Alcott, Crane, Stoddard, and others along *with* him. As Cary Nelson has reminded us recently, "Texts that were either widely read or influential at key moments need to retain their place in our sense of literary history" (Elliott 914). Quite aside from the fact that Stoddard's *Morgesons* seems worth reading as much as any of James's novels, we will miss much of James's literary history if we do not read the much less impressive Alcott and Crane.

Of course, to exhume dusty texts is not to claim that everyone must at once begin reading them. As Nelson has pointed out, writing literary history is not the same as canon building. *Making* literary history, how-ever, is a different matter. It is clear from James's ambitious program of correcting and appropriating the Civil War women agonists that a canon-making project was implicit in his very act of composition.[3] Howells's editorial support and public praise of James, the 1934 issue of *Hound & Horn* devoted to him, Rahv's and Trilling's and Howe's post-World War II establishment of *The Bostonians* as a classic American political novel may all, in varying ways, constitute important moments of canon-formation. But these external moves are to some degree later reenact-ments of the dynamic within James himself as he conceived and executed his works. If contemporary and later readers have made James a major American writer, they have done so partly because *James* has shown them how to define what major American writing is to *be*.[4]

As Howells predicted, James's texts *have* created their own readers. This fact adds a wrenching twist to one's effort to try to sketch James's objective location in the past, since one's own political and aesthetic formation is a partial consequence of the past that he created. Any rehistoricizing of James requires a corresponding act of self-questioning by the literary historian. As Gerald L. Bruns has said so well in his discussion of canon and power in Deuteronomy and Jeremiah, "A text, after all, is canonical, not in virtue of being final and correct and part of an official library, but because it becomes *binding* upon a group of people" (von Hallberg 67). It is for that very reason that the most difficult task the literary historian must attempt is to unshackle himself or herself from binding canonical chains. There are many ways to do this. My way of undoing James's canonical authority is to find documentary evidence to expose the processes by which he constructed it.

Another problem is that, whereas canons operate by excluding, liter-ary history must scrupulously try to leave nothing out. Yet it is clearly impossible to include everything. My own study has not only had to omit many American women writers James reviewed – Harriet Beecher Stowe, Adeline Whitney, Rebecca Harding Davis, Helen Hunt Jackson, Julia Constance Fletcher – but also many American men, and not just William R. Alger, the author of *The Friendships of Women* (1867). And quite aside from the preposterousness of attempting to trace James's development without reference to various European writers (the George Sand connection would alone require several hundred pages and a couple of years), there is the whole problem of James's relation to Hawthorne. Richard Brodhead's recent summation of this matter in *The School of Hawthorne* shows with fine insight and subtlety that "one of the peculiarities of James's fiction is its strong and persistent orientation toward the works of other writers" (116), and that Hawthorne's novels functioned as an "organized process of instruction" (vii) for James, who was inspired through his recently canonized predecessor by a new idea of the "*highness* of writing*" (110). If Brodhead's study occasionally makes too exclusive a claim for Hawthorne, that is because *any* limited perspective (my own much more egregiously, I am afraid) brings with it its own inevitable train of distortions and exaggerations.

The single most frustrating exclusion in my own study is that I do not have the time or space to follow the story of James and the "woman business" down through time. James's later writing makes it obvious that he was not snatched once and for all by his father's revenant in *The Bostonians*. He moved on, developing in unprecedented ways and always responding with remarkable fullness to new currents of thought and literature in England and France in the 1880s and 1890s.

A key event in the continuation of this story would be the bankruptcy of James R. Osgood and Company, the firm that was to have paid James four thousand dollars for serial and book rights to *The Bostonians*.[5] One of the ventures that probably contributed to this bankruptcy was none other than *The Literary Remains of the Late Henry James*, brought out by Osgood a month or so before James's novel began its serial run. Thus, the father's remains not only haunted the son's text, they may have injured his material prosperity as well. James himself felt the parallel between the failure of his father's last testament and that of his own novel. Writing Godkin, he indulged his "pious melancholy" and lamented the passing of his father's spirit "into darkness and silence forever, the waves of time closing straight over it, without one or two signs being made on its behalf." In the same way, writing William, James complained that he had received "not a word, echo or comment on the serial" (thus forgetting, or choosing not to mention, John Hay's cheering note); there was only "deathly silence." Then James added, "But how can one murmur at one's success not being what one would like when one thinks of the pathetic, tragic ineffectualness of poor Father's lifelong effort, and the silence and oblivion that seems to have swallowed it up?" (*Letters* 3: 73, 102). The writing and early publication history of *The Bostonians* are rightly interpreted as a bizarre and not wholly accidental instance of filial suttee. The episode recalls Ralph Touchett's hope that he would not outlive his father.

After this symbolic death, James's story becomes one of self-resurrection and a renewed artistic life. In view of his continuing productivity and development (in spite of setbacks during the years in the theater), James could proudly have chanted Walt Whitman's lines in the pivotal thirty-eighth section of "Song of Myself": "Somehow I have been stunned. Stand back!" James, too, remembered that he "could forget the mockers and insults," and after 1895 he did indeed "troop forth replenished with supreme power." In this inspired labor of self-replenishing, the effective agents, as Leon Edel first realized, were the disturbing novels and novellas James wrote in the last five years of the century. Most of these texts focus on girls or young women who face extreme danger or exposure. Edel interprets the narratives as epiphenomena accompanying James's inner reintegration following his unsuccessful social novels of the 1880s and his frustrations with the theater in the first half of the 1890s. James rebuilt himself, so to speak, by imagining what it would be like to grow up as a girl in a world full of cold and even cruel aliens. But we may also interpret these narratives as contributions, weird and late, to the broad tradition of women's fiction.

From the beginning the wild card in James's conservative approach to women was a deep identification with them. His rebirth came partly through this identification: The very act of living his way into the experience of Maisie Farange, initially so helpless, spurred him into working out in narrative a hard-won state of freedom. Another way to put this is that James was rethinking the whole problem of female independence in the terms established by the mainstream midcentury tale of the abandoned or neglected daughter. Fleda, Maisie, and Nanda are all versions of those sturdy and upright early heroines, and they all take on the world without being able to avail themselves of some traditional female sanctuary. They all fail to get the man they want – Owen Gereth, Sir Claude, Vanderbank – and they all achieve a sad liberation. In *The Portrait of a Lady* James had told how a callow independent girl grows up by acquiring a painful sense of entangling duty, but in *What Maisie Knew* the heroine grows up by attaining a painful state of detachment. Maisie's hard-won independence expresses itself in the conditions she learns how to impose, as when she consents to leave Mrs. Wix and live with the weak man she loves only if he consents to leave Mrs. Beale. This proposed reciprocal sacrifice shows that Maisie has developed a mature sense of moral justice, one capable of striking a balance between obligation and desire, giving and taking. We look in vain for this sense of justice in either Isabel's return to Rome or Verena's surrender to sentiment.

The usual way of schematizing James's late development has been to see his novels of the latter 1890s as essentially preparatory, psychologically as well as artistically. Oscar Cargill's label – "The Augean Stable" – eloquently evokes this particular point of view. I would argue, however, that *What Maisie Knew* remains James's most living novel, precisely because it begins with an act of divorce, the collapse of the legal institution the senior James had criticized yet clutched. The novel has a power to move, shock, and stir that is missing from the more studied – and, yes, better-rounded – novels of the so-called major phase.

The bizarreness of *What Maisie Knew* results from the contrasts between its hard modernity and its systematic Victorian echoes. James was engaged in the curious project of dredging up the past in order to contribute to a specifically nineties project. Similarly, in writing *The Turn of the Screw*, he conjoined his memory of a serial read in childhood with an up-to-date appropriation of psychic research,[6] and in *The Spoils of Poynton* he reached back to Susan Warner's 1852 novel, *Queechy*, for his heroine's unusual first name, Fleda. James's delayed adolescent rebellion came from a revisitation of his youth, and even more of his youth's literature.

The critical side of this inner revolution shows up in James's 1897 and 1902 essays on George Sand, the writer he returned to more obsessively than any other. Back in 1868, writing the first of his nine pieces on her and confessing that "we believe we have read . . . all" of her tales, he insisted that her "restless, nervous, and capricious" imagination was essentially that "of a woman." In 1877 he could not decide whether her "want of veracity" and delicacy meant she was feminine or whether her sexual adventures made her "more masculine than any man she might have married." By 1897 the feminine part of her endowment had shrunk to "her immense plausibility," and her masculinity had become so dominant that "her *liaison* with Mérimée" was "almost like a union against nature." The 1902 essay, as Corse has shown, represented an extraordinary breakthrough for James. Now he not only admired George Sand for being a Bohemian man "not superstitiously haunted by the conception of the gentleman," but he saw her as a pioneer in the "evolution and transformation" of women:

> The approximation of the extraordinary woman has been practically . . . to the ordinary man. George Sand's service is that she planted the flag much higher – her own approximation at least was to the extraordinary. She reached him, she surpassed him, and she showed how, with native dispositions, the thing could be done. So far as we have come these new records will live as the precious textbook of the business. (*Literary Criticism* 2: 697, 699, 712, 716, 749, 748, 773–75)

But *this* line of business was too daring for James. *What Maisie Knew* and *The Awkward Age* had taken their brave new heroines only up to the border of sexual experience. Now, moving beyond this boundary with the character of Madame de Vionnet, James had to retreat. Just as Strether recoils to Woollett, the French lady lacks George Sand's gay resilience and daring. *The Ambassadors* is about drawing back after going as far as one can possibly manage. In this novel, as in *The Wings of the Dove* and *The Golden Bowl,* James once again took it upon himself to defend the costs the civilized order exacts. The latter two novels have at their center a female character who acts as the effective agent in cultivating or reclaiming or domesticating a man. Compared to *What Maisie Knew* and *The Awkward Age,* these novels (like *The Outcry*) reveal a much heavier investment in the enterprise of conservation than in that of "evolution and transformation." Woman is once again a sublime suffering servant, as in *The Lamplighter, St. Elmo,* the theology of Henry Sr., and *The Portrait of a Lady.*

The gender-based ideology that is implicit in the novels of the major phase became queerly explicit after James's visit to the United States in 1904–5. His essays on the speech and manners of American women that appeared in *Harper's Bazar* in 1906 and 1907 brought his lifelong anti-feminism to the surface more clearly than any other public writing of his. He praised the mid-Victorian governess or schoolmistress who served as "the closed vessel of authority, closed against sloppy leakage," and he praised her because her strict primness was "one of the ways in which authority can be conveyed." She was "an exquisite, an almost unconscious instrument of influence to a special end – . . . embodying, for her young companions, a precious ripe tradition." James had not shown much affection for the older New England speech when he wrote *The Europeans* in the 1870s, but now he extolled this speech precisely because it represented "the expressional effect of the few capable of taking themselves, and of keeping themselves, in hand – *capable even of taking and of keeping their wives, their daughters, their sisters*" (italics mine). James feared that the whole system of cultural authority transmitted by well-trained female subordinates was vanishing. He recalled from the spring of 1882 his shocked observation of the noisy recess at "the 'most fashionable' " girls' school in Boston, and he concluded the essay on speech by recalling in detail his effort to persuade a young lady of 1904 to mend her speech ways.[7] The climax of the essay occurs when James utters a supreme appeal: " 'Don't let us have women like that,' I couldn't help quite piteously and all sincerely breaking out; 'in the name of our homes, of our children, of our future, of our national honor, don't let us have women like that!' " (*French Writers and American Women Essays* 42–49).

This strange outburst has no parallel in James's writing yet articulates a position that is implicit in most of his narratives. The finely conscious young woman was the heiress of the ages for him in the sense that she was the crucial figure in the transmission of civilization. The real meaning of her inheritance, as we see in the lives of Isabel, Milly Theale, and Maggie Verver, is that she has a painful work to perform. What is noble about her is that she performs it even after seeing through the shabby deceptions of those who have represented culture for her. James's "breaking out" is an irrepressible personal statement that gets reported with a degree of shame partly because the point of his speech is to implore the young lady *not* to break out. She *must* become and remain a "closed vessel of authority." It is because the vessels are not sealed any more that James himself unbottles the authoritarian doctrine his narratives keep corked. Unlike Basil Ransom, who threatens and denounces and resorts to muscular force, James uses a pleading imperative: "Don't let us." The distressing sight of the modern woman's sloppy leakage makes him leak in protest. He spills in order to try to stop the spilling.

There is much more emotional violence in this scene than in the cautious statement James ventured twenty years earlier, when he endorsed Basil's speech defending marriage by declaring that it showed "more reason . . . as well as more appreciation of a very considerable mystery" (*Bostonians* 390). The violence comes from James's desperate feeling that the mystery has been pretty well desecrated, that cultural authority has lost its property rights, bindingness, and hiddenness. The moment in which James pops his cork in conversation with an American girl represents the climactic scene of unveiling – of apocalypse – in his writing. What gets revealed is his reactionary ideal of civilized female influence, and even more his understanding of literary authority. For James, canonical transmission depends fundamentally on restraint, which is both the means of propagation as well as the thing transmitted. James's violence results from the opposed impulses at work in the whole process: Expression gets passed on from generation to generation through an unexpressed restraint on expression. His use of the colloquial phrase, "keeping in hand," is itself terribly expressive. To keep in hand is, variously, to keep in one's possession, to keep one's hand on, to restrain, to make behave. James is affirming the importance and the relatedness of all of these. That is to say, he is revealing what he understands to be the rightful connection between property in women, civilized decorum, and literary history.

It is precisely because James did not "break out" (except for this one instance) that his readers have tended not to be aware of the nature of his authority over them. His contribution to American and British literature was in part to combine a high cultural seriousness with the realists' elimination of the commenting narrator, and one consequence of this program is that the kind of appropriation (of history, of other people) his texts engage in remains basically invisible to those who read them in the way that they ask to be read.

This book has attempted to break the seal – to read James's narratives in the light of his private letters, the books he read and reviewed, the teachings of his father, the writings of contemporaries. One of the originating impulses that made James a writer, made him the particular writer he became, was a need to resist the liberalizing or democratizing tendencies of his time. In particular, James was concerned to master the challenge posed by insurrectionary women in life and art. So successful was he in absorbing and rewriting their narratives that they not only became extremely inconspicuous in the nineteenth-century literary landscape, but his own narratives ended up mapping that landscape for us. In appropriating the work of lesser writers, he produced a repressive response to the very struggle much of that work engaged in – the struggle to end a gender-specific caste distinction. While he himself gave a benign cast to this act of appropriation by figuring it as a gardener's pruning – "it is at the cost of . . . certain obscured, hindered, sacrificed growths, that the happiest examples of any rich human efflorescence have hitherto managed to bask in the light" (*French Writers* 35) – we are more likely to prefer Walter Benjamin's darker version: "There is no document of civilization which is not at the same time a document of barbarism" (*Illuminations* 256). It would be naive to imagine that the justice we rarely find in history is somehow going to be the basic story line of literary history.

At the end of "Song of Myself" Whitman, our friendly advance man, promises to be waiting for us down the road. At the end of "The Speech of American Women," James leaves a similar message with the girl he is pleading with. Her self-satisfaction has persuaded him that she is locked up in a vulgar fools' paradise, like the rest of the "imprisoned mass," and that escape will be possible "for individuals" only. American women are infatuated and unreachable. Their only hope is in

> . . . quietly slipping out one by one. . . . You want to know how that may be managed? . . . Well, by letting me just hover at the gate and have speech of you when you can steal away. Only look out for the gleam of my lantern, and meet me by this low postern. I'll take care of the rest. (52–53)

How remote this strange assignation is from the spirit of Whitman's beautiful valedictory! Instead of offering a friendly arm and a bold spirit, James sets up an escape that is framed in archaic language and that is to be managed, taken "in hand" (46), by him alone. The postern gate, the assurance that he will "take care of the rest," shows that his promised rendezvous is designed to be far less empowering than Whitman's. As a matter of fact, James's Europe-haunted determination to rescue someone who already happens to be free definitely resembles Tom Sawyer's insistence on certain pointless arrangements for Jim's "evasion." Tom would have liked that postern gate.

It is clear from the careers of several poets that Whitman has kept his promise to meet us down the road. It is less well understood that James has kept his own pledge to help American women light out for civilization. Cynthia Ozick writes that "in early young womanhood I believed, with all the rigor and force and stunned ardor of religious belief, in the old Henry James, in his scepter and his authority." This belief led her into a "black hole of a microfilm cell" where she found despair and revulsion, and she was then saved from her foolish worship by reading Leon Edel's biography, which taught her that even James was not born a master. Now, writing from what she understands as a hard-won state of wisdom, she warns beginning writers not to imitate the Master's "cathedral tones." They must instead be content to sound their "paltry, oafish, feeble, simple, skeletal, single note" (Ozick 185, 183, 187). The language of force, injury, and confinement and the paralyzing series of adjectives suggest that one final reason it is impossible to end the story of James and the "woman business" is that the business is not over.

Notes

<hr/>

1. INTRODUCTION

1   In *Mabel Vaughan* the chief lesson, voiced by the heroine's teacher Mrs. Herbert, is that "there is nothing so insidious as self-love, nothing so noble and so womanly as that divine love which finds its happiness in duty" (10).

2   In fact, any number of critics claim this, even Kaston, who allows that *The Bostonians* "may be the most explicitly feminist of James's works" (17).

3   Two good but sketchy accounts of HJ and the woman question appeared in the middle 1970s. Veeder (154–62) considered HJ's response to the women's issues that were implicit in midcentury fiction; Niemtzow showed that he derived a conservative sense of woman and marriage from his father and that these views informed *The Portrait*. Most of the recent studies that treat some of the women's themes in James's fiction do not attend to biography, history, or the contemporary literary context. The best of these studies is by E. Allen, who begins with the contradiction between woman as cultural sign and woman as subjectivity and then shows how HJ sought over time to reconcile this contradiction. Thus, in "Daisy Miller" the heroine is a sign to be understood by male consciousness; in *The Portrait* the heroine herself grows painfully aware of her sign function; and later heroines try to control and exploit this contradiction in themselves. Fowler focuses on the psychological effect on HJ's heroines of the gap between their apparent freedom and their unpreparedness for experience in a male-controlled world. Rowe's suggestion in *Theoretical Dimensions* that HJ "was a pioneer among the nineteenth-century writers in the representation of the psychological effects of woman's subordination in a patriarchal culture" ignores the real pioneers, the women writers, whose work he repeatedly categorizes as "domestic romance or popular melodrama" (88). Rowe's questioning of HJ's mastery in *The Bostonians* proves disappointing in comparison with the theoretical method outlined in his chapter, "Feminist Issues," and in Rowe, "Correspondence."

4   HJ believed the papers composing *Modern Women* were written by "three or four sapient connoisseurs" (*Literary Criticism* 1: 20), presumably male. In fact, the author was Eliza Lynn Linton, a journalist. In countering her claim that modern women prostituted themselves, HJ declared that they were "still

remarkably patient, submissive, sympathetic – remarkably well-disposed to model themselves on the judgment and wishes of men" (ibid. 25). Stone's pioneering "Victorian Feminism" proposed that it was not the women novelists who defended the New Woman but the men – Grant Allen, George Moore, Meredith, Gissing, and (with qualifications) Hardy and James.

5 Corse's study of HJ's criticism of women novelists argues that he developed "from a conventional denigrating of women as inferior" (58) to a more enlightened view. The key texts for Corse are HJ's later discussions of George Sand, gathered in *Literary Criticism* 2: 736–98.

6 The letter was preserved because it retracted the advice later on. Alice's letters to HJ do not survive, and there are many other missing items. From 1869, for instance, the following letters sent to HJ may have been burned by him: HJSr's of 18 May, MJ's of 25 May, HJSr's and MJ's of 21 and 22 June, WJ's of 28 June, HJSr's of an unspecified day in July and of 27 Aug., WJ's "short note" of Oct. or Nov., MJ's of 23 Nov. HJ acknowledged receiving all these in letters dated 13 June, 17 and 26 July, 17 Sept., and 7 and 21 Dec.

7 For HJ's comments on Benson, see ch. 2, this volume. Higginson has been called "the most important American male feminist of his generation" (Leach 302). One of MT's letters to HJ hints at the tone the two cousins took in talking about him: "I think now that we can afford to turn up our noses at him, in future" (3 June 1869, MH-H). Higginson had criticized HJ and in *Short Studies* (56–57) later attacked his rendering of American life in *The Europeans*. Two decades later HJ summed up Higginson's democratic advocacy with conspicuous hauteur, identifying him with the midcentury "agitations on behalf of everything, almost, but especially of the negroes and the ladies. Of a completely enlarged citizenship for women the author has been an eminent advocate, as well, I gather, as one of the depositaries of the belief in their full adaptation to public uses – the universality of their endowment" (*Literary Criticism* 1: 687).

8 See Orr, "Mr. Henry James, Senior," and HJ, *Letters* 2: 297, 306, 313 and 3: 62.

9 HJ's 3 May 1907 letter to Elizabeth Jordan mentions *The Initials* (and *Robinson Crusoe* and *Nicholas Nickleby*) but not *Uncle Tom's Cabin* or *The Lamplighter*. *The Initials* is the one novel he comments on – "a novel 'of manners,' new & much esteemed at that time" (Howells, *Double Billing* 50) – as if to justify having read it. Veeder (16–17) provides a useful list of HJ's pre-1881 references to novels by British and American women. HJ's 1885 revision of an early tale makes his only known reference to a Southworth novel, *The Missing Bride* (*Tales* 1: 436). His 31 Jan. 1877 letter to his mother mentions "that novel you used always to be reading, to the neglect of your household duties (*A House of Cards*)" (MH-H). This novel by Frances Sarah Hoey was serialized in 1868 in *Littell's Living Age*.

10 Interestingly, in "Madame de Mauves" Longmore thinks the corrupt Baron de Mauves would be likely to have a taste for the same pair (*Tales* 2: 305).

11 In an 1858 report in the *American Publishers' Circular* of the "greatest successes in recent publishing," *all* the novels were by women: *Uncle Tom's Cabin, The*

Lamplighter, The Shady Side, Ruth Hall, Alone, The Hidden Path, Moss Side (Geary 369–70).

12 I use "woman's fiction" (generally without quotation marks) to designate the subset of women's fiction that Baym described. Numerous paths from women's writing to realism have been marked out. Colby has argued that authors like Hannah More and Charlotte Yonge, who dealt with the torment of conversion and dutiful living, prepared the way for "the novel of psychological realism" (209). Eakin (*New England Girl*) traces a continuity between Harriet Beecher Stowe's treatment of the American girl and that of Howells and HJ.

13 Fanny Fern, Harriet Beecher Stowe, and Emma Southworth were the only popular novelists from the 1850s who supported female suffrage. On the first two, see Kelley 332–33. In 1871 Southworth tried to register to vote in Washington, D.C., according to W.P.E., "Why Is It?" *Woman's Journal* 2 (29 April 1871): 130. The more usual position was expressed by Marion Harland in *Alone:* "If there is an enjoyment, which is purely of the intellect, its usurpation is man's high prerogative; the sticklers for woman's 'equal rights' will never establish her title to it" (222).

Tompkins argues in *Sensational Designs* that Ellen's submissiveness in *Wide, Wide World* must be understood in terms of nineteenth-century evangelicalism: In "the spiritual order . . . women hold dominion over everything by virtue of their submission on earth" (163). But in her afterword to her edition of the novel, Tompkins says that "we" are moved because Ellen "*is* us" (Warner 597). Then there is this: "The love of power even when it is not our own, the love of seeing power displayed, power triumphant, crushing everything in its path, even – and perhaps especially – when what it crushes happens to be us is at the core of the novel's attraction" (599).

14 I first made the case for this novel in "Well Hidden Hand." Dobson, "Hidden Hand," argues that the book resists the feminine ethos of obedient submission. The novel, edited by Dobson, was reprinted in 1988 by Rutgers Univ. Press.

15 See Dodge, *Gail Hamilton's Life* 1: 479, and Alcott, *Louisa May Alcott* 162.

16 The agonists bear comparison with the contemporary British sensation novelists, who, according to Hughes, yoked melodrama with realism, coincidence with "concern for accuracy and authenticity" (16).

17 LeClair in *Young Henry James* doubted that HJ "was consumed with desire to go to Europe" (426) at the beginning of his writing career. That he published no fiction in British magazines until 1878 implies he aimed his early writing at American readers. Aziz suggests that even in 1873 HJ was still "afraid of English readers" (HJ, *Tales* 2: xliv).

Before Daugherty's 1981 study of HJ's criticism, his early reviews of minor American writers were ignored. Edel's 1956 selection, *The American Essays*, claimed to have "collected all of Henry James's essays on American letters" (v), but left out all his early reviews of American fiction. Shapira's edition, *Selected Literary Criticism*, stressed HJ's criticism of major British and French writers but omitted everything on Americans except the early review of *Drum-Taps* and the 1887 essay on Emerson. Buitenhuis in *The Grasping Imagination: The American Writings of Henry James* considered HJ a commentator on American life and tried to deal with all his American writing, yet ignored the early reviews of American novels. In 1984 all of HJ's reviews of American books were gathered by Edel and M. Wilson for the Library of America (*Literary Criticism* 1: 183–702).

18 The evidence, sifted in ch. 3, is found in Alcott, *Moods* (1865) 181–82; HJ, *Literary Criticism* 1: 192; HJ, "Watch and Ward" 339.

19 Jeffrey M. Masson argued in 1984 that when Freud abandoned the belief that some of his women patients had been seduced by an older male in the family, theorizing instead that this memory was deluded and expressed a repressed incestuous desire, he was himself repressing a dangerous truth. Masson has been attacked from several sides, most notably by defender of Freudian orthodoxy Janet Malcolm and debunker of Freudian science Frederick Crews. I think a more fruitful response to Masson would be to try to discern the full historic meaning of incest in nineteenth-century women's lives. AJ, for instance, was frequently "courted" by her father and brothers. Jean Strouse emphasizes her relationship with her father; Howard M. Feinstein, that with WJ. Linda Schierse Leonard has recently argued that patriarchy does widespread damage to the father–daughter relationship, that a "father–daughter wound is a condition of our culture" (25). In the feminist revision of the psychoanalytic theory of incest, "the common product of female socialization under patriarchy is an adult woman who may deeply resent her feminine identity but . . . seeks confirmation of her importance in sexual relations with men who are more powerful than herself" (Herman and Hirschman 58). The most interesting discussions since Masson of father–daughter incest in literature are by Sandra M. Gilbert and Christine Froula, who connect patriarchal material from the *Iliad* and the Bible with nineteenth- and twentieth-century narratives by women.

2. THE LESSONS OF THE FATHER

1 See particularly Anderson and Brooks. For studies of HJSr see Kellogg, Grattan, Warren, Perry, Matthiessen, Young, Edel (*Untried Years*), LeClair, Hoover, Gunn, and Feinstein. See also Strout, who used Erikson's *Young Man Luther* to develop the thesis that HJSr selected WJ "as the particular child who must justify the parent" (207). Although marred by factual errors, Bell's exposition of the effects on HJSr's children of his "vision that expressive selfhood was evil" (120) may be the best essay-interpretation of the James family.

2 Sayre pioneered the analysis of James's memoirs, and Hoffa, Tompkins ("Redemption"), and Tintner ("Autobiography") have made helpful contributions. Holly ("Drama of Intention" and " 'Absolutely Acclaimed' ") makes good use of unpublished materials and therapeutic concepts. Eakin ("Henry James and the Autobiographical Act") offers the state-of-the-art reading, sympathetic and sophisticated.

3 Attribution by Haskell. In 1934 Warren gave a few good pages to HJSr's views on marriage and free love, concluding that he showed less "consistency and clarity" (109) than Andrews, his opponent in controversy. Strouse gave the first clear demonstration that the father's doctrines on women were inconsistent and demeaning and were probably responsible in part for AJ's instability (44–47). See also Hoover 74–77, 115–17. The most perceptive discussion of HJSr's views on marriage and their effect on HJ is by Niemtzow, who recognizes HJSr's hostility to feminism and his exaltation of marriage.

4 These manuscript materials, classified at the Houghton among HJSr's "Compositions," are of many kinds: rough drafts of letters of controversy, drafts of articles and books, lectures written in a large hand on folio sheets, and numerous miscellaneous fragments. "Marriage" and "Free Love – Marriage" are evidently lectures, as are "Woman" and "Woman in Revelation & History" [bMS AM 1094.8 (9), (11), (72), and (74)]. The latter begins: "I propose to offer you a few observations upon Woman: first as she is given in the Bible, which is the letter of Revelation; and then as she is given in History, which is its spirit or fulfillment."

5 *Love in the Phalanstery* first shows up in a bookseller's advertisement as early as 29 May 1847 (*Harbinger* 4: 400); the English title notwithstanding, this may have been the untranslated French text. For a summary of the Fourierists' prior difficulties over marriage, see Delano 19–22. "No aspect of Fourier's thought was more scrupulously avoided by his disciples than his reflections on love and sexuality," according to Beecher (297), who gives a valuable exposition of Fourier's *Le Nouveau monde amoureux*, which remained unpublished until 1967. The *Observer*'s series of articles assailing his views on marriage ran from March to September 1846, and included such titles as "New York Associationists on Marriage," "New York Fourierites on Marriage," and "Fourierism: Women and Children." See also "Statement." Recounting years later his discovery of Fourierism, HJSr still displayed his headlong imprudence: "They told me, Ripley and the rest, that [Fourier] was an enthusiast: I found him only wrong by defect in that particular." Hence, refusing to draw a line like other American Associationists, HJSr endorsed Fourier's harmonies "in *every* sphere whether of . . . passions or active administration" (HJSr to Mrs. Francis G. Shaw, 10 May 1859, in Catharine Walsh's hand, MH-H; italics mine). In *The Secret of Swedenborg* he could not see "how any consistent religionist is ever to stop short of fanaticism." Such a person may rightly wish an "*exemption . . . from the ordinary limitations that impend over human freedom*" (240; italics his). For Swedenborg's view of the legitimacy of mistress keeping, see Wilkinson 169–70.

6 A.E.F. was identified as Ford by Warren (108). Among the relatively few clippings of HJSr's ephemeral writings preserved with his papers at the Houghton is "Observer and Hennequin," which identifies HJSr as the translator.

7 In addition to Ford's letters, see "Few Words" and "Love Question." Although George Ripley had quoted "the whole of the admirable preface" in his review of *Love in the Phalanstery*, he did not intervene in the controversy between Ford and HJSr. Parke Godwin's reply to the *Observer* reiterated that

American Associationists drew a firm line "between the organization of Industry as such and the organization of the domestic and sexual relations." Frances Macdaniel was one of the few readers who approved of HJSr's "lucubrations in the Harbinger" (HJSr to Macdaniel, 10 March 1849, from a typescript copy made March 1931, MH-H). A writer at the Oneida Community felt that these lucubrations "exhibited powers of logic and analysis which we have rarely seen surpassed" ("Movements and Changes").

8 On nineteenth-century communal societies, see Veysey, Estlake, Carden, and Noyes (*Dixon and His Copyists*). This last item points out some of the many factual errors in Dixon's accounts of free-love communities and in the pseudonymous John B. Ellis's *Free Love & Its Votaries*. The most valuable contemporary accounts remain Noyes's *History of American Socialisms* and Nordhoff's *Communistic Societies*.

9 Emerson too was tarred by Lazarus, who approvingly quoted "Give All to Love" and other poems. Emerson refrained from replying, but the following year, 1853, he evidently looked into *Love vs. Marriage* and some other books listed in its bibliography, including Andrews's *Science of Society* and *Love in the Phalanstery* (*Journals* 13: 211). Apparently neither Emerson nor his modern editors realized that HJSr had a hand in the latter pamphlet.

10 HJSr had shown a tendency all along to exalt divine sovereignty at the expense of individual freedom. In Dec. 1845 he said: "He whose will is subject to the law of his being, or the will of his Creator, is a form of love, of neighborly love, enjoying according to his capacity of reception, the ceaseless inflow of divine delights. He who is insubmissive to that law, is a form of self-love" (*What Constitutes* 29). In time he would identify love with woman, self-love with man. Stoehr shows that many nineteenth-century sex radicals ended in reaction (39). Matthiessen's comments on HJSr's controversy with Andrews – that the former was "an uncompromising egalitarian" and the latter was actuated by "the natural distrust of the poor man for the well-to-do" (12, 13) – reflects some staggering class-related biases.

11 Kern argues that Oneidan practices basically reflected male defense mechanisms. Male continence, for instance, was designed less out of consideration for the female than from "fear of debilitation, desiccation, or dementia arising through the loss of semen" (224). This argument rests on an unconvincing Freudian interpretation of Noyes's life and thought.

12 Strouse 5, 13. MJ and AHJ were each a refuge for their husbands. "I should be . . . terribly tossed [between heaven and hell] . . . if I were not a married man; that is if I were not able when the celestial powers . . . were in *flight* to run to the bosom of your mother, the home of all truth and purity, and deafen my ears to everything, but her spotless worth till the pitiless inflowing infamy had spent itself" (modern typescript of HJSr to Robertson James, 10 Dec. [no year], italics apparently his, Vaux). After WJ died, AHJ said she had tried "to make my life serve his, to stand between him and all harmful things" (letter to Frances Rollins Morse, 4 Feb. 1911, MH-H).

13 What are we to make of this ambiguous confession? "I have been tolerably blameless in all the literal righteousness of the law. It is probable, no doubt,

that I have borne actual false-witness on occasion, or committed here and there actual theft, adultery, and murder. I am not in the least interested either to admit or deny any literal imputations of this sort" (*Secret* 172).

14 An earlier account of HJSr's breakdown is found in his 10 May 1859 letter to Mrs. Francis G. Shaw: "What troubled me in my hereditary theology was, *the dishonour it left on the Divine name*. . . . My heart revolted before my head was able to see any extrication for it. In this state of conflict, my nerves gave way, and I was obliged to abandon thought and betake myself to the water-cure" (copy in Mary James's hand, italics hers, MH-H). His 1 May 1844 letter from Windsor to his mother, shortly before his breakdown, reveals both his inner unrest and his determination not to recognize it. After boasting about his lodgings, he concluded: "I confess to some potent pullings now and then dear Ma in your direction – 'nursery' remembrances, and 'little back-room' remembrances come over me not infrequently which make Windsor Castle seem a great ghastly lie, and its parks an endless sickness not to be endured a moment longer. But these are only *feelings*, which do not commend themselves to my judgment in sober moments, and *they* therefore will not decide the question of our return" (MH-H). Feinstein rightly emphasizes the supreme importance of will for the Jameses: WJ, for instance, "habituated himself to stifling his own desires with self-deforming discipline" (230). But the manner in which HJSr's will overrode his infantile feelings and memories about his mother belies Feinstein's claim that his "intergenerational" story is "primarily . . . about men, not because women are unimportant, but because the sources tell it that way" (16). The sources tell of women present – but forcibly denied.

15 In 1863 WJ sent AJ a photograph of Sickles for her "amusement" and asked, "Is n't he a bully boy?" (*Letters of WJ* 1: 51). Apparently the James children were aware of their father's role in this crime-of-passion case, and thus of his public contentions on marriage and divorce.

16 The queerness of HJSr's opinions on reform becomes conspicuous when he is read in the light of contemporary liberals who shared his concerns. See, e.g., the English barrister Sheldon Amos, whose *Difference of Sex as a Topic of Jurisprudence and Legislation* pushed for divorce without litigation and turned the familiar idea of women's superiority into an argument for female suffrage. HJSr knew of this pamphlet (HJSr to Julia A. Kellogg, 29 Sept. [no year], MH-H).

17 HJSr thought he had been lucid: "I am writing my lecture on *the Symbolism of Woman* & . . . have finished 25 pages, and am so far clear as a crystal, without being at all shallow either" (to Julia A. Kellogg, 18 Oct. [1868], MH-H). He was less euphoric after his lukewarm reception: "I am going to finish a lecture on Woman which I will send you when published. It was given two or three times in Boston last winter in crude form, but I shall reshape it" (to Parke Godwin, 12 Aug. 1869, MH-H). As late as 1878 he was still reading the "paper on woman" (MJ to HJ, 9 March [1878], MH-H). Although some of his lectures were well received (see MJ to AJ, 14 Jan. [1870?], MH-H, and HJSr to HJ, 4 March 1873, MH-H), most were not:

"Father came back comfortably from his Providence spree, but rather discouraged, I think, as he always is after giving a lecture – All that he has to say, seems so good and glorious, and easily understood to him, but it falls so dead upon the dull, or skeptical ears who come to hear him that I do not wonder he feels so" (MJ to HJ, 17 March 1874, MH-H).

18 See the fine discussion of this episode in Strouse 98–110. Taylor also wrote "Diseases of Women" (1859), "Effect on Women of Imperfect Hygiene of the Sexual Function" (1882), "Genital Irritation" (1881), and " 'Spinal Irritation'; or, The Causes of Back-Ache among American Women" (1864).

19 The list of books at the back of WJ's 1868–70 diary (MH-H) includes consecutively Mill's book and Bushnell's "Woman [sic] Suffrage." This entry was made soon after 21 June 1869; the entire list probably represents books read. On 12 July 1869, HJ added a postscript to a letter to WJ: "My one intellectual feat is having read J. S. Mill on the subjection of women at Vevey[?]" (MH-H).

20 WJ accused Mill of supporting "divorce at will" yet shirking the problem of "the tremendous changes such divorce must entail upon the relation of children to society" (564). Here WJ echoed one of his father's most frequently reiterated claims: Those who support free divorce must show how society will not be entailed with the responsibility of supporting the children of divorced couples. Writing to Julia A. Kellogg on 8 Sept. [1869], HJSr approved of WJ's review: "It is very just. He wallops Bushnell in a moderate way, & criticizes Mill while doing justice to him" (MH-H).

21 For a bibliography of Benson, see Scholnick. Benson privately advised the editors of the *Galaxy* to publish HJSr and certain other writers in a letter of 6 Jan. 1867 (William Conant Church Papers, NYPL). Several years later HJ identified Benson as "your little admirer" in a letter to HJSr (4 March [1873], *Letters* 1: 347). By this time Benson had been frozen out of American magazines and, taking up painting once again, had moved to Italy, where he and HJ eventually became friends.

22 WJ's letter, dated 8 Feb. according to HJ's acknowledgment, has not survived. WJ rarely let differences of opinion drop with his younger brother. Possibly his letter had tried to show HJ just where father's *Atlantic* essay was weak. If so, then HJ's later praise of father's article may have been an indirect rejoinder to WJ. When WJ assembled a bibliography of his father's works after his death, he omitted "The Woman Thou Gavest with Me" (*Literary Remains* 470).

23 For a good exposition of HJSr's views on divorce, see R. White 61–62.

24 The *Nation* also had a private reason for regarding HJSr as a nuisance. In 1867, when a *Nation* writer had briefly and tactfully suggested that his essay on Swedenborg's ontology was unclear, HJSr answered the charge by reiterating his points at tedious length. His letter, as printed in the *Nation,* is ten times longer than the criticism calling it forth. (WJ, reading the original essay in Germany, also considered it obscure; Howells wrote that HJSr's writings on Swedenborg "had sometimes a collective opacity which the most resolute vision could not penetrate.") Late in 1869 HJSr again availed himself of the

Nation's pages for a belligerent controversy with a Swedenborgian. Following his blast of 16 December the editors let it be known they would not continue the exchange. They gave HJSr the last word, but two weeks later, as if in revenge, they printed the satiric notice of his *Atlantic* essay. See [Dennett?], "North American Review"; HJSr, "Mr. Henry James's Theory"; *Letters of WJ* 1: 92, 96–97; Howells, *Literary Friends* 223–24; "Emanuel Swedenborg"; HJSr, "Mr. Henry James and the Swedenborgian Church" and "Mr. James and the Swedenborgians." For HJSr's peremptory tone in addressing the *Nation*'s editors, see his letters to Julia A. Kellogg, 5 June and 22 Aug. [no year], MH-H.

25   In editing this letter Edel renders "Dennet" as "Drouet" and then provides the information that this person "was a minor member of the *Nation* staff" (*Letters* 1: 217, 218). I searched through all published sources on the *Nation* and its editors without turning up a single reference to "Drouet." I then suspected that HJ may have been thinking of Dennett, the editor of the monthly magazine reviews in the *Nation* (Mott, *History* 344; Armstrong, *Godkin* 100). Dennett *had* recently moved to Cambridge ([Godkin], "Dennett" 362–63), as HJ reported hearing. When I finally had the opportunity to examine the holograph of the letter at the Houghton Library, I saw that the name as written is "Dennet." The second letter superficially resembles an *r* but is obviously the peculiar *e* HJ formed around 1870. Other examples of this *e* are to found in "heard," one line above "Dennet," and in HJ's opening salutation to his parents on 17 July 1869.
        This was HJ's first written reference to Dennett, as far as I know. If Edel's transcriptions are accurate in *Letters* 1: 262, 342, 383, 444, HJ's later references spelled the name correctly. MJ hated Dennett (*Tales* 2: xl), as did her husband (HJSr to HJ, 8 Aug. 1873, MH-H).

26   Did HJ know that his father had a history of wearing out editors' patience? In an 1859 letter to Greeley at the *New York Tribune*, HJSr stooped to crude insult: "You are by no means a stupid man: and yet at times how very stupidly you talk!" ("Marriage – Divorce"). James Redpath referred to the letter containing this sentence as "the Second Epistle of James" ("Free-Love in the Tropics"). Greeley's reply to HJSr: "We have had about enough of" the discussion. Henceforth, I believe, the *Tribune* was closed to HJSr's "paradox and moonshine" (Greeley, "Reply to the Above").

27   The *Nation* editors replied that if HJSr could explain why marriages were unhappy he would know "the secret of the universe." HJSr's rejoinder exhibited true megalomania: "For aught you know, . . . so far as marriage is concerned, I may be in possession of that secret *now;* but evidently, so long as you disbelieve the fact, there is no chance of your coming to know the secret" ("Reply of Mr. James" 404; italics his).

28   Russell began working for the *St. Paul Pioneer* in 1852. His obituary supplies no information on his radicalism or his connections with HJSr. See "Veteran Officer of Civil War Dies," *St. Paul Pioneer Press*, 4 October 1920, 14. Stern first identified Russell (*Pantarch* 132) as *Woodhull & Claflin's* correspondent.

29 HJSr's essay "Modern Diabolism" had appeared the previous year in the *Atlantic*. Mary James considered this "a most interesting paper – perhaps the best thing he ever did" (letter to HJ, 1 April [1873], MH-H).

30 In addition to *The Bostonians*, *The Reverberator*, and "The Aspern Papers," there are "Sir Dominick Ferrand" (1892), "The Real Right Thing" (1899), and "The Abasement of the Northmores" (1900).

31 This last acknowledges another nonextant letter, from WJ on 1 June. Only six James family letters to HJ survive from his final four months in Europe (May to late Aug.): from WJ on 25 June and 26 July; from MJ on 18 May, 6 and 13 July; and from HJSr on 21 June. Seven of HJ's own letters home survive from the same period: to MJ on 17 May, 3 June, and 28 July; to WJ on 13 June and 6 July; and to HJSr on 23 June.

32 No surviving HJ letter acknowledges WJ's of 26 July. WJ, living at home, had no doubt been reading the latest Beecher–Tilton coverage in the James family newspaper, the *Boston Daily Advertiser*. The 22 July issue gave two columns to Tilton's statement accusing Beecher of adultery. On 23 July there were two columns on Beecher's reply; 24 July told Mrs. Tilton's side. HJSr wrote Emerson: "Even our own Daily Advertiser, habitually so clean, grew foul in that reflected smut/ordure, and failed of its usual welcome at the breakfast table" (Draft, sheet 4, MH-H). Perhaps WJ had to read the paper in his bedroom. (The *Daily Advertiser* is Bromfield Corey's paper in *The Rise of Silas Lapham* – "the only daily there is in the old-fashioned Bostonian sense" [43].)

33 It is unlikely that "young man Henry" has some connection with Henry Ward Beecher or HJ himself. I doubt that HJ thought of Beecher by his first name and can think of no telling similarities between Oneidan Charles and HJ.

34 By this time there had been other invasions of the Jameses' privacy. The *Boston Daily Advertiser* ran a story on 16 May 1879 headed "Henry James, Junior and Senior," which amused and disgusted his mother (MJ to Bob, 20 May 1879, Vaux). HJSr had more than once denounced "that witless rage of gossip which seems to be organizing the correspondence of so many of our papers" ("Emerson, Fourier and 'Warrington' "). In 1883, writing Lizzie Boott about Du Maurier's eye trouble, HJ added: "Don't repeat this – please; I have such a horror in the U.S.A. of everything getting into the papers" (*Letters* 3: 9).

3. PRECOCIOUS INCEST

1 Alcott's private comment on this ending reveals her complex feelings about it. "Publishers wont let authors finish up as they like but insist on having people married off in a wholesale manner which much afflicts me. 'Jo' should have remained a literary spinster but so many enthusiastic young ladies wrote to me clamorously demanding that she should marry Laurie, *or* somebody, that I didnt dare to refuse & out of perversity went & made a

funny match for her. I expect vials of wrath to be poured out upon my head, but rather enjoy the prospect" (*Selected Letters* 125).

2 See Auerbach, *Communities of Women* 55–73. Showalter, who follows others in dividing Alcott's productions into self-sacrificial and feminist writings, edits some of the latter in *Alternative Alcott*.

3 All quotations come from the first edition, except where noted.

4 Another ambiguous reaction is to be found in a letter from L. W. Brown to Caroline Dall dated 28 Jan. [1865], Dall Papers, MHS: ". . . one of those fascinating Books that a body cant leave until finished. . . . Sylvia is such a mixture of contradictions that one is constantly anxious about her. I am not quite clear yet about her position between the two men who both adore her but think upon the whole she got out of the snarl as well as anybody could. I couldnt but feel sorry that longer time was not allowed her to enjoy life and repay Geoffrey after the mists had cleared away. I was not satisfied with Miss Yule's marriage – it seemed to me the feeblest scene in the Book, and rather degrading the institution after the ideal brought forward by Adam & Faith. The Golden Wedding scene was splendid." On HJ's response, see Tintner's very helpful discussion in Stern, *Critical Essays*.

5 Long, *Henry James* 12, shows that HJ was also influenced by Oliver Wendell Holmes's *Guardian Angel*. Veeder (106), argues that *The Initials* was the novel HJ drew the most from in writing *Watch and Ward*. Veeder expertly dissects HJ's "tired language" in the novel – personification, "the formula, the epithet, the noun entity, the cliché, and circumlocution" (57).

6 My quotations are from the 1871 serial edition, which reflects HJ's original intent more accurately than the 1878 revision.

7 The Shakespearean phrase was proverbial, as Mary Chesnut's description of a Confederate officer fresh from the war shows (*Mary Chesnut's Civil War* 139).

8 Here HJ's ridicule leads him into distortion. Alcott nowhere implies that Warwick's act was "naughty."

9 Some of HJ's early tales preserved their heroines from unworthy suitors. In "A Day of Days" a gentlewoman is briefly swept off her feet by a chance encounter with "a genuine democrat," " 'the vulgar son of vulgar people' " (*Tales* 92, 104). In "Poor Richard," the unworthy Major Luttrell, who at thirty-six has attained "middle age," has nearly won the twenty-four-year old Gertrude (*Tales* 133, 163) when young Richard intervenes.

10 For a good discussion of the revision from a different perspective, see Mac-Donald's "*Moods*, Gothic and Domestic" in Stern, *Critical Essays*.

4. THE CHAINS OF LITERATURE

1 For this and many other facts about Stoddard, I am indebted to James H. Matlack's invaluable dissertation, "The Literary Career of Elizabeth Barstow Stoddard (1823–1902)" and articles derived from it, "The *Alta California's* Lady Correspondent" and "Hawthorne and Elizabeth Barstow Stoddard."

2 From a 22 June 1862 letter by Stoddard, as quoted in Matlack, "Hawthorne" 284–85.

3 See Howells, "Editor's Study" 987, and *Literary Friends and Acquaintance* 77; and Lathrop, "Mrs. Stoddard's 'Two Men' " 173–74.

4 Whipple's review was probably unfavorable, judging from the omission of Stoddard's name from his Centennial 1876 survey of American authors (see *American Literature and Other Papers*). The Dickinson household subscribed to the *Atlantic* from 1857 on (Capps).

5 *Morgesons* (1862) 32–33. Quotations are from this edition unless otherwise noted.

6 See particularly the discussion of *Uncle Tom's Cabin, The Wide, Wide World,* and the canonization of Hawthorne in *Sensational Designs*. Buell and Zagarell (xvii–xix) give a lucid exposition of *The Morgesons'* bold challenge to existing feminine norms.

7 Letter dated 2 Feb. 1855, quoted from Hull, " 'Scribbling' Females" 40. See also Wood, " 'Scribbling.' "

8 [Howells], review of *Two Men* 537–38. Earlier, evidently after a favorable review came out in a Boston publication, Stoddard wrote Howells a defiant note: "Who dares to praise me in Boston! There's an 'if' attached, I'll be bound. If it wasn't for Mrs. Howells I would say darn the Bostonians" (25 March 1866, MH-H). For Howells on burlesque, see his "New Taste in Theatricals"; on Byron, see Stowe, "True Story," and Howells, *Selected Letters* 1: 335–36.

9 *Two Men* (1865) 56. Quotations are from this edition unless otherwise noted.

10 For another treatment of the egalitarian potential of the island, see Antoinette Blackwell's 1871 novel, *The Island Neighbors: A Novel of American Life,* in which a romance between an Irish serving-woman and a self-reliant Yankee blossoms into marriage only because it occurs on an island, away from Boston. For commentary, see William Leach, *True Love and Perfect Union* 108–11.

5. ANNE MONCURE CRANE SEEMULLER

1 The only modern criticism of this writer comes from students of HJ who have followed up his review of *Emily Chester* by reading the book. "The novel is badly over-written and lacks the courage of its convictions, but it is much more interesting than James allows" (Jones 33). "The theme of the novel, though obscured by the author's prudishness and bad prose, may be simply stated: it concerns a woman who loves and remains faithful to her husband despite her sexual aversion to him and her attraction to another man" (Daugherty 14–15).

My bibliographical entry for Seemuller lists all her publications known to me. The only private papers I know of are her letters to Francis P. or William Conant Church, Church Papers, NYPL. Other sources of information are a 10 Jan. 1873 funeral notice in the files of the Museum and Library of Maryland History; the anonymous untitled note in the *Nation* of 30 Jan. 1873; Boyle, *Biographical Sketches;* Shepherd, *Representative Authors;* the sketch by John Donald Wade in *Dictionary of American Biography;* a clipping provided me by the Enoch Pratt Free Library from the *Baltimore News-Post* of 13 Oct. 1944; and the unsigned article, "Mrs. Anne Moncure Crane Seemuller," from the Woman's Edition of the Baltimore *American* of 29 Feb. 1896.

2 " 'She is handsome,' some one would remark, hesitatingly, 'but *really* I don't see – ' and here she would stop, 'finding it difficult to formulate her objection,' as Mr. Howells somewhere admirably puts it" ("Little Bopeep" 478).

3 It is out of the question to try to consider the many other books and authors that influenced *The Portrait* – Emerson, Turgenev (see Peterson), George Eliot (see G. Levine), Flaubert, George Sand's *Indiana,* Cherbuliez's *Le Roman d'une honnête femme,* Charles Reade's *Griffith Gaunt.* See Cargill 78–119; Long, *Henry James: Early Novels* 104–7; Grover. Tintner, *Book World* 118–25, 146–50, traces Osmond to Sir Willoughby Patterne in Meredith's *Egoist* and a Paterian character in a novel by W. H. Mallock. Elizabeth Stoddard's *Two Men* has a character named Osmond.

4 There is a curious interpolation in Edel's transcription of this passage in *Letters* 1: 55. The holograph shows nothing between "sufficient" and "notoriety," but Edel inserts "cont" between the words and then interprets this as "cont[inental]," evidently forgetting his own abbreviation for *continued.*

5 A chronology, based on HJ's letters to Perry and Norton (who noted on the backs when he received and answered them):

15 Oct.   HJ writes Norton offering to review *E.C.*
28 Oct.   HJ, still waiting for Norton's reply, has not yet begun to read *E.C.*
29 Oct.   Norton finally gets HJ's letter of 15 Oct.
30 Oct.   Norton answers, accepting the offer.
11 Nov.   HJ replies, promising to send the review of *E.C.* before Dec. 1. His threat to be "severe" (MH-H) indicates he has read or is reading the novel and has perhaps begun the review.
? Nov.   Norton acknowledges receiving the review and comments on it.
1 Dec.   HJ acknowledges Norton's letter.

6 Also, as Howells no doubt realized, "Reuben Dale" was a flat and mediocre narrative. For discussion see Doyle 42–47.

7 Lecture manuscript titled "An Essay upon the Philosophic Significance of man & Woman," sheet 1, MH-H.

8 See HJ's favorable remarks on perfect men in Mrs. Craik's *John Halifax* and *A Noble Life* (*Literary Criticism* 1: 845). All undocumented quotations in this section are from HJ's review of *Emily Chester* as reprinted in *Literary Criticism* 1: 588–95.

9 If it seems unconvincing to link a review written in 1864 with a novel conceived in 1883, I can only point to the 1884 letter in which HJ three times wrote 1865 for 1885. See ch. 8 ("Elizabeth Peabody Revived") for a discus-

sion of this lapse and the two-decade-old time warp attending his composition of *The Bostonians*.

10   Review of *Emily Chester* 697. HJ could have read this British review in *Littell's Living Age* 84 (Jan.–March 1865): 603–5.

11   In 1884 HJ described *The Portrait of a Lady* as "before all things a study of character – descriptive, analytic, *psychological*, concerned with fine shades, emotions, etc." (*Letters* 3: 46; italics mine). Baym shows that fiction classed as "psychological" was often seen as deriving from *Jane Eyre* and was felt to reflect "a female viewpoint," and she also points out that it was standard for three decades before HJ to use reviews of fiction in order to urge on women "a true and generous *forgetfulness of self*, a lowly spirit of pious submission" (*Novels* 94–95, 190).

12   Other reviewers got less excited. The *New York Times* blandly summed up the novel's "psychological purpose" ("a vindication of the supremacy of the affections over the counter claims of the intellect") and awaited "the reappearance of its authoress" (10 Dec. 1864). The *Saturday Review*'s long sarcastic summary attributed the novel's excesses to its transcendentalism and "that extraordinary mixture of electro-biology and the Family Bible which is so delightful to the American mind" (697). A dogmatically favorable response is found in a Feb. 1865 letter of Gail Hamilton's: " 'Emily Chester' I have read, and do not feel myself tainted in the smallest degree by so doing. There is no tainting element in the book. It is pure as the snow . . . and no one can see anything impure there unless his organ of vision is impaired. . . . Of all the criticisms of 'Emily Chester' which I have read, very few show any real comprehension of the book" (M. Dodge 1: 479).

13   All undocumented quotations in this section are from HJ's review of *Opportunity* as reprinted in *Literary Criticism* 1: 595–99. The *Putnam's* critic saw that although Grahame "is represented as the most brilliant and fascinating of men," neither his speech nor his actions bore out this claim (review of *Opportunity* 256).

14   In HJ's "Daniel Deronda: A Conversation," Constantius, the author's stand-in, says he "enjoyed" the Daniel segments because "my fancy often warms cold things" (*Literary Criticism* 1: 987).

15   Constantius considers Gwendolen "at the first a little childish for the weight of interest she has to carry" (*Literary Criticism* 1: 989).

16   *Literary Criticism* 2: 1077, 1076, 1081, 1071, 1075. After Scribner's complimented HJ on his prefaces for *Portrait* and *Roderick Hudson*, he replied: "As far as material or 'inspiration' for them goes, I have decidedly rather too inconveniently much than too little" (H. Parker 502).

17   Brodhead (54–58) shows that Fields and his publishing apparatus, Ticknor & Fields and the *Atlantic Monthly*, played a key role in establishing the canon of "distinguished" American writers that prevailed until the 1920s. This apparatus was clearly *not* used to support Seemuller.

18   In view of her violent denouement, it may have seemed to Seemuller's readers that she had drawn on a crime that dominated public attention the year before *Reginald Archer* appeared. On 25 Nov. 1869, at the offices of the

New York Tribune, Daniel McFarland shot Albert D. Richardson, who had recently married McFarland's former wife. Richardson died a week later. When the trial took place in April 1870, it was "almost the only topic of conversation" (*Tribune*, 6 May 1870). (HJSr commented on the case in his June 1870 *Atlantic* essay, "The Logic of Marriage and Murder.") The defense lawyer had defended Sickles, another crime-of-passion murderer, twelve years earlier (and HJSr had written about *that* crime too). The defense's argument was that McFarland's wife had been corrupted by "Fourierites, Agrarianites, Mormons, Spiritualists, free lovers" (*Tribune*, 9 April 1870) so that it was easy for Richardson to seduce her. She became an actress and got an Indiana divorce, and McFarland, a lawyer and former college professor, inevitably went mad. Many prominent witnesses were called – Whitelaw Reid, Horace Greeley, Fitz Hugh Ludlow. Feminist opinion was with the woman (*Tribune*, 12 May 1870). McFarland was found not guilty.

19 She could write with true distinction. In *Opportunity*, when Rose Carvel realizes that the man she loves regards her as a kind of sister or daughter, "she had a sensation of being an automaton wound up to run for a certain time, and her most distinct idea concerning herself was a vague wonder as to how soon she would be allowed to run down" (260–61).

20 "Mrs. Anne Moncure Crane Seemuller." That Anne ate some green paint at the age of three may explain her liver trouble ("Colored" 295).

6. MINNIE TEMPLE'S DEATH AND THE BIRTH OF HENRY JAMES'S IMAGINATION

1 Excerpted in Lubbock's edition of HJ's *Letters* 2: 416–18.

2 These documents along with various other items belonging to the de Kay and Gilder families (Gilder Papers) will probably be deposited in the New York Public Library. I quote from them with the kind permission of Gilder and W. deKay Palmer.

3 All letters identified solely by date in this chapter were written by Temple to Gray and survive in fair copies made by Alice H. and Margaret Mary James. They are quoted with the permission of the Houghton Library.

4 MT's full sentence: "For if morality, virtue, were the test of a Christian, certainly Christ would never have likened the Kingdom of Heaven to a little Child, in whose little heart is certainly no struggle, no conscious battle between right & wrong, but only unconsciousness of self, love & trust" (25 Jan. 1870). HJ's version (*Notes of a Son* 510) replaced the phrase his father might have written, "unconsciousness of self," with "unthinking."

5 HJ's replacement of "natural Religion" with "naturalism" (*Notes of a Son* 512) altered MT's statement considerably. Did he confuse these two very different things?

6 The reason HJ once gave Grace Norton for not marrying – "I should pretend to think just a little better of life than I really do" (Edel, *Conquest of London* 358) – may owe something to MT's views. Also, she evidently encouraged him to travel in Europe (*Notes of a Son* 467).

7   MJ wrote HJ: "Poor little Elly she certainly has great pluck – She is perhaps safer than she would be with an older man – I have no doubt she thinks so" (6 Sept. [1869]). HJ disapproved of the marriage in letters to HJSr (17 Sept. 1869), WJ (25 Sept. [1869]), and AJ (6 Oct. [1869]). Bob Temple wrote HJ: "The idea of that young & lovely girl tied down to a man, *28* years her senior, is to me simply *revolting*" (17[?] Sept. 1869).

8   "Female Writers" 168. In *The Bostonians* Mrs. Luna would also glibly reverse Pope's formula, saying, "Whatever is, is wrong, and all that sort of thing."

9   MT's 21 Nov. 1869 letter to Gray gives an appreciative account of this visit. *Notes of a Son* (499) omits a veiled passage about the impressions she took away: "I can't write them to you, at any rate – I must have a sympathetic look now and then from you, a glance of approval – or disapproval, to feel my way by – and my impressions are not sufficiently unalterable to bear seeing them down, once for all, in black & white." Some of her later letters (30 Nov. and 12 Dec. 1869) imply that HJSr's assault on her egotism shook her self-confidence.

10 For further discussion of MT's relationship with WJ, see Habegger, "New Light."

11 Did Henry draw a connection between MT and the orphaned heroine of *The Lamplighter?* This novel, published in March 1854, was given to him as a substitute for the spicy *Hot Corn,* published that winter. MT's father died in July; her mother, in October.

12 It may be because of HJSr's teaching that WJ and HJ both quoted the line from *Faust* that demands renunciation: "*Entbehren sollst du! sollst entbehren!*" (*Varieties* 51; *Bostonians* ch. 11). HJ gave the line to Olive, who substitutes *entsagen* for *entbehren.*

13 HJ to WJ, 8 March 1870. For discussion of HJSr's "*Marriage* paper" and "the three female papers on Woman," see ch. 2 ("Your Article on the Woman Business I Decidedly Like").

14 Forty-two years later, working on *Notes of a Son and Brother,* HJ wrote his nephew Henry James III about these letters, which had collapsed in his memory into a single document: "Apropos of this there is one small thing that besets me. *Is* there in Irving Street, accidentally standing over, either the original or the copy of a certain letter that I wrote home (either to your Dad or to one of your Grandparents) from this country (Malvern, early in 1870) after receiving the news of Minny Temple's death? We had that out in Irving Street, to *be* copied, winter before last; we judged it of distinct value for the Record (it struck even me as highly so!) and I think I am capable of reproducing it in the Book, apropos of her so touching early end, under the guise of a letter from a person, a near relative, not named" (HJ to HJ III, 19 Jan. 1913, MH-H). Not using the letters, HJ had no need for this subterfuge.

15 "Souls" is wrongly transcribed as "hearts" in *Letters* 1: 221.

16 Edel inaccurately has "absolute" (*Letters* 1: 221).

17 To WJ, 29 March [1870]. Where I read "our friendship," Edel reads "one friendship" (*Letters* 1: 224).

18 Date of composition of "Travelling Companions" determined by Maqbool

Aziz (*Tales* 2: xxxii). Annie Fields's journal shows that the manuscript submission reached the *Atlantic* by 16 July 1870.

19   See my discussion of "The Story of a Year" (1865) and "A Most Extraordinary Case" (1868) in ch. 7 ("The Dying Man").

7. THE FATHERLESS HEROINE AND THE FILIAL SON

1   *The Portrait of a Lady* (Boston: Houghton Mifflin, 1882 [1881]), 19. Subsequent citations are to this, the first American book edition, unless otherwise specified.

2   HJ's 1867 story, "Poor Richard," had attributed the same weak reaction to its strong, independent orphan-heroine: "An immense weariness had somehow come upon her, and a sudden sense of loneliness. A vague suspicion that her money had done her an incurable wrong inspired her with a profound distaste for the care of it" (*Tales* 1: 165).

3   The provisional title was mentioned as early as 24 Oct. [1876] and as late as 23 July [1878] (*Letters* 2: 72, 179).

4   The Howells letters are dated 24 Oct. [1876] and 2 Feb. [1877]; that to WJ, 12 Jan. [1877] (*Letters* 2: 72, 97, 91).

5   The reviewer in *Penn Monthly*, possibly Elizabeth Stuart Phelps, considered Isabel "a very clever mechanical drawing of an automaton, who moves perfectly in every part, but who, after all, is not alive" (Phelps [?] 233). Writing HJ, Woolson called Phelps "your poor serious soul-to-soul enemy" (*Letters* 3: 528). Among modern critics who stress the novel's unadmitted tendentiousness is Adele Wiseman, who argues that Isabel "is destined by the writer to epitomise and validate a particular cultural ideal of feminine heroism" (459). Baym's "Revision" historicizes *The Portrait* as "one of an increasing number of works about 'the woman question' " (183).

6   HJ to AJ, 22 Feb. [1876] (*Letters* 2: 30).

7   HJ to Norton, 28 Dec. 1880, MH-H. Edel misreads "mark" as "work" and then attempts to render the sentence intelligible by inserting "in" before "the work of art" (*Letters* 2: 324). For earlier doubts of the accuracy of HJ's reproduction of MT, see Henry James III in *Letters of William James* 1: 36, Cargill 79–81, and Sandeen.

8   "H. de K & Minnie Temple roomed together at school" (Rosamond Gilder, binder labeled "Early Notes on H.G.'s Letters/Tyringham III," Gilder Papers).

9   Rosamond Gilder's typescript, 3 April 1863, Gilder Papers. The friendship cooled during MT's last year. After her death Helena wrote somewhat boastfully about her feelings to her new friend, Mary Hallock: MT "was to me a passion – lasting forever as my passions do I think – So was I to her – but someone came between us & her love cooled and it seemed to me as if death were better" ([Spring 1870?], Gilder Papers). Four decades later Helena identified this person as Katherine ("Kitty") Emmet, the sister at whose home in Pelham, New York, MT lived in 1869–70. Yet a November [1869] letter

from MT to Helena says, "Kitty sends her love and says to come on Wednesday or Thursday" (Rosamond Gilder's typescript, Gilder Papers), and Helena's daughter later wrote that "H.[elena] went to see her [MT] just before her abortive trip to California" (working notes for "Two Pictures," n.p., Gilder Papers). Mary Hallock evidently felt rather jealous: "I dont suppose I shall ever have a chance to forgive anything in you – except an exaggerated estimate of your friend M." (to Helena de Kay, Dec. 1869, Foote Papers, Stanford Univ.). Mary's letters to Helena inspired Smith-Rosenberg's influential article, "The Female World of Love and Ritual: Relations between Women in Nineteenth-Century America" (*Disorderly Conduct* 27). In 1894 Helena wrote an antisuffrage pamphlet, *A Letter on Woman Suffrage: From One Woman to Another*. In 1909 she was president of the Executive Committee of the National League for the Civic Education of Women, an antisuffrage group.

10 In her teens, in 1862–63, Clymer belonged to the Minerva Society, a pioneering women's club of New Harmony, Indiana (Glynes, "Minerva Society" 2; G. Courtney, *History* 12). Marrying at the age of sixteen or seventeen, she apparently separated from her husband and took up residence in her mother's home in New York. In a historic meeting of Sorosis in 1868, Clymer "brought in a resolution" (Croly, *History* 20) to restore the club's name, a move that rebuffed the Boston-supported faction that wanted the new organization to be a sort of female auxiliary. (Earlier, Annie Fields, who recalled Clymer as that "pretty little niece" [M. Howe 81], had been one of those who persuaded Sorosis to change its name to the conservative-sounding "Woman's League" [Croly, *Sorosis* 13].) In an 1871 meeting of Sorosis Clymer "recited a dreadful slur on the fidelity of both sexes, called the 'Faithful Lovers' " ("Sorosis" 8), and about the same time she got a good part in an Augustin Daly production. Mary Hallock and Helena de Kay were lukewarm about her theatrical ambition: "I dont believe in 'Careers' but I cannot help believing in a beautiful innocent woman. But Helena, the mother, (tell it not in Gath) is a cold blooded calculating worldly woman, and Ella [Clymer] is like wax in her hands" (Hallock to de Kay, ca. 1864–69, Foote Papers, Stanford Univ.). MT, on the other hand, "always liked" the mother, feeling that Clymer "had a very nice way with her mother, & they seemed to be very fond of each other" (fair copy, MT to Gray, 20 May 1869, MH-H). In *Notes of a Son* HJ excised MT's two passages about Clymer.

11 *Notes of a Son* introduces the letter containing this statement by repeating for the second time in ch. 13 that MT would have found life an agony if she had lived (491).

12 For a good conventional account of the differences between Ralph and HJ, see Hutchinson, who writes: "Ralph is indeed very close to James. . . . Watching Ralph perform . . . James understands how drastically more compromising it is to try to fulfill the requirements of one's imagination in life, than it is by writing a novel" (280). Working at a time (1954) when few biographical materials were available, Sandeen pointed out some important connections between Ralph and James – their ambiguous love for their

cousin, their assumption of control over her destiny, their struggle for health.

13 Brodhead puts this well: "James as I read him begins as and long continues to be a highly derivative author." "Expressing his own most powerful patterns of consciousness in fiction . . . is precisely what James does not do in his earliest writing; instead it is what he comes to be able to do, as the result of a practical program of literary apprenticeship" (175, 131).

14 This 1866 story shows how early HJ had a firm ideal of noble womanhood: Adela's "part was still to be the perfect young lady. For our own part, we can imagine no figure more bewitching than that of the perfect young lady under these circumstances" (*Tales* 1: 102). For an argument that Stendhal's *Chartreuse de Parme* was the "armature" on which HJ built "Most Extraordinary Case," see Tintner's "In the Footsteps."

15 After WJ criticized some of HJ's early stories, the latter wrote: "I should be quite at [a] loss to explain their obscurities or justify their shortcomings. They are the poor unripe fruits of *the house of bondage*" (HJ to parents, 17 July 1869, MH-H; italics mine). WJ's letter, dated 28 June according to HJ's acknowledgment, has not survived.

16 Of course, Isabel does not live up to all of HJSr's dogmas. It is out of the question that she should redeem Osmond, and she does not at all submit as he expects. But as Niemtzow shows, HJSr's views "guide the last hundred pages" (380), so that Isabel is required "to satisfy the moral code that the elder James prophesied would come if legal marriage contracts were dissolved and she does so 'freely' and 'consciously' " (388). R. White argues that HJ faces and resolves the problems of human sexuality by assuming HJSr's sacramental view of marriage.

17 See Tintner's good discussion of HJ's "ironic" use of 1876 ("Centennial"). Feidelson's brilliantly developed argument for the tragic freedom of Isabel's consciousness has, to my eyes, an insubstantial glitter. Freedom that is merely "intrinsic" – Sisyphus's freedom in Camus's parable, HJSr's freedom in slavery – seems a rationalization for servitude.

8. THE RETURN OF THE FATHER IN THE BOSTONIANS

1 One of several justifications for loosely equating author and narrator in *The Bostonians* is the passage apologizing for the lengthy description of Basil's New York neighborhood: "I mention it . . . for old acquaintance sake" (186).

2 But HJ does the same thing with another word that was standard English by 1885: "He had rallied, as the French say" (13).

3 On HJ's class loyalty, M. Green shows that *The Bostonians* often identifies poverty and moral failure. Grewal's brilliant dissertation sees HJ as the heir to a certain tradition of "conservative-liberal" culture criticism: "Whenever he has to deal with conditions very much below the level of 'civilized ease,' he shows a nervous uneasiness which blocks the normal flow of his sympathy" (228).

4 On HJ's alterations in course of composition, see Habegger, "Disunity" and "Introduction" xxxii–xxxv, and Heaton.

5 According to Smith and Peinovich, who also point out that HJ "deleted
   parenthetical authorial comments" (304). This article must be used cau-
   tiously as it has many factual errors and misquotations.

6 HJ's phrase in an 1899 letter to Mrs. Humphry Ward, *Letters of Henry James*,
   ed. Lubbock, 1: 333: "I 'go behind' right and left in . . . The Bostonians."
   Mizruchi tries to salvage the novel's damaged authority by seeing it as self-
   conscious egalitarianism. The narrator is one of Frye's *eirons* whose "fluctua-
   tions between criticizing others and self-deprecation reflect an ambivalence
   toward power" (211). His proclivity "to resist the authority of his narrative"
   (213) and his reluctance to take "power over the reader's perceptions" (214)
   furnish evidence that he is " 'democratic' " (215).

7 On the influence of *The Bostonians* on the New York Intellectuals, see
   Habegger, *Gender* 289–302.

8 In 1909, HJ would maintain "that it was impossible for any woman to write
   a good criticism" of Whitman (N. Page 45). Similarly, while writing the last
   chapters of *The Bostonians* HJ disagreed with Grace Norton's view of Balzac's *Contes Drolatiques* by "taking refuge in the general statement that a
   woman *can't* speak properly of Balzac . . . ; the feminine point of view here
   is inadequate!" (*Letters* 3: 75). In 1867 he wrote: "We speak, of course, of a
   first-class imagination – as men occasionally have it, and as no woman (unless it be Mme. Sand) has yet had it" (*Literary Criticism* 1: 1156). Even with
   Sand he had reservations: "There is something very liberal and universal in
   George Sand's genius, as well as very masculine; but our final impression of
   her always is that she is a woman and a Frenchwoman. Women, we are told,
   do not value the truth for its own sake, but only for some personal use they
   make of it. My present criticism involves an assent to this somewhat cynical
   dogma" (*Literary Criticism* 2: 712).

9 HJ may have been spurred by the critique of *The Portrait* in the *Atlantic*.
   Horace Scudder had drawn a damning parallel with "The Emperor's New
   Clothes" in order to question the novel's illusion of life: "Only when one is
   within the charmed circle of the story is he under its spell" (128). Scudder
   unfavorably compared the novel with Howells's *Doctor Breen's Practice*,
   which HJ himself had greatly admired.

10 Many political conservatives have done so. C. Anderson sees the novel as a
   "fable championing the institution of marriage" (311) and faults HJ for criticizing Basil and not understanding Southern character. Miller sees Basil's
   victory as a sign of HJ's new but still unsettled conservatism: His "liberalism . . . grows sick" (337). Gooder expresses the more widely accepted
   conservative view: "*The Bostonians* shares with *Huckleberry Finn* . . . the
   distinction of doubting the capacity of human nature and human society to
   sustain the democratic ideal" (xxxiii). For an illuminating discussion of Matthiessen's uneasiness with HJ's political attitudes, see Cain; for a discussion
   of Howe's and Trilling's credulous acceptance of HJ's account of anarchism,
   see Lucas. Torsney has recently presented fresh evidence of HJ's evolving
   response to British imperialism.

11 Some other inconsistencies: At first Pardon works (implausibly) for the

Boston Evening Transcript (43); later the name is silently altered to *Vesper* (422). Olive's mother's death "preceded" (116) her father's, but earlier (13) HJ implies that the mother had been the surviving parent. HJ implies in ch. 36 that no one, including Olive, has servants at Marmion; later, as she and Verena sit together in the dark, a "parlor-maid" (413) materializes. Mrs. Burrage's gathering takes place 26 March (246); two days later the month is April (324). Even those critics who focus on the temporal aspects overlook the inconsistencies in chronology.

12   See ch. 3 for a brief consideration of this central Jamesian image, which appears in his review of Alcott's *Moods* and in his own *Watch and Ward,* "The Aspern Papers," and *Notes of a Son and Brother.* Henry Burrage adds a complicating twist. This gentle, refined young man is not only one of HJ's few characters to bear his own first name, but the young man's deceased father also was called Henry (246).

13   Facts from Burger and Bettersworth. Lamar broke the news to the disbelieving Mary Chesnut that George Eliot was living with Lewes (*Mary Chesnut's Civil War* 543, 581, 661).

14   See *Complete Notebooks* 30 and the 18 April [1885] letter to Osgood, *Letters* 3: 78. The review appeared June 1883.

15   HJ also saw his father as expressive. Writing in 1896 to his nephew Edward (son of Bob), he composed an interesting genealogy: "You have probably an heredity of expression in your blood (from your father through his father)" (Maher 183).

16   HJSr to Caroline Dall, "Wed. evening" [1865?], Dall Papers, MHS.

17   HJSr to Julia A. Kellogg, n.d., MH-H. Catalogued as bMS Am 1092.9 (4248).

18   On her opinion of HJSr's brain disease, see Maher 145. Strouse, *Alice James* 207–8, was the first to report the facts about this death with any fullness. Edel, *Henry James: A Life* 283, mentions the refusal to eat but reverts to the old euphemistic picture: "He had turned his sickroom into a place of joy." Hastings (112) wrongly gives 19 Dec. as the date of death.

19   According to Perry, *Thought and Character* 2: 325, WJ first presented his concept of pragmatism in connection with religion.

20   In the serial Basil elsewhere smiles at Verena "as men smile when they are perfectly unsatisfactory (through being, perhaps, in the right)" (*Century Magazine* 30: 566). The book version (229) drops the phrase in parentheses.

21   Emerson's essay "Woman" (called to my attention by Ian F. A. Bell) begins by voicing similar views: "Man is the will, and Woman the sentiment" (338–39); "the omnipotence of Eve is in humility" (344); by their conversation women "finish society, manners, language" (341). But the last half of the essay vigorously defends women's right to vote. Originally delivered in 1855, the essay was collected in *Miscellanies* the year HJ began writing *The Bostonians,* 1884.

22   On occasion HJ himself showed a hidden streak of orthodox theology. "Don't," he wrote his brother Bob, "let your periodical mania for change – which is simply a temptation of the devil – attack you; or rather if it does attack you, don't on any account let it get the better of you, for if it does the

devil will get possession of you altogether. . . . Excuse my preaching" (6 Dec. [1876?], Vaux).

23 Thus, HJSr saw the husband as a Christ figure: "In marriage the man so freely makes himself over to the woman, so cordially endows her with all his substance, as to make a spiritual resurrection or glorification for him in his offspring logically inevitable" (*Secret of Swedenborg* 125).

24 HJSr to Dall, 13 Jan. [1865], Dall Papers, MHS. Cf. HJ's remarks on the gender of George Sand's mind, quoted in note 8, this chapter, and ch. 9. The dinner was on 9 January. Was that when Louisa May Alcott dined with the Jameses (see ch. 3)? If so, Dall may have been present when HJ lectured the author of *Moods*. Dall had acquired an advance copy of this novel just before Christmas, and she discussed it with a class of young ladies soon after the dinner. Her record of her class is intriguing: "great fun over Moods & Mr James's visit to me yesterday" (journal entry for 14 Jan. 1865, Dall Papers, MHS).

25 "When he [HJSr] proceeds to talk of 'the family bond' as entitled to 'divine honor,' to tell us what [*sic*] 'this institution is bound to insist on its own prerogative,' and to 'stigmatize' and 'scourge' the opposing idea of freedom, it sounds so like the old and familiar crack of the whip over the heads of another school of abolitionists, that a slip of the pen which transfers the technicalities of slavery to marriage will, I trust, be readily condoned. There is such an echo of seeming congruence between 'sacred family institution' and 'peculiar institution,' between 'bond' and 'bondage,' between 'divine honors' and 'divine institution,' and between 'scourging' and 'stigmatizing' in the one interest and 'scourging' and 'stigmatizing' in the other . . . that one has fairly to rub his eyes open, not, indeed, to confound the two things" ("Free-Love Controversy. – Continued" 4).

26 Had James been so inclined, he could have heard Hatch, now named Tappan, again in 1871. According to "What Women Are Doing," *Woman's Journal* 2 (1 April 1871): 97, "Mrs. Cora L. V. Tappan is giving a course of lectures . . . in New York."

27 Dickinson's *What Answer?* attacked white American racism with more conviction than artistry. Annie Fields wrote, "Read Anna Dickinson's fine story – What Answer? Thank God for such as she!" (journal entry for 1 Oct. 1868, Fields Papers, MHS). When the novel was advertised with Harriet Beecher Stowe's praise, "a brave, noble book," HJ took offense. Admitting he had not yet read it, he attacked both it and Stowe's "criticism" (*Literary Criticism* 1: 224). The following week, John Richard Dennett, writing anonymously in "Injurious Works and Injurious Criticism," joined HJ's assault on the "thoroughly bad novel," which lacked character and plot. Dennett lectured Dickinson that she should be quiet on the subject of race until "certain laborious ethnologists and physiologists" reach their conclusions. As it is, she is "very ignorant and very illogical," "as entirely unqualified . . . as a peri would be . . . to make a commentary on Wheaton's books concerning international law." Dennett was answered by Isabella B. Hooker, who called the book "the most emphatic protest against the spirit of caste that has appeared in American

literature." Speaking of Dickinson's beginnings as a lecturer, Hooker wrote that she "flamed out, to the surprise of herself and everyone else, in a little speech in defence of women." This controversy underlies HJ's conception of his improvisational and idealistic young speaker – and also discloses his own caste affiliations.

   S. Davis sums up some of the events in Dickinson's life that run parallel to the novel – a triangular relation among Dickinson, Susan B. Anthony, and Wendell Phillips, and later the well-publicized contention for her by Phillips and Whitelaw Reid. Long, *Great Succession* 120, 186–87, suggests that Victoria Woodhull "looms in the background of *The Bostonians*." Neither scholar satisfactorily establishes what HJ knew, when he knew it, or how he felt about the two orators.

28 HJ's sense of political activism is staggering. Are we supposed to believe that a Northern abolitionist traveled clandestinely in the South in order to carry the slaves *the Bible* (215)?

29 See Edel, *Henry James: The Middle Years* 142–43; Long, *Great Succession* 184–85.

30 The poem was later published as a broadside. Two copies at MHS have the identities penned in. The "porpus" was Ednah D. Cheney, Louisa May Alcott's friend. HJSr was not among McDowell's targets. See also McAlexander 68–71. According to Lewis, "Courtship" 181, AHJ sent WJ a copy of the poem early in their courtship.

31 Dall's journal for 19, 23, 24 March 1866, and HJSr to Dall, "Wednesday evening" [25 April 1866] and 27 Aug. [1866], all in Dall Papers, MHS. The second letter has been wrongly assigned to 1859. It was written in 1866, from Swampscott, Mass., shortly before the Jameses settled in Cambridge: "We are wholly unsettled, not knowing whither to turn for the winter. Alice goes to New York for the winter with her aunt. It is probable that we ourselves shall find a shelter in Cambridge."

32 In view of Feinstein's thesis that HJSr compelled WJ to give up painting for medicine, Peabody's advice that he attend art anatomist Rimmer's lectures takes on a somber point (and HJSr's ridicule of her suggestion looks rather sinister). Minnie Temple wanted to attend one of Rimmer's classes (Rosamond Gilder's typescript, Minnie Temple to Helena de Kay, Nov. [1869], Gilder Papers). Helena de Kay did attend and left behind detailed notes.

33 "The notion that he is dated is quaint. The portrait of the feminist in 'The Bostonians' could have been sketched today." H. Moss, "The Last of James," *New Yorker* 63 (9 March 1987): 103.

34 WJ, Review of Bushnell 561–63; HJ to WJ, 30 Oct. [1869], MH-H. Discussed in ch. 2.

35 HJ had almost certainly read this passage by his friend Woolson: "I myself have seen tears of joy, the uttermost faith, and deepest devotion, in mature, well-educated, and cultivated women, for some other woman whom they adored. . . . But – but! there is a monotonous certainty that follows on, which arouses to laughter the unregenerate masculine mind and makes it deny the whole (which is a mistake; it *is* there), namely, the certainty that

once let loose an agreeable *man* in this atmosphere, and, ten to one, the whole cloud-structure topples over" (Untitled Essay 503).

36 Fair copy of MT to John Chipman Gray, 25 Jan. 1870, MH-H; M. Howe 80–81; Field 31–33. For discussion, see ch. 2.

37 An early letter from MJ to her mother-in-law defended HJSr's ideas, especially his revelation of the "true spiritual significance" of the Scriptures (to Catharine Barber James, 14 Jan. [1849 or 1855], MH-H). When HJ visited old family friends in London in 1869, "Mrs. W[ilkinson] inquired whether 'my mamma read & studied much now – she used to have such a splendid head' " (HJ to HJSr, 2 March 1869, MH-H). A letter from MJ to HJ and AJ, 26 July [1872?], MH-H, shows how little time she found to read: "As an evidence of the free domestic atmosphere that prevails in the house, *I* have been *absorbed* for the last two days in the Eustace Diamonds! peacefully absorbed!" Eventually MJ felt "free" only when able to devote herself to HJSr: "I feel that I must keep myself free that I may go and come with Father at pleasure" (MJ to HJ, 18 May 1874, MH-H).

38 Letter of 25 Jan. 1864, MH-H. The same dogmatic formula shows up in a letter to his youngest son: "I have my own very decided convictions upon the subject, and I can have no objections to sharing them with you, provided your own conclusions favour them" (typed copy, HJSr to Bob, [summer 1874], Vaux).

39 During Bob's marital troubles in the mid-1870s, HJSr insisted that he return East from Wisconsin: "It is simply indispensable in my opinion that you fix yourself . . . where you can have intercourse with home once a year . . . and oftener if need be. This thing is necessary to my happiness. I can't stand this tremendous separation from you" (typed copy, 10 Dec. [no year], Vaux).

40 See "The Little Girls" in Edel, *Henry James: A Life* 480–83. HJ's 1877 *Galaxy* essay on George Sand regards her, like Verena, as a gifted *improvisatrice* from an irregular home, and shows a fascinated distaste for her treatment of her mother's lightness in *L'Histoire de ma vie:* "a startling absence of delicacy, of reticence, of the sense of certain spiritual sanctities and reservations" (*Literary Criticism* 2: 714).

41 In his preface to *The Tragic Muse* HJ called those novels he considered formless (*The Three Musketeers, War and Peace*) "loose baggy monsters" (*Literary Criticism* 2: 1107).

42 Attribution by me on circumstantial evidence. See Willard & Livermore 23–24 and Kuehl 2: 520–22. On Boston reformers in general, see Mann and Huggins.

9. CONCLUSION

1 Butler's essay is in McGann (ed.), *Historical Studies.* On the linkages between historical excavation, interpretation, and evaluation, see McGann's *Beauty of Inflections.* Tompkins's chapter, " 'But Is It Any Good?' The Institutionalization of Literary Value" (*Sensational Designs*), represents a dismissal of the question and thus avoids the important work of comparative evaluation.

2   Of the many recent discussions of canon and literary history, I single out
    Lauter, von Hallberg, Tompkins, Bercovitch, Reising, Froula, Brodhead,
    and the "Diversity" chapters in the *Columbia Literary History of the United
    States*.

3   Hence the radical incompleteness of von Hallberg's apparently thorough
    summing up: "Canons are discussed from three perspectives here: how art-
    ists determine canons by selecting certain styles and masters to emulate; how
    poet-critics and academic critics, through the institutions of literary study,
    construct canons; and how institutionalized canons effectively govern liter-
    ary study and instruction" (1–2). These categorizations leave out (1) the fact
    that HJ rewrote "minor" writers as well as the "masters," and (2) that HJ's
    fiction often emerged *from* his criticism.

4   Brodhead is one of the few critics who are able to focus on "major" writers
    even while emphasizing their limited cultural roles. He calls attention to HJ's
    "excruciatingly condescending" treatment of "the popular lady novelists"
    (110), and he more than once reminds us that there are multiple "schools" in
    American literature and that the reason one "past" rather than another gets
    kept alive has to do with later keepers of the flame. Yet Brodhead's book
    shows little familiarity with the school of Susan Warner. Also, like many
    other critics, he has a tendency to conceive of nineteenth-century women
    novelists as intrinsically "popular," a curious distortion. (I take it that Tuttle-
    ton's review, which transforms Brodhead's literary history into a defense of
    "an elitist curriculum" [364], represents a willful misreading.)

5   See Anesko, ch. 5, and Weber.

6   See Edel, *Henry James: A Life* 463–67, and Biedler.

7   HJ opens his account of this conversation by recalling, "I have mentioned
    that several of my young friends had clearly not at all liked my plea for the
    mild effort of differentiation" (*French Writers* 47). But no such mention oc-
    curs in the three earlier sections of the essay. Was a segment omitted by HJ or
    his editor, Elizabeth Jordan? Did the "young friends" happen to be students
    at Bryn Mawr, twice visited by HJ in 1904–5? Could the final conversation
    be in some way a rejoinder to the noisy girls at the select Boston school in
    1882?

Works Cited

In addition to the manuscript depositories listed in my acknowledgments, this study has made occasional reference to three other collections:

William Conant Church Papers, NYPL

James T. Fisher Papers, MHS

Books owned by Henry James, Sr., now at the Swedenborg School of Religion, Newton, Mass.

In assembling the following bibliography, I have attributed a number of unsigned pieces to their known or probable authors. A question mark after an author's name (in brackets) indicates that I know of no firm external proof of authorship. Every other attribution is justified within the entry, except for attributions based on these reference works:

Atlantic Index: A List of Articles, with Names of Authors Appended. Boston: Atlantic Monthly, 1889.

Eppard, Philip B., and George Monteiro. *A Guide to the* Atlantic Monthly *Contributors' Club.* Boston: Hall, 1983.

Haskell, Daniel C. *The Nation . . . Indexes of Titles and Contributors.* New York: New York Public Library, 1951, 1953.

Indexes to individual volumes of *Harbinger.*

Alcott, Louisa May. *Alternative Alcott.* Ed. Elaine Showalter. New Brunswick, N.J.: Rutgers Univ. Press, 1988.

  Behind a Mask: The Unknown Thrillers of Louisa May Alcott. New York: Morrow, 1975.

  Little Women. New York: Grosset & Dunlap, 1947.

  Louisa May Alcott: Her Life, Letters, and Journals. Ed. Ednah D. Cheney. Boston: Roberts, 1889.

  Moods. Boston: Loring, 1865.

  Moods. A Novel. Boston: Roberts, 1889. Revised version, first published 1882.

  Plots and Counterplots: More Unknown Thrillers of Louisa May Alcott. New York: Morrow, 1976.

  The Selected Letters of Louisa May Alcott. Ed. Joel Myerson, Daniel Shealy, and Madeleine B. Stern. Boston: Little, Brown, 1987.

"Thoreau's Flute." *Atlantic Monthly* 12 (Sept. 1863): 280–81.

Allen, Elizabeth. *A Woman's Place in the Novels of Henry James*. New York: St. Martin's, 1984.

Allen, Gay Wilson. *William James: A Biography*. New York: Viking, 1967.

A[mes], L[ucia] T[rue]. "*The Bostonians*." *Woman's Journal* 17 (13 March 1886): 82–83. Attribution by Habegger.

Amos, Sheldon. *Difference of Sex as a Topic of Jurisprudence and Legislation*. London: Longmans, Green, 1870.

Anderson, Charles R. "James's Portrait of the Southerner." *American Literature* 27 (1955): 309–31.

Anderson, Quentin. *The American Henry James*. New Brunswick, N.J.: Rutgers Univ. Press, 1957.

Andrews, Stephen Pearl. "Comments and Reply." *Woodhull & Claflin's Weekly* 7 (9, 16 May 1874): 4–6, 4–5.

"Free Love Controversy. – Continued./Stephen Pearl Andrews on Henry James." *Woodhull & Claflin's Weekly* 8 (27 June 1874): 3–5.

Andrews, Stephen Pearl, Henry James, Sr., and Horace Greeley. *Love, Marriage, and Divorce, and the Sovereignty of the Individual*. Boston: Tucker, 1889. First published in New York in 1853.

Anesko, Michael. *"Friction with the Market": Henry James and the Profession of Authorship*. New York: Oxford Univ. Press, 1986.

Anthony, Katharine. *Louisa May Alcott*. New York: Knopf, 1938.

Armstrong, William M. "Additions to the *Nation Index*." *Bulletin of the New York Public Library* 73 (April 1969): 267–74.

E. L. Godkin: A Biography. Albany: State Univ. of New York Press, 1978.

Auerbach, Nina. *Communities of Women: An Idea in Fiction*. Cambridge: Harvard Univ. Press, 1978.

Austin, James C. "Success and Failure of Rebecca Harding Davis." *Midcontinent American Studies Journal* 3 (Spring 1962): 44–49.

Baym, Nina. "The Madwoman and Her Languages: Why I Don't Do Feminist Theory." In *Feminist Issues in Literary Scholarship*, ed. Shari Benstock. Bloomington: Indiana Univ. Press, 1987.

Novels, Readers, and Reviewers: Responses to Fiction in Antebellum America. Ithaca, N.Y.: Cornell Univ. Press, 1984.

"Revision and Thematic Change in *The Portrait of a Lady*." *Modern Fiction Studies* 22 (Summer 1976): 183–200.

Woman's Fiction: A Guide to Novels by and about Women in America, 1820–1870. Ithaca, N.Y.: Cornell Univ. Press, 1978.

Bedell, Madelon. *The Alcotts: Biography of a Family*. New York: Potter, 1980.

Beecher, Jonathan. *Charles Fourier: The Visionary and His World*. Berkeley: Univ. of California Press, 1986.

Bell, Millicent. "Jamesian Being." *Virginia Quarterly Review* 52 (Winter 1976): 115–32.

Benjamin, Walter. *Illuminations*, trans. Harry Zohn. New York: Schocken, 1969.

Benson, Eugene. "About the Literary Spirit." *Galaxy* 1 (15 July 1866): 487–92.

"French and English Art-Writers." *Atlantic* 24 (July 1869): 119–25.

"A Woman in the Pulpit." *Nation* 1 (27 July 1865): 121. Attribution by Armstrong, "Additions."

"Women Writers and Mrs. Edwards." *Galaxy* 5 (June 1868): 788–91.

Bercovitch, Sacvan, ed. *Reconstructing American Literary History.* Cambridge, Mass.: Harvard Univ. Press, 1986.

Bewley, Marius. "*The Blithedale Romance* and *The Bostonians.*" In *The Complex Fate.* London. Chatto & Windus, 1952.

Biedler, Peter G. "The Governess and the Ghosts." *PMLA* 100 (Jan. 1985): 96–97.

Blackwell, Antoinette. *The Island Neighbors: A Novel of American Life.* New York: Harper, 1871.

"Books of the Week." *New-York Daily Tribune,* 18 March 1871, 6.

Boyle, Esmeralda. *Biographical Sketches of Distinguished Marylanders.* Baltimore: Kelly, Piet, 1877.

Brodhead, Richard H. *The School of Hawthorne.* New York: Oxford Univ. Press, 1986.

Brooks, Cleanth, R. W. B. Lewis, and Robert Penn Warren, eds. *American Literature: The Makers and the Making.* New York: St. Martin's, 1974.

Brown, Antoinette L. " 'Woman and the "Woman's Movement." ' " *New-York Daily Tribune,* 26 April 1853.

B[rowne], W[illiam] H[and]. Review of *Reginald Archer. Southern Magazine* (July 1871): 113–16.

Brownell, W. C. "The 'Nation' from the Inside." *Nation* 101 (8 July 1915): 42–44.

Buell, Lawrence, and Sandra A. Zagarell. "Biographical and Critical Introduction." In *The Morgesons.* New York: Oxford Univ. Press, 1984.

Buitenhuis, Peter. *The Grasping Imagination: The American Writings of Henry James.* Toronto: Univ. of Toronto Press, 1970.

Bunce, Oliver. *A Bachelor's Story.* New York: Rudd & Carleton, 1859.

Burger, Nash K., and John K. Bettersworth. "L. Q. C. Lamar: Artificer of Reconciliation." In *Mississippi Heroes.* Jackson: Univ. Press of Mississippi, 1980.

Cain, William E. "Criticism and Politics: F. O. Matthiessen and the Making of Henry James." *New England Quarterly* 60 (June 1987): 163–86.

Capps, Jack L. *Emily Dickinson's Reading 1836–1886.* Cambridge, Mass.: Harvard University Press, 1966.

Carden, Maren Lockwood. *Oneida: Utopian Community to Modern Corporation.* Baltimore: Johns Hopkins Univ. Press, 1969.

Cargill, Oscar. *The Novels of Henry James.* New York: Macmillan, 1961.

C[hanning], W[illiam] H[enry]. "Tendencies of Socialism." *The Spirit of the Age* (N.Y.) 2 (9, 16, 23 March, 13 April, 1850): 152–55, 168–71, 184–87, 232–36.

Chesnut, Mary. *Mary Chesnut's Civil War.* Ed. C. Vann Woodward. New Haven, Conn.: Yale Univ. Press, 1981.

Clarke, Edward H. *Sex in Education; or, A Fair Chance for the Girls.* Boston: Osgood, 1873.

Clemens, Samuel. See Twain, Mark.

Colby, Vineta. *Yesterday's Woman: Domestic Realism in the English Novel.* Princeton, N.J.: Princeton Univ. Press, 1974.

Corse, Sandra. "Henry James on Eliot and Sand." *South Atlantic Review* 51 (1986): 57–68.

Courtney, Grace Gates. *History: Indiana Federation of Clubs.* Fort Wayne, Ind.: Fort Wayne Printing, 1939.

Crane, Anne Moncure.

NOVELS

Emily Chester. A Novel. Boston: Ticknor and Fields, 1864.

Opportunity. A Novel. Boston: Ticknor and Fields, 1867.

Reginald Archer. A Novel. Boston: Osgood, 1871.

SHORT FICTION

"Little Bopeep." *Galaxy* 8 (Sept.–Oct. 1869): 384–98, 477–89.

"My Courtship." *Galaxy* 1 (15 July 1866): 501–12.

"My Note-Book." *Galaxy* 5 (June 1868): 733–45.

POETRY

"Arbutus." *Galaxy* 9 (May 1870): 671–72.

"Barbarossa and Bismarck." *Galaxy* 12 (Nov. 1871): 612–13.

"Edwin Booth." *Galaxy* 7 (Jan. 1869): 87.

"Winter Wind." *Galaxy* 3 (1 Jan. 1867): 23.

"Words to a 'Lied ohne Worte.' " *Galaxy* 1 (1 Aug. 1866): 588 [misnumbered as 688].

ESSAYS

"Colored Photographs." *Old and New* 6 (Sept. 1872): 289–97.

"Novelists' Poetry." *Galaxy* 2 (15 Nov. 1866): 512–15.

"Private Bohemias." *Putnam's* N.S. 2 (Aug. 1868): 138–43.

Crews, Frederick. "The Freudian Way of Knowledge." *New Criterion* 2 (June 1984): 7–25.

Cridge, A. "Gems from Fourier." *Woodhull & Claflin's Weekly* 10 (22 Oct. 1875): 2–3.

Croly, J. C. *The History of the Woman's Club Movement in America.* New York: Henry G. Allen, 1898.

Sorosis: Its Origin and History. New York: J. J. Little, 1886.

Cummins, Maria S. *The Lamplighter.* Boston: Jewett, 1854.

Mabel Vaughan. Boston: Jewett, 1857.

Daugherty, Sarah B. *The Literary Criticism of Henry James.* Athens: Ohio Univ. Press, 1981.

Davidson, James Wood. *The Living Writers of the South.* New York: Carleton, 1869.

Davis, Rebecca Harding. "Men's Rights." *Putnam's* N.S. 2 (Feb. 1869): 212–24.

"A Story of To-Day." *Atlantic Monthly* 8–9 (Oct. 1861–March 1862): 471–86, 582–97, 707–18, 40–51, 202–13, 282–98.

Davis, Sara deSaussure. "Feminist Sources in *The Bostonians.*" *American Literature* 50 (Jan. 1979): 570–87.

Deck, Raymond H., Jr. "The 'Vastation' of Henry James, Sr.: New Light on James's Theological Career." *Bulletin of Research in the Humanities* 83 (Summer 1980): 216–47.

Delano, Sterling F. *The Harbinger and New England Transcendentalism.* Rutherford: Fairleigh Dickinson Univ. Press, 1983.

———. and Rita Colanzi. "An Index to Volume VIII of *The Harbinger.*" *Resources for American Literary Study* 10 (Autumn 1980): 173–86.

[Dennett, John Richard]. "Injurious Works and Injurious Criticism." *Nation* 7 (29 Oct. 1868): 346–47.

[?]. "The Magazines for January." *Nation* 9 (30 Dec. 1869): 588–91.

[?]. "The North American Review for July." *Nation* 5 (18 July 1867): 48.

Desroche, Henri. "Introduction: Fouriérisme écrit et Fouriérisme pratiqué." In Emile Poulat, *Les Cahiers manuscrits de Fourier: Etude historique et inventaire raisonné.* Paris: Editions de Minuit, 1957.

Dickinson, Anna. *What Answer?* Boston: Fields, Osgood, 1869.

Dickinson, Emily. *The Letters of Emily Dickinson.* Ed. Thomas H. Johnson. Cambridge, Mass.: Harvard Univ. Press, 1958. 3 vols.

Dixon, William Hepworth. *Spiritual Wives.* London: Hurst & Blackett, 1868. 2 vols.

Dobson, Joanne. "The Hidden Hand: Subversion of Cultural Ideology in Three Mid-Nineteenth-Century American Women's Novels." *American Quarterly* 38 (Summer 1986): 223–42.

[Dodge, Mary A.]. *Gail Hamilton's Life in Letters.* Boston: Lee & Shepard, 1901. 2 vols.

Doyle, James. *Annie Howells and Achille Fréchette.* Toronto: Univ. of Toronto Press, 1979.

Eakin, Paul John. "Henry James and the Autobiographical Act." *Prospects* 8 (1983): 211–60.

———. *The New England Girl: Cultural Ideals in Hawthorne, Stowe, Howells and James.* Athens: Univ. of Georgia Press, 1976.

Edel, Leon. *Henry James: A Life.* New York: Harper & Row, 1985.

———. *Henry James: 1843–1870 The Untried Years.* Philadelphia: Lippincott, 1953.

———. *Henry James: 1870–1881 The Conquest of London.* Philadelphia: Lippincott, 1962.

———. *Henry James: 1882–1895 The Middle Years.* Philadelphia: Lippincott, 1962.

———. "Introduction." *Watch and Ward.* London: Hart-Davis, 1960.

Elbert, Sarah. *A Hunger for Home: Louisa May Alcott and Little Women.* Philadelphia: Temple Univ. Press, 1984.

Elliott, Emory, general ed. *Columbia Literary History of the United States.* New York: Columbia Univ. Press, 1988.

Ellis, John B. *Free Love & Its Votaries: American Socialism Unmasked.* San Francisco: Bancroft, 1870.

Ellmann, Richard. *James Joyce.* New York: Oxford Univ. Press, 1965.

"Emanuel Swedenborg." *Nation* 4 (25 April 1867): 329–31.

Emerson, Edward. "William James." *Later Years of the Saturday Club.* Ed. M. A. DeWolfe Howe. Boston: Houghton Mifflin, 1927.

Emerson, Ralph Waldo. *Emerson in His Journals.* Ed. Joel Porte. Cambridge, Mass.: Harvard Univ. Press, 1982.

The Journals and Miscellaneous Notebooks. Cambridge,Mass.: Harvard Univ. Press, 1977. Vol. 13.

Miscellanies. Boston: Houghton Mifflin, 1884.

Estlake, Allan. *The Oneida Community.* London: Redway, 1900.

Evans, Augusta J. *Beulah.* New York: Derby & Jackson, 1859.

St. Elmo. A Novel. New York: Carleton, 1868.

Feidelson, Charles. "The Moment of *The Portrait of a Lady.*" In James, *The Portrait of a Lady.* New York: Norton, 1975.

Feinstein, Howard M. *Becoming William James.* Ithaca, N.Y.: Cornell Univ. Press, 1984.

"Female Writers." *Literary World* 1 (1 April 1871): 168.

Fetterley, Judith. *Provisions: A Reader from 19th-Century American Women.* Bloomington: Indiana Univ. Press, 1985.

The Resisting Reader: A Feminist Approach to American Fiction. Bloomington: Indiana Univ. Press, 1978.

"A Few Words on Hennequin." *Harbinger* 8 (16 Dec. 1848): 54. Signed "N."

Fidler, William Perry. *Augusta Evans Wilson 1835–1909: A Biography.* Tuscaloosa: Univ. of Alabama Press, 1951.

Field, Kate. "The New England Women's Club." *Woman's Advocate* 1 (Jan. 1869): 25–33.

Fischer, Sandra K. "Isabel Archer and the Enclosed Chamber: A Phenomenological Reading." *Henry James Review* 7 (Winter–Spring 1986): 48–58.

[Ford, Alfred E.]. "Letter from A.E.F." *Harbinger* 8 (2 Dec. 1848): 36.

"Love in the Phalanstery." *Harbinger* 8 (11 Nov. 1848): 12–13.

Foster, Richard. "Introduction." *The Morgesons.* New York: Johnson Reprint, 1971.

Fowler, Virginia C. *Henry James's American Girl: The Embroidery on the Canvas.* Madison: Univ. of Wisconsin Press, 1984.

French, Marilyn. *The Book as World: James Joyce's Ulysses.* Cambridge, Mass.: Harvard Univ. Press, 1976.

[Frothingham, Octavius B.]. "Is There Such a Thing As Sex?" *Nation* 8 (4 Feb. 1869): 87–89.

"Women vs. Women." *Nation* 5 (3 Oct. 1867): 276–77.

Froula, Christine. "The Daughter's Seduction: Sexual Violence and Literary History." *Signs* 11 (Summer 1986): 621–44.

Gannett, William C. *Ezra Stiles Gannett. Christian Minister in Boston, 1824–1871.* Boston: American Unitarian Association, 1893. First published 1875.

Gay, Peter. *Education of the Senses.* New York: Oxford Univ. Press, 1984.

Geary, Susan. "The Domestic Novel as a Commercial Commodity: Making a Best Seller in the 1850s." *Papers of the Bibliographical Society of America* 70 (1976): 365–93.

Gilbert, Sandra M. "Life's Empty Pack: Notes toward a Literary Daughteronomy." *Critical Inquiry* 11 (March 1985): 355–84.

Gilder, Helena de Kay. *A Letter on Woman Suffrage: From One Woman to Another.* New York: [no publisher], 1909. First edition 1894.

Gilder, Rosamond. "Two Pictures." Unpublished ms. Gilder Papers.

Glynes, Ella M. Dietz. "The Minerva Society and Sorosis." *Woman's Journal* 35 (2 Jan. 1904): 2–3.

Godkin, E. L. *Life and Letters.* New York: Macmillan, 1907.

[Godkin, E. L.]. "Baby Suffrage." *Nation* 10 (14 April 1870): 236–37.

" 'Female Influence.' " *Nation* 5 (25 July 1867): 73–74.

"John Richard Dennett." *Nation* 19 (3 Dec. 1874): 362–63. Obituary, attribution in Godkin, *Life,* 308–9.

"Mr. Mill's Plea for Women." *Nation* 9 (22 July 1869): 72–73.

"A Neglected Side of the Woman's Rights Question." *Nation* 7 (26 Nov. 1868): 434–36.

"The Other Side of the Question." *Nation* 5 (17 Oct. 1867): 316–17.

"Society and Marriage." *Nation* 10 (26 May 1870): 332–33.

"Thomas Carlyle." *Nation* 5 (5 Sept. 1867): 194–95.

Godwin, Parke. *A Popular View of the Doctrines of Charles Fourier.* New York: Redfield, 1844.

[Godwin, Parke]. "The Observer Once More." *Harbinger* 7 (21 Oct. 1848): 196. Attribution by Delano.

Gooder, R. D. Introduction. *The Bostonians.* Oxford: Oxford Univ. Press, 1984.

Grattan, C. Hartley. *The Three Jameses: A Family of Minds.* New York: New York Univ. Press, 1962. First published 1932.

Greeley, Horace. "Reply to the Above." *New-York Daily Tribune,* 23 April 1859. Answers HJSr's "Marriage – Divorce."

"Reply to the Foregoing." *New-York Daily Tribune,* 4 May 1859. Answers HJSr's "Marriage – Divorce – H.J."

Green, Martin. *Re-appraisals: Some Commonsense Readings in American Literature.* New York: Norton, 1965.

Grewal, Om Prakash. "Henry James and the Ideology of Culture: A Critical Study of *The Bostonians, The Princess Casamassima,* and *The Tragic Muse.*" Diss: Univ. of Rochester, 1969.

Gribben, Alan. *Mark Twain's Library: A Reconstruction.* Boston: Hall, 1980. 2 vols.

Grover, Philip. *Henry James and the French Novel: A Study in Inspiration.* London: Paul Elek, 1973.

Gunn, Giles, ed. *Henry James, Sr.: A Selection of His Writings.* Chicago: American Library Association, 1974.

Habegger, Alfred. "The Disunity of *The Bostonians.*" *Nineteenth-Century Fiction* 24 (Sept. 1969): 193–209.

Gender, Fantasy, and Realism in American Literature. New York: Columbia Univ. Press, 1982.

"Henry James's Rewriting of Minny Temple's Letters." *American Literature* 58 (May 1986): 159–80.

Introduction. *The Bostonians.* Indianapolis: Bobbs-Merrill, 1975.

"New Light on William James and Minny Temple." *New England Quarterly* 60 (March 1987): 28–53.

"A Well Hidden Hand." *Novel* 14 (Spring 1981): 197–212.

Harland, Marion. [pseud. of Mary Virginia Terhune.] *Alone*. Richmond: Morris, 1855.

Harlow, Virginia. *Thomas Sergeant Perry: A Biography and Letters to Perry from William, Henry, and Garth Wilkinson James*. Durham, N.C.: Duke Univ. Press, 1950.

Harris, Susan K. "Stoddard's *The Morgesons*: A Contextual Evaluation." *ESQ* 31 (1985): 11–22.

Hart, James D. *The Popular Book: A History of America's Literary Taste*. New York: Oxford Univ. Press, 1950.

Haskell, Daniel C. *The Nation . . . Indexes of Titles and Contributors*. New York: New York Public Library, 1951, 1953.

Hastings, Katharine (Bagg). "William James (1771–1832) of Albany, N.Y., and His Descendants." *New York Genealogical and Biographical Record* 55 (April, July, Oct. 1924): 101–19, 222–36, 301–13.

Heaton, Daniel H. "The Altered Characterization of Miss Birdseye in Henry James's *The Bostonians*." *American Literature* 50 (Jan. 1979): 580–603.

Henke, Suzette. "Gerty MacDowell: Joyce's Sentimental Heroine." In *Women in Joyce*. Ed. Henke and Elaine Unkeless. Urbana: Univ. of Illinois Press, 1982.

Hennequin, Victor. *Les Amours au Phalanstère*. Paris: Librairie Phalanstérienne, 1847.

Love in the Phalanstery. New York: Dewitt & Davenport, 1849 [1848]. Anonymously translated by HJSr.

"Henry James." *New York Daily Tribune*, 20 Dec. 1882.

"Henry James." *New York Post*, 20 Dec. 1882.

"Henry James, Junior and Senior." *Boston Daily Advertiser*, 16 May 1879.

Herman, Judith Lewis, with Lisa Hirschman. *Father–Daughter Incest*. Cambridge, Mass.: Harvard Univ. Press, 1981.

Higginson, Thomas Wentworth. *Cheerful Yesterdays*. Boston: Houghton Mifflin, 1898.

"Emily Dickinson's Letters." *Atlantic Monthly* 68 (Oct. 1891): 444–56.

Short Studies of American Authors. Boston: Lee & Shepard, 1880.

Hoffa, William. "The Final Preface: Henry James's Autobiography." *Sewanee Review* 77 (April–June 1969): 277–93.

Holly, Carol. " 'Absolutely Acclaimed': The Cure for Depression in James's Final Phase." *Henry James Review* 8 (Winter 1987): 126–38.

"A Drama of Intention in Henry James's *Autobiography*." *Modern Language Studies* 13 (Fall 1983): 22–31.

Holmes, Mary Jane. *Lena Rivers*. New York: Miller, Orton, 1857.

Tempest and Sunshine; or, Life in Kentucky. New York: Appleton, 1855.

Holt, Henry. "A Young Man's Oracle." *Nation* 101 (8 July 1915): 45–48.

H[ooker], I[sabella] B. "Miss Dickinson's Novel." *Nation* 7 (12 Nov. 1868): 391–92.

Hoover, Dwight W. *Henry James, Sr., and the Religion of Community*. Grand Rapids, Mich.: Eerdmans, 1969.

Howard, David. "*The Bostonians*." In *The Air of Reality: New Essays on Henry James*. Ed. John Goode. London: Methuen, 1972.

Howe, Irving. Introduction. *The Bostonians*. New York: Modern Library, 1956.

H[owe], J[ulia] W[ard]. "A Merited Lesson." *Woman's Journal* 3 (9 Nov. 1872): 356.

Howe, M. A. DeWolfe. *Memories of a Hostess: A Chronic of Eminent Friendships Drawn Chiefly from the Diaries of Mrs. James T. Fields.* Boston: Atlantic Monthly Press, 1922.

Howells, W. D. "Editor's Study." *Harper's New Monthly Magazine* 78 (May 1889): 982–87.

"Henry James, Jr." *Century Magazine* 25 (Nov. 1882): 25–29.

Literary Friends and Acquaintance. Bloomington: Indiana Univ. Press, 1968.

"The New Taste in Theatricals." *Atlantic Monthly* 23 (May 1869): 635–44.

Review of *Two Men. Nation* 1 (26 Oct. 1865): 537–38.

"Reviews and Literary Notices." *Atlantic Monthly* 24 (Dec. 1869): 762–63.

The Rise of Silas Lapham. Bloomington: Indiana Univ. Press, 1971.

Selected Letters. Boston: Twayne, 1979–83. 5 vols.

Howells, W. D., and Henry James. *A Double Billing: Novel-Writing and Novel-Reading: An Impersonal Explanation/Henry James and the Bazar Letters.* Ed. William M. Gibson, Leon Edel, Lyall H. Powers. New York: New York Public Library, 1958.

Huggins, Nathan I. *Protestants Against Poverty: Boston's Charities, 1870–1900.* Westport: Greenwood, 1970.

Hughes, Winifred. *The Maniac in the Cellar: Sensation Novels of the 1860s.* Princeton, N.J.: Princeton Univ. Press, 1980.

Hull, Raymona E. " 'Scribbling' Females and Serious Males: Hawthorne's Comments from Abroad on Some American Authors." *Nathaniel Hawthorne Journal* (1975): 35–58.

Hutchinson, Stuart. "Beyond the Victorians: *The Portrait of a Lady.*" In *Reading the Victorian Novel: Detail into Form.* London: Vision Press, 1980.

James, Henry. *The American Essays.* Ed. Leon Edel. New York: Vintage, 1956.

"The Bostonians." *Century Magazine* 29–31 (Feb. 1885–Feb. 1886).

The Bostonians: A Novel. London and New York: Macmillan, 1886.

The Complete Notebooks of Henry James. Ed. Leon Edel and Lyall H. Powers. New York: Oxford Univ. Press, 1987.

French Writers and American Women Essays. Ed. Peter Buitenhuis. Branford, Conn.: Compass, 1960.

Hawthorne. London: Macmillan, 1879.

Letters. Ed. Leon Edel. Cambridge, Mass.: Harvard Univ. Press, 1974–84. 4 vols.

The Letters of Henry James. Ed. Percy Lubbock. London: Macmillan, 1920. 2 vols.

Literary Criticism. Ed. Leon Edel with Mark Wilson. New York: Library of America, 1984. 2 vols.

Notes of a Son and Brother. New York: Scribner's, 1914.

"The Portrait of a Lady." *Atlantic Monthly* 46–48 (Nov. 1880–Dec. 1881).

The Portrait of a Lady. Boston: Houghton Mifflin, 1882 [1881].

The Portrait of a Lady. Ed. Robert D. Bamberg. New York: Norton, 1975.

Roderick Hudson. Harmondsworth: Penguin, 1986.

Selected Literary Criticism. Ed. Morris Shapira. London: Heinemann, 1963.

A Small Boy & Others. New York: Scribner's, 1913.

The Tales of Henry James. Ed. Maqbool Aziz. Oxford: Clarendon Press, 1973–84. 3 vols.

"Watch and Ward." *Atlantic Monthly* 28 (Aug.–Dec. 1871): 232–46, 320–39, 415–31, 577–96, 689–710.

Watch and Ward. Boston: Houghton, Osgood, 1879.

James, Henry, Sr. "Concluding Remarks on A.E.F.'s Letter." *Harbinger* 8 (23 Dec. 1848): 60–61.

"Dialogue between a Parent and Child." 9 pages. MS. in MH-H.

Draft of 1874 letter to Emerson. 15 pages. MS. in MH-H.

"Emerson, Fourier and 'Warrington.' " *Springfield Daily Republican*, 2 Dec. 1868, 2.

"An Essay upon the philosophic significance of man & Woman." Ms.

"Free Love Controversy. – Continued. Henry James to Stephen Pearl Andrews." *Woodhull & Claflin's Weekly* 8 (20 June 1874): 4–5. HJSr letter dated 20 May 1874.

"Free-Love Controversy Continued. Letter from Henry James." *Woodhull & Claflin's Weekly* 7 (9 May 1874): 3–4. First part of HJSr letter of 16 April 1874.

"Free-Love Controversy Continued. Letter from Henry James to S. P. Andrews – Continued." *Woodhull & Claflin's Weekly* 7 (16 May 1874): 4. Conclusion of HJSr letter of 16 April 1874.

"Further Remarks on A.E.F.'s Letter." *Harbinger* 8 (9, 16 Dec. 1848): 44–45, 53–54.

"Is Marriage Holy?" *Atlantic Monthly* 25 (March 1870): 360–68.

"The Lesson of the Sickles Tragedy." *New-York Daily Tribune*, 16 April 1859. Letter dated 3 April 1859.

The Literary Remains of the Late Henry James. Ed. William James. Boston: Osgood, 1885.

"The Logic of Marriage and Murder." *Atlantic Monthly* 25 (June 1870): 744–49.

"Love and Marriage." *Harbinger* 7 (23 Oct. 1848): 202–3.

"Marriage – Divorce." *New-York Daily Tribune*, 23 April 1859. Letter dated 20 April 1859.

"Marriage – Divorce – H.J." *New-York Daily Tribune*, 4 May 1859. Letter dated 26 April 1859.

"The Marriage Question." *New-York Daily Tribune*, 18 Sept. 1852.

" 'Modern Diabolism.' " *Atlantic Monthly* 32 (Aug. 1873): 219–24.

"Morality vs. Brute Instinct/Marriage vs. Free Love." *St. Paul Daily Press*, 19 Feb. 1874, 2.

"Mr. Henry James and the Swedenborgian Church." *Nation* 9 (2 Dec. 1869): 482–83.

"Mr. Henry James on Marriage." *Nation* 10 (9 June 1870): 366–67. Letter dated 28 May 1870.

"Mr. Henry James's Theory of Creation." *Nation* 5 (1 Aug. 1867): 95–96.

"Mr. James and the Swedenborgians." *Nation* 9 (16 Dec. 1869): 534.

"The N.Y. Observer and Mr. James." *New-York Daily Tribune,* 16 Nov. 1852, 5.

"The Observer and Hennequin." *Harbinger* 7 (21 Oct. 1848): 197–98.

"The Philadelphia Saturday Post and Fourier." *Harbinger* 8 (18 Nov. 1848): 20. Authorship acknowledged in following item.

"Philadelphia Saturday Post and Fourier Again." *Harbinger* 8 (25 Nov. 1848): 28 [29].

"The Philosophy of Marriage: or an attempt to show the ground of the sacredness of Marriage." 77 pages. MS. in MH-H.

"Postscript to Y.S.'s Reply to A.E.F." *Harbinger* 8 (30 Dec. 1848): 68–69.

"Preface." *Love in the Phalanstery.* New York: Dewitt & Davenport, 1849 [1848].

"Remarks." *Harbinger* 8 (2 Dec. 1848): 36–37.

"Reply of Mr. James." *Nation* 10 (23 June 1870): 404–5. Letter dated 11 June 1870.

"Reply to A.E.F. in last week's Harbinger." *Harbinger* 8 (10 Feb. 1849): 116–17.

"Reply to A.E.F.'s Article of Last Week." *Harbinger* 8 (3 Feb. 1849): 107–8.

The Secret of Swedenborg: Being an Elucidation of His Doctrine of the Divine Natural Humanity. Boston: Houghton Mifflin, 1869.

"Some Personal Recollections of Carlyle." *Atlantic Monthly* 47 (May 1881): 593–609.

"Spiritualism New and Old." *Atlantic Monthly* 29 (March 1872): 358–62.

What Constitutes the State? A Lecture Delivered before the Young Men's Association of the City of Albany. New York: John Allen, 1846. Lecture was read "December last."

"Woman and the 'Woman's Movement.'" *Putnam's* 1 (March 1853): 279–88.

"The Woman Thou Gavest with Me." *Atlantic Monthly* 25 (Jan. 1870): 66–72.

James, Henry, Sr., Harvey Y. Russell, and Stephen Pearl Andrews. "Morality vs. Brute Instinct. Marriage vs. Free Love. Correspondence and Comments." *Woodhull and Claflin's Weekly* 7 (18 April 1874): 5–6. Reprints and responds to HJSr's letter to Russell of 23 Dec. 1872.

James, William. *The Letters of William James.* Ed. Henry James III. London: Longmans, Green, 1920. 2 vols.

Review of Bushnell's *Women's Suffrage* and Mill's *Subjection of Women.* *North American Review* 109 (Oct. 1869): 556–65.

The Varieties of Religious Experience. New York: Longmans, Green, 1925.

Jones, Vivien. *James the Critic.* London: Macmillan, 1985.

Joyce, James. *Ulysses. The Corrected Text.* New York: Random House, 1986.

Kaledin, Eugenia. *The Education of Mrs. Henry Adams.* Philadelphia: Temple Univ. Press, 1981.

Kaston, Carren. *Imagination and Desire in the Novels of Henry James.* New Brunswick, N.J.: Rutgers Univ. Press, 1984.

Kelley, Mary. *Private Woman, Public Stage: Literary Domesticity in Nineteenth-Century America.* New York: Oxford Univ. Press, 1984.

Kellogg, J[ulia]. A. *Philosophy of Henry James . . . : A Digest.* New York: John W. Lovell, 1883.

Kern, Louis J. *An Ordered Love: Sex Roles and Sexuality in Victorian Utopias – the*

Shakers, the Mormons, and the Oneida Community. Chapel Hill: Univ. of North Carolina Press, 1981.

Kerr, Howard. *Mediums, and Spirit-Rappers, and Roaring Radicals: Spiritualism in American Literature, 1850–1900*. Urbana: Univ. of Illinois Press, 1972.

Kraft, James. "An Unpublished Review by Henry James." *Studies in Bibliography* 20 (1967): 267–73.

Kuehl, Warren F. "Mead, Lucia True Ames." In *Notable American Women 1607–1950*, ed. Edward T. James et al. Cambridge, Mass.: Harvard Univ. Press, 1971. Vol. 2.

la Rose, Pierre de Chaignon. "Preface." *Notes and Reviews by Henry James*. Freeport, N.Y.: Books for Libraries, 1968. First published 1921.

"The Last Meeting of Sorosis." *Woman's Journal* 2 (17 June 1871): 192.

Lathrop, George Parsons. "Mrs. Stoddard's 'Two Men'." *Epoch* 4 (12 Oct. 1888): 173–74.

Lauter, Paul. *Reconstructing American Literature: Courses, Syllabi, Issues*. Old Westbury, N.Y.: Feminist Press, 1983.

[Lazarus, Marx Edgeworth]. *Love vs. Marriage. Part I*. New York: Fowlers & Wells, 1852. Part II was apparently not published.

Leach, William. *True Love and Perfect Union: The Feminist Reform of Sex and Society*. New York: Basic Books, 1980.

LeClair, Robert C. "Henry James and Minny Temple." *American Literature* 21 (March 1949): 35–48.

Young Henry James 1843–1870. New York: Bookman, 1955.

Leonard, Linda Schierse. *The Wounded Woman: Healing the Father–Daughter Relationship*. Athens: Swallow Press, 1982.

"A Letter to Mr. James." *New-York Observer* 30 (25 Nov. 1852): 382.

Levine, George. "Isabel, Gwendolen, and Dorothea." *ELH* 30 (Sept. 1963): 244–57.

Levy, Leo B. "The Comedy of *Watch and Ward*." *Arlington Quarterly* 1 (Summer 1968): 86–98.

Lewis, R. W. B. "The Courtship of William James." *Yale Review* 73 (Winter 1984): 177–98.

Edith Wharton: A Biography. New York: Harper & Row, 1975.

Long, Robert Emmet. *The Great Succession: Henry James and the Legacy of Hawthorne*. Pittsburgh: Univ. of Pittsburgh Press, 1979.

Henry James: The Early Novels. Boston: Twayne, 1983.

"The Society and the Masks: *The Blithedale Romance* and *The Bostonians*." *Nineteenth-Century Fiction* 19 (Sept. 1964): 105–22.

"Love in the Phalanstery." *New-York Observer* (7 Oct. 1848): 162.

"The Love Question." *Harbinger* 8 (6 Jan. 1849): 77–78. Signed "G.F.T."

Lucas, John. "Conservatism and Revolution in the 1880s." In *Literature and Politics in the Nineteenth Century*, ed. John Lucas. London: Methuen, 1971.

"The Magazines of the Month." *Independent* 21 (30 Dec. 1869): 6.

Maher, Jane. *Biography of Broken Fortunes: Wilkie and Bob, Brothers of William, Henry, and Alice James*. Hamden: Archon, 1986.

Malcolm, Janet. "Trouble in the Archives – 1." *New Yorker* 59 (5 Dec. 1983): 59–152.

"Man and Woman." *New-York Daily Tribune,* 7 March 1853.

Mann, Arthur. *Yankee Reformers in the Urban Age.* Cambridge, Mass.: Harvard Univ. Press, 1954.

"Marriage and Reformers." *New-York Observer* 30 (11 Nov. 1852): 366.

Marsh, George Perkins. "The Education of Women." *Nation* 3 (30 Aug. 1866): 165–66.

Martin, Theodora Penny. *The Sound of Our Own Voices: Women's Study Clubs 1860–1910.* Boston: Beacon Press, 1987.

Masson, Jeffrey M. "Freud and the Seduction Theory." *Atlantic Monthly* 253 (Feb. 1984): 33–60.

Matlack, James H. "The *Alta California's* Lady Correspondent." *New-York Historical Society Quarterly* 58 (Oct. 1974): 280–303.

——. "Hawthorne and Elizabeth Barstow Stoddard." *New England Quarterly* 50 (June 1977): 278–302.

——. "The Literary Career of Elizabeth Barstow Stoddard (1823–1902)." Diss: Yale, 1967.

Matthiessen, F. O. *The James Family.* New York: Knopf, 1948.

McAlexander, Hubert Horton. *The Prodigal Daughter: A Biography of Sherwood Bonner.* Baton Rouge: Louisiana State Univ. Press, 1981.

[McDowell, Katherine]. "The Radical Club. A Poem, Respectfully Dedicated to 'The Infinite.' By an Atom." Boston *Times,* 8 May 1875.

——. *The Radical Club. . . .* Boston: Times, 1876.

McGann, Jerome J. *The Beauty of Inflections: Literary Investigations in Historical Method and Theory.* New York: Oxford Univ. Press, 1985.

——. ed. *Historical Studies and Literary Criticism.* Madison: Univ. of Wisconsin Press, 1985.

[McKim, James Miller]. "The Vexed Question." *Nation* 10 (24 & 31 March, 14 April 1870): 189–90, 205–6, 237–38.

McMaster, Juliet. "The Portrait of Isabel Archer." *American Literature* 45 (March 1973): 51–66.

Miller, Theodore C. "The Muddled Politics of Henry James's *The Bostonians.*" *Georgia Review* 26 (Fall 1972): 336–46.

"Minor Book Notices." *Literary World* 1 (1 April 1871): 172.

Mizruchi, Susan L. "The Politics of Temporality in *The Bostonians.*" *Nineteenth-Century Fiction* 40 (Sept. 1985): 187–215.

Monteiro, George. *Henry James and John Hay: The Record of a Friendship.* Providence: Brown Univ. Press, 1965.

Moody, Loring. "Free Love and Its Accusers./No. 1./Henry James." *Woodhull & Claflin's Weekly* 8 (13 June 1874): 5–6.

Moss, Howard. "The Last of James." *New Yorker* 63 (9 March 1987): 101–4.

Moss, Mary. "The Novels of Elizabeth Stoddard." *Bookman* 16 (Nov. 1902): 260–63.

Mott, Frank Luther. *Golden Multitudes: The Story of Best Sellers in the United States.* New York: Macmillan, 1947.

——. *A History of American Magazines 1865–1885.* Cambridge, Mass.: Harvard Univ. Press, 1957.

"Movements and Changes." *Spiritual Magazine* 2 (31 Aug. 1849): 232.

"Mrs. Anne Moncure Crane Seemuller." *Baltimore American,* Woman's Edition, 29 Feb. 1896.

"Mrs. Stoddard's 'Two Men.' " *Literary World* 19 (21 July 1888): 227.

Muncy, Raymond Lee. *Sex and Marriage in Utopian Communities.* Bloomington: Indiana Univ. Press, 1973.

"New Publications." *New-York Daily Tribune,* 28 Sept. 1848.

Niemtzow, Annette. "Marriage and the New Woman in *The Portrait of a Lady.*" *American Literature* 47 (Nov. 1975): 377–95.

[Noble, Lulu Gray]. "Notes on the Woman's Rights Agitation. By a Looker-on." *Nation* 10 (20 Jan., 10 & 17 Feb., 1870): 38–39, 88–89, 101–3.

Nordhoff, Charles. *The Communistic Societies of the United States.* New York: Schocken, 1965. First published 1875.

[Norton, Charles Eliot]. "Female Suffrage and Education." *Nation* 5 (22 Aug. 1867): 152.

"Nothing Unreasonable. Miss Dickinson's Lecture." *New-York Daily Tribune,* 29 May 1869, 7.

Noyes, John Humphrey. *Dixon and His Copyists. A Criticism of the Accounts of the Oneida Community in "New America," "Spiritual Wives" and Kindred Publications.* Wallingford, Conn.: Oneida Community, 1871.

History of American Socialisms. New York: Dover, 1966. Reprint of 1870 ed.

[Noyes, John Humphrey?]. "Mr. Andrews and the Tribune." *The Circular* 2 (13 May 1853): 210.

Nye, Russel B. "The Novel as Dream and Weapon: Women's Popular Novels in the 19th Century." *Historical Society of Michigan Chronicle* 11 (4th Quarter, 1975): 2–16.

Obituary of Henry James, Sr. New York *Post,* 19 Dec. 1882.

An Official Report of Mordaunt v. Mordaunt, Cole, and Johnstone. As Tried before Lord Penzance, in the Divorce Court, February 16 and Following Days. London: Published at the Office, 317, Strand, 1870.

Olsen, Tillie. "A Biographical Interpretation." *Life in the Iron Mills.* Old Westbury, N.Y.: Feminist Press, 1972.

Orr, A. "The Future of English Women." *Nineteenth Century* 3 (June 1878): 1010–32.

"Mr. Henry James, Senior." *Athenaeum* 2752 (24 July 1880): 113–15.

Ozick, Cynthia. "The Lesson of the Master." In Stephen Berg, ed., *In Praise of What Persists.* New York: Harper, 1984.

Page, Norman, ed. *Henry James: Interviews and Recollections.* London: Macmillan, 1984.

Page, Philip. "The Curious Narration of *The Bostonians.*" *American Literature* 46 (Nov. 1974): 374–83.

Parker, Gail, ed. *The Oven-Birds: American Women on Womanhood, 1820–1920.* Garden City, N.Y.: Anchor, 1972.

Parker, Hershel. "Henry James 'In the Wood': Sequence and Significances of his Literary Labors, 1905–1907." *Nineteenth-Century Fiction* 38 (March 1984): 492–513.

Peabody, Elizabeth Palmer. *Letters of Elizabeth Palmer Peabody.* Ed. Bruce A. Ronda. Middletown, Conn.: Wesleyan Univ. Press, 1984.

Perry, Ralph Barton. *The Thought and Character of William James.* Boston: Little, Brown, 1935. 2 vols.

"Personal." *Round Table* 2 (7 Oct. 1865): 70.

Peterson, Dale E. *The Clement Vision: Poetic Realism in Turgenev and James.* Port Washington: Kennikat, 1975.

P[helps], E[lizabeth] S[tuart]? Review of *The Portrait of a Lady. Penn Monthly* 13 (March 1882): 233–34. Attribution by Linda J. Taylor.

Porter, Charlotte. "The Serial Story." *Century Magazine* 30 (Sept. 1885): 812–13.

The Radical Club. A Poem Respectfully Dedicated to an Atom. By a Chip. Boston: Gill, 1876.

Rahv, Philip. Introduction. *The Bostonians.* New York: Dial Press, 1945.

"Recent Fiction." *The Critic* 9 N.S. (23 June 1888): 305.

"Recent Fiction." *Literary World* 9 (1 Aug. 1878): 47.

"Recent Novels." *Nation* 27 (22 Aug. 1878): 117–18.

"Recent Novels." *Nation* 47 (9 Aug. 1888): 118.

Redpath, James. "Free-Love in the Tropics." *New-York Daily Tribune* (4 May 1859). Answers HJSr's "Marriage – Divorce."

Reising, Russell J. *The Unusable Past: Theory and the Study of American Literature.* New York: Methuen, 1986.

"Remarks." *Harbinger* 8 (11 Nov. 1848): 13. Signed "For the Harbinger." Mistakenly attributed to HJSr by Delano and Colanzi.

Review of *Emily Chester. New York Times,* 10 Dec. 1864, 2.

Review of *Emily Chester. Saturday Review* 18 (3 Dec. 1864): 697–98.

Review of *The Lamplighter. New-York Daily Tribune,* 28 March 1854.

Review of *Moralism and Christianity. Free Church Circular* 3 (13 April 1850): 88–91.

Review of *The Morgesons. Independent* 41 (17 Oct. 1889): 1355.

Review of *Opportunity. New York Times,* 6 Dec. 1867, 2.

Review of *Opportunity. Putnam's* N.S. 1 (Feb. 1868): 256.

Review of *Reginald Archer. Galaxy* 11 (June 1871): 896–98.

Review of *Reginald Archer. Nation* 12 (11 May 1871): 325–26.

Review of *Watch and Ward. Athenaeum* 2650 (10 Aug. 1878): 177.

Review of *Watch and Ward. Library Table* 4 (1878): 301–2.

[Ripley, George?]. "The March Magazines." *New-York Daily Tribune,* 3 March 1853.

[Ripley, George]. Review of *Love in the Phalanstery. Harbinger* 7 (23 Sept. 1848): 167.

Rollins, Alice Wellington. "Woman's Sense of Humor." *Critic* N.S. 1 (29 March 1884): 145–46.

Rowe, John Carlos. "Correspondence." *Henry James Review* 6 (Winter 1985): 153–54.

——. *The Theoretical Dimensions of Henry James.* Madison: Univ. of Wisconsin Press, 1984.

Sandeen, Ernest. "*The Wings of the Dove* and *The Portrait of a Lady:* A Study of Henry James's Later Phase." *PMLA* 69 (Dec. 1954): 1060–75.

Sargent, Epes. *The Woman Who Dared*. Boston: Roberts, 1870.

Sargent, Mary Elizabeth (Fiske) ["Mrs. J. T. Sargent"]. *Sketches and Reminiscences of the Radical Club of Chestnut Street, Boston*. Boston: Osgood, 1880.

Saxton, Martha. *Louisa May: A Modern Biography of Louisa May Alcott*. Boston: Houghton Mifflin, 1977.

Sayre, Robert F. *The Examined Self: Benjamin Franklin, Henry Adams, Henry James*. Madison: Univ. of Wisconsin Press, 1988. First published 1964.

Scholnick, Robert J. "Between Realism and Romanticism: The Curious Career of Eugene Benson." *American Literary Realism* 14 (Autumn 1981): 242–61.

[Scudder, Horace]. "*The Portrait of a Lady* and *Dr. Breen's Practice*." *Atlantic Monthly* 49 (Jan. 1882): 126–30.

Seemuller. See Crane, Anne Moncure.

Senn, Fritz. "Nausicaa." In *James Joyce's* Ulysses: *Critical Essays*. Ed. Clive Hart and David Hayman. Berkeley: Univ. of California Press, 1974.

Sewall, Richard B. *The Life of Emily Dickinson*. New York: Farrar, Straus & Giroux, 1974.

Shepherd, Henry E. *The Representative Authors of Maryland*. New York: Whitehall, 1911.

Smith, Herbert F., and Michael Peinovich. "*The Bostonians*: Creation and Revision." *Bulletin of the New York Public Library* 73 (May 1969): 298–308.

Smith-Rosenberg, Carroll. *Disorderly Conduct: Visions of Gender in Victorian America*. New York: Knopf, 1985.

"Some Recent Novels." *Atlantic Monthly* 88 (Dec. 1901): 848–50.

"Sorosis – A May-Day Meeting." *New-York Daily Tribune*, 2 May 1871, 8.

Southworth, Emma D. E. N. *The Curse of Clifton*. Philadelphia: Peterson, 1852.

The Hidden Hand; or, Capitola the Mad-Cap. New York: Dillingham, 1888.

Spiller, Robert E., et al., eds. *Literary History of the United States*. New York: Macmillan, 1948.

"Statement of the 'American Union of Associationists,' with Reference to Recent Attacks." *Harbinger* 3 (15 Aug. 1846): 154.

Stedman, Edmund Clarence. "A Critical Estimate of Mrs. Stoddard's Novels." In *Two Men: A Novel*. Philadelphia: Coates, 1901.

Stern, Madeleine B., ed. *Critical Essays on Louisa May Alcott*. Boston: Hall, 1984.

Louisa May Alcott. Norman: Univ. of Oklahoma Press, 1950.

The Pantarch: A Biography of Stephen Pearl Andrews. Austin: Univ. of Texas Press, 1968.

Stoddard, Elizabeth. *The Morgesons*. New York: Carleton, 1862.

The Morgesons. New York: Johnson Reprint, 1971.

The Morgesons. Ed. Lawrence Buell and Sandra A. Zagarell. New York: Oxford Univ. Press, 1984.

Temple House. A Novel. New York: Carleton, [1867].

Two Men. A Novel. New York: Bunce & Huntington, 1865.

Two Men: A Novel. New York: Cassell, 1888.

Two Men: A Novel. Philadelphia: Coates, 1901.

Stoehr, Taylor. *Free Love in America*. New York: AMS Press, 1979.

Stone, Donald D. "Victorian Feminism and the Nineteenth-Century Novel." *Women's Studies* 1 (1972): 65–91.

Stowe, Harriet Beecher. *The Pearl of Orr's Island*. Ridgewood, N.J.: Gregg, 1967. "The True Story of Lady Byron's Life." *Atlantic Monthly* 24 (Sept. 1869): 295–313.

Strouse, Jean. *Alice James: A Biography*. Boston: Houghton Mifflin, 1980.

Strout, Cushing. "William James and the Twice-Born Sick Soul." In *The Veracious Imagination*. Middletown, Conn.: Wesleyan Univ. Press, 1981.

Stubbs, Patricia. *Women and Fiction: Feminism and the Novel 1880–1920*. Brighton: Harvester, 1979.

Taylor, Charles Fayette. "Emotional Prodigality." *Dental Cosmos* 21 (1879): 359–71.

Taylor, Linda J. *Henry James, 1866–1916: A Reference Guide*. Boston: Hall, 1982.

Thoreau, Henry D. *Walden*. Princeton, N.J.: Princeton Univ. Press, 1971.

Tintner, Adeline R. "Autobiography as Fiction: 'The Usurping Consciousness' as Hero of James's Memoirs." *Twentieth Century Literature* 23 (May 1977): 239–60.

The Book World of Henry James: Appropriating the Classics. Ann Arbor, Mich.: UMI Research Press, 1987.

"The Centennial of 1876 and *The Portrait of a Lady*." *Markham Review* 10 (Fall–Winter 1980–81): 27–29.

"In the Footsteps of Stendhal: James's 'A Most Extraordinary Case' and *La Chartreuse de Parme*." *Revue de Littérature Comparée* 55 (April–June 1981): 232–38.

Tompkins, Jane P. "The Redemption of Time in *Notes of a Son and Brother*." *Texas Studies in Literature and Language* 14 (Winter 1973): 681–90.

Sensational Designs: The Cultural Work of American Fiction, 1790–1860. New York: Oxford Univ. Press, 1985.

Torsney, Cheryl B. "The Political Context of *The Portrait of a Lady*." *Henry James Review* 7 (Winter–Spring 1986): 86–104.

Trilling, Lionel. "The Bostonians." *The Opposing Self*. New York: Viking, 1955.

Tuttleton, James W. Review of Richard H. Brodhead's *The School of Hawthorne*. *Nineteenth-Century Literature* 42 (Dec. 1987): 362–65.

Twain, Mark. "The Facts Concerning the Recent Carnival of Crime in Connecticut." *Atlantic Monthly* 37 (June 1876): 641–50.

"Mental Telegraphy. A Manuscript with a History." *Harper's New Monthly Magazine* 84 (Dec. 1891): 95–104.

Untitled Note on Anne Moncure Crane Seemuller. *Nation* 16 (30 Jan. 1873): 75.

van Gogh, Vincent. *The Letters of Vincent van Gogh to His Brother*. Boston: Houghton Mifflin, 1927. 2 vols.

Veeder, William. *Henry James – The Lessons of the Master: Popular Fiction and Personal Style in the Nineteenth Century*. Chicago: Univ. of Chicago Press, 1975.

Veysey, Laurence, ed. *The Perfectionists: Radical Social Thought in the North, 1815–1860*. New York: Wiley, 1973.

von Hallberg, Robert, ed. *Canons*. Chicago: Univ. of Chicago Press, 1984.

Ward, J. A. *The Search for Form: Studies in the Structure of James's Fiction.* Chapel Hill: Univ. of North Carolina Press, 1967.

Warner, Susan. *The Wide, Wide World.* Philadelphia: Lippincott, n.d.

The Wide, Wide World. "Afterword" by Jane Tompkins. New York: Feminist Press, 1987.

Warren, Austin. *The Elder Henry James.* New York: Macmillan, 1934.

Weber, Carl. *The Rise and Fall of James Ripley Osgood: A Biography.* Waterville, Maine: Colby College Press, 1959.

Weir, Sybil. "*The Morgesons:* A Neglected Feminist *Bildungsroman.*" *New England Quarterly* 49 (Sept. 1976): 427–39.

Whipple, Edwin Percy. *American Literature and Other Papers.* Boston: Ticknor, 1887.

White, Allon. *The Uses of Obscurity: The Fiction of Early Modernism.* London: Routledge & Kegan Paul, 1981.

White, Robert. "Love, Marriage, and Divorce: The Matter of Sexuality in *The Portrait of a Lady.*" *Henry James Review* 7 (Winter–Spring 1986): 59–71.

Wiesenfarth, Joseph. "A Woman in *The Portrait of a Lady.*" *Henry James Review* 7 (Winter–Spring 1986); 18–28.

Wilkinson, James John Garth. *Emanuel Swedenborg: A Biography.* London: Newbery, 1849.

Willard, Frances E., and Mary A. Livermore. *American Women.* New York: Mast, Crowell, & Kirkpatrick, 1897.

Wiseman, Adele. "What Price the Heroine?" *International Journal of Women's Studies* 4 (Nov./Dec. 1981): 459–71.

Wood, Ann Douglas. "The 'Scribbling Women' and Fanny Fern: Why Women Wrote." *American Quarterly* 23 (Spring 1971): 3–24.

[Woolson, Constance Fenimore.] Untitled Essay. "Contributors' Club." *Atlantic Monthly* 42 (Oct. 1878): 502–3.

"A Word about H.J. and W.H.G." *New Church Independent and Monthly Review* 28 (April 1880): 187–89.

Young, Frederic Harold. *The Philosophy of Henry James, Sr.* New York: Bookman, 1951.

Ziff, Larzer. *Literary Democracy.* New York: Viking, 1981.

Zuckert, Catherine H. "American Women and Democratic Morals: *The Bostonians.*" *Feminist Studies* 3 (Spring–Summer 1976): 30–50.

Index